S0-BZT-360

Ecological Economics

Ecological Economics

Energy, Environment and Society

JUAN MARTINEZ-ALIER
with Klaus Schlüpmann

Basil Blackwell

Copyright©J. Martinez-Alier 1987

First published 1987

Basil Blackwell Ltd
108 Cowley Road, Oxford, OX4 1JF, UK

Basil Blackwell Inc,
432 Park Avenue South, Suite 1503
New York, NY 10016, USA

British Library Cataloguing in Publication Data
Martinez-Alier, Juan
Ecological economics: energy,
environment and society.
1. Economic development   2. Human ecology
I. Title   II. Schlüpmann, Klaus
III. L'Ecologisme i l'economia. *English*
330.9   HD82

ISBN 0-631-15739-5

Library of Congress Cataloging-in-Publication Data
Martinez-Alier, Juan
Ecological economics.
Expanded and rearranged translation of:
L'ecologisme i l'economia.
Bibliography: p.
Includes index.
1. Economic development – Environmental aspects.
2. Environmental policy.   3. Natural resources.
4. Man – Influence on nature.
I. Schlüpmann, Klaus.   II. Title.
HD85.S7M363513   1987   333.7   87-14512
ISBN 0-631-15739-5

Typeset in 10 on 12pt Sabon
by Dobbie Typesetting Service, Plymouth, Devon, England
Printed in Great Britain by T. J. Press (Padstow) Ltd

Contents

Preface

Since the early 1970s, economists have paid increasing attention to the ecological analysis of economic processes. This was at first focused on the definition of ecological limits to growth, followed by more systematic examination of the pattern of flows of energy and materials in the economy, with emphasis on the inter-generational allocation of energy and material resources and on the valuation of externalities (which Kapp had already studied in detail). As in all newly founded branches of science, so will it happen in ecological economics: historiographic reviews of its own disciplinary tradition will now begin to appear, such as the present book which traces the history of the relations between economics and human ecology (more precisely, human ecological energetics). One of the first empirical ecological studies, by Möbius in 1879, was called *The Economy of the Oysters*. This book, however, does not deal with the application of concepts of economics to the study of nature (Worster, 1977) but, on the contrary, with the ecological approach to the study of human society and economy.

We have all too often heard that histories of sciences attempt sometimes to legitimize new paradigms. But why did ecological (or biophysical) economics, which has old traditions, appear in the 1970s as something new? This book takes back to the mid-nineteenth century the history of a subject, ecological economics, which was generally thought to have come into existence in the 1970s, and the reality of which mainstream economists would still dispute nowadays. Sociologists, historians and perhaps philosophers of science may find something valuable in this attempt at reconstructing the history of an interdisciplinary current of thought which never found an institutionalized academic niche. However, this book does not aim at glibly pushing paradigms of economics on and off the stage in response to audience applause, but rather at engaging economists in rational argument about the principles of their science. It will also be useful to some economic historians, environmental sociologists, human geographers and ecologists, social anthropologists, and also to ecological Marxists and practical environmentalists.

This book is an expanded and rearranged version translated mostly by myself, of my *L'ecologisme i l'economia: Història d'unes relacions amagades* (1984). My friend Klaus Schlüpmann wrote some paragraphs of the introductory chapter, apart from patiently introducing me to the history of natural sciences. He also wrote a draft for the second part of chapter 3 (Podolinsky's biography) and most of chapter 5 on Clausius; I could not have written the book without his help. Other major sources of inspiration have been J. M. Naredo, who has published a book on the ecological critique of National Income Accounting (Naredo, 1987); R. N. Adams, who kindly sent to me in 1984 the typescript of his new book on energy and society; and Jacques Grinevald. The present version was mostly written at St Antony's College, Oxford, in 1984, on a grant from the Fundación Juan March. Other sources of financial support have been the CIRIT (Catalonia) and the Energy Research Group of the IDRC (Ottawa) led by my friend Ashok Desai.

Georgescu-Roegen remains the leading author in the field of ecological economics. His visit to Barcelona in the initial stages of my work and his collegial benevolence and interest gave me the push I needed in order to go on with a research project which I could not carry out in the deplorable local libraries. I was bibliographically much helped by happy stays in Berlin between 1980 and 1983, for which I am thankful to Marta Giralt, Dorothea Hartung, Urs and Clarita Müller-Plantenberg, and to the Latin American Institute of the Free University. For help during a fruitful visit to the United States I am particularly grateful to Martha Ackelsberg, Arnold Bauer, Fred Buttel, Paul Christensen, Bob Costanza, Herman Daly, Loren Goldner, Dick Norgaard and Ben Orlove. My ex-students Maite Cabeza, Antoni Estradé, Carmen Matutes and Emilio Quintana contributed references and ideas at various stages of this work.

J. M.-A.

1

Introduction

Ecology studies the flow of energy and the cycles of materials in ecosystems. Although Georgescu-Roegen's views against the 'energetic dogma' are accepted here, and although human ecologists and ecological anthropologists no longer suffer from calorific obsessions, this book deals mainly with the study of energy flow, a useful unifying principle in ecological analysis and also in the analysis of the economy from the ecological point of view. Economics is the study of the human allocation of scarce resources to alternative ends, a definition with which (tactically, so to speak) we have no quarrel.

The evaluation of the use of energy in the economy seems perhaps a recent preoccupation, which some readers would trace back to the 'energy crisis' of 1973, and other readers – better informed – would associate with Georgescu-Roegen's *The Entropy Law and the Economic Process* (1971) which heralded a conceptual overturn in economics. There is in fact a long history of interaction between human ecological energetics and economics. This history remains to be written. Each chapter of this book considers at least one author who did some work on the relations between economics and the study of the flow of energy in human societies. Therefore, the part of economics of particular interest is the economics of exhaustible resources, and the part of human ecology considered in this book is ecological energetics. What the book loses in amplitude, it gains in sharpness of focus.

Human ecology is wider than the study of energy flow. The point has been made with great force by Alfred Crosby (1986), who studied the expansion of European plants, animals, humans and, not least, diseases such as smallpox and measles throughout the world. This book places a somewhat one-sided attention on exhaustible sources of energy, and not so much on the ecological effects of increased energy use, such as the growth of carbon dioxide in the atmosphere, nor on the availability of materials and on pollution effects arising from the use of such materials.

This limitation is in part a matter of convenience, since it is easy to seek out the writers who have counted calories. In any case, as the reader shall see, not much is lost analytically by focusing on the use of energy as the central point in ecological economics.

The period covered in this book is, roughly, that between Jevons' *The Coal Question* (1865) and the 1940s. It seems appropriate to start at a time when the laws of thermodynamics had been established. The physiocrats, Smith, Malthus and Ricardo, should not therefore be blamed for disregarding the use of energy in the economy. It is more difficult to choose a date for the conclusion of the history of ecological economics. The best-known early attempt to work out the economic theory of exhaustible resources was made by Hotelling (1931), and this could be taken to be the culmination of the dialogue between natural scientists and economists, because economists had finally agreed that some resources were exhaustible, although this fact would still take a long time to appear in the textbooks. The economic theory of exhaustible resources took into account the physical characteristics of this type of resource. The 1930s could be a convenient ending point also on the grounds that 'short run' problems associated with 'excess capacity' came to dominate in macro-economics, and therefore the question of whether the availability of resources would stop economic growth was not on the agenda. However, Keynesian economics, starting with Harrod (1939), became also an economics of long-run growth, the categories of which (national income, investment, consumption, incremental capital/output ratio) paid no attention whatever to physical realities, as John Ise pointed out as early as 1950 (pp. 415–16).

By choosing the 1940s as the final period I have been able to consider Hayek's extremely derogatory views on some of the writers under study. But there is no end in sight to the ecological critique of economic theory, to which this book makes a further contribution by resurrecting the arguments of half-forgotten authors.

One could in addition take Georgescu-Roegen's *The Entropy Law and the Economic Process* as a final point, and see this present book as a history of his precursors, about most of whom he did not know – in itself a fact not attributable to sloppy standards of scholarship in such a careful author, but to the lack of social atmosphere before 1973, inside or outside the academic world, for the formation of a school of ecological economics. That there was no concerted action to create a school of ecological economics is made clear by Boulding's inane critique of Georgescu-Roegen (Boulding, 1972).

Courses on the 'economics of natural resources', 'energy economics', and the like, have been introduced in many universities, and the study of the substantial contributions by some natural scientists and a few economists in the period between 1865 and the 1940s ought to provide a background to such courses. One of the most immediate applications of this book, then, will be in the teaching of economics, helping to shape the field of ecological economics. This book should also be useful in courses on human ecology, ecological anthropology, and human geography, because in it is presented the earliest work on the flow of energy in human societies, which ecologists have ignored. One of my most persistent questions is why the recognition of the school of ecological economics which has objectively existed since the 1880s, is unacknowledged even by its own members. Thus, this book may help to foster the growing awareness among scientists of the origins of their disciplines and also of the ideological uses to which natural sciences are put. The main themes and authors will now be introduced.

Agricultural Energetics

Applied work on the economics of energy use did not become a branch of economics until very recently. The best work was still being done, not only in the period covered by this book, but also in the 1950s, 1960s and 1970s, by non-economists (Cottrell, 1955; Rappaport, 1967; Odum, H., 1971; Pimentel, 1973; Leach, 1976; Chapman, 1975; Foley, 1981). One striking finding of energy analysis was that the efficiency of modern agriculture was less than that of traditional agriculture. This will be considered in the next chapter, again with some attention being paid to questions of measurement. But, in principle, energy analysis and conventional economic analysis seem to give contradictory judgements of the same process. The productivity of agriculture has not increased, but decreased, from the point of view of energy analysis. This does not mean that a new criterion of economic efficiency, such as energy return to energy input, should be introduced, which would be substituted for the usual criterion of economic efficiency. It is a fact, for instance, that different agricultural products have use values which are not always related to their energy content, and even less to their energy cost, but rather to their protein or vitamin content, or simply to the pleasure to be gained by eating or drinking them. Nevertheless, such studies of the flow of energy in agriculture show that it is not appropriate to analyse economic growth in terms of an increased productivity of agriculture (said to be based upon technical progress or upon the development of productive forces) which, because of the relatively low income-elasticity of demand for agricultural produce, frees labour to other sectors of the economy.

Here again, we must emphasize that the study of energy flow is not the only ecological approach. There is a current debate on whether the lack of diversity of modern agriculture threatens its stability. Clearly, the higher productivity (in money terms) of modern agriculture is due not only to cheap energy inputs but also to the substitution of a handful of new crop varieties for the many ancestral types (Brush, 1986). Is the cost of seed banks lower than their future benefits, discounted perhaps at present value? Energetics leaves aside this aspect of ecological agricultural economics.

The increase in agricultural productivity gained by using oil appears to be so only at the oil prices that have obtained. If oil has been undervalued from the point of view of its conservation for future generations, then the increase in productivity is fictitious. To economic theorists, the question might appear to be one of finding a means of giving values across the generations to the flows from the stocks of fossil fuels and other exhaustible resources, in such a manner that an acceptable, or even an optimal, path of depletion would be achieved. This would require the reserves to be known, the future demand of all generations to be known, and future changes in available techniques to be known. When the rate of depletion of exhaustible resources is being discussed, an appeal is usually made to Hotelling's rule, which compares, assuming the existence of a futures' market, the difference in net return (price minus marginal cost of extraction) between now and a future date with the interest to be gained by selling now and investing the proceeds. But this criterion appears to beg the question, since interest will only accrue continually if the economy grows – a point emphasized by Soddy in 1922, arguing explicitly against Keynes. In other words, while there are grounds for discounting the future if it is assumed that the future will be more prosperous than the present (as assumed in theories of economic growth, where the sacrifice of current consumption in order to invest makes sense insofar as the investment will increase future consumption, and where the rate of interest makes the present discounted value of consumption equal, over time), the present use of exhaustible resources should perhaps be kept to a minimum if a long life for humanity is assumed. In any case, it seems clear that there is no way of escaping an ethical choice, sometimes hidden away in the assumptions of the models. One chapter of this book is devoted to a critique of the orthodox economic theory of exhaustible resources. 'Time-preference' will be discussed; this is often introduced in economic theory as a 'revealed preference' in agreement with the introspective, subjective individualism which characterizes methodologically economic theory. This methodology is somewhat awkward since, as is the nature of the case, economic agents who are not yet born cannot bid in today's markets.

The first chapters of this book do not deal, however, with such abstruse methodological questions, but provide a straight narrative of the history of energy accounting in agriculture, after an initial chapter, which introduces the reader to some practical work on agricultural energetics. It appears that Serhii Podolinsky, a Ukrainian socialist physician, first developed the concept of energy return to energy input in different types of land use, trying to combine, in articles published between 1880 and 1883, this ecological approach with the Marxist theory of economic value. Although one of the versions of Podolinsky's article was published in *Die Neue Zeit*, there has been no discussion of his views in the Marxist literature on agricultural development. The relations between Marxism and ecology (centred on the notion of *Produktivkräfte*) is one of the main topics studied in this book. Another crucial episode in these relations was Lenin's reaction to Bogdanov's writings, in 1909. Lenin attacked not only Mach's theory of knowledge, but also Ostwald's energetics.

When Podolinsky wrote from the ecological point of view on the 'conditions of human life on earth', he was using Marx's terminology: 'the eternal natural condition of the human life'.[1] Marx did not formulate this question in terms of human ecology (studying the flow of energy and materials) and in any case his particular interest was in showing how the conditions of existence would *vary*, that is, how they adopted different social forms in history. For instance, direct appropriation from nature in primitive society (*produktive Konsumption*), or consumption of commodities bought with wages earned by selling labour, in capitalism. The ecological view of the conditions of human existence *could* have been easily connected with Marxism through an adequate definition of productive forces or productive powers. This was *not* done by Marx. Despite the superficial similarity between an ecological approach and an approach in terms of 'reproduction' of social systems, there has been a long-standing divorce between Marxism and ecology. Of all Marxist concepts, that which fits better with the main theme of this book is commodity fetishism, or, in my vocabulary, the fiction of commensurability; in Neurath's example, the fact that we 'cannot' compare kilograms of coal and hours of human labour in the same units.

The energy analysis of agriculture was not picked up, either, by populist, pro-peasant authors. Chayanov did not read Podolinsky. An argument could have been developed in favour of peasant farming. Energy analysis could have been put into service in the ideology of pro-peasant populism, which might have pleased Podolinsky himself. Many years later (Buttel,

---

[1] For instance, *Das Kapital*, vol. I, MEW edn, p. 198: *die Bedingungen des menschlichen Lebens* or *die ewige Naturbedingung des menschlichen Lebens*.

1980; Palerm, 1980; and of course Georgescu-Roegen) it was pointed out that the Green Revolution in agriculture of the 1960s was not 'green' at all, either in the old East European populist sense or in the new 'German' sense, because it seemed to favour rich peasants or farmers over poor peasants and landless labourers, and because it also meant 'farming with petroleum'.

While Podolinsky had at least a non-enthusiastic report from Engels on his intellectual efforts, and considerable attention later both in his own country and abroad, complete silence appears to have greeted Eduard Sacher, who, in books published in 1881 and 1899, also studied the flow of energy in agriculture. Sacher was aware of the increase in the energy input that chemical fertilizers and the use of the steam engine for threshing implied. He also had the idea of correlating stages in the history of humankind with energy use per caput.

There is also interesting material on agricultural energetics in the work of another Austrian writer, Josef Popper-Lynkeus, who in 1912 published *Die allgemeine Nährpflicht als Lösung der sozialen Frage*, the fundamental early text of ecological economics. This book, full of detailed computations of the use of resources, will be considered in chapter 13 on 'ecological utopianism'. Popper-Lynkeus proposed an economy which would make a decreasing use of exhaustible resources, and he considered to what extent renewable energy from agricultural crops could be substituted for coal, taking a 'pessimistic' view, because he quite properly included in his accounts the energy cost of growing crops. Such analysis is directly relevant, as shall be seen, to discussion today on 'energy cropping' versus food production, for instance in Brazil. The question is certainly not one of choosing between 'economics' and 'sentiment' (as Patrick Geddes would have said ironically), but rather of what is the ethical 'input' from outside economics proper which would enable the view to be accepted that the price mechanism leads to an acceptable allocation of scarce resources to alternative ends.

Popper-Lynkeus was a physicist, a friend of Ernst Mach, and he influenced the Vienna Circle and particularly Otto Neurath, whose economics based upon a *Naturalrechnung* and whose proposals for a 'unified science and cosmic history' are considered in this book. Another influence on Otto Neurath's economics was that of Karl Ballod-Atlanticus, a Berlin economist, and, like Popper-Lynkeus, a left-wing ecologist and the author of another 'ecological Utopia', *Der Zukunftsstaat*, first published in 1898.

About 1840, that is, before the laws of energetics were established, the new 'agricultural chemistry' had started with Liebig in Germany and with Boussingault in France. Liebig often appears in textbooks as a founding father of ecology (cf. Kormondy, 1965) because of his work on the cycles of carbon and of some plant nutrients. He liked to think that his own work, of which he became a commercial propagandist, was of great relevance in order to avoid a 'subsistence crisis' in Europe, which would occur unless 'heaps of dung and guano deposits of the size of English coalfields' were discovered (a phrase quoted by Kautsky (1899) in *Die Agrarfrage*, praising Liebig), or unless the new gospel of inorganic chemical fertilization were adopted. The reception of Liebig's doctrines in some countries has been well studied (Rossiter, 1975; Krohn, 1978). The question remains: was it often pointed out that European agriculture was starting to draw upon non-renewable material subsidies? Did perhaps some contemporary economists and agronomists point out that imports of guano from Peru meant an increase in the energy intensity of European agriculture and meant a worsening of its energy balance? Did anybody point out that Peru was exporting much more energy than it was getting back in return? Or did perhaps some economists discuss (though not yet using such technical terms) the 'shadow-price' of guano which would ensure an 'optimal rate of depletion' over time? Such questions are clearly rhetorical; about 100 years later, the exports by Peru of enormous amounts of basically the same resource, though at an earlier stage in the trophic chain (this time in the form of fishmeal for North Atlantic animals), did not prompt a debate on such terms.

Around the turn of the century, the discussion on the substitution of Chilean saltpetre by nitrogen taken from the air with the aid of hydro-electricity was indeed carried out in terms of its energy cost, so that the analysis of the flow of energy in modern agriculture could have become a well-trodden field of study much earlier than it did. The trivial use of the concept of 'technical progress' in economics and economic history, would then be questioned. An economic history of agriculture should be, at the same time, a history of agricultural science and technology, and a history of the social factors which influenced agricultural science and its applications.

The 'Entropy Law' and the Economic Process

Leaving aside the history of agricultural energetics (which takes up about one-quarter of this book), and going back to the more general theme of the relations (or lack of relations) between economics and the study of the flow of energy in human society, Jevons' views have also been considered carefully, a task which the edition of his correspondence by Collison Black (Jevons, 1972) facilitates. Jevons, one of the progenitors of marginalist economic theory, was up to date in science as shown in his exchanges with John Herschel, Clerk Maxwell and others, and also by his treatise on the *Principles of Science* (Jevons, 1879). Jevons addressed himself in *The Coal Question* (Jevons, 1865), to the substantive issue of coal reserves, and of improving the thermodynamic efficiency of coal-driven machines, expressing the view that as thermodynamic efficiency increased, so would the use of coal increase. Jevons certainly cannot be dismissed as one professionalized economist ignorant of natural sciences. The question that shall be asked is why, despite his interest in coal, did he not consider the intertemporal allocation of exhaustible resources in his work on marginalist economics?

Walras' work shall also be touched upon briefly, he who rarely mentioned physical matters except to remark often on the formal analogy (which also pleased Jevons) between the equations of mechanics and of economic equilibrium. But the most interesting point of contact between Walras and ecological economics was the correspondence he had with Patrick Geddes, the Scottish urban and regional planner.

Geddes is an author difficult to classify, and certainly difficult to read. He criticized the notion of 'utility' on the grounds that it was tautological. He believed that a part of consumption could be explained by biology, but he was by no means a reductionist, his favourite economist being John Ruskin who had emphasized aesthetic values above all. The new economics – as Geddes wrote to Walras in 1883 – was unsatisfactory also on the 'supply' side, since production should be studied with the help of physics. He developed the basic principles of a sort of *Tableau Économique* in physical terms, and he criticized economic accounting because it did not keep trace of the losses of energy and materials in the economic process. Geddes was also one of the first authors who tried to interpret the course of human history in terms of changes in the use of energy. One other author who, at the turn of the century, also had this idea, was the American historian Henry Adams, to whose views one chapter shall be devoted.

There might have been more discussions of the economy among the professional physicists than have been found. One discussion was by Rudolf Clausius, who in 1885 wrote on the energy reserves in nature and on their use for the benefit of humankind. Was he the first author to use the metaphor of the prodigal heir, which appears so often in the literature on limits to growth? 'We have found' (he wrote) 'stocks of coal from old times . . . These we are now using and we behave just as a happy heir eating up a rich legacy'. It is tempting to adopt Clausius not only as an ecological economist, but also as a 'green' father-figure. However, not only his social context should be considered, but, in general, the issues involved in the ideological transference of concepts and findings from natural sciences to social sciences and to social struggles.[2] I have tried to avoid writing this book in the form of an a priori exercise in legitimation of a putative discipline of ecological economics which would have been *in statu nascendi* for about 100 years. I have also tried not to alter the other authors' ideas in order to turn them into background support for today's left-wing 'ecologism'.

While, in general, economists and economic historians were clearly not interested in studying the flow of energy in human societies, physicists, on their side, seem to have been more willing to engage in theological speculation than in economics, deriving views on the divine creation of the world from thermodynamics, and threatening mankind with a rather swift 'heat-death'. There are many examples of blatant ideological use of science even by scientists themselves. Such words of caution are, however, not an answer to the basic question: why did many other natural scientists not 'trespass' onto the economists' field? Natural scientists, mathematicians and engineers (Watt, Lazare and Sadi Carnot, Coriolis, Babbage, Zeuner, Rankine, Herschel, Thomson, Clausius) had been concerned with the efficiency of the steam engine for a long time. Some of them, for example, Babbage, are also catalogued as economists. The connection between the discovery of the mechanical equivalent of heat and the role of the steam engine in the economy was phrased by Boris Hessen in a foundational text of the sociology of science:

by its very essence the steam engine is based on the transformation of one form of movement (thermal) into another form (mechanical). Thus, together with the development of the steam engine we get inevitably also the problem of the transition of one form of movement into another, which we do not find in Newton and which is closely bound with the problem of energy and its transformation. (Hessen, in Bukharin, 1931, p. 194).

The physiologists came to consider from the mid-nineteenth century onwards the efficiency in the transformation of energy by plants and animals (and by the human body) as a central question in their research. How to feed industrial workers at minimum cost, and assuring some standards of health, was a relevant consideration, and time and again references have been found to the diet of a soldier at war, which the Prussian wars of 1866 and 1870 against Austria and France made topical. Such research did not arise from idle scientific curiosity.

[2] The statement 'the entropy law shows that there will be no sustained economic growth, and therefore available resources should be shared equally' reminds me of the touching proposition from an Andalusian anarchosyndicalist leader in the 1910s that the laws of gravitation attracted them to the earth with such force that a redistribution of the latifundia became a necessity of nature.

The question can then be asked, why did 'the entropy law and the economic process' not become a well-established field of study in the 1850s, as might have happened? Clearly, in order to answer this question – which provides a common thread through all the chapters in this book – studies are required of the ideological and political background of scientists, and particularly of the separation between sciences and of their institutionalization and professionalization.[3] For instance, in the case of Clausius, work has been done on his views on physics and the foundations of science (Truesdell, 1980), and part of his biography has been written (Ronge, 1955; Daub, 1971) but in chapter 5 the economic, political, and cultural context will be described.

One other physicist (of minor importance in his own discipline) who wrote on the economy was Leopold Pfaundler. In a brief and clearly written article (Pfaundler, 1902) he analysed the carrying capacity of the earth, with calculations of the solar energy falling on the soil and being converted by plants through photosynthesis, and also of the needs of food energy for human nutrition. His article suggests that the expression 'energy crisis' should be reserved for situations in which there are humans who are unable to obtain the 2,000 or 2,500 kilocalories per day that they would need for minimum sustenance, and that the cause of such 'energy crises' is, in the last resort, not the niggardliness of nature, but the restrictions in geographical mobility (because of frontiers, passports, visas): frontier police are like Maxwell's demons working in reverse.

Social-Darwinism and Ecology

Pfaundler's main thesis was that the carrying capacity of the earth was not determined by the availability of materials, but by the availability of free energies, since materials could be completely recycled because of the law of conservation of matter. One other contribution by Pfaundler (following Boltzmann's steps) was his awareness of the links between social-Darwinism and the study of the use of energy and materials by humanity. Social-Darwinism has inevitably cropped up in my research, against my wishes, and against the wishes of some of the other authors (for instance, Popper-Lynkeus and Podolinsky), who held strongly egalitarian views.

Although I certainly understand Podolinsky's principle, that a society is not viable unless the energy return to human energy expenditure covers

---

[3] These are themes developed by writers such as Cannon, 1976; Gregory, 1977; Krohn et al. (eds), 1978; Graham et al. (eds), 1983.

the energy cost of human labour, and while I realize that the idea of arranging societies in a scale according to such parameters might be useful, I am annoyed by statements such as one can find in the pages of *Human Ecology* where, for instance, the very low level of energy use by highland shepherds in the Andes is commended as an adaptive device.[4] One could as well say that the shepherds not only 'adapt' to ecological conditions, but to the land tenure system, that is, they have used natural resources in a manner compatible with their own survival and reproduction and with the delivery of a surplus to the landowners, the value of which has been assessed in calories (cf. Brooke Thomas, 1976, p. 403). Peruvian peasants have attempted time and again, at least from the Spanish conquest onwards, *not* to adapt to the destiny that the colonial power, the authorities from Lima, the local landowners, and the world economic and political system, reserved for them. While the patterns of migration of animals can probably be explained to a great extent by ecologists (who else?), the preventing of Mexicans from entering the United States, and the export of oil from Mexico to the United States are social, political phenomena. The openness of Saudi Arabia and Iran to visiting oil tankers, even the relative isolation of the Tsembaga-Maring or the Kung San in the 1960s, are facts of human history which energetics and biology do not explain. The dynamics of human history is better understood as the result of a struggle between rich and poor, the forms of which vary according to the changes in relations of production, than as a history of social organisms which 'adapt' to ecological conditions.

Although a dog may be envisaged travelling across the Atlantic by Concorde with a great expenditure of fuel, the intraspecific differences in the use of energy and materials are small in all species, if human intervention is excluded, compared to the differences for humankind. It is distinctive of the human species that at one given moment the use of energy and materials by its members can show enormous differences. The struggle between groups of humans (inside each society – or, rather, state – and between states) is *not* a biological 'struggle for life'.

A classic statement of the connection between energetics and natural selection theory was made by Alfred Lotka (1880–1949):

'If we had only the animal kingdom to consider we should in the first instance be disposed to conclude that the cosmic effect of the scrimmage for available energy

---

[4] e.g. Smith, 1979; or Weinstein et al., 1983, 'The Quechua Indians of the Peruvian high Andes are an example of a human population which has developed special cultural adaptations to deal with hypocalorie stress imposed by a harsh environment', referring to their use of dung as fuel and to their "vertical" economy where meat and wool from the highlands is traded for cereals and other produce from lower levels.

would be to increase the total energy flux, the rate of degradation of the energy received from the sun. But plants work in the opposite direction. And even among animals, greater efficiency in utilizing energy, a better husbanding of resources, and hence a less rapid drain upon them, must work to the advantage of a species talented in that direction. There are thus two opposing tendencies in operation, and it is difficult to see how any general principle can be applied to determine just where the balance will be struck (Lotka, 1925, p. 357).

In Lotka's view, however, the 'law of evolution' (i.e. of reproductive success of a species) took the form of a 'law of maximum energy flow':

This at least seems probable . . . so long as there is an abundant surplus of available energy running 'to waste' over the sides of the mill wheel, so to speak, so long will a marked advantage be gained by any species that may develop talents to utilize this 'lost portion of stream'. Such a species will therefore, other things equal, tend to grow in extent (numbers) and this growth will further increase the flux of energy through the system. It is to be observed that in this argument the principle of the survival of the fittest yields us information beyond that attainable by the reasoning of thermodynamics. As to the other aspect of the matter, the problem of economy in husbanding resources will not rise to its full importance until the available resources are more completely tapped than they are today. Every indication is that man will learn to utilize some of the sunlight that now goes to waste. The general effect will be to increase the rate of energy flow through the system of organic nature. . . . (Lotka, 1925, p. 357)

The success of the human *species* could therefore be analysed in terms of its learning to use sources of energy. But, could the link-up between energetics and evolution, could the notion that 'the life contest is primarily a competition for available energy' (Boltzman, 1886, cited by Lotka, 1925, p. 355) be applied *intraspecifically*? Unfortunately, an intimation of such social-Darwinist energetics is found in Lotka's influential book:

An impartial judge, if such could be produced, would doubtless concede to the human species, as it stands today, an unique and predominant position in the scheme of nature. For, civilized man has achieved the distinction of practically clearing the board of all foes of a stature in any way comparable to his own. This has resulted for him in a very special form of the struggle for existence. With the conflict against other species relegated to the back-ground, man's combat with his own kind has been forced to the center of the stage. . . . (Lotka, 1925, p. 417)

This line of thought is unsound, because natural selection theory cannot be applied intraspecifically except in a metaphorical way. The subject will be considered again in the chapters on Pfaundler and on Henry Adams.

Ecological and Pecuniary Economics

In the list of authors, Frederick Soddy, a well known chemist, deserves a prominent place. In order to emphasize (in a very 'green' way) the role of agriculture in the economy, Soddy drew a distinction between the 'vital use' of energy and its 'laboral use', similar to that of Lotka between 'endosomatic' and 'exosomatic' uses of energy. From 1903 onwards he had told economists to study the use of energy by humanity. He blamed economists for mistaking chrematistics for economics.

It is difficult to classify Soddy either as an 'optimist' or as a 'pessimist' on the question of economic growth. He certainly believed in the progress of scientific knowledge, but he did not believe that this necessarily entailed technical progress, though he was sometimes carried away by the vistas of energy opened up by radioactivity. Soddy's main point was that the economists were mistaking real capital for financial capital. He pointed out that the payment of interest could only arise either from growth of the economy or from impoverishment of debtors, and that there was no pure economic theory of growth, since growth depended, in the last analysis, on physical factors, that is, on the availability of energy. The exhausting of the stock of fossil fuels could only be called squandering, even if fossil fuels were spent in the construction of so-called 'capital goods' by which the present generation would presumably increase 'productive capacity' to the benefit of future generations. Soddy's critique was *not* only that *rentier* capitalists could not go on earning interest merely by loaning out their capital, none of them using it 'productively' in order to extract profits from wage-labour. His point was also that it was impossible for capitalists to go on earning interest (or profit) even though their capital were invested 'productively' – unless they spoliated exhaustible resources. It is the definition of 'production' which is in question.

Ostwald's contribution to ecological economics was less polemical against the economists than Soddy's, and directed more to the historians. He also failed in his rather high-handed attempt to engage in dialogue with historians and with social scientists, though he later became one of the recognized forebears of evolutionary ecological anthropology in the United States (through Leslie White). The true heads of this lineage ought to be Podolinsky, Sacher, and Geddes.

Ostwald, also a chemist, was president of the Monist League (founded by Haeckel) between 1911 and 1914. Haeckel himself, though credited with the introduction of the word 'ecology' in science, is not featured in this book because he did not study the flow of energy in human societies. He was a most important figure in the doctrine that the theory of natural selection and evolution is applicable to human struggles. His colleague in the Monist League must certainly appear in this book. It is true that Ostwald was not a believer in the egalitarian ecologism, robustly and explicitly based on an appeal to reason, of most of the authors in this book; but to conflate social energetics and social-Darwinism in all cases is a mistake. Many of the German Monists showed social-Darwinist tendencies similar in kind and in degree to the racial and class eugenic thought in Britain and the United States (Hofstadter, 1944; Greta Jones, 1980; Stepan, 1982). Sometimes this went together with the desire to offer a new religion based on science and the study of nature; in the German context, Darwinism and social-Darwinism had played a role in the anti-clerical *Kulturkampf* (Gasman, 1971). One of Ostwald's books is entitled *The Sunday Sermons*, and given to the Monist faithful.[5]

Nevertheless, it will be shown in this book that empirical human ecology, as a critique of economics, originated in thoroughly rationalist authors. A crucial position in this argument is occupied by Popper-Lynkeus, who worshipped neither the sun nor the steam engine, neither the Virgin Mary nor the electric dynamo; he did not worship at all. He was not in the least a Germanic romantic nationalist, he was an Austrian Jewish Machian empirio-criticist. Ostwald, though younger than Popper-Lynkeus, was epistemologically more ancient and politically more conservative, a good German would-be imperialist, though not a strident social-Darwinist.

The approach to Ostwald's social energetics will be by way of Max Weber's detailed and little-known critique of 1909, not yet translated into English. Of particular interest is Max Weber's discussion of the relations between the sciences. Ostwald was a Comtean, and Comte did not understand (Weber wrote) that each science dealt separately with an object of knowledge, using a set of hypothetical – theoretical propositions whose validity did not depend on the findings of any other discipline. Discussing Ostwald's view, that the development of culture went with an improvement in the efficiency of the transformation of energy, Max Weber cleverly pointed out that it was energetically cheaper to weave a piece of cloth by hand than mechanically; nevertheless mechanical weaving is presumably a sign of cultural progress. A similar reply can be imagined, addressed to those scientists (and/or to these peasant ideologues) who nowadays point out to economists that modern agriculture implies worsening the energy output/input ratio: 'nothing to do with economics'.

---

[5] There was little distance from such religious nature-loving to the quackery of Rudolf Steiner. The tendency to mix up ecology and religion reappears now and then (for instance, in the work of Capra, 1983).

In contrast to Max Weber, I shall put forward in chapter 14 of this book the following view, which bears no relation to Comtean 'pyramidism': the natural sciences study 'natural history' – to use an old word – while the social sciences study (or at least should be useful for the study of) the history of humankind, and together they could be integrated in a study of truly universal history, which would also comprise the 'history of the future'. This view, proposed by Neurath, is not reductionist, and it does not imply either a *holistic* approach (whatever irrationalities or mysteries the word might hide) or a *Ganzheitslehre*.

'Social Engineering' and the 'History of the Future'

Before 1973, and even in 1987, many volumes of economic history of different schools (Marx, Schumpeter, Polanyi, Hicks, Kuznets, to give some examples), could be perused without finding as a central question the use of energy and of material resources. A. G. Frank (1959) showed that there was a perfect correlation between the given measures of growth of industrial capital stocks and the consumption of energy from fossil fuels both in the USA and in the UK. But neither Frank nor Wallerstein wrote the kind of ecological history which is now developing (cf. Debeir, Deléage, and Hémery, 1986).

Concepts of economics such as production and productivity, technical progress, net investment as growth of productive capacity, and value added, seem nowadays singularly metaphysical. The belief in economic growth, and the concomitant possibility of disqualifying redistributive compulsions, help to explain the resilience of economics (both in the academic and political worlds) faced with the ecological critique. Charles Maier's dictum (Maier, 1978, p. 70) that the ideology of economic growth was the last great conservative ideology can be interpreted in this sense. In the 1980s the neo-liberal faith in the market did not emphasize growth to the same extent that the corporatist Keynesianism of the 1960s did, and it was tempted by the customary social-Darwinist (or sociobiologist) rationalization of social inequality.

Economics is unable to deal convincingly with the ecological critique. Therefore, it was paradoxical that the renewed faith in the market coincided with the 'energy crisis' of 1973 and its aftermath. However, a reductionist methodology which would attempt to explain the human utilization of energy and material resources with the exclusive help of the natural sciences would be unsuccessful. Some use perhaps one ton of petroleum yearly (in the form of fuel for tractors, fertilizers, herbicides, transport, fridges, electric kitchens, etc.), in order to feed themselves while other members of humanity do not use a single drop of petroleum. The human allocation of energy and material resources to different uses cannot only be explained by natural sciences. Economics should *not* become merely human ecology. However, conventional economics (or Marxist economics) could not explain for instance, why it is unlikely that the present ratio of automobiles to population of North Atlantic countries (and Japan) be extended to the world at large. Using cars as an example, Carnap, 1938, wrote in the *Encyclopaedia of Unified Science*: 'very often a prediction cannot be based on our knowledge of only one branch of science'.

In such an encyclopaedia it would certainly not do if, under an article on 'Agriculture, development of', one simply read: 'the economists say that there has been an increase in productivity, while agricultural energetics shows that there has been a decrease in the output/input ratio'. If the value of exhaustible resources were counted at an opportunity cost which took 'adequately' into account the demand of future generations, then the economic and ecological judgements might come closer. Nevertheless, economists will say – as Max Weber said – that market prices (which arise from the interactions of many agents, whose aggregate information is the best that exists) are decisive elements in explaining the allocation of resources.

In a planned economy, a 'social' rate of discount of the present value of future demands could perhaps be used, which would value future demands to a greater extent that the market rate of interest does. Prices of exhaustible resources in the Soviet Union have been criticized by economists because average cost and not marginal cost is used for pricing, thus pushing up production in 'inefficient' mines and in the sector as a whole. But no attempt has yet been made in economic literature to apply Hotelling's rule to the depletion path of natural resources in the Soviet Union; it will be interesting to see the necessary discussion of the appropriate rate of discount of the (more? or less?) radiant future (cf. Sen, 1961; Marglin, 1963; Parfit, 1985).

In the case of the agricultural economy, the contradiction between propositions from the different sciences would have to be removed, if it were required to be able to predict whether the numbers of peasants and agricultural workers in the world as a whole would fall, or whether, on the contrary, they would rise. 'Prediction' is clearly a far-fetched word, in this context. The question would be rather whether *narodism* is a rational political ideology for the 1990s and beyond.

Also of use in making the 'history' of achievable futures, would be a general history which would co-ordinate the propositions from the different sciences, eliminating the contradictions between them. An Encyclopaedia of Unified Science would be the same (as Neurath put it) as a truly universal history, within the perspective of scientific utopianism.

As noted above, Hayek, (1941, 1942, 1943, 1944) (and also Popper, (1944, 1945)), in articles published in the early 1940s which later became famous books, linked 'historicism', 'objectivism', 'social engineering' and 'utopianism' to totalitarianism. Karl Popper drew a difference between 'holistic utopian social engineering' and 'piecemeal social engineering', and not being such a fundamentalist believer in the market as Hayek, agreed with 'piecemeal social engineering' while seeing in 'utopian social engineering' the gravest threat to the 'open society'. Some of the authors considered in this book are listed by Hayek in those articles and in *The Counter-revolution of Science* (1952) as typical representatives of 'scientism', 'neo-Saint-Simonism', 'technocratic collectivism', 'social engineering', 'social energeticism'. This list, together with that provided by Žmavc (1926, p. 42), has been most useful.

The arguments of ecological economics could be placed in the context of a discussion on possible 'market failures' – a formulation which assumes 'market success' as the rule – that is, whether the price mechanism allocates exhaustible resources successfully among the generations. In this book, a general diatribe against the market economy is not necessary; a restricted, technical point is made, that is, that in the economics of exhaustible resources, most potential buyers *cannot* come to the market. The methodological individualism pushed with such fervour by Hayek and Karl Popper runs into an impasse when it is considered that individuals not yet born have ontological difficulties in making their presence felt in today's market for exhaustible resources.

Marx's tendency to disbelieve in the benefits of the market could, in principle, facilitate a fruitful dialogue between Marxism and ecological economics, along the lines that Otto Neurath (one of Hayek's *bêtes noires*) tried to develop. This is the subject of one chapter of this book, and it is probably its most important message, at least for historians and anthropologists, and perhaps also politically.

It was certainly abusive on Hayek's part to qualify several of the authors studied as 'neo-Saint-Simonians', when their point was precisely to question economic growth. Both Saint-Simonism and Marxian 'utopianism' would be characterized by the confusion between the advance of scientific knowledge and the boundless expansion of technology, and by the lack of analysis of the exhaustibility of resources. This notion of Marxian utopianism is taken from Steven Lukes, who wrote in 1984: 'What united them (Marx and Engels) with Saint-Simon and his followers has been well described by the Manuels:[6] an endlessly dynamic prospect founded upon the boundless expansion of science and technology, exploitation of the inexaustible resources of the globe, and the flowering of human capacities'. In the Marxist view, future abundance (once capitalist relations of production no longer prevented the growth of productive forces) would eventually allow humanity to reach the communist stage: 'from each according to his abilities, to each according to his needs', as Marx wrote in 1875 in the *Critique of the Gotha Programme*. There also existed another left-wing utopianist current which denied this vision of future overflowing abundance, and which therefore (in some cases at least) asked for a more urgent consideration of equality than mainstream Marxism. This current could be called ecological utopianism. It has existed for some time, although almost nobody seems to have noticed it.

The ecological critique of economics might have effects on the attitudes of socio-political actors of each country, and internationally. For instance, will corporatist agreements on incomes policies and on so-called restructuring of industry, be undermined by the potential discredit of National Income Accounting and of theories of economic growth? Will the resurrected faith in the market lose some of its believers? Will struggles on international trade policies and on commodity prices be affected by an ecological approach to the definition of 'unequal exchange'?

If modern agriculture is studied from the point of view of the ecological energetics first developed by Podolinsky and Sacher, then it must be concluded that in the over-developed countries, even such minimal requirements of human life as a loaf of bread, might have become 'positional goods' (in the sense of Hirsch, 1976), at least towards future generations. This is what lies behind the recommendation, no doubt well-intentioned, that 'in a time when advanced nations are ever more intensively searching for renewable alternatives to their fossil-fuelled economies, it would be at least ironic if the Chinese were to abandon completely their solar energetics' (Smil, 1979, p. 131). On the contrary, in this book, the following proposal is put forward: that universal egalitarian ecological utopianism is one 'appropriate ideology' for the poor people of the world (against both the ideologies of 'waiting for economic growth while preserving inequality' and 'to each country, its adaptive, appropriate technology'). Though it is an ideology which could be called 'ecological neo-narodism', it can find much support in the tradition of rational-empiricist study of human ecology.

To sum up, the detailed study of the questions raised by the authors listed will make clear that ecological economics could have been developed long ago. The question remains why so few natural scientists wrote on the economy in the second half of the nineteenth century and at the beginning of the twentieth century. I do not believe that a complete census

[6] Cf. Lukes, Steven, 1984, p. 156; Manuel, F. E. and Manuel, F. P., 1979, p. 707. The Manuels are anti-utopianists.

has been established, but it is clear that there were not many such scientists.[7] A related question is, why did economists pay so little attention to such attempts at interdisciplinarity, including among the economists also the economic historians, who should have known better? And, finally, why was the left-wing ecological critique of economics not adopted as an ideology by any social group? These are questions about the separation and the relationships between the sciences, about the social functions of science, and about the sociology and the history of science.

[7] Although my research on Russian human ecology both before and after 1917 has been most cursory. For a short, competent survey of the history of ecology with emphasis on Russian authors, see Budyko, 1980, pp. 13–15; also Major (1969), Bakuzis (1969), Susiluoto (1982), and G. A. Novikov et al., (1970). Ecology is a science which abounds in Russian names: Dokuchaiev (who developed soil science), Vernadsky, etc. Podolinsky was probably not the only author in Russia to make the link between economics and ecological energetics. The word 'ecosystem' itself dates from 1935, given by Tansley, of Oxford, but the study of ecosystems, including human ecosystems, had begun much earlier.

2

'Modern' Agriculture:
A Source of Energy?

Introduction

Sometimes it is said that agriculture might become a source of energy, by which it is meant that biomass might be used as fuel, not merely in the form of wood or dung. It is difficult to understand the physics (as distinct from the sociology) of simultaneously excluding sugar production from the 'energy sector' and including ethanol from sugar cane. It is only an 'urban bias' (or an 'upper class' bias) of the most potent sort, which allows people who are perhaps worried about an excess of calories in their diet, to exclude food production from the 'energy sector' of the economy.

In this chapter, as an introduction to the history of agricultural energetics, three contemporary case studies of agriculture as a source and as a user of energy will be examined: the Brazilian ethanol programme; the Chinese agrarian economy (as described by Smil, 1979); and the energy balances of Spanish agriculture before and after 'modernization' (Naredo and Campos, 1980). The methods of analysis are in essence identical to those developed much earlier by Podolinsky and Sacher. They will provide a contemporary lens for a retrospective vision of the beginnings of 'modern' agriculture from the 1840s onwards, when 'agricultural chemistry' really started to develop, as will be described in the last section of this chapter. Some distinctive moments in the history of the (non-existing) discipline of ecological agricultural economics are seen tentatively: the study of the cycles of materials during the 1840s and 1850s; the beginning of agricultural energetics in about 1880; the explosion in the number of studies of the flow of energy in the 1970s, and the interest in genetic variability in agroecosystems in the 1980s.[1]

---

[1] Preceded by calls against the excessive use of pesticides, in Carson's *Silent Spring* (1963). The next stage will probably be the study of the socio-economic and ecological impact of the new agricultural biotechnologies.

Ethanol from Sugar Cane

In the context of the general awareness since the 1970s that modern agriculture means 'farming with petroleum', the Brazilian programme allegedly for substituting part of its oil imports by the distillation of massive quantities of ethyl alcohol from sugar cane, presents a paradox, worth exploring for its own sake and to help clarify some of the procedures of energy accounting in agriculture. The question obviously arises of whether the programme will not mean converting oil into ethyl alcohol with little gain in energy availability. However, it has been argued that for each calorie used as input, some four calories are obtained as output, in the form of ethanol, the reason being that sugar cane is a very productive crop in energy terms, and also that bagasse is used as fuel in the distillation process.

Ethanol is used as fuel for cars. This means that while one relevant comparison is between the energetic efficiency of ethanol production and other types of agriculture, another relevant comparison is between the energy cost of ethanol and the energy cost of other sources of energy such as coal, oil, and hydroelectricity; in this sense, ethanol from sugar cane appears to be quite expensive.

The 'extra-energy' obtained from the ethanol programme at its most ambitious, even assuming that the large amount of land needed is in fact available, would not modify substantially the general energy situation in Brazil. If shared equally among Brazilians, average energy consumption would increase by such a small amount that it is quite unlikely that the average Brazilian family would dispose of enough energy to be able to run a car. If made generally available, this extra-energy would probably be used by some as an increase in the food energy intake, and by others in the form of products and services which are more necessary than cars. However, the point is that the extra-energy from the ethanol programme takes the specific form of fuel for cars, and it will not be available to the population in general, but only to a small sector of the population. In that way, ethanol is more like an expensive whisky than beer or cheap wine. Of course, the aim of the ethanol programme has never been to increase general availability of energy, but specifically to increase the supply of fuel for cars, without at the same time increasing the import requirements of oil. The ethanol programme would thus be complementary to other programmes which would increase energy availability to a level which would make it possible to turn Brazil into a generally motorized country. The likelihood of this prospect will be examined.

Production of ethanol in Brazil in 1985 was of the order of eleven billion litres (11×10^9). As a tentative exercise, the land requirement and the contribution to gross energy availability from three different programmes, of 10, 30 or 90 billion litres will be estimated. The yield from cane is about 54 tons/hectare, and 66 litres of ethanol are produced per ton of cane (Gomes da Silva et al., 1978; Hopkinson and Day, 1980). This means a production of 3,564 litres of ethanol per hectare/year. This would be enough to run between two or three cars (taking a consumption of the order of 10 litres/100 kilometres, and 15,000 kilometres/year). Such programmes would require also, of course, as will be seen later, inputs of energy in order to produce the ethanol itself, and in order to produce and maintain the cars and the new roads. Land is also required beyond that needed to grow the cane, since cars imply characteristic patterns of urbanization. In table 1 this is left aside, for simplicity.

Table 1   Three hypothetical plans of ethanol production in Brazil

			Gross energy availability from ethanol, per head/year			
Ethanol production	Direct land requirement	Number of ethanol cars	Population, 150 million		Population, 200 million	
			litres	kcal	litres	kcal
$(10^9 litres)$	$(10^6 hectares)$	(10^6)		(10^6)		(10^6)
10	2.8	5.6– 8.4	66.6	0.350	50	0.263
30	8.4	16.8–25.2	200.0	1.052	150	0.789
90	25.2	50.4–75.6	600.0	3.156	450	2.267

For comparison, direct food consumption per head/year of a well-fed adult person is roughly one million kilocalories. *Sources*: As in text

The figures for the contribution of ethanol to primary energy availability (in kilocalories per head/year) are computed by taking the value of 5,260 kilocalories per one litre of ethanol. Thus, taking the extremely ambitious programme of 90 billion litres of ethanol (which nobody has proposed), this would be enough to provide fuel for between 50 and 75 million cars, that is, the number of cars which a Brazil 'motorized' to North-Atlantic standards would have when the population (which was about 140 million in 1985, growing at almost two per cent per year) reached 200 million. The per head contribution of ethanol would be, in this hypothetical case, 450 litres of ethanol per head/year, that is, 1.23 litres per head/day, that is, about 6,500 kilocalories per head/day, that is, somewhat less than one kilogram of coal. The gross energy from this hypothetical, enormous, ethanol programme of 90 billion litres, would therefore provide an increase in consumption equivalent to about 0.3 TEC or 0.2 TEP (tons equivalent of coal, or tons equivalent of oil) per head/year, which can be compared with current primary non-food energy use in Brazil of about 1.5 TEC or 1 TEP per head/year (roughly one-half from oil, one-quarter from hydro-electricity, and one-quarter still from wood). As an energy programme, this extremely optimistic plan of 90 billion litres is not impressive. As an agricultural programme, it is extremely impressive. Even the smallest programme, of 10 billion litres, requires nearly 3 million hectares of cane (more than the area of cane in Cuba), and would add about 700 kilocalories per head/day, for a population of 200 million. In the form of alcohol for drink, this would be excessive (50 litres per head/year, 0.14 litres per head/day). In the form of food, it would certainly provide a welcome supplement, or an opportunity for a diversification of the diet to most Brazilians. The essence of the ethanol programme, however, is not that it will provide energy in the form of food (or drink), but that energy will be provided specifically in the form of fuel for cars. And the fact is that most Brazilians will not have a car, since this depends on the general level of energy availability, to which the ethanol programme will make a minute contribute. The current availability of primary energy per head/year in Brazil is of the order of 1.5 TEC or 1 TEP. In the less over-developed countries (such as Spain) which have a relatively high level of motorization, it exceeds 3 TEC or 2 TEP. Since the ethanol programme has been presented to the public as a way of reducing oil consumption, it might be assumed that Brazil would not increase imports of oil: in such a case, it is unlikely that Brazil would ever reach levels of motorization consistent with a 90 billion litre or even a 30 billion litre ethanol programme.

A 90 billion litre ethanol programme would supply enough fuel for 50 million or 75 million cars. There would be enough energy for the cars, but not nearly enough for the people, to enable them to have cars. The general availability of energy in Brazil depends on new important oil and natural gas discoveries and on hydroelectricity. Potential capacity of hydroelectric power has been given (Goldemberg, 1978) as 120 gigawatts (equivalent to 120 large power stations, of one thousand megawatts each), with a potential annual generation of about 515,000 gigawatts/hour.[2] Assuming a population of 200 million, the total contribution of hydro-electricity could reach 2,575 kilowatt-hours per person/year, or a little over

---

[2] Hydroelectric installations do not run 24 hours a day, every day of the year, at full capacity.

two million kilocalories per person/year (1 kilowatt hour = 860 kilocalories), or 6,020 kilocalories per person/day.[3]

Electricity is usually measured at its generation energy cost, that is, the energy content of the coal or oil which is used, or would be used, to produce it. This accounting convention is also applied to hydroelectricity, multiplying the energy delivered by a factor of 3. The total contribution of hydroelectricity, in terms of conventionally accounted primary energy use, would then reach (for a population of 200 million) 21 kilowatt hours or 18,060 kilocalories per person/day.

Oil imports have been of the order of 50 million tons per year. If this level is maintained, this would mean, for a population of 200 million, 250 kilograms per person/year, that is, some 0.7 kilogram per person/day, that is, some 7,000 kilocalories per person/day. Thus, from hydroelectricity (measured at alternative generation cost) and from imported oil, primary energy use would be in the region of 25,000 kilocalories per head/day, far from the level of 70,000 kilocalories corresponding to the primary energy consumption per head of the less over-developed countries where motorization is pretty general. Ethanol production would not make any appreciable difference to this general picture, even assuming the hypothetically enormous programme of 90 billion litres. From where should the additional energy come?

The notion that, because of the ethanol programme, general motorization will be compatible with oil imports remaining the same, let alone decreasing, makes little sense. Even assuming hydroelectricity to be developed to its physical limit, general availability of energy in Brazil would make general motorization impossible, unless new sources of domestic oil and gas change the outlook. Assuming however a rather distorted distribution of energy use (because of the distorted distribution of power, of property and of income) then a relatively large market for cars may develop, consistent with an ethanol programme of up to some 20 or 30 billion litres.

The energy requirements of ethanol production are other reasons why it is misleading to present the ethanol programme as an oil-saving programme, which at the same time allows motorization. Ethanol is a very expensive (with respect to energy) source of energy, compared with

---

[3] When 1 kilowatt hour = 860 kilocalories is written, this means that with the power of one kilowatt in one hour (equivalently, with 3,600,000 joules, or with 860 kilocalories) one can produce enough heat to increase the temperature of 860 kilograms of water one degree centigrade (between 14°C and 15°C). One horse-power is approximately equal to 0.75 kilowatt. The energy delivered by one (very strong) horse in one hour would be equal to 0.75 kilowatt hour, or 645 kilocalories. However, in order to deliver this energy, the horse has had to eat food containing an amount of energy six or eight times larger.

oil or coal. The initial balances presented by Goldemberg (1978) and Gomes da Silva et al. (1978) were as follows (table 2).

Table 2 Energy balance, ethanol from cane, 10^6 kilocalories/hectare/year

Outputs			Inputs		
Ethanol	Bagasse	Total	Into agriculture	Into industry	Total
18.7	17.5	36.2	4.2	10.8	15

Since part of the output of bagasse is used as fuel for the distilleries, a consolidated balance would be as in table 3.

Table 3 Energy balance, ethanol from cane, 10^6 kilocalories/hectare/year

Outputs		Inputs
Ethanol	(Unused bagasse)	Into agriculture
18.7	(6.7)	4.2

The energy output/input ratio, excluding unused bagasse, appears to be 4.4:1. However, in table 3 the energy cost of building and running the distilleries is missing. Also missing are the energy costs and benefits of disposing of stillage (*vinhaça*). From the output, the energy cost of transporting the ethanol to the markets should be subtracted. Finally, the net energy output that the land produced before being taken over by the ethanol programme should also be subtracted. For instance, if the land had been used as pasture, its energy output would have been smaller than would now be achieved. If the land had been used for sugar cane to produce sugar, there would be no energy gain whatever, rather the reverse.

The energy input into agriculture (of 4.2 million kilocaries/hectare/year) can be considered in a comparative context.[4] Pimentel calculated an input of 7 million kilocalories/hectare/year for maize growing in the United States (Pimentel, 1973, 1979), with an output of about 5,000 kilograms of maize/hectare (equivalent to about 18.5 million kilocalories, not counting stalks). Naredo (1980) gave an input of about 3.5 million

---

[4] One convenient equivalence is that the heat energy released in burning one ton of oil is about 42,000 megajoules = 10 million kilocalories. Thus, to say that the energy input into agriculture (excluding of course solar energy) is 4 million kilocalories, or 7 million calories per hectare/year, is like saying that it is equivalent to 0.4 or 0.7 tons of oil.

kilocalories/hectare/year for a wheat–sunflower rotation in southern Spain, with an output of about 8.5 million kilocalories/hectare/year (without straw, or 11 million kilocalories/hectare/year, counting straw). It can also be compared, for instance, to Mexican peasant maize growing, with an energy input of about 0.5 million kilocalories/hectare/year, for an output of about 7 million kilocalories/hectare/year (Pimentel, 1979, p. 40). And it can also be compared to the more energy-intensive and labour-saving method of growing cane in Louisiana, which takes 8.4 million kilocalories/hectare/year, for an output similar to that of Brazil, because of a much higher level of nitrogen fertilization, and because cane is not only loaded, but also harvested, by machine (Hopkinson and Day, 1980).

The energy efficiency of ethanol production would of course increase with a more manual method of farming. On the other hand, mechanization of cane cutting – which is likely if unions are allowed to be active – will increase the energy input substantially, since cane is a very bulky crop.

According to Gomes da Silva et al. (1976, 1978), about 50 per cent of the energy input into agriculture of 4.2 million kilocalories/hectare/year would be accounted for by fuel for machinery, 30 per cent by fertilizer, 10 per cent by machinery and other agricultural equipment corresponding to the annual energy cost over their lifetime, and the rest to seed, pesticides, and human labour.

The energy efficiency of ethanol production in this authoritative Brazilian study[5] is much higher than that calculated for ethanol production in Louisiana, of 1.5:1 instead of 4.4:1 (Hopkinson and Day, 1980). For sugar production, the Barbados Sugar Producers' Association (Hudson, 1975) considered two systems, one fully mechanized and another only partly mechanized, both with the same input of fertilizer and the same industrial process. With yields, in both systems, of 70 tons of cane/hectare (and 7 tons of sugar/hectare), the energy output/energy input ratios are, respectively, 2.7 and 5.4. Another balance for cane sugar (Gifford, 1976, cited by Slesser, 1979, p. 112) shows an energy input per hectare of about 40 gigajoules (GJ), equal to 9.6 million kilocalories, and a ratio energy output/energy input of about 2.7. The comparatively favourable ratio in Brazil in Gomes da Silva's study is partly explained by the relatively low level of energy input in agriculture (because of a lower level of fertilization and mechanization), but it is also explained by failure to consider the energy cost of building and running mills and distilleries. Though the main energy input in the industrial process is bagasse, building

[5] Gomes da Silva became in the early 1980s the Secretary of Agriculture of the São Paulo government under the Franco Montoro administration; Goldemberg is *the* energy expert of Brazil.

the distilleries implies some extra energy cost. The most common type of new distillery in Brazil is the 120 cubic metres/day, 18 million litres per season (of five months, working three shifts), which takes cane from about 5,000 hectares (Conselho Nacional, 1980).

If the mechanization of cane cutting, and the energy cost imputable to the building of the distillery (plus the cost of disposing of stillage) are taken into account in the energy input, and if some energy to be spent on the transport of the ethanol and the net energy output lost because of the change in land use are subtracted from the output, then the energy balance of ethanol production would change substantially. There is no point in risking a figure, because so much depends on the estimate of net energy produced in the same area previous to the change in crop, and also on the estimate of energy benefits from stillage.

Considering the ethanol industry as one more branch of the so-called 'energy sector' of the economy (coal and oil extraction, hydroelectricity, etc.), the energy cost of ethanol production could then be compared with other sources of energy. In this respect, ethanol appears to be much more expensive than either coal or oil, and comparable to gasoline from coal or gasoline from oil shale (Slesser, 1978, p. 70). In coal or oil extraction, transport and refining, an expenditure of one calorie would be needed in order to produce five to ten calories; in ethanol production, with the appropriate corrections, an optimistic ratio would be two or three calories produced per calorie spent.

Finally it should be considered whether the workers in the cane fields and in the distilleries would be able to run ethanol cars. How much energy does a car use per year? Not only the fuel must be taken into account, but also the energy spent in building the car, spread over the car's lifetime. Then, how much energy does a worker in the ethanol industry 'produce'? Would he (and his family) be able to run a car, if he were entitled to the full energetic fruits of his labour? If this were the case (in a semi-mechanized system) the ethanol programme would defeat its aim, which is to provide a surplus of energy for middle-class town-dwellers to run cars (cf. Freitag and Martinez-Alier, 1982).

The Energy Cost of Modernizing Chinese Agriculture

The primary energy consumed per head/year in industrialized over-developed countries is of the order of 100,000–400,000 megajoules, that is, some 25–100 million kilocalories, that is, some 2.5–10 tons of oil equivalent. Food energy is usually excluded from such statistics. It is properly excluded, since in industrialized countries most food (except that produced in domestic gardens, possibly with few energy inputs apart from human labour and energy from the sun) is not really primary energy, but energy from oil or other sources converted into food (with an efficiency, which on average for all foods, is smaller than unity). To count food energy as primary energy would thus imply double counting. Moreover, direct food energy consumption would be of the order of one million kilocalories per person/year, which is negligible compared with 25, 50 or 100 million kilocalories.

If, however, countries which make a less splendid use of fossil fuels are considered, then the exclusion of food and wood energy produces some bizarre statistics. For instance, international statistics give the primary energy consumption of Bangladesh at 1,200 megajoules per person/year, which is less than 300,000 kilocalories, less than 1,000 kilocalories per person/day. This figure excludes of course the primordial primary energy, that is, food and the so-called 'non-commercial biofuels'. It seems more sensible to use Sacher's methodology developed in 1880: he included, as will be discussed later, not only coal, but also wood and foodstuff and feedstuff energy. He considered the minimum energy requirement to be in the region of three million kilocalories per person/year, that is, 12,600 megajoules. The exclusion from the 'energy sector' of most food, feed and fuel of most people from most countries not only betrays an 'urban, upper-class bias', but also makes comparisons difficult, and it is in fact quite absurd even from the point of view of so-called 'economics of the energy sector', if it is considered that agriculture and forestry are able to demand and to supply commercial fuels.

International statistics show an average level of primary energy consumption per head/year in so-called developing countries of the order of 12,000 megajoules (ten times the Bangladesh figure) that is, about three million kilocalories or 0.3 TEP, to which should be added non-commercial fuels and also food and feedstuffs (excluding double-counting of the feed fed to animals). There are in fact in the world people living on less than three million kilocalories per person/year, including both commercial and non-commercial energy. They are not much featured in books on so-called 'energy economics' because most of this very low consumption is necessarily in the form of food and 'non-commercial biofuels'. They should certainly appear in books on human ecological energetics.

The energetics of Chinese agriculture (based on Smil, 1979) will now be discussed. Human energy input and animal energy input into Chinese agriculture will be considered first. Human energy input can be measured in several ways. It could be thought that the total energy expenditure of workers (food and non-food) should be included. The 'social reproduction' of workers includes not only the physical energy to keep them in working order, but a variable historical element, which can be many times higher than the food and fuel energy physiologically needed. In this sense it has been pointed out that the substitution of energy-extensive sectors (such as tourism, or teaching, or the service sector in general) for energy-intensive sectors (such as steel making) would not necessarily diminish the energy-intensity of the whole economy, since workers in the service sector will use a lower energy input in the job, but not outside the job, in their leisure hours. A corollary of this interesting viewpoint (Puntí, 1983) is that the low energy intensity per unit of 'value added' of economies based on services is deceptive, since such economies consume imported high-energy products. The high energy efficiency of traditional agriculture depends upon a low level of energy consumption by the peasants. If Chinese peasants had a similar standard of living to North American farmers, then there would be no surplus of energy from renewable sources to feed the towns; on the contrary, an external subsidy from fossil fuels into the rural areas would be needed. Exosomatic energy consumption beyond that needed for subsistence must not be counted as cost. If we do that, then we might conclude with Loomis that 'given our [North Atlantic] standard of living, fossil fuel may be conserved by replacing labour by machines' (Loomis, 1984). This paradox, which Puntí (1983) had already pointed out, and which Loomis sees as a devastating critique of Pimentel's work, arises only if the high level of household energy consumption by US farmers (as compared, for instance, to Asian peasants) is included as an input into the agricultural economy. Loomis' accounting fallacy is analogous to counting the energy dissipated by landlords' households living on Ricardian rents as a cost for eighteenth- and nineteenth-century English farms. A surplus is not a cost.

Human energy input could also be measured strictly by the food energy consumed, and here it would have to be decided whether all food consumed is referred to, or only the extra food needed for working. The word 'working' would also need to be clarified, since a child who plays also works, in a physical sense, by moving himself or herself and other things about. Thus, to take Lotka's example (1925, pp. 346–7), of a daily food energy intake of 3,000 kilocalories, 2,500 kilocalories would be spent to maintain the body's temperature, and the rest – 500 kilocalories – could be devoted to other activities. Unless somebody else is working for us, at least part of these 500 kilocalories should be devoted to balance this account, to cover the energy cost of living, collecting or earning a replacement amount equal at least to the total expenditure of 3,000 kilocalories. In Podolinsky's and Sacher's pioneering accounts, the human energy input into agriculture was measured (as will be seen) not as total food energy intake (3,000 kilocalories, for instance) but as work performed (that is, 500 kilocalories, in Lotka's example). This is also the method used by Smil (1979).

What is the yearly human energy input into Chinese agriculture? Even after a decision has been made to compute it as work performed and not as food energy intake, this is not the end of the matter, because work performed can be calculated in different ways (the results of which should agree with each other). One way would be to multiply a reasonable estimate of work rate – for the Chinese men and women, Smil puts it at 6 and 5 kilogrametres per second – by the number of hours worked per year, taken to be 2,400. For a man, this would equal 120,000 kilocalories of useful work output per year, for a woman, 100,000 kilocalories. (Remember the equivalent, 430 kilogrametres = 1 kilocalorie.) Another approach is to calculate useful work as a share of food energy input: assuming the all-day energetic efficiency to be about 15 per cent for eight hours of work, this procedure would give annual energy outputs of between 97,000 and 130,000 kilocalories per person, according to the estimate of food consumption which Smil had previously calculated. Finally, useful work can be computed as a residual, after subtracting maintenance energy cost from average food intake, and this method gives figures which broadly agree. Taking 100,000 kilocalories of useful energy per agricultural worker per year, the total work performed by the 390 million active persons in Chinese villages (in 1974) would amount to 39×10^{12} kilocalories. The figure of agricultural active population is high, based on the realistic view that most women work both at home and in the fields.

Chinese animal energetics will now be considered. One important point to keep in mind is the low number of hours worked per animal in China. There were (in 1974) about 100 million draught animals, 130 million sheep and goats, more than 250 million pigs, and nearly 1.3 billion chicken, ducks and geese. Assume an average daily ration of 4.5 kilograms of dry matter per head for large animals, 1.5 kilograms for sheep and goats, 2 kilograms for pigs, and 0.1 kilograms for poultry, most feedstuffs being in the form of leftovers from the crops or of pasture; the official Chinese practice being at the time to use at most, 6 per cent of the total harvest of (unmilled) cereals, pulses and tubers for feedstuffs (this ratio is above 50 per cent in North Atlantic countries, including the Soviet Union).

The total energy equivalent of China's animal feed would have amounted in 1974 to about $2,000 \times 10^{12}$ kilocalories, that is, almost three times as much as the total *food* energy (for a population of the order of 850 million). Some two-fifths of this is consumed by draught animals (that is, 800×10^{12} kilocalories), although they work few hours.

So, it can be seen that the useful work performed in agriculture per year would be 39×10^{12} kilocalories, corresponding to 390 million active persons, plus 21.2×10^{12} kilocalories (table 4) corresponding to 113.8 million animals. The energy contribution from traditional fuels will now be considered (which in a 'modern' economy would be substituted by other fuels), and also the contribution of pigs and other animals as sources of fertilizer, which in a 'modern' economy would be substituted by chemical fertilizer.

Table 4 *Calculation of useful work performed by animals in China (1974)*

Animals	Average weight, kg	Average draught, kg	Average speed of work m/sec	Average horse power	Hours worked per year	No. of animals (10^6)	Useful work $(10^{12}$ kcal)
Cattle	385	39	0.70	0.36	1000	63.5	9.7
Buffaloes	500	50	0.70	0.46	1200	30.0	7.0
Asses	350	35	0.70	0.32	1100	11.7	1.7
Horses	350	53	1.00	0.70	1100	7.0	2.3
Mules	350	53	0.95	0.66	1100	1.6	0.5
Totals						113.8	21.2

Average draught, 10% or 15% of weight.
Source: Smil (1979)

In 1974, the fuelwood consumption in the countryside would have reached some 380×10^{12} kilocalories, the equivalent of roughly 140 million cubic metres, while the consumption of crop by-products as fuel was even more important, reaching perhaps 700×10^{12} kilocalories.

Thus it can be seen that the Chinese countryside consumed annually:

as food, approximately 600×10^{12} kilocalories;
as feed, $2,000 \times 10^{12}$ kilocalories; and
as fuel, $1,080 \times 10^{12}$ kilocalories.

This total of biomass energy could be compared to the direct fossil fuel and hydroenergy used in agriculture, in 1974, for water pumping and for machinery, to which Smil adds locally mined coal, and local hydroelectricity, for a total of 500×10^{12} kilocalories. The Chinese countryside utilized about seven times more biomass energy than other forms of energy. It is, as Smil puts it, 'a solar-dominated ecosystem'. Not only the countryside, but China as a whole, still was so in 1974; about $4,100 \times 10^{12}$ kilocalories of phytomass were consumed as food, feed, fuel and raw materials, while 'modern' primary energy reached less than $2,700 \times 10^{12}$ kilocalories (equivalent to some 400 million tons of coal, that is, about 0.5 TEC per person/year).

Figures on fertilizers do not modify this general picture, but they are of interest in themselves. In China, in 1974, the amount of inorganic nitrogen available from domestic factories and from imports, some 4.2 million tons, was equivalent to the amount of nitrogen returned to the fields from fermented animal and human wastes.

The total area of China was divided in 1974 into:

agricultural area, 1,090,000 square kilometres;
grasslands, 4,150,000 square kilometres;
forests, 1,100,000 square kilometres; and
other land, 3,220,000 square kilometres.

Agricultural area has then about 100 million hectares, and nitrogen application per hectare would be quite high, about 84 kilograms. This has to be so, fitting in with the picture of a very intensive agriculture in terms of human labour (over 3 workers/hectare), though not at all intensive in terms of other auxiliary energies.

The nitrogen contribution from animal and human wastes will now be considered in detail. For large animals, dry dung output (about 20 per cent of fresh manure) was taken to be 1,000 kilograms per head/year for a total of 114 million tons; for pigs, dry dung output was taken to be 250 kilograms per head/year, and for poultry, 6 kilograms. Of the total output of 180 million tons of dry dung, it was assumed that 70 per cent was available as fertilizer, that the nitrogen content of pig manure was 2.5 per cent, and that of large-animal manure was 2 per cent, thus reaching a figure of 2.7 million tons of nitrogen. With respect to human wastes, a daily average of 0.15 kilograms of dry wastes per person was assumed, for a population of about 850 million and 66 per cent availability. Since the nitrogen content of human waste is 5 per cent, the human fertilizer output would be 1.5 million tons of nitrogen, for a total for both animal and human output of 4.2 million tons of nitrogen.

The alternative energy costs of 'modernizing' Chinese agriculture will now be calculated, starting by computing the cost of replacing animal and human nitrogen supply by synthetic nitrogen. Taking the feedstock and process energy cost of one kilogram of synthetic nitrogen to be 17,000 kilocalories (Smil quotes Leach and Slesser), the energy cost of 4.2 million tons of nitrogen would be approximately 71×10^{12} kilocalories or some 10 million tons of equivalent coal, taking a value of 1 kilogram coal $= 7,000$ kilocalories.

Assuming that machinery would be substituted for about 70 per cent of the useful work from humans and animals (which is equivalent, per year, to some 60×10^{12} kilocalories), this would imply 42×10^{12} kilocalories of work. Taking an efficiency of between 10 per cent and

15 per cent, this would require from 280×10^{12} kilocalories to 420×10^{12} kilocalories of fossil fuels and primary electricity, that is, some 40–60 million tons of equivalent coal to which should be added the annual energy cost of making the machinery.

Finally, assuming a reduction of 50 per cent in use of fuel from forests and crop residues, and its substitution by other energies, this would represent some 60 million tons of coal equivalent, even when taking into account a great increase in combustion efficiency.

One evident conclusion is that the alternative energy costs all seem rather low, by world comparison. Coal extraction in Great Britain is of the order of 100 million tons per year, with an energy content which would suffice for this 'modernization' of Chinese agriculture.[6]

Though the alternative energy input seems quite practicable, it must nevertheless be taken into account that the 'modernization' of agriculture cannot take place by itself – if a 70 per cent reduction in human work is assumed, it is being assumed implicitly that this work will not be turned into leisure, but into activity in other sectors of the economy, whose energy requirements might be quite high, or even if turned into leisure there will be an expectation of increased consumption.

Nevertheless, Smil's work on Chinese agriculture is useful in order to clarify the question of whether the contribution of peasant agriculture is essential in order to feed the world's population. The substitution of the work given by humans and animals, of the organic fertilizer they provide, and of the fuel they collect from forests and agricultural by-products, would not put an appreciably greater burden on world fossil-fuel reserves. The programme of modernization of agriculture considered would add just about 10^6 kilocalories per person/year to 'modern' primary energy consumption, or in oil equivalents, 0.1 tons; this is negligible compared to primary energy consumption of upwards from 5 tons of oil equivalent per person/year in the most over-developed countries. The recommendation that Chinese peasants should go on using renewable forms of energy, as their contribution to world conservation of resources, deserves a wry peasant smile.

The Energy Balances of Spanish Agriculture (1950s–1970s)

In the 1940s and early 1950s, Spanish agriculture (which then gave some sort of employment to over 50 per cent of the active population, the share

---

[6] In actual fact the Chinese rural population are making increasing use of methane gas from the fermentation of animal and human wastes, which does not prevent their subsequent use as fertilizer, so that these accounts should be modified accordingly.

being higher in the 'hungry forties' than in the 1920s and 1930s) was still based on human and animal work, and on dung as fertilizer, to an extent that (apart from a much lower pressure on the land, and lower yields) made it technically more similar to Chinese agriculture than to the agriculture of North Atlantic countries. It was not until the 1970s that the number of tractors exceeded the number of mules.

The number of tractors grew from about 10 thousand to over 400 thousand; the active agricultural population decreased from over 5 million to 2.5 million, the number of draught animals (including cattle in some regions) decreased from 3.2 million to 1.1 million. This change is shown in table 5.

Table 5 *Installed horsepower per arable hectare, Spanish agriculture*

	1947	1977
Humans	0.04	0.02
Draught animals	0.09	0.03
Machines (including combine harvesters, pumps, etc.)	0.03	1.40
Totals	0.16	1.45

Source: Naredo and Campos, (1980, p. 176)

Production also increased, though not *pari passu* with the increase in mechanical power, nor with the increase in chemical fertilizer.[7] However, here is a familiar case of simultaneous increase in production, and decrease in active agricultural population, which (as Marx pointed out long ago) makes the notion of diminishing returns inapplicable, unless it is modified out of all recognition.

Excluding the inputs produced by agriculture itself (straw, seeds, feedstuffs, dung, and also human and animal work), and considering therefore only the inputs coming from outside agriculture, the change is reflected in table 6, which also includes the net energy value of agricultural production (excluding seed, straw, pastures, etc. re-employed in the same sector).

There is one clear conclusion which remains, even if the effect of increased meat, eggs and milk production is subtracted. Not counting solar energy, the energy input into agriculture has increased more than production. While in 1950–51, one calorie of a 'modern' type of energy

---

[7] Production of meat grew more than any other sector, based to a large extent on American feedgrains.

Table 6 Energy value of inputs from outside agriculture and of net agricultural production, Spanish agriculture, 10^{12} kilocalories

	Average 1950–1	Average 1977–8	Index 1977–8 (base 100, 1950–1)
Inputs			
Fertilizers	2.46	17.84	725
Machinery	0.11	2.90	2,630
Fuel	0.90	26.42	2,930
Electricity	0.52	2.44	469
Pesticides	0.43	1.90	441
Imported feedstuffs	–	30.81	–
Total	4.42	82.31	1,862
Production of vegetable			
products	26.97	49.22	183
of animal products	3.44	12.59	366
Total	30.41	61.81	203

The energy value of imported feedstuffs excludes process energy in country of origin; it includes energy content and process energy in Spanish factories. Output of vegetable products, if seed, straw, pastures were included, would be 96×10^{12} kilocalories in 1950–1 and 160×10^{12} kilocalories in 1977–8. Animal products (meat, milk, eggs, etc.) do not include animal work, nor dung.
Source: Calculated from Naredo and Campos, (1980, pp. 196, 198, 214)

would help to 'produce' six calories of vegetable production, the ratio would in the late 1970s be down to one calorie per calorie. This is not explained by changes in product mix but in production techniques. For instance, fruit and vegetables increased their share in net production only from 14 per cent to 15 per cent (measured in calories, not in money), while cereals increased from 41 per cent to 47 per cent, because of the increase in barley and maize. Olives (for oil), wine, and leguminous crops lost some ground; sunflower and other so-called 'industrial crops' (sugar-beet, for instance), increased.

Have the new techniques increased productivity? There has been an increase of productivity of land and labour, and a decrease in the efficiency of Spanish agriculture in terms of conversion of 'modern' energy inputs. The doubt might arise whether overall energy efficiency has not in fact remained more or less the same, should gross agricultural production be compared with total energy input (excluding only solar energy), and should human and animal work not be costed as energy delivered, but as food energy intake. Even then, there is a small deterioration in the output/input ratio. In any case, the point of the analysis is to show the substitution of non-renewable forms of energy for renewable energy. In this respect, on a per head basis, Spain is now using over 0.2 tons of equivalent oil per head/year for feeding her inhabitants (this figure includes agricultural exports, but excludes all energy expenditure from the fields to the table).

However, the extra-energy input needed to substitute for most of the active agricultural population left behind, getting it down to a British level of two or three per cent, would not alter the order of magnitude of present primary energy consumption, upwards of 2 TEP per head/year. Spain could certainly continue along the same path (at least for a long time) and could feed herself (as indeed the world could feed itself) without 'manual' agriculture. Not only could Spain feed herself, she would be able, with some little extra energy input, to contribute substantially to Common Market surpluses.

Have peasants and agricultural workers really become expendable all over the world? Could the world feed itself, converting fossil-fuel calories into food calories with the sort of efficiency which the disappearance of manual work implies? For how long? Is this, anyway, a useful approach to the study of the world economy? This theme will be picked up again, at the end of the book, in the political epilogue.

How should the change in Spanish agriculture, between the 1950s and the 1970s as depicted by Naredo and Campos, be judged? Could it be described in terms of increased production and of much greater productivity? In the 1960s and early 1970s, there was a debate in Spain (similar to debates in Brazil and in India) on whether the latifundist agrarian structure (which some Marxists and some liberals liked to call feudal or semi-feudal) was an obstacle to the growth of production. This is not the place to enter (again) this debate, which requires empirical studies of relations of production and forms of class struggle in agriculture, while this present book deals only with productive forces. In any case, in Spain (as also, in Brazil), the debate receded because in the 1960s and at least until the mid-1970s the growth of the economy and of agricultural productivity (chrematistically measured) proved that the 'feudal' side was in the wrong. Not that this changed the terms of the general political debate: the feudal image was used for political tactics, to signal the willingness on the part of the moderate left to reach a pact with the bourgeoisie. In the late 1970s, this same willingness was no longer expressed in terms of a common anti-feudal struggle, which had become too ridiculous, but in terms of modernization, consensus politics, social pacts, austerity policies, national solidarity: euro-communism became indistinguishable from social-democratic euro-corporatism.

Both the liberal-moderate left and the ultra-left in the 1960s and 1970s missed one important point, as much in Spain as in Brazil or in India: an unambiguous definition of productive forces, of production, of productivity was lacking. In the Spanish debate, the ultra-leftists made the point that land redistribution was a good thing, not in order to remove obstacles to growth, since the existing agrarian structure seemed quite capable of promoting growth (as conventionally measured), but because agricultural workers, threatened by unemployment, wanted to have either land of their own, or a secure employment in collectivized agriculture. This argument still stands to some extent today, reinforced by the end of emigration, the increased unemployment (because of continuous 'productivity' growth), and by the doubts on whether production is adequately measured.[8] For example, Sudrià's work on primary energy consumption in twentieth-century Spain shows a fictitious increase between the 1930s and the 1980s from about 450 kg of equivalent coal per head and year to about 2900 kg (Sudrià, 1987, pp. 324, 352). The accounts exclude food energy consumed not only by humans but also by animals. Sources of renewable energy so typically Spanish as mules, windmills and charcoal are entirely left aside, as the author himself states. This is not ecological history but merely a new line in conventional economic history which does not yet take into account the ecological critique of economics. It cannot even be said that what is being measured is simply the destruction of fossil fuels in the Spanish economy, since the figures include hydroelectricity (though they exclude water power used directly!). The new economic history should start from sunshine, of which fortunately there is plenty in Spain.

Boussingault, Liebig, Guano and Agrarian Chemistry

Technical progress has meant that agriculture, which has always been a source of energy, is no longer such a source in some countries of the world. Modern agriculture transforms fossil energy into food. The beginning of the change in agricultural practices came with mechanization (especially with the internal combustion engine, since the steam engine was not so important to the countryside) and with agrarian chemistry. Changing agricultural practice, whilst increasing harvests, at the same time has produced a spectacular decline in the number of agricultural workers.

---

[8] My book on Spanish latifundist agriculture carried the subtitle 'A study of relations of production and class consciousness in the latifundist system', a phrase quite removed from vulgar materialism-energeticism. The book as it stands is an analysis of land tenure, use of labour, and landowners' and labourers' values, but it included no discussion of the productive forces. This had to wait until Naredo and Campos (1980).

The high energetic intensity of modern agriculture derives not only from the energy required to run machines, but also from the manufacture of fertilizers, pesticides, and insecticides. Nitrogen fertilizers were first produced with hydroelectricity at the end of the nineteenth-century in Norway. The nitrogen, phosphorus and potassium cycles had been discovered only a few decades before. Many economists thought that agrarian chemistry, understood as technical progress, would reverse the tendency towards decreasing returns or, to put it another way, would move the production function upwards.

The new agrarian chemistry was inaugurated in the 1840s by Boussingault (1802–87) in France and by Liebig (1803–73) in Germany. Liebig liked to say that his research was crucial in order to prevent a subsistence crisis in Europe. The development of agrarian chemistry admits an externalist, sociological interpretation of scientific and technical advances.

Liebig's basic idea was that of changing from an agriculture of spoliation to an agriculture of restitution. He was obliged to understand first that plants are nourished by minerals. Liebig was the phosphate man; Boussingault was the one to analyse the nitrogen cycle, which Liebig did not understand. Both of them carried out analyses of Peruvian guano. Boussingault explained that Fourcroy and Vauquelin were the first to draw attention to the nature of guano, and that the specimen Fourcroy and Vauquelin examined had been brought to Europe by Humboldt (Boussingault, 1845, p. 380).

Mayer' article, *Bemerkungen ueber die Kraefte der unbelebten Natur* (Observations concerning the forces of inanimate nature), which established the mechanical equivalence of heat and the law of conservation of energy, had been published in 1842, in the *Annalen* which were edited by Liebig. The idea of a flow of energy in agriculture had appeared in Mayer's booklet of 1845, which Liebig had refused to publish. What interested Liebig and Boussingault about guano was its chemical composition; neither of them studied the flow of energy in agriculture, costing fertilizers in energy terms, though Boussingault did research on nutrition and on photosynthesis. In order to defend the need to develop agrarian chemistry, they often remarked that guano supplies would run out (and that saltpetre, which is nitrate of sodium and potassium, would not last indefinitely either). Boussingault noted that from the calculations made by Humboldt it was plain that it would take three centuries to form a layer of the excrement of the birds no more than a centimetre thick. An astonishing lapse of time was necessary for guano layers of 20–30 metres thick to accumulate. Such layers had existed until quite recently, but now the guano was disappearing rapidly since it had become an object for commercial enterprises (Boussingault, 1845, p. 381).

Strange commercial and financial enterprises have made guano a favourite subject of Peruvian historians (such as Bonilla, 1974) aiming to demonstrate the misdeeds of imperialism which left Peru without guano and receiving almost nothing in exchange (since the money from guano remained in Europe to pay off loans or was spent on imported consumer goods, Hunt, 1984), while other historians have attempted to show the universal benefits achieved by the 'imperialism' of free trade. There is another point of view: the heteronomy of European agriculture from an energetic and material subsidy from outside – did it provoke no ecological arguments similar to those of today? Did no-one say that the increase in the productivity of European agriculture was the reverse side of the increase in the destruction of exhaustible resources and human lives in a place as distant and desolate as the guano islands in the middle of the Humboldt stream? In order to avoid an agriculture of spoliation in Europe, and in order to restore to the soil the nutrients incorporated in plants, other territories were spoliated. An energetic and materialistic economic history could complete the research into prices paid, and the financial transactions and political struggles of an incipient, but failed, national bourgeoisie in Peru, with a calculation of that spoliation in physical terms.

Students of agricultural economics still learn nowadays about Liebig's 'law of the minimum', which he explained as follows: 'no single element of the indispensable minerals is superior to any other, but all have equal value for the life of the plant. Therefore, if one element is missing from the soil, the others cannot produce a properly developed plant until the missing element has been supplied' (Liebig, 1859, p. vi). They are not taught his own opinions about the political economy of agriculture. For example: 'agriculturalists' (he wrote) 'must not rely upon guano; its price was double what it had been before; no man with any sense would want the production of his country to depend on the supply of a foreign manure' (Liebig, 1859, p. 269). It was therefore necessary to develop chemical fertilizers, in spite of his pride in the fact that 'science' (that is to say, Liebig himself) 'guided by a careful study of the elements of the food of plants', pointed out in 1840 to the agriculturalists that guano was 'one of the most infallible means of raising the produce of corn and flesh, and most urgently recommended its application' (Liebig, 1859, p. 265). One hundredweight of guano contained the mineral elements necessary to produce between 25 and 30 hundredweight of wheat; this led to the belief that 'guano beds of America' possessed an 'immense value with reference to the production of corn in Europe' and that guano would come to have a decisive role in the history of Europe unless it were replaced in time: 'bloody wars have sometimes sprung from causes of much less importance' (Liebig, 1859, p. 269–70).

Liebig and Boussingault believed in replacement, perhaps because they were chemists rather than physicists; the dissipation of matter is not an established law of physics, whereas the degradation of energy is. However, they believed in replacement, not by hypothesis, but because they thought they would be able to manufacture chemical fertilizers which possessed virtues similar to those of guano, or other manures, which had long been known, but whose chemical constituents they had analysed. They never said that if the price of guano rose steeply enough, there would undoubtedly be an alternative fertilization technology (a back-stop technology, according to the terminology of the economic theorists of today).

Guano had been known as a fertilizer since before the Incas. The analyses of its chemical composition and the analyses of the composition of manures and human excrement and other fertilizers already known to agriculturalists laid the foundations of agrarian chemistry, especially in Liebig's laboratory in Giessen. Liebig's name can be associated, obviously, with a new leading sector of the chrematistic economy: the manufacture of fertilizers. It can also be associated with a more 'ecological' vision, because he developed an argument against latifundist agriculture and in favour of a ruralized urbanism. He wrote that when two thousand people live in one square mile, it is impossible to export cereals and meat from that land, since the produce of the land is just enough to feed them.[9] Also, all the mineral elements contained in the products consumed can easily be returned without loss to the fields from which they were taken. But suppose that this land falls into the hands of the big owners; in this case a system of spoliation will take the place of the system of restitution and compensation. The small owner gives back to the land almost all he takes from it; the big owner, on the other hand, sends the grain and the meat to be sold in the major centres of consumption, and so loses the conditions necessary to reproduce them. Good luck brought guano, but guano would run out, and what would happen then? (Liebig, 1859, pp. 229–31). Quoting Carey, he pointed out that in the United States there were distances of hundreds and thousands of miles between the centres of production of cererals and the markets. The result was that the soil was becoming almost exhausted everywhere (Liebig, 1859, p. 220).[10]

[9] A German square mile was about 50 square kilometres. Liebig was thinking of the poor soils in northern Germany.

[10] Henry Carey (1793–1879) was an American protectionist theorist who argued against the existence of decreasing returns in the extensive margin, but who saw the economy very much in physical terms and was worried by the depletion of the fertility of the soil caused by agricultural exports. He was influenced by Liebig and by his fellow protectionist economist Erasmus Peshine Smith (1814–82) who was a student of Liebig's agricultural chemistry and who came close to depicting economic activity in terms of energetics in his *Manual of Political Economy* 1853; cf. Michael Hudson, 1975, p. 212–37.

The estimates which Liebig gave of the phosphoric acid and the potassium taken from the fields in the United States without restitution were used as an opportunity to defend chemical fertilizers again – for example, super-phosphates, manufactured with sulphuric acid. At the same time, however, he praised the Chinese practice of fertilizing the fields with human excrement and thought that the landowners of the great countries should form societies to set up *reservoirs* where human and animal excrement would be collected and prepared for transportation to the fields (Liebig, 1859, p. 268). The urbanistic problem of rubbish, excrement and refuse accumulated in the big cities was the other side of the problem of an agriculture of spoliation. From this, two clear lines of argument emerged: an ecological line and a line of economic growth based on agrarian chemistry and the great sewers, and the chemical treatment of urban refuse which large-scale urbanization required.

The interpretation of the history of agrarian technology eventually triumphant was not the ecological interpretation, *also* found in Liebig, even though he did sell patents for fertilizers. His digressions on the recycling of excrement were considered to be the rhetorical exaggerations of a learned scientist, or to refer to the eccentricities of the Chinese; while most Chinese were taking excrement to their own fields in China, some thousands of coolies held in debt peonage were taking bird excrement in Peru and sending it on to Europe.[11]

What was appreciated about Liebig was the promise of an agriculture with great yields, separated from the big cities and based on chemical fertilization. That made him a famous man, which was very much to his liking.[12]

The discussion about the substitution of industrial fertilizers for Chilean nitrate came after Liebig. Chilean saltpetre was imported in great quantities; for example, about 10 kilograms per person per year in Germany towards 1900.[13] Boussingault remarked early on that nitric acid was the result of the combining of azote and oxygen, and that in order to achieve the combination of these two gases with an electric spark, the mixture must

[11] Liebig's opinions about the agriculture of China (and Japan) were formed under the influence of the Prussian scientific missions which were then investigating the possibilities of establishing colonies, and in which the geographer Richthofen (1833–1905) later participated.

[12] The edition of his *Letters on Modern Agriculture* which has been quoted announced the sale of busts of the author. There is a book on Liebig and English agriculture in preparation by Vance M. D. Hall (cf. *Centaurus*, (1982–83), 26, p. 232), to be added to the excellent studies by Rossiter, Krohn, and Schaefer.

[13] Which is far less, for example, than the present quantity of petroleum and petroleum products: about 4 kilograms per person per *day*.

be moist according to Cavendish (Boussingault, 1845, pp. 323–4). Boussingault did not then envisage the practical possibility of industrial nitrogen fertilizers manufactured by electricity. That discussion would come later, explicitly in terms of the energetic costs of substitution. For example, there are detailed calculations of the kilowatt-hours necessary to 'manufacture' nitrogen in Popper-Lynkeus' book (1912, p. 714) and particularly in Jurisch's (1908). The First World War gave great impetus, since nitrogen was necessary for making explosives, thus fulfilling Joseph Henry's prediction of seventy years before that one day the bolt of Jove (that is, electricity) would come to the aid of Mars, the god of war.

Soddy also referred to Cavendish's 'great discovery of the eighteenth century'. In the Birkeland-Eyde process, instead 'of the energy of a patient attendant turning the handle of a frictional electric machine . . . the power of hundreds of thousands of horses, derived chiefly from the "white fuel" of the Norwegian and Swiss hill-sides, are ceaselessly at work, turning dynamos which produce powerful high-tension arcs in the air, so converting it partially into nitrous and nitric acids'. As did so many other British writers in the years after 1900, he referred to Sir William Crookes' famous presidential address to the British Association for the Advancement of Science, where Crookes had drawn attention to the probable future failure of the wheat supply unless chemists succeeded in solving the problems of the fixation of atmospheric nitrogen. They had indeed succeeded (with the Haber process they were to succeed further), but

the question, as to how long the Chile saltpetre beds will last, has simply been merged into the more general problem of how long the natural resources of energy of the globe will hold out. Insofar as such developments utilize the natural energy running to waste, as in water power, they may be accounted as pure gain. But insofar as they consume the fuel resources of the globe they are very different. The one is like spending the interest on a legacy, and the other is like spending the legacy itself. The wheat problem . . . is one particular aspect of a still hardly-recognized coming energy problem.

Soddy therefore anticipated 'a period of reflection in which awkward interviews between civilization and its banker are in prospect' (Soddy, 1912, pp. 135–9).[14] The alarm about agricultural yields in the absence

[14] Soddy made this point in an article in *Scientia: International Review of Scientific Synthesis*, IX, 1912, pp. 186–202, and in the same year in his book *Matter and Energy*. This book was translated and published in 1913 in Moscow with a preface and notes by Nicolai Morozov, an ex-member of Narodnaya Volya who had spent the years 1881–1905 in prison and who later became a writer on scientific topics. Cf. A. N. Krivomazov, 'The reception of Soddy's work in the USSR', in Kauffman, 1986, p. 121. Morozov must have been familiar with Podolinsky's work, and he might have emphasized the similarity between Podolinsky's and Soddy's energy economics. (Nicolai Morozov is not to be confused with G. F. Morozov, the forest ecologist.)

of chemical fertilizers was as old as Liebig, if not Humphry Davy (1778–1829), but the view that modern agriculture was energy-intensive agriculture was still a novelty in 1912, and surprisingly remained a novelty until the 1970s. Recent discussion on new agricultural practices such as non-tillage shows that savings in fuel for tractors must be compensated by greater nitrogen fertilization (Randall, 1982, p. 363).

The increase in agricultural production is doubtful, certainly not because there is not enough nitrogen in the air, but because the increase in agricultural production implies the expenditure of fossil energy in the manufacture of fertilizers. And so, a modern discussion of rural economy (the title which Boussingault used for his book, which is not about chrematistic or catallactic economics but about agricultural chemistry) would have to consider the possibility of manufacturing nitrogen fertilizers with a smaller expenditure of energy (using appropriate catalysts) and endowing cereals, by means of genetic engineering, with bacteria such as those associated with pulses. A discussion on the ecological effects of the new biotechnologies, including their impact on energy use, seems more useful than an orthodox economic discussion of decreasing or increasing returns in agriculture or on the belief of some economists in ineluctable 'technical progress'. For the moment, looking at the evolution of the last hundred years in the over-developed countries, it is difficult to say whether agricultural productivity is greater or smaller. The expenditure of fossil energy (and of minerals, which are not renewable, since they cannot in practice be totally recycled) has risen more than proportionately. Measured in money, there is no doubt of the increase in agricultural productivity, but where do the prices of exhaustible resources come from? From supply and demand? Can we *really* explain the temporal pattern of use of exhaustible resources by employing the methodology of economic theory, meant to explain the exchanges between individuals who are now alive, and who hold views on the history of science and on technical progress, who possess given purchasing powers, and who exhibit subjective preferences whose origins are all unexplained?

Some writers think that, because of the decrease in the price of oil in the mid-1980s, energy considerations are no longer relevant. Commenting on Pimentel's work of the 1970s on the energy intensity of modern agriculture, it has been asserted: 'In retrospect it appears that these concerns about energy dependence, although not without foundation, were overdrawn' (Hayami and Ruttan, 1985, p. 221). The proof is supposed to be that the fears about the impact of a presumed energy shortage on fertilizer prices have failed to materialize. However, a decrease in the price of oil does not mean that oil reserves in the world have increased.

The argument against mainstream economics is *not* that the market is wrong because it is based on subjective valuations instead of being based on objective geological facts. Geology is a human science. The argument, to be fully developed in chapter 11, is simply that the market for exhaustible resources cannot operate unless agents have some estimates about present and future availability, and unless they attribute a certain present value to future demand.

3

The History of Agricultural
Energetics: Podolinsky

Introduction

'The beginning of the influence that the second law of thermodynamics
was to have on ecological theory' has been traced back to Lotka (1925)
by E. P. Odum (1968, p. 15). In fact, the study of the flow of energy and
of energetic efficiencies in human societies started earlier, though it did
not become an academic discipline. There is nothing very startling in this.
All too often a rich past of ideas, concepts, controversies, personal failures
and successes falls into oblivion as the history of disciplines which have
finally found their academic niches is written. Thus, 'the ecosystem
approach to ecology which was developed by the Odum brothers out of
the thoughts of Lindeman . . . (based upon) food chains, energy flow,
trophic levels, and ecological efficiencies' (Colinvaux, 1976; cf. also Ellen,
1982, p. 95) began much earlier than the names quoted would suggest.
Some writings will now be introduced which, although published about a
hundred years ago, read like recent contributions to ecological anthropology,
human ecology and energy economics, since they were based on computations of the energy returns to inputs in different human activities. Such
initial attempts (around 1880) were generally received with silence, and
one cannot therefore exclude the existence of other precursors in the 1850s,
1860s and 1870s.

The work being considered could have been a foundation stone for
human ecology, for ecological anthropology, and for energy economics,
and I would be reluctant to classify it as belonging to only one of these
disciplines. The study of the flow of energy and the cycles of materials
in small human groups (Rappaport, 1967; Lee, 1979) is usually classified
as ecological anthropology while, for instance, the study of energy flows
in rural China (Smil, 1979) (discussed in chapter 2) would belong to human
ecology. However, anthropologists like Leslie White and, more recently,
R. N. Adams, have also attempted work of the widest scope (see White,

1943; 1948; 1959; and Adams, R. N., 1975; 1982; 1984). Moreover, some small-scale studies, for instance that by Brooke Thomas (1976) on the flow of energy in a settlement of Quechua shepherds in Puno, Peru, to which reference has been made in the introduction, are classified as human ecology, perhaps because they do not attempt to link up the study of ecology with that of other levels of reality – social organization, religious beliefs and rituals – as the anthropologists do. Although comparative studies on energy flows in agriculture (Pimentel, 1973, 1979; Leach, 1976) clearly belong to the category of agricultural energy economics, they make use of the findings of ecological anthropologists on the output/input ratios in energy terms in traditional systems, such as tropical slash-and-burn agriculture, or Chinese rice- or Mexican maize-growing.

From the 1850s and 1860s onwards, it was possible to adopt a quantitative view of the flow of energy from the sun (though that sun worked by nuclear fusion was not understood until the 1930s), and it was also possible to determine how much of the energy from the sun intercepted by the earth was radiated back into space, and how much (or, rather, how little) could be transformed by plants into carbon, which they took from carbon dioxide in the atmosphere. The process of nutrition as oxidation of carbon was also understood, as was the use of energy in metabolism and in work.

Therefore, it is not surprising that somebody should have attempted to measure the output/input ratio in agriculture in energy terms. One of the first such attempts was made by Serhii Podolinsky. This has been known for some time, mainly because of Engels' letters to Marx on Podolinsky, which had already been mentioned in the 1920s, both in the literature on the relations between Marxism and natural sciences, and in biographical works on Podolinsky's role in Ukrainian populism and socialism of the 1870s. Engels had some knowledge of the elementary energetics of human physiology, and in a note of 1875 (later included in *Dialectics of Nature*) he refers to Fick's and Wislicenus' experiment in climbing the Faulhorn in 1865, which became popularized under the name of 'A day of hunger for science'. Adolf Fick (1829–1901) had already written in 1857 and 1858 on the number of kilocalories (2,700) that a man would spend and need per day, when not working (Fick, 1906, **IV**, p. 418). Different types of work would imply different energy expenditures over that rate. An idea being circulated at the time (for instance, in an article in *Das Ausland* in 1877, 50, p. 298, without author's name) was that the economic values of different types of work could be established in physical terms. Engels already had rejected explicitly this notion in 1875.

On 19 December 1882, Engels wrote to Marx that Podolinsky had 'discovered' the following facts, already well known. If the food intake of one person per day were equal to 10,000 kilocalories, then the physical work done would be a fraction of this energy. This physical work would become economic work if employed in fixing solar energy, for instance through agricultural activity. Whether the energy fixed by the work of one person per day were equal to 5,000, 10,000, 20,000 or one million kilocalories, would depend only on the degree of development of the means of production. Establishing an energy budget was in any case possible only in the most primitive branches of production, such as hunting and fishing.

In agriculture (here Engels was most perceptive) one would have to reckon, among the energy inputs, the energy value of fertilizers and other auxiliary means, a difficult thing to compute. In industry, all energy accounting had to stop; it was impossible to calculate in energy terms the costs of production of a needle, a screw or a hammer. The wish to express economic relations in physical terms could not be carried out. All that Podolinsky had managed to show (wrote Engels to Marx on 22 December 1882) was the old story that all industrial producers have to live from the products of agriculture; this well-known fact could, if one so wished, be translated into the language of physics, but little would be gained by it. Engels' letters to Marx on Podolinsky were first published by Bebel and Bernstein (1919, vol. IV, pp. 499–502) and they have since then been published several times, in all major European languages.

Podolinsky's original article appeared in similar Russian, French, Italian and German versions between 1880 and 1883. It will be summarized in the following pages. He began by explaining the laws of energetics, quoting from Clausius that although the energy of the Universe was a constant, there was a tendency towards the dissipation of energy or, in Clausius' terminology, there was a tendency for entropy to reach a maximum. 'Entropy' referred to the quantity of energy which would no longer be transformed into other forms of energy. Podolinsky did not discuss the difference in thermodynamics between open, closed and isolated systems, although he stated explicitly, as the starting point of his analysis, that at the present time the earth was receiving enormous quantities of energy from the sun, and would do so for a very long time. All physical and biological phenomena were expressions of the transformations of this energy. He did not enter into the controversies regarding the creation of the Universe and its 'heat-death', nor did he discuss the relations between thermodynamics and the theory of natural selection and the evolution of species. In March 1880 he had published an article against social-Darwinism. He certainly realized that the availability of energy was a crucial consideration for the increase (or decrease) of population. However, he thought that the distribution of production was explained by the relations between social classes, i.e. poverty could not be explained by ecological analysis: 'in the countries where capitalism triumphs, a great part of work goes towards the production of luxury goods, that is to say, towards a gratuitous dissipation of energy instead of towards increasing the availability of energy'.

The energy available to humankind came mainly from the sun. Podolinsky gave figures for the solar constant.[1] He explained how coal and oil, wind energy and water power, were transformations of solar energy, and after mentioning tides as another possible source of energy, he went on to his main piece of analysis. He wrote that a very small part of the flow of energy from the sun was assimilated by plants, though without explicit discussion

Table 7 Annual production, and energy input (from work from humans and domestic animals only), per hectare, averages for France, 1870s, according to Podolinsky

	Production (kg)	Production (kcal)	Energy input (kcal)
Forest	900 (dried wood)	2,295,000	nil
Natural pastures	2,500 (hay)	6,375,000	nil
Sown pastures	3,100 (hay, excluding seed)	7,905,000	37,450 (corresponding to 50 horse-hours and 80 man-hours)
Wheat agriculture	800 (wheat) 2,000 (straw) (excluding seed)	8,100,000	77,500 (corresponding to 100 horse-hours and 200 man-hours)

Energy values of wood, hay and straw, 2,550 kcal/kg, of wheat 3,750 kcal/kg. To convert hours of work into kcal, Podolinsky used these values: 645 kcal/hour of horse-work, 65 kcal/hour of man-work.

Sources: The sources he used were Statistique de la France, 1874, 1875, 1878; Ch. Laboulaye, Dictionnaire des arts et de l'agriculture, 4th edn, 1877, articles on agriculture (by Hervé Mangon) and on carbonification; Pelouze et Frémy, Traîté de Chimie; Hermann, Grundzüge der Physiologie, 5th edn, 1877.

[1] The remarks of Mouchot (1879, 2nd edn, pp. 62–64) are relevant: la constante solaire ou la quantité de chaleur reçue normalement par un centimètre carré en une minute aux limites de l'atmosphère, avait été estimée par Pouillet. . . . Crova was le savant professeur de la faculté de Montpellier (qui) vient de publier récemment le travail le plus complet qu'on aît encore sur la mesure des radiations calorifiques du soleil. Podolinsky must have been aware of this work, but he quoted Secchi, the director of the Observatory in Rome, and not Crova. See also chapter 7, p. 108.

of photosynthetic yield, a subject which had already been under scrutiny for some years. Human work, and the work of animals directed by humans, were able to increase the energy budget on the surface of the earth by agricultural activity. This he showed by comparing the productivity of different types of land use in France. His accounts are summarized in table 7.

Podolinsky's figures correspond to the biologists' 'net production', and he mentioned nothing of the energy expended by plants in respiration which, although of great interest to the biologist, has less interest for the ecological anthropologist or economist. He compared wheat agriculture and sown pastures with natural pastures and forest, concluding that production was higher when there was an input of human and animal work. Thus, comparing sown pastures to natural pastures, there was an increase of 41 kilocalories for each kilocalorie of human and animal work employed. Podolinsky measured human (and animal) *work*, that is, he counted the energy input as the equivalent to work done, and not as the food energy intake, which is the measure sometimes taken in contemporary studies in ecological anthropology.

Comparing wheat agriculture to natural pastures, each kilocalorie put in contributed to an increase of 22 kilocalories. If forests were taken as the term of comparison, the energy productivity of human and animal work was, of course, even higher. Labour could increase 'the accumulation of energy on earth'. Energy accounting thus gave a scientific basis to the labour theory of value, a point that neither Marx nor Engels appreciated.

Although Podolinsky mentioned guano, and although he must have been keenly aware of the war then raging for the Peruvian or Chilean saltpetre of Tarapacá, he did not subtract from output, or include in the input, the energy contents and cost of fertilizers. Nor did he consider the energy input of steam engines in agriculture, though he was aware of their use for threshing. In its essentials, though, his methodology was that used later in order to establish the energy balance for particular crops, or for small-scale societies, or for the entire agricultural sector of particular countries (e.g. Cottrell, 1955; Rappaport, 1967; H. Odum, 1971; Pimentel, 1973, 1979; Leach, 1976; Brooke Thomas, 1976; Naredo and Campos, 1980; Fluck and Baird, 1980). Podolinsky did not include solar radiation in the energy input, and here he anticipated too the agricultural energy economics of today. If the energy economics of domestic heating were to be studied, the fossil fuels, wood or dung used in order to increase the temperature up to (say) 15°C from – 10°C or – 20°C would be considered, but the first long tranche, up from – 273°C, which is mostly due to solar energy, would be taken for granted. Although solar radiation was not included as input, Podolinsky was of course interested in how much of this energy could be transformed by plants. He attributed the energy of the sun to 'dissociation' (quoting Secchi and H. Saint-Claire Deville), and he explained Kirchhoff's law of radiation. He quoted not only Clausius but also W. Thomson on the degradation of energy.

There were two parallel processes, he explained, by which plants assimilated energy, and animals fed on plants and degraded energy. Both processes together formed the *Kreislauf des Lebens*, a much-used expression probably taken from Moleschott's book of this title, of 1852. Podolinsky wrote:

We have in front of us two parallel processes which together form the so-called circuit of life. Plants have the property of accumulating solar energy, but the animals, when they feed on vegetable substances, transform a part of this saved energy into mechanical work and dissipate this energy into space. If the quantity of energy accumulated by plants is greater than that dispersed by animals, then stocks of energy appear, for instance in the period when mineral coal was formed, during which vegetable life obviously was preponderant over animal life. If, on the contrary, animal life were preponderant, the provision of energy would be quickly dispersed and animal life would have to go back to the limits determined by vegetable wealth. So, a certain equilibrium would have to be built between the accumulation and the dissipation of energy.

Not only plants, also human labour had the virtue of retarding the dissipation of energy on the surface of the earth. Human labour achieved this by agriculture, but the work of a tailor, a shoemaker or a builder also qualify, in Podolinsky's view, as productive work, since they afford 'protection against the dissipation of energy into space'.

Podolinsky, in the second part of his article, considered the question of how the human organism is capable of doing work, since 'we have not yet said anything on the capacity of the human organism to do work, without which it would be difficult to explain the accumulation of energy on the surface of the earth under the influence of labour'. Quoting from Hirn and Helmholtz (but not, though he could have, from Adolf Fick, Pettenkofer and Voit) he concluded correctly that 'man has the capacity to transform one-fifth of the energy gained from food into muscular work', giving to this ratio, in accordance with normal practice at the time, the name of 'economic coefficient', remarking that man was a more efficient transformer of energy than a steam engine. Taking into account that not everybody can work (because of health and age), and that there are other human needs beyond food energy, perhaps the best possible 'economic coefficient' would be 1/10. He then used a metaphor to put across a general theoretical principal on the minimum 'natural conditions of human existence': humanity was a 'perfect machine' in Sadi Carnot's sense, that is:

humanity is a machine that not only turns heat and other physical forces into work, but succeeds also in carrying out the inverse cycle, that is, it turns work into heat and other physical forces which are necessary to satisfy our needs, and, so to speak, with its own work turned into heat is able to heat its own boiler.

Now, for humanity to ensure its conditions of existence, each calorie of human work must have then a productivity (this is his own term) of at least ten calories or, in more general terms, the energy productivity of human work must be equal to or greater than the 'economic coefficient', i.e. than the efficiency of the human body as a heat engine. If that minimum necessary energy productivity of work is not achieved, then, of course, 'scarcity appears and, many times, a reduction in population'.

In economics Podolinsky thought that he had reconciled the Physiocrats with the labour theory of value. He knew that the Physiocrats could not have made a study of energy flows, since the mechanical equivalent of heat was established only in the early 1840s. His combination of an energy theory of value and a labour theory of value was his distinctive contribution. Sending his article to Marx in 1880, he explained that he wanted to bring the doctrine of surplus labour (and implicitly, of surplus value) into harmony with physical theory.

It is of course a simplification to say that the human body has an efficiency of 20 per cent, which would become 10 per cent, taking into account other needs apart from food and the fact that not everybody works. But what matters in the present context is the idea that one could determine the necessary minimum conditions of human survival on earth through an analysis of energy flows and energy efficiencies. The first thoughts on the physiological applications of the laws of energy had been voiced in the 1840s. Podolinsky here was on solid ground. Thus, Tait (1864, p. 344), writing for the general public in his usual patriotic mood, had stated that Joule had preceded Helmholtz's famous work *Ueber die Erhaltung der Kraft* of 1847 when he said in April 1847, in a public lecture, that

the knowledge of the equivalency of heat to mechanical power is of great importance in solving a great number of interesting and important questions. In the case of the steam engine, by ascertaining the quantity of heat produced by the combustion of coal, we can find how much of it is converted into mechanical power, and thus come to a conclusion how far the steam engine is susceptible of further improvement. Calculations made upon this principle have shown that at least ten times as much power might be produced as is now obtained by the combustion of heat. Another interesting conclusion is that the animal frame, though destined to fulfil so many other ends, is, as a machine, more perfect than the best contrived steam engine; that is, is capable of more work with the same expenditure of fuel.

Neither Joule nor Helmholtz could have really calculated the theoretical efficiency of a thermic machine before the second law of thermodynamics was established in 1850 and 1851 by Clausius and W. Thomson. But the comparison in thermodynamic terms between the steam engine, and domestic animals and the human body, was made before 1850 and had become a commonplace by the 1860s. Thus Tait could give as a homely example of the application of conservation of energy to animal processes 'the greater supply and choicer quality of food required by convicts in penal servitude, than by their less (sic) fortunate comrades who are merely imprisoned' (1864, p. 362). Although Podolinsky was writing a few years before Max Rubner's classic experiments of 1889–94, the elementary energetics of the physiology of nutrition and work was therefore well established before the 1880s. All that was required for inspiration of the idea that the basic principles of human ecology and economy could be analysed in terms of the concept of energy return to human energy input, in a framework of reproduction of social systems, was to bring together the well-known facts that biomass could be measured in energy units, and that the human body is a thermic machine.

Podolinsky also saw clearly the difference between using the flow of solar energy and the stock of energy in coal. The task of labour was to increase the accumulation of solar energy on earth, rather than the simple transformation into work of energy already accumulated on earth, more so since work done with coal was inevitably accompanied by a great dissipation of heat-energy into space. He was not, however, at all 'pessimistic' about the prospects for the economy, and he was hopeful for the direct use of solar energy for industrial purposes, referring to the 'solar engine of M. Mouchot'. One could envisage that solar energy would one day be used directly to make chemical syntheses of nutritive substances, by-passing agriculture. Thus, a proper discussion of the demographic question had to take into account 'the relation between the general quantity of energy on earth and the quantity of humans who live on it', and this was a more relevant consideration, in his explicit view, than the Malthusian prognosis.

Podolinsky's contribution to human ecology, ecological anthropology and economics could have been taken up much earlier in the scientific debate. For instance, any of the many students of the Russian and Ukrainian peasantry could have had the idea of using the agricultural energetics of this sympathetic author. An argument in favour of the greater energy efficiency of peasant agriculture (which Podolinsky himself did not develop) could then have been made several decades before Georgescu-Roegen. Moreover, the Marxists could have paid greater attention to him. His article was published in socialist journals in France and Italy and in the theoretical organ of the German socialist party. The channels it followed on its way to *Die Neue Zeit*, edited by Kautsky are not yet known. Engels might have recommended its publication, despite his lack of enthusiasm for it, though it was probably Bernstein who had it published. But when Kautsky published *Die Agrarfrage* in 1899 he did not include a study of energy flow.[2] Thus, although Podolinsky can be placed at the crossroads of well-trodden intellectual paths (*narodnik* thought, Marxism, ecology), his work can still be presented as a novelty. I do not claim, however, to have 'discovered' him, since he has never been forgotten by his countrymen. An account of his intellectual and political background will follow, in the belief that histories of science should be set in a social context.

One of the *Narodniki*

Serhii Podolinsky (1850–91) was described as a 'Ukrainian socialist and a friend of Lavrov' in the edition of the letters between Marx and Engels by Adoratski. In the *MEW* edition however, Lavrov does not appear, but it is explained that Podolinsky knew Marx and Engels, and exchanged letters with Marx. He is not mentioned in the several editions of the *Great Soviet Encyclopaedia*, but he appears in both the 'native' and 'exiled' Ukrainian encyclopaedias.[3]

Podolinsky was influential in the Ukrainian and Russian resistance to tsarism in the short period of his active life, from 1867 to 1882. He was known in Kiev, Lviv, Vienna, Zürich, Geneva, Paris and London. He was not a *rasnotschinetz*, a *déclassé* upstart, one of the types of social rebel of the time. Rather, he was a member of the 'repentant gentry'. His father had been educated in St Petersburg and was Postmaster-General of the southern provinces. He later retired to his estates; a gentleman poet, he was the last of 'Pushkin's Pleiades'. His mother's mother was born Choisseul-Gouffier, daughter of the French ambassador to the Porte in Napoleon's time.

Podolinsky's infancy was characterized by the agrarian question. The Crimean War, 1853–6, had dealt a blow to the *ancien régime*. The emancipation of the serfs, in 1861, initiated a process of differentiation of the peasantry. In the Ukraine the sugar industry became industrialized and there was investment of foreign capital in iron production in the

[2] In Lenin's magnificent *Development of Capitalism in Russia*, published in 1900 shortly after Kautsky's *Agrarfrage*, there is no trace of energy-accounting of agriculture, but his opponents, populist theoreticians, missed the occasion (available since the 1870s or 1880s) of making a pro-peasant argument out of it.

[3] Roman Serbyn, in Montreal, is working on a biography and an edition of his works.

Donetz basin. The railway network grew in the context of the colonial dependence of the southern provinces of Great Russia. In the atmosphere of relative political freedom of 1857–63, even liberals like Herzen had to give the reforms of the young Tsar a chance. After 1863, the Polish resistance was defeated; in Europe, Prussian military might was in the ascendant, and generalized repression was the norm, culminating in the defeat of the Paris Commune in 1871. After a new period of relative political freedom in Russia from 1873 to 1876, there came the war with the Turks, and the great political trials of 1877–8, which finally led to the assassination of Alexander II in 1881.

The young Podolinsky, a student of natural sciences in Kiev, gravitated towards N. I. Ziber (1844–88), who was the first teacher of economics at a university to become a Marxist.[4] He was also connected with Mikail Drahomanov (1841–95), a radical democrat federalist and Ukrainian nationalist, in the steps of the poet Schevtschenko and the brotherhood Cyril and Methodius of 1845–7 (of Kostamarov, Kulisch and others). This left-wing group built a hromada, or commune, in Kiev. Their young, left-wing countrymen on the other side of the border, Ruthenians of Austrian Galicia, were also organizing themselves in a similar way, building up communes which they called sich, after the legendary Cossack commune of the sixteenth to eighteenth centuries.

In 1872, Podolinsky finished his studies in Kiev and travelled with Ziber to the West. They visited Heidelberg, and also workers' housing in the Dreifus-Mieg factories in Mulhouse. Podolinsky met Engels and Marx in London in the summer of 1872, through Lavrov, and in September he attended as an observer the Congress of the International in The Hague, where the Marxist-Bakuninist split occurred. He wrote a letter (on 7 September 1872) to Rosalia Idelson (at the time a fellow student of medicine in Zürich, and a friend of Valerian Smirnov, who was also a medical student and close collaborator of Lavrov), with disparaging words for Marx's and Engels' overpowering behaviour at the Congress, and praising the anarchist James Guillaume.[5] The combination of a rather negative attitude towards Marx as a politician with a deep reverence for him as a theorist was typical of Russian populists (Walicki, 1969, p. 137). Podolinsky was to write two articles on the history of the International in the first issues of the journal *Vperiod*.

[4] And who was mentioned by Marx, as N. Sieber, in the preface of 1873 to the second edition of vol. I of *Das Kapital*. Ziber has been seen as a forerunner of the 'legal Marxists' of the 1890s, partisans of capitalist industrial growth and favourable to the destruction of the peasant communes (Walicki, 1969).

[5] French translation of this letter in Lehning (ed.) 1974, *Archives Bakounine*.

Podolinsky was registered in Zürich as a medical student between May 1872 and August 1873 (Meijer, 1955), and he was described at the time as having 'an attractive appearance, with an interesting social and financial background'. Olga Lubatovitsch later recollected sailing trips on the lake, and his talks on philosophy and science with her, then a girl of eighteen.[6]

In Zürich, the collaboration of Lavrov was sought in order to found a socialist journal. Herzen had died, Chernichevsky was in prison, Bakunin was too compromised. Mikhailovsky lived in Russia, and was still too young and perhaps too moderate. Lavrov (1823–99) had been a mathematician and philosopher at the military academy in St Petersburg, but had lost his chair in 1866 (after Karakozov's attempt on the Tsar, and the repression unleashed by Muravev, also known as the 'scourge of Poland'), and he had been exiled from Russia. His *Historical Letters* had been the gospel of the youth of the 1870s. He was living in Paris. Podolinsky (together with Smirnov) was one of the main participants in the production of this journal, *Vperiod* (Forward). He also intervened as a 'Lavrist' in the conflict with the Bakuninists, specifically with Sazhin-Ross, for the control of a Russian library which had been set up in Zürich. In the lists of readers and of participants in lectures in the Russian library (where politics was the main subject), two of the names which appeared most often were Podolinsky and Sofia Bardina (Meijer, 1955, p. 132). After the tsarist government put Zürich out of bounds to Russian female students (by enacting a decree in June 1873 according to which their degrees would not be recognized), and after most Russian students had left, *Vperiod* continued its publication in London. Podolinsky had been one of the most active members of the Russian student colony in Zürich, which included a remarkable group of girls (attracted to this university because it was open to women). One of Podolinsky's teachers was the physiologist Ludimar Hermann (1838–1914), mentioned by Vera Figner in her memoirs as a competent teacher, although mildly opposed to women's training in medicine.

After Zürich, Podolinsky studied in Paris for some time and then returned to Kiev, where in 1873 it had proved feasible to found a section of the Imperial Geographical Society. Studies of regional history and

[6] Herself a medical student (and a member of the Fritschi group of Russian girls in Zürich), she was described by a contemporary as 'an enigmatic being whose biological character was at first all but clear . . . a roundish, boyish face, short-cut hair, parted askew, enormous blue glasses, a quite youthful, tender-coloured face, a coarse jacket . . . absorbed in a large book, every now and then rolling a cigarette which was finished in a few draughts . . . the phenomenon was a seventeen-year-old Russian girl from Moscow, Miss Ljubatovic (Meijer, 1955, pp. 59–60). See an English translation of part of her autobiography published in *Byloe*, 1906, in B. A. Engel and C. N. Rosenthal (1975).

geography, and of folklore flourished. The high period of populism was beginning, culminating in the summer of 1874. The young intellectuals became teachers, midwives, and doctors, and 'went to the people', to live with the peasants in order to promote literacy, to improve hygiene and public health and to raise social consciousness.

In 1875, Podolinsky was in Austria and in a letter of 4 May to Valerian Smirnov (1848–1900), he drew up a balance of the experience of 'going to the people':

For six months I lived in the village (of Iaroslavka, between Kiev and Odessa, where the family estate was) and in Kiev. In the village I devoted myself almost exclusively to practising medicine and saw almost no one beside the peasants. My success as a physician greatly exceeded my expectations. People came to see me from forty to fifty villages, and on some days I had more than fifty patients. And I also constantly visited neighbouring villages. Nevertheless, my noble rank was, of course, spoiling everything, and therefore I decided to relinquish it. I began by renouncing all income, and I intend in the autumn, after returning to Russia, to buy a peasant homestead somewhere and to settle down on it.

The reason he had again gone abroad was primarily to learn farming, which he could do in Serbia or in Galicia (that is, western Ukraine, under Austrian rule) better than in Russia, where 'it is now most inconvenient for a man of the gentry to learn a trade' because of police surveillance. But he planned eventually to go back to the Ukraine, despite the failure of the movement of 'going to the people'. The overwhelming majority of its members either got caught by the police as a result of bad luck or carelessness, or gave up soon, 'reducing it' – wrote Podolinsky – 'to a highly emotional summer excursion' (Serbyn, 1982).

At that time Podolinsky was already a Ukrainian nationalist. He wrote and published in Vienna a 'socialist fairy tale', *Parova-Maschina*, (The Steam Engine).[7] A rural worker is severely wounded while threshing, and dreams in his bed of a golden future when the workers will own the land and machines, will not have to work so hard and will eat delicious food. This story, criticized as naïve by Drahomanov, was considered scandalous in high places. In his dream, the worker talks to his young brother, who gives him a highly coloured account of the revolutionary history of the Ukrainian people, from the revolution of the Haydamak in 1768 and the Cossack commune of Zaporoga to the recent protests against the Jewish and German owners of the sugar factories, with a glorious revolution at

[7] Cf. George Hume, *Thirty-five years in Russia* (London, 1914), the memoirs of an Englishman who introduced the reaping machine and the steam thresher into Russia, in 1861, and who was based in Kharkov. *Parova-Maschina* was also published in French, some years later.

the end under the motto of 'the Commune is a giant'. In another pamphlet, Podolinsky brought out a popularized version of Lassalle and Marx in Ukrainian, and he also translated Vasilii Varzar's *Khitraia mekhanika* (The Cunning Trick) into Ukrainian, a pamphlet against usury.

In 1874 there had been an archaeological congress in Kiev, which in fact became a meeting of populists, a demonstration in favour of Ukrainian life with all political shades represented. At the same time, links were established with Galician socialists and nationalists, that is, with the Pavliks (brother and sister), with the young writer Franko in Lviv, and with Terletsky in Vienna. In 1875, Podolinsky was bringing out his pamphlets in Vienna in collaboration with Terletsky. In 1876, the ukase of Bad Ems forbade all writings in Ukrainian; while things were going badly in the eastern part of the Ukraine, in the western part (under Austrian rule) there was some agitation. Drahomanov, exiled in Geneva in 1876, maintained links with the Hromada group in Kiev through Pavlik in Lviv, who was also involved in the introduction into Russian territory of the series of revolutionary pamphlets put out in Vienna by Podolinsky and Terletsky. After some harassment from the authorities starting in October 1876, Mikhailo and Anna Pavlik, Terletsky, Franko and others were brought to trial in Lviv in January 1878 – a trial which is seen as the beginning of the socialist movement in Galicia (Himka, 1983, pp. 64–6) – and in which they received sentences milder than they would have had on the other side of the border, had they been Russian instead of Austrian subjects.

Despite Podolinsky's instrumental view of the medical profession merely as a means to make contacts with the peasantry, as explained in his letters to Smirnov of 1875 (in which he wrote that being a 'paramedic' or *Feldsher* was just as useful as being a qualified doctor), he went on to complete his studies, receiving his doctorate in medicine in Breslau in 1876 with a thesis on pancreatic enzymes and protein digestion written in German under the supervision of Heidenhain (1834–97).

Rudolf Peter Heinrich Heidenhain was a member of a family of physicians, educated at Könisberg, Halle, and Berlin, where he had worked with Emil Du-Bois Reymond (1818–96). In 1859 he had been appointed to a chair at Breslau where he stayed for the remainder of his career. Heidenhain made important contributions to histology. His prime interest was physiology, and he published a long essay on kidney function in Ludimar Hermann's *Handbuch der Physiologie* (1879–83, 6 vols). Since Hermann had been Podolinsky's teacher in Zürich, the connection is clear.[8]

---

[8] Podolinsky's thesis (there is one copy in the Bodleian) is entitled *Beiträge zur Kenntnis des pancreatischen Eiweissfermentes*. Heidenhains' biography has been taken from Fulton and Wilson, 1966.

In 1877 Podolinsky was back in Kiev. He had not joined the many young people who willingly enlisted for the war against the Turks in Herzegovina, motivated by Slav patriotism, but instead married Maria Andreeva, a landowner's daughter. They went into exile and settled in Montpellier. They were certainly not poor. The materials collected over the preceding years were used by Podolinsky to write a study, published in Ukrainian in Geneva in 1878, *The Life and Health of the Ukrainian Population*. This was a scientific work with statistical results and specific recommendations. Infant mortality in the Ukraine was 20 per cent; between 10 and 15 per cent of the population had lice; there should be a doctor for every ten or fifteen thousand people; and a sum of 1,500 to 2,000 roubles should be made available yearly for medical expenses.

The years 1877–8 saw not only the Turkish War but also the trials of the hundreds of young people arrested since 1874, whose cases were grave enough not to be dealt with by purely administrative processes. There was the trial of the fifty in Moscow and of the 193 in St Petersburg. At the beginning of 1878, Vera Zasulich's shot at Trepov, the chief of police who had abused political prisoners, reverberated all over Europe, and her trial in April 1878 ended in a verdict of 'not guilty' – it was also the last political trial by jury. In the summer of 1879, the Land and Freedom movement was split between the Black Repartition group of Axelrod, Plekhanov, Zasulich – later orthodox Marxists, and Mensheviks – and the People's Will (*Narodnaya Volya*) fraction, no longer interested in working with the peasants, but city-based, impatient, preaching violent direct action and with an 'executive committee' bent on killing the Tsar, and formed by Zhelyabov, Perovskaya, Vera Figner, Morosov and others. Olga Lubatovitsch was a member of it. Zhelyabov (1850–81) was a Ukrainian, and he attempted to persuade Drahomanov to become a spokesman abroad for Narodnaya Volya, but Drahomanov refused to do so. He later wrote a life of Zhelyabov, as if to make his excuses and to pay his respects. Drahomanov was more of a federalist radical democrat, who then edited in Geneva the journal *Hromada* in which Podolinsky was financially and personally involved.

In 1880 Podolinsky wrote the manifesto for *Hromada*. This appeared, signed by Drahomanov, Mykhaylo Pavlik and Podolinsky on 1 September 1880, but it was work of Podolinsky, and possibly a bit too radical for Drahomanov's taste. Here are some long extracts from this manifesto:

... The political, economic and educational enslavement of our country by Russia and Austria–Hungary curtails the freedoms of speech and publication to such an extent that it is almost impossible for those who favour freedom for the Ukrainian people, the socialists in particular, to speak or write unhampered on topics pertaining to human welfare and progress.

Our ideas and proposals are as follows:

I – In political matters:
  1 – Equal rights for men and women of all races.
  2 – Inviolable freedom of speech, publication, education, assembly, and organization.
  3 – Inalienable self-government for every community.
  4 – Complete independence for the Ukraine, organized into a federation of free communities.

. . . Every nation suffers under foreign rule; neither can a nation prosper when it is forced to support large segments of the population which are non-productive. In reality it makes little difference whether the Ukrainian people get rid of these because they are exploiting groups or because they are foreign elements. Whatever their nationality, they should either contribute their share of work, or else they should leave the country.

The settlement of Rumanians, Bulgarians, Serbs, Greeks, Russians, Germans, Polish artisans and peasants, Jewish tradesmen, etc., who contribute toward the well-being of the country is a different matter. They must share equal rights and freedoms with the Ukrainians. Their communities and organizations should not be coerced into adopting the language and customs of the Ukrainian commonwealth. They should have the freedom to organize their own schools, from the primary to the university level, and the freedom to join in all sorts of activities with people in their own home countries. These constructive foreign elements will be the links that bind the Ukraine to the neighbouring nations, with whom the Ukrainians should unite in a great free international federation. . . .

II – In economic matters:
  5 – All the important natural resources and means of production, such as land, water, machines, and factories, should be owned by the workers and peasants, organized into co-operative associations. People should not be placed in the position of selling their labour. They should work directly for themselves.

We believe that co-operative or collective ownership and labour are much more worth while than a system of private ownership.

At the same time we believe that the manner in which private ownership becomes collective and the manner in which a system of co-operative labour is set up and the produce divided will have to be solved through the goodwill of each community. It is to be hoped that both theory and practice in the economic field will show the individual communities how to organize co-operative labour and a just distribution of goods, not only on the local level, but also on the national and even international levels.

III – In educational and cultural matters:
  6 – We are in favour of empirical methods in the natural and social sciences, and in related fields of knowledge.

We think that science and the arts (literature, the theatre, painting, sculpture, and music) will some day replace the religions of today, which have caused and still cause so much enmity among peoples. Until education and persuasion have brought this about, all individuals and communities should have the freedom to worship as they choose . . . Here we cannot go into details concerning the ways and methods of realizing our programme. By using the printed word we show that we do not evade our part in the peaceable ways of furthering human progress. At the same time, we have no vain hopes. At no time in history were radical changes in social life brought about by peaceable means. Perhaps even less in the Ukraine than in other countries can we expect the voluntary abdication of power by existing rulers. Therefore it will be difficult for the people of the Ukraine to escape the necessity of an armed revolutionary struggle. Only such a revolution will finally transfer the natural resources and means of production into the hands of societies and communities of peasants and workers. To prevent the old ruling groups from seizing again their usurped wealth and power, it will be necessary to abolish the State army and introduce instead a Cossack militia in which every citizen will be trained to carry arms and use them when necessary. . . .[9]

In 1880 Podolinsky published in Geneva, for the journal *Hromada*, his study 'Manufactures and Industry in the Ukraine', which has been described as the first history of the Ukrainian economy, and as the first piece of scholarly writing in economics in the Ukrainian language. This

[9] The source from which this English translation has been taken (*The Annals of the Ukrainian Academy of Arts and Sciences in the US*, vol. II, New York, Spring 1952, special issue on Mikhaylo Drahomanov. A Symposium and Selected Writings, edited by Ivan L. Rudnytsky) refers to Drahomanov's 'Selected Works' (Bohatsky, 1939) where the manifesto is reprinted, and to the original source (i.e. the review *Hromada*, published in Geneva, 1881). The source of the English translation also includes an editor's note which makes the point that this manifesto had a maximalist flavour, more to Podolinsky's than to Drahomanov's taste, and which says (p. 223):

We must explain briefly the history of *Hromada*. Since 1877 Drahomanov had been publishing this magazine, at irregular intervals. This was part of the political task entrusted to Drahomanov by the illegal Hromada group in Kiev. In all Drahomanov had published five thick volumes. But political and personal differences arose between Drahomanov and his Kiev friends, who suspended their remittances, and the further issues were stopped. At this point Drahomanov, who was then living with Mykhaylo Pavlik, a journalist from Galicia, was approached by Serhii Podolynsky. Podolynsky (1850–91), a doctor and economist, a member of the Ukrainian Hromada in Kiev, and a militant socialist, had been living in France as a political emigrant since 1878. His parents were rich, and he had at his disposition substantial means, with which he wished to finance a new series of *Hromada*, transformed into a bi-monthly. Although Drahomanov had certain doubts about this, he agreed to co-operate. But the project soon broke down. Under police pressure Podolynsky's family ceased to send money. Soon thereafter Podolynsky became mentally ill, and was taken back to Russia by his parents. Only two numbers of the new *Hromada*, with Drahomanov, Podolynsky and Pavlyk as editors, ever appeared.

too was the year which saw the publication of the first versions of this article on energy accounting (in Russian, in *Slovo*, and in French, in the *Revue Socialiste* edited by Benoît Malon), and it was also the year when he wrote to Marx. Podolinsky published two other articles in the *Revue Socialiste*, in 1880, one against social-Darwinism, where he attacked Haeckel; one on 'Nihilism, Terrorism and Socialism' where, under his own name, he openly defended some 'terrorists', either dead or in prison, although he expressed hopes that the movement would turn towards socialism. His name appeared on the board of editors of the *Revue Socialiste* and other international socialist journals together with the best-known socialist writers of the time. Bernstein had praised his article against social-Darwinism in a letter to Lavrov of 31 August 1879.[10]

In Kiev, his writings were now banned; after the successful regicide of March 1881, it appears that his sources of finance were cut off. The last letter from Podolinsky to Lavrov, from Montpellier, dated 26 March 1881, asked for a full set of the Narodnaya Volya publications, in order to issue a popular book in Geneva.[11] In Montpellier, at about this time, his second child, and a child of Olga Lubatovitsch and Nikolai Morozov who had been left by Sergei Kravchinski in his care, died of meningitis. Olga Lubatovitsch was in prison in Russia after attempting to free Morozov. The marriage to Maria Andreeva was not a success. Podolinsky became ill and underwent psychiatric treatment, first in Montpellier and later in Paris, and apparently did not recover before his death in 1891. His parents obtained special permission to repatriate him in 1885 and his father wrote a poem on the sorrows that all mothers suffer.

His last writings were about a journey to Spain when he was still living in Montpellier. Roman Serbyn's assessment is adequate: 'As a political thinker Podolinsky combined Marxist economics, a Ukrainian orientation on the peasantry, and Russian revolutionary populism' (1982, p. 7). To such political views, not uncommon at the time and in his country, he added a satisfactory understanding of the basic principles of the natural sciences.

He was full of expectations on the reaction he would produce in Marx to his article on ecological economics. On 24 March 1880 he had written to Lavrov asking for Marx's address. He then wrote two letters to Marx

---

[10] He might have been connected also to Kropotkin and to Réclus (whom he quoted in his work, and who had enlisted Drahomanov to write on the Ukraine for his *Géographie Universelle*). This is one possible connecting line to Patrick Geddes (who, however, did not quote Podolinsky's work in his articles of 1884, cf. chapter 6).

[11] The edition of Lavrov's letters by Boris Sapir (1974) includes about fifty pages of Podolinsky's letters to Lavrov, in Russian.

from Montpellier. Marx replied to the first; over two years later he apparently asked Engels to give him a report on Podolinsky's economic views. In the first letter to Marx, dated 30 March 1880, Podolinsky had written:

It gives me a special pleasure to be able to send to you a small work, for which your work *Das Kapital* gave the first stimulus. Perhaps you will still remember that I had the honour of meeting you in the summer of 1872, at Herr Engels' home, through Herr Lavrov. I hope to be able to publish soon some applications of my thoughts to the development of diverse forms of production, in the *Revue Socialiste*. Apart from this, I am preparing a longer work, with examples, although I am still unsure whether I should use the French or the German language.

Marx's reply is unknown to us, and may have been lost (it does not appear in the *MEW* edition). On 8 April 1880, Podolinsky wrote again:

I do not think I can thank you better for your letter than by telling you that it gave me such a deep joy as very rarely has ever happened to me. Your worries about my health have moved me especially, and I hasten to let you know that it is not so bad as you perhaps have heard. Unless my knowledge as a doctor deceives me, I possess a lasting organism which will allow me sufficient time to work. With particular impatience I wait for your opinion on my attempt to bring surplus labour and the current physical theories into harmony.[12]

Though a good biography of Podolinsky is still lacking, his main connections, with Lavrov, with Drahomanov, his friendship with Narodnaya Volya members, his ecological Marxism, his cosmopolitism compatible with the defence of a threatened language, his socialist federalism and communalism, make his life and ideas very attractive: a remarkable 'doctor and economist' who perhaps could not cope with the strain in the disastrous aftermath of the assassination of the Tsar in March 1881.

What Podolinsky would have done in the 1880s and 1890s is, of course, speculation. His Lavrism and his Marxism had already led him to a belief in the political value of science, away from the extremely intense political activism of many members of his generation. The route of direct violent action was shown to be unprofitable, at least in the short run. Podolinsky had had misgivings all along. He probably went through a moral agony in seeing so many of his friends and acquaintances abandon plans for the study of medicine and turn to revolutionary action, and to execution or prison. In 1880 he mentioned by name, with admiration, in his article on terrorism, nihilism and socialism, Sofia Bardina, born in 1853, the

---

[12] These letters, written in German, are at the Institute of Social History in Amsterdam. I am grateful to the Institute and to my friend Rudolf de Jong for allowing me access to them. They have been published before in Ukrainian writings on Podolinsky. The new MEGA edition will probably provide more materials on the exchange between Marx and Podolinsky.

heroine of the 'trial of the fifty' in 1877; Ossinsky, born also in 1853, active in Kiev, executed in 1879; and Myshkin (1847–85), the hero of the 'trial of 193' in 1877 and 1878, who had attempted to free Chernishevski and who was to escape from prison in 1882 finally to be executed in 1885.

Podolinsky, after his period in Zürich as an active Lavrist in 1872–3, and after a spell of 'going to the people' in 1874, had clearly turned towards Ukrainian federalist socialism in 1875. After 1880, perhaps he would have become a politically orthodox Marxist, as other Russian populists became. A part of his heart was Ukrainian nationalist, and another part was sympathetic to the rather anarchist idea of a 'federation of free communes'. Ukrainian nationalism would not prosper in the 1880s and 1890s, and Drahomanov was to die in relative obscurity in Bulgaria in 1895, escaping economic penury only through a contract with the university in Sofia to which his competence as a folklorist entitled him.

In the 1880s, 'the all-consuming desire to serve others at all costs yielded to a concern to pursue selfish interests and insulate oneself from the misfortunes which a harsh reality could inflict. Students in the higher educational institutions began to think not of abandoning their courses in order to go to the people in a spirit of self-sacrifice or to devote their lives to revolutionary struggle, but rather of completing their courses and then living within the law. The great expectations of the previous decade were replaced by a preoccupation with trivia' (Offord, 1986, p. 78). Because of Podolinsky's profession of medicine, and because of his growing reputation as an economist, it is unlikely that he would have been tempted by practical farming, along the lines of Englehardt on his estate at Batishchevo, as an outlet for the failure of the great hopes of the 1870s. He might have become a 'legal populist' writer, in the mould of Nikolai Danielson, the translator of *Das Kapital*.

One writer explained that the youth of the 1860s had attended lectures in physiology, that of the 1870s on political economy, and that of the 1880s was becoming enthralled by disquisitions on Christianity (Wortman, 1967, p. 192). It seems unlikely that Podolinsky would have reached the third stage, although he shared the interests of many Russian radicals in religious dissent. He might have become an important intellectual figure living abroad, adding an essential ecological element to the kind of populist Marxism for which Marx himself was groping in the last years of his life, so much influenced by the events and discussions in Russia (Shanin, 1983).

4

Eduard Sacher's Formulation of Podolinsky's Principle

In 1881 the reputable house of Gustav Fischer in Jena published a book by a somewhat obscure author, Eduard Sacher, entitled *Foundations of a Mechanics of Society*. Sacher (1834–1903) published another book in 1899 with a similar title and many of the same numerical examples. It is not known whether there were any connections between Sacher and other members of a sort of 'Austrian school' of ecological economics (Pfaundler, 1839–1920; Josef Popper, 1838–1921) or with Mach (1838–1916) and Boltzmann (1844–1906). Ostwald, younger than any of them, did not do empirical work on energy accounting for human societies, although he is usually given the major role in 'social energetics'. Hayek (1952), himself an Austrian, certainly included Ostwald, but did not include any of his countrymen (except Neurath) in his list of 'social energeticists' (nor did he include Podolinsky). Eduard Sacher was discovered through Žmavc (1926), who barely mentions him and explains that his work had no impact, and goes on to say that it was he, Žmavc, influenced by Pfaundler, who introduced Ostwald to 'social energetics'. Be that as it may, Sacher is, with Podolinsky, one of the earliest authors who wrote on energy and human society.

Eduard Sacher was born in Bohemia of parents who were not rich. His father was a school teacher. Eduard Sacher became a teacher of physics and mathematics in secondary schools and in the teacher training colleges in Salzburg between 1869 and 1883, and later in Krems until his death. Apart from his two books on energy economics, he also published a book on the causes and remedies of pauperism. He was active in mountaineering circles. His attempts at giving the social sciences a base in the natural sciences, and the lack of response among both the official representatives of economics and the Marxists, were known to some of his colleagues and were mentioned in his obituary in 1903 in the journal of the Teachers' Association of the Salzburg region.[1]

In the preface to his book of 1881, Sacher stated that the natural sciences could provide a basis for a rational economy and in the introduction he went on to explain the mechanical conversion of heat, introducing the energy unit 1 kilocalorie or 424 kilogrametres, which Clausius called 1 *Werk*. Throughout the book he used 1 W as a unit, where W stands both for *Wärmeeinheit* (that is, kilocalorie) and for *Werk*. He began his analysis by considering human beings as thermic machines, with their capacity to do work. Physiology explained the amount of work that a person could do. From the different estimates of Poisson, Dupin and Saussure, and Christian, he concluded that the maximum that one worker could achieve in one day is the equivalent of 1,000 kilocalories, and that in order to do this work he would need at least 3,000 kilocalories in the form of food. Not all activity which is work in the physical sense is work in the economic sense. Therefore, it could be estimated (after various considerations on the share of the population economically active, number of holidays, etc.), that the work performed per worker/day would be equivalent perhaps to 450 kilocalories. He then put forward an initial conclusion, which he later argued in more detail: 'The economic task of the available labour force consists of winning from nature the greatest possible amount of energy' (p. 24). This would depend on the skill of the labour force, its instruments, on the fertility of the soil, on the availability of waterfalls, and on the climate: the northern nations were poor, because of lack of sunshine.

The sources of energy were agricultural and forest production; water power; minerals such as coal; wind power; domestic animals; and the products of hunting and fishing, all of them ultimately traceable to solar radiation. He then attempted to quantify the energy available per person/year in central Europe, possibly the first such estimate. Thus, 1 hectare of pine forest would produce per year some 8.3 cubic metres of wood, equivalent to 4,980 kilograms of dried wood, which, reckoning 3,600 kilocalories/kilogram, amounted to nearly 18 million kilocalories/hectare/year. No sources were quoted, but usual equivalents, given for instance by Ramage (1983), are:

1 ton of wood is equivalent to 15,000 megajoules and 3.6×10^6 kilocalories

1 m^3 of wood is equivalent to 9,000 megajoules, and 2.1×10^6 kilocalories

[1] *Zeitschrift des Salzburger Landes-Lehrervereines*, Jg. 33, 1903, p. 16. I am grateful to Dr Eva Obermayer-Marnach, Austrian Biographical Dictionary, Academy of Sciences, Vienna, for a photocopy of this source.

which agree with Sacher's. Sacher compared this output of energy with that which had arrived on that hectare of land during the year, and remarked on the small percentage which was converted. This image of an immense flow of energy from the sun being reflected back into space, with only a minute amount being assimilated by plants, moved him to write, as if making a point in his classroom: 'Nature is incredibly rich'. From one hectare of wheat, 2,590 kilograms of wheat and 3,000 kilograms of straw would be harvested – such high yields were consistent with the very high labour input, which Sacher assumed, perhaps realistically for Eastern European conditions, of 180 workdays/hectare/year. Subtracting 3 million kilocalories from the production to account not only for the seed but also for the fertilizer (unfortunately, no details were given either in the 1881 or in the 1889 versions), 15 million kilocalories/hectare/year would be obtained. Considering the use of land in Austria and in Prussia (Prussia had 17.25 million hectares of arable land, 6.25 million hectares of pasture land, and 8 million hectares of forest, for a population of 26 million), about 19 million kilocalories per person/year would be available.

He then went on to compute the energy available from domestic animals. One horse per day can do work equivalent to 2,160,000 kilogrametres, equivalent to 5,100 kilocalories (this is not the calorie intake, but the equivalent to the work carried out). This amounts to 1.5 million kilocalories/year, assuming about 300 days of work. Since there were two million horses in Prussia, their work during one year would be equivalent to $3 \times 10^6 \times 10^6$ kilocalories, that is, some 115,400 kilocalories per person/year. There were many other domestic animals, and using the equivalents one cow $= \frac{2}{3}$ horse $= 10$ sheep $= 4$ pigs $= 12$ goats, it could be calculated that Prussia had the equivalent of 557,000 kilocalories per person/year from domestic animals. Sacher's energy analysis should have counted the calories made available as food (and not as work) by all animals except horses, but this would have changed his general results on energy availability only by a small amount. Whether they are counted as work or as food energy, there is also the problem of double counting, since the animals will feed on the pastures, will use the straw, etc. Sacher dealt later with this problem. Another point is that cows, pigs, and so on, are not kept for work nor even primarily as a source of food energy, but rather as a source of protein.

In addition, Sacher gave an unexplained estimate for energy from waterfalls, 'which could become a significant source of wealth' (p. 29) directly, or in the form of electricity. Fourthly, he considered coal. Reckoning only 6,000 kilocalories/kilogram, the amount of energy available per person/year in Prussia would be 9 million kilocalories, since Prussia obtained yearly 40 million tons of coal, that is, 1.5 tons per person/year. Sacher was aware of the difference between primary energy and final energy, which for coal used in steam engines would be very large indeed; here he was concerned with primary energy from coal.

According to Sacher, the chemical energy in the metals produced should also be calculated, but he confessed that he did not know how to estimate this – a clear attempt at valuing metals on an irrelevant scale. Finally, figures were given without explanation on the energy made available from hunting and fishing. Sacher then presented the table reproduced here as table 8. However, he considered that domestic animals required, in the form of food energy, fifteen times the energy delivered by them, and therefore to avoid double counting one should subtract 8.3 million kilocalories, thus some 20.3 million kilocalories per person/year remained available.

Table 8 *Energy available per person/year in Central Europe, c.1880, according to Sacher (10^6 kcal)*

From agriculture, pasture and forests	19.000
From domestic animals	0.557
From water power	0.036
From coal	9.000
From hunting	0.005
From fishing	0.020
Total	28.618

How was this energy used by society? Sacher discussed nutritional needs, and gave as an example the diet of a German soldier at war, concluding that at least 1 million kilocalories per person/year (at about 3,000 kilocalories per day) would be needed as food. Adding the food wasted at different stages, the minimal food energy use per person/ year could be estimated at 2 million kilocalories. The energy spent on housing, clothing and other minimal necessities of life would perhaps amount to 1 million kilocalories more. The difference between 20.3 million kilocalories and 3 million kilocalories for subsistence could be used for all the amenities of civilization, and to build machines, that is, for investment.

Sacher then made an attempt to correlate stages in cultural progress and energy availability; this before Geddes and long before Henry Adams and Wilhelm Ostwald. Podolinsky had wished to correlate modes of production and energy availability, but this was not done in any of the versions of his article, and illness prevented him from further work. Sacher was unaware of Podolinsky's work.[2]

Sacher gave the following figures on kilocalories available per person/ year: 'savages', 3 million; 'nomads', 6 million; 'agriculturalists', 14 million; contemporary Central Europeans, 20.3 million (1881, p. 33). While he had discussed in some detail the figures corresponding to 'savages' and to 'Central Europeans', he did not give any explanation for the other two categories. Consistency would have demanded that Sacher subtract all the energy derived from coal in his estimate for agriculturalists. The figure of 14 million kilocalories per person/year for agriculturalists is also inexact in the sense that there is great variation in this group of people. Research into human ecology many years after Sacher (Hardesty, 1977; Ellen, 1982) shows that many agricultural peoples survive and even give up a surplus to landowners or to the State with a lower level of available energy. As was said in the introduction, the history of the resistance of many such peoples to exploitation is well known.

Sacher not only developed this view of the stages of history, a clear antecedent of evolutionary ecological anthropology, but also paid great attention to the way that surplus energy, beyond the needs of subsistence, was appropriated by some groups of society to the exclusion of others. A large part of his books (particularly that published in 1899) is devoted to a discussion of the economics of distribution, with an attack on the categories of interest, profit and rent.

Sacher went on to calculate the energy return on human energy input into agriculture. For wheat agriculture he drew up the following balance:

Net energy output/hectare/year (excluding seed and fertilizer, including straw): 15,000,000 kilocalories

Human energy input/hectare/year (corresponding to 180 workdays/ hectare/year): 81,000 kilocalories

The labour input is high, but plausible, and each day of work is counted as 450 kilocalories. Sacher did not consider the energy input from domestic animals in this balance, and with such high labour input he may have been thinking of a purely manual agriculture. The ratio energy output/human energy input is then 185.

---

[2] Though the preface to his book is dated May 1881, one year after Podolinsky's article appeared in French in the *Revue Socialiste*.

The first requirement in comparative work in ecological anthropology is to normalize the method of measuring the human energy input. Sacher did not count the calorie intake, but the work done. The figure of 185 still appears to be very high, but this is because the energy output includes straw. It is a figure comparable to those found in much modern work on ecological anthropology.[3]

Sacher explained that, in order to do work equivalent to 450 kilocalories per day, workers have not only to be fed, but also to be clothed and housed. Perhaps the minimum expenditure of energy per person/day would be 9,000 kilocalories (this was the standard of a 'savage', in his view) converted into 450 kilocalories of effective work, with an efficiency, therefore, of 1:20. Thus, for every 20 kilocalories which the agricultural worker, working on wheat cultivation, uses as food, clothing or housing, she or he delivers 185 kilocalories. In other words, 'one person working on wheat-growing can feed nine other persons', a finding which Sacher later amended by subtracting the energy value of the straw.

The energy productivity of labour would be the cause for the share in different countries of their active agricultural population in their whole populations. In Britain, the remarkably low share of agricultural population was due not only to food imports but also to the fact that 'many agricultural machines are used, therefore saving labour power, which is substituted in part by the chemical energy of coal, in the steam plough' (p. 35). This tantalizing remark shows that Sacher was on the brink of doing a comprehensive output/input analysis of energy flow in agriculture, since he was also aware of fertilizers as part of the energy input. He almost quantified the view that the high productivity of labour in energy terms, in a country such as Britain, was the consequence of the substitution of energy from stocks (of Chilean nitrates, of coal) for the flow of human and animal energy.

Sacher also tried to link energy analysis with the theory of economic value, defining three types of value, all in terms of energy. This is not a very useful part of his analysis, but it is included for the sake of completeness. The example of coal will clarify Sacher's definitions of his

[3] But not – for instance – to the figure given by Ellen (1982, p. 152) of an energy return/human energy input of 2.4 for agriculture among the Nualu, which is not comparable with figures which measure human energy input not as food intake, but as work done. As Podolinsky and Sacher already knew, a ratio of 2.4 would not allow the reproduction of even the most simplified society, if the human energy input is measured as work done. For a discussion on the energy valuation of labour, see, for instance, Fluck and Baird, 1980, Puntí, 1983, Loomis, 1984.

three types of value. In Prussia, one miner obtained, on average, 198 tons of coal per year (Sacher, 1881, p. 59).[4] If the daily work of a miner is set at equal to 750 kilocalories (it being heavy work), with 300 workdays per year, then the total amount of work done per year would be equivalent to 225,000 kilocalories. This would mean 1,136 kilocalories per ton of coal, and this could be called the 'exchange rate' of a ton of coal, on a human energy theory of value. The 'absolute value' of a ton of coal would be 6,500,000 kilocalories (that is, its enthalpy, though Sacher did not use the term), but its 'use-value' would be much less because of various losses and especially because of the low efficiency of the steam engine. Thus the energy gained from a ton of coal which really could replace human labour would only be around 180,000 kilocalories.

Taking one house as an example, its 'exchange-value' would again be its human energy cost; its 'use-value' would be the energy (not gained, in this case, but) saved by living in the house, compared to the extra energy required if living in the open air. Similar considerations would apply to clothes. Hypothetical figures were given by Sacher (1881, p. 74). In agriculture, the 'use-value' produced from a hectare of wheat would amount to 4,810,000 kilocalories per year (with the yields that Sacher had assumed), once the production of straw had been reduced fifteenfold because it was used as feed for animals, and taking other losses into account. The human energy input would be, as he had already explained, 81,000 kilocalories/hectare/year, and this was the 'exchange-value'. The ratio (4,810:81 = 59) between 'use-value' and 'exchange-value' was given the curious name of 'specific value'; it is in fact the energy productivity of human labour.

The energetic efficiency of an agricultural worker (his or her 'value as a machine', as Sacher put it) would be of the order of 1:20, because one cannot consider food energy only and because not everybody is available for work. For an economy to be viable, the 'use-values', (i.e. energy gained, or saved) must be on average at least twenty times greater than 'exchange-values', (that is, human energy costs, measured as work done) (1881, p. 63). Here, Sacher's analysis, though expressed in his quaint terminology, states again Podolinsky's principle. In other words, the energy productivity of human work must be equal to or greater than the efficiency of human beings as heat engines. Agriculture fulfilled this condition very amply, and so did coalmining, as the figures showed.

Sacher was an 'energetic dogmatist', in Georgescu-Roegen's sense, since he did not consider the availability of material resources, such as water, or

---

[4] This could be compared to the foreseen 'productivity' of 2,500 tons/worker per year in the new coal field of Selby, in Yorkshire. Figures are not available on the energy input needed from non-human sources in this coal field.

metals. He was nevertheless aware that an energy theory of exchange-value was not really tenable; he devoted many obscure pages to explain why prices differed from such energy values, and he mentioned explicitly that artistic work had value which could not be expressed by its human energy cost. The role of skill and innovations he considered to be very important in economic development, beyond energy availability. Thus, from Charlemagne, who had introduced new field rotations, to the inventors of the steam engine, who had made coal useful for work, 'mental work' had contributed much to wealth, and it could not be measured by energy cost. A corollary of this view was that it was inappropriate to set wages proportionally to the expenditure of human energy, since skill and training play a great role in the value of human work.

With such provisos in mind, Sacher thought nevertheless that the 'wealth of nations' (1881, pp. 77–8) was basically determined by the energy return to human energy input. The higher the energy gained (or spared), which he called 'use-value', and the lower the human energy cost, which he called 'exchange-value', the more energy was available beyond pure subsistence, and the wealthier was the nation. Of course, the viability (or reproduction capacity) of a socio-economic system should include a time perspective, but whether this wealth was permanent or transient was not discussed by Sacher, who, unlike Podolinsky, did not mention the second law of thermodynamics – although there is perhaps no need to go beyond practical experience and the first law (the principle of conservation of energy) to see that burnt-out coal cannot burn again.

Since there were physical limits to the wealth of nations (despite the important role of human skill and innovations), how this wealth was to be distributed became an acute question. Chapters 7–14 of Sacher's first book, and most of the second, are devoted to a discussion of theories of rent, interest and profits. The real 'capitalists' were the plants which assimilated solar energy (1881, p. 84). Sacher was strongly anti-*rentier* and anti-capitalist, which might go some way to explaining his theories' lack of reception in academic circles, though not in the socialist or anarchist *demi-monde*.

As we shall see, Podolinsky's and Sacher's basic principles of human ecology reappear time and again, their initial contributions having been ignored. Why were they forgotten? To point to the separation between the natural and the social sciences is really to explain nothing, because this separation itself needs explaining and it did not always prevent, as shall be seen in the next chapter, and also in chapter 7, some physicists from engaging in discussions of the economy. Although the difference between the painstaking counting of energy and material flows by modern ecologists and Sacher's and Podolinsky's 'armchair' accounts is plain, the continuity in method and the discontinuity in time and intellectual tradition between their work and modern human ecology and ecological anthropology should be stressed. As for economic history, the first academically successful attempt at this kind of approach was not made until Cipolla (1962).[5]

---

[5] Many recent works of historical energy economics emphasize industrial use, and they forget food energy, fuel from biomass, and the contribution from domestic animals. There is now a flourishing school of such studies, a common finding being that, in what is seen as the age of the steam engine, water power (even before transmission of electricity was thought of) was a very important source. Refer to, for instance, Hunter, 1979; also, J. Carreras, J. Maluquer de Motes, J. Nadal, and C. Sudrià, on energy use in Catalan industry from 1830 to the present (Carreras, 1987).

A vigorous debate continues on the relation between economic growth and the level of energy use. For opposite viewpoints, see Hall, Cleveland and Kaufman (1986) and José Goldemberg et al. (1986).

5

Rudolf Clausius: 'On the Energy Stocks in Nature'

Introduction

In 1885 Rudolf Clausius had a booklet published in Bonn, *On the Energy Stocks in Nature and their Valorization for the Benefit of Humankind*. The contents are easily summarized. In the first five pages Clausius described the history of the steam engine, as he had done many times as a teacher, as a student, and even as a schoolboy in 1838–40 in Stettin. On page seven he remarked that electricity was beginning to compete with steam but that it would be 'uneconomic' if produced from zinc batteries. 'Our countryman (Werner) Siemens, a true genius' had invented the dynamoelectric machine which made available the force of waterfalls by making possible the interconversion of mechanical energy and electrical energy. But why were waterfalls needed when coal was available? Clausius analysed here once again the coal question:

> With respect to the consumption of mechanical energy we are living today in a marvellous age. In economics there is the general rule that consumption in one period of any good should not exceed its production in the same period. Therefore, we should consume only the fuel that is reproduced through the growth of forests, although in practice we go about things in a completely different way.
>
> We realize that there are coal stocks under the earth from ancient times, massively accumulated through the growth of plants then existing on earth during such long periods of time that compared to them, historical time appears as infinitely short. We are now consuming such stocks, behaving as happy heirs. So much is taken from the soil as human strength and technical means allow, and it is consumed as if it were inexhaustible. The amount of railways, steam boats and factories equipped with steam engines increases astonishingly so that when we look at the future the question inevitably arises of what will happen once coal reserves are exhausted.
>
> This is not a superfluous question despite the abundance of coal deposits. There are certainly very large stocks in the planet which up to now have not been measured but we may estimate the magnitude of reserves in particular countries and we may guess how long they will last.

William Siemens (*Inaugural Address at the General Meeting of the Iron and Steel Institute*, March 1877, p. 7) reckoned that, should extraction of coal in England continue at the same rate, the coal fields would last for 1,100 years longer, but should the annual rate of extraction increase as in the last twenty years, then coal reserves would last only 250 years. Although such figures are not exact, they show however the beginnings of a crisis. We are dealing with periods of time which are relatively short compared to the life of nations. (Clausius, 1885)

Clausius then discussed briefly the impossibility of a *perpetuum mobile*. After explaining why an economy based on the use of hydrogen as a fuel was not practicable because electrolysis did not give a net energy gain, he concluded:

We ought to separate with absolute clarity the possible from the impossible. Energy cannot be created without use of energy. The reserve of potential energy contained in coal fields owes its origin to that energy which the sun sent to us as radiant heat, necessary for the sustenance of plants, throughout long periods of time before the existence of humankind. Science will not be able, however advanced, to originate a new source of energy once that resource, coal, is exhausted. On the contrary, men will be condemned to manage with the energy which the sun will continue to radiate for a very long time. (Ibid.)

Clausius was wrong, and not only because he forgot to mention oil. Less than twenty years after 1885, Frederick Soddy would speculate on the social consequences of the use of radioactive energy,[1] and sixty years later, Clausius' colleagues, as physicists, had commited the crime of the nuclear bomb. Other forms of atomic energy, possibly quite destructive, possibly impracticable, such as the breeder reactor or nuclear fusion, today are offered for the future. But such options are not attractive or convincing to all, and therefore the 'coal question' and, in general, the question of exhaustible energy resources is no less topical than in Clausius' time. He favoured hydroelectricity as a substitute: 'solar energy is offered to us on the one hand in the form of matter which can be oxydated and which has come into being by the growth of plants, and on the other hand in the movement of water, which can produce so much energy that waterfalls could be substituted for large coal mines'. 'A lover of nature', he wrote, 'will find it ugly that waterfalls, the foaming savagery of which constitutes the main source of beauty of alpine landscapes, be captured and harnessed to machines, but this is their inevitable destiny. The active industrial life that will develop near each waterfall will have to substitute for the foresaken beauty'. Clausius added:

[1] See chapter 9.

Such forces of nature should be efficiently used in great scale as soon as possible in order to protect coal reserves against quick depletion. Coal reserves will not deteriorate if kept under the earth.

Due to the invention and improvement of machines such as the steam engine, the century which is now ending has been characterized by the use of the natural sources of energy to an extent never known before. The next centuries will have as their main task that of introducing a wise economy in the consumption of natural resources, mainly those we have found as a heritage of past ages and which we should not waste because they cannot be restituted. The quicker the change comes, the better. The most civilized nations should act in concert in order to control the extraction of coal in a manner alike to the control of forest exploitation in well organized states. (Ibid.)

Clausius was assuming a large degree of international goodwill. One of the analogies he chose, the collaboration among national post offices, sounds less ridiculous than, as he wrote, the creation of 'the great neutral state of the Congo'.

The Electrical Revolution

We have seen that Clausius' short text emphasized two points: the exhaustibility of coal, and the reliance on the new possibilities of transmission of hydroelectrical energy by dynamos. The second point was then very much in fashion. Thus, Josef Popper,[2] engineer of steam engine boilers, who was to be respected as a student of aerodynamics and also as a social reformer by older and younger colleagues such as Ernst Mach, Richard von Mises, Theodor Karman and Albert Einstein, was able to explain the principles of the transmission of electrical energy when only twenty-four years old, in 1862. In the 1880s the magic of electrical exhibitions was brought out in public: Paris 1881, Munich 1882, Vienna 1883. In Munich, Marcel Deprez demonstrated the transmission of electrical energy by moving a vehicle from a stationary dynamoelectric machine 60 kilometres away. Electricity gave rise to an 'orgy of voltaic arcs', and 'in order to make such magic even more complete, there now arrived the enormous clouds from the chimney of the boiler room, where steam performs the work of 2,000 horse-power', since electricity could also be made by burning coal.[3]

Josef Popper wrote in his autobiography (published posthumously in 1924) that he did not presume to compare his article of 1862 (which he

[2] See also chapter 13.
[3] *Die Neue Zeit*, edited by Karl Kautsky, vol. I, October 1883.

deposited unpublished in the Viennese Academy of Sciences) to Werner Siemens' or Deprez's inventions. He had rather been interested in the ethical and socio-economic impacts of technical change, and he had soon realized that electricity could help regions and nations which still suffered from pauperism: if they lacked coal or oil, they could profit from hydroelectricity. Would the analogy with Robert Oppenheimer's and Fréderic Joliot's statements in 1945–55 in favour of the peaceful use of nuclear energy be far-fetched?

In the 1880s nobody was better qualified to talk on the economy of steam and electrification than Rudolf Clausius, and it is strange that he did not make his views on the economics of energy known earlier, louder and more often. It was he who in 1850 had axiomatically determined the 'economic coefficient', the *Wirkungsgrad* of thermic machines, starting his career in thermodyamics. In the thirty-five years between 1850 and 1885 which he had spent as professor at the Artillery School in Berlin, at Zürich Polytechnic and at the Universities of Würzburg and Bonn, he never ceased to work on the subject. He had also worked on electrodynamics. James Clerk Maxwell (1831–79) had left a stumbling stone to the scientific community with his *Treatise on Electricity and Magnetism* (1872). Electromagnetic phenomena as implied by the dynamoelectric machine were under discussion long since (Oersted, Faraday, Wilhelm Weber) and gave rise to a controversy of lasting repercussions. Today's common understanding of electromagnetic phenomena in terms of 'fluids', a description in mathematical terms borrowed from fluid mechanics, was much debated in comparison to an 'atomistic' description or one in terms of centres of the forces and their action at a distance, familiar from gravitation and electrostatics. A continuous field of action with curls, springs and sinks obviously depended on the presence of a medium, called the 'ether', for which there was no direct experimental evidence. Only with the experiments (1887–9) by Heinrich Hertz (1857–94) on 'wireless waves' did the description in terms of Maxwell's equations seem convincing and become more generally accepted.

Rudolf Clausius entered this controversy in 1875 with a paper on 'A fundamental law of electrodynamics' in which he attempted to retain some of the ideas developed in 1846 by Wilhelm Weber (1804–91), by now a 'grand old man' of the exact sciences and widely known for his constitutionalism in politics. For Clausius he might have been a kind of mentor, and he had once given a very favourable judgement on demand of the young man's Swiss employers. A delicate detail is that there was not only Clerk Maxwell (and others, among them Hermann Grassman, a son of one of Clausius' teachers in Stettin) taking part in the controversy, but once more his old adversary Hermann Helmholtz (1821–94). It would be of great interest for German intellectual history to elucidate the opposition of these two men of different social backgrounds, which occasionally shine forth in their scientific pronouncements.

When he spoke in 1885 about the importance of the electrical transmission of force and the significance of the dynamo for energy economics, Clausius had not ceased publishing scientific articles on electrodynamics and the dynamo and he was certainly an expert on their fundamental principles. He realized that the impressive characteristic of electrical power is its transportability and since the costs of transport are an integral part of the (energy) costs of energy, electrification offered a technically promising outlook: electrification and 'white coal' versus steam and fossil fuels, all the more so as in Germany the level of consumption of energy was still not that incompatible with the potential supply of hydroelectricity as it very soon became (and in Britain presumably already was), and lacking exact figures one could believe that fuel could be replaced.

The Club of Ideologists

A taste for some machines is easily recognized in Clausius. He was aware of their epochal significance for the economy and society. He had worked successfully since 1850 on a fundamental law governing the performance of the steam engine and, as we have seen, he worked with less success in later days on the principles of the dynamo-electric machine. His famous paper of 1850 on the motive power of heat and on the laws derived thereof for a theory of heat, began by stating:

> Since, by the help of the steam engine, heat is used as motive power and, based upon this, it has been practically noticed that a certain amount of energy may be considered equivalent to the heat required to produce it, it was rather obvious that a fixed theoretical relation could be determined between the amount of heat and the work produced by it, and from this relation conclusions could be drawn on the nature and the laws of heat.

At that time, the result was the 'second law of thermodynamics': heat does not go from cold bodies to warm ones by itself. By this axiom, the theoretical efficiency of heat engines could be ascertained: it would only depend on the temperatures at which the machine worked and of the heat sink. Some scientists in the engineering tradition, such as Clausius' colleague in Zurich, Gustav Zeuner, teacher of a whole generation of builders of steam engines and locomotives, were not impressed by the theoretical principle because the theoretically determined efficiency was not reached in practical conditions by a long way. In the 1880s Clausius was still discussing the correct interpretation of his findings, with, among others, the Alsatian entrepreneur, engineer and experimenter Gustave Adolphe Hirn. Practical engineering doubts did not diminish in the least the importance of Clausius' law, which was not really questioned either by Ludwig Boltzmann's attempt since 1866, and also Maxwell's and Clausius' himself, to 'deduce' the second axiom of thermodynamics inside the framework of the molecular kinetic theory of gases, that is, 'statistical mechanics'. In this view, the stochastical movement of the molecules should explain the functional quantities defined by thermodynamics within the framework of (quantum-) mechanical calculus. In this context the 'second law' became an enigma, since it was considered derivable from other principles. But indeed, since the first attempt by Boltzmann, all such trials, including Clausius', failed: the second law of thermodynamics persisted as an axiomatic principle to be included in one of its many forms in any attempt to describe relevant phenomena. In kinetic theory one had to live in particular with the seeming paradox that the mathematics used to describe the individual statistical event, the impact of two molecules, produces no asymmetry at all, whereas the statistical ensemble does show the asymmetry of the heat flow according to the second law.

The asymmetry of the heat flow with respect to the time variable, its unidirectional character, in a sense the 'time-pointer' that it represents, is an observation of far reaching consequences. A machine driven by heat is not a watermill. A heat engine cannot 'transport' a quantity of heat, by which it was driven, back to the original temperature level, without additional work. And why should it? Heat is not moving matter, like water, it is, in the picture drawn by kinetic theory, energy of molecules, yes, but also a characteristic of the ensemble of a large number of molecules, the temperature of which indicates a potential of 'rearrangements', of 'changing order', where order is an instantaneous attribution of energy and location to each molecule. This potential of rearranging possibilities increases with temperature (and number of molecules, and also depends on their kind), and it was given a name by Rudolf Clausius in the sense that 'entropy' increases with the decrease in this rearrangement potential. Hence, heat scientifically is always referred to by two functions: energy and entropy. The Jena physicist Felix Auerbach published a book in 1902 on 'The Mistress of the World and Her Shadow'. The title expresses not so much the optimistic connotations of having energy as a mistress as the pessimistic ones of entropy. Human work, however, can be 'ektropic', it can decrease the entropy of a partial system. Of course it can. Another way of stating Clausius' law is by saying that entropy in a closed system cannot but increase: 'entropically' thus became synonymous with irreversibly. To repeat once more the practical conclusion: any use of heat to produce work is accompanied by an irrecoverable loss of energy, to be seen as an increase in entropy.

When it is said that heat flows, by itself, only from warm bodies to cold bodies but not vice versa, there is obviously something totally 'irreversible', something 'entropic' in the process, an 'arrow in time'. Care must be taken in expression. Irreversibility is an attribute which equally applies to an irrevocable progress as to the sad aspects of ageing and death, there is in general no need to refer to thermodynamics. However, within the framework of a social philosophy which tries to exploit scientific principles politically, the second law of thermodynamics may have considerable significance.

That the 'Industrial Revolution' implied going beyond the limits of the 'circuit of life' and that it allowed humankind to break out of the agrarian cycle of abundance and hunger, impressed many students of social and economic history. Thus, Patrick Geddes wrote in 1884 of production in the 'age of energy' (which, in ways to be discussed in chapter 14, is not in contradiction to seeing the period as the 'age of capital'), and he felt a duty to 'physicalize' sociology, economics and geography.[4]

James Watt (1736–1819), an engineer, was to become the symbol of the Industrial Revolution, shown in this light by many authors, for instance by Stuart Chase (later, one of the intellectual mentors of the Technocrats)[5] and by Lewis Mumford in the 1920s. Michel Serres wrote of the 'Carnotian revolution' (Grinevald, 1976): a literary metaphor or perhaps another politico-ideological construction? Lazare Carnot had made a name for himself as a organizer of the Revolutionary Army and as a researcher on hydraulic machines. His son, Sadi Carnot (1796–1832) devoted his short life to the study of the steam engine, and his work was to culminate in the formulation of the second law of thermodynamics in 1850 and 1851. His paper of 1824 became famous in retrospect. Between father and son there was the watershed of the 'Industrial Revolution'. James Watt had been a practical man. Should Sadi Carnot, a theorist, personalize a higher historical abstraction, in a fictitious personification of historical periods? Human life is above all empirically irreversible and finite: do we need to appeal to a 'law of entropy', or perhaps have we been driven away from Paradise?

Economists such as Nicholas Georgescu-Roegen would wish to quantify the industrial economic process which dissipates enormous quantities of raw materials and energy, analogously to thermodynamic processes so that the growth of entropy might be measured and slowed down by recycling.

[4] See chapter 6.
[5] See chapter 9.

Such economists are at least aiming, if nothing else, to provide a rational base in order to calculate the costs of our economy. Why not? On the other hand, the thermodynamics of Ilya Prigogine and some synergetics emphasize the ektropic, entropy-reducing possibilities of open systems.[6] Daring comparisons are made between anthropological-social processes and biophysical processes, by using the key word of biophysical thermodynamics, 'self-organization'. Such analyses, or rather analogies, do not seem convincing; they are too rough, up to now and perhaps for ever.

Thermodynamics had from the beginning ideological connotations. Clausius' formulation is also to blame, since it ran: the energy of 'the world' remains constant, while its entropy strives towards a maximum. What was meant by 'the world'? He should perhaps have said, 'the world in the sense we use the word here', simply as a 'closed system'. In 1851 William Thomson had already written of the 'heat-death' towards which the world was proceeding and, however astonishing it now seems, such a cheap 'philosophy of the future' did not fail to have consequences. The reasons for William Thomson's eschatological futurology and for his 'theological handling' – to use Josef Popper's phrase – of the second law will be considered briefly. Around 1860, Henry Thomas Buckle had written his *History of Civilization*, an influential book which proposed simple 'scientific' laws of historical development based on the climate and the fertility of the soils. Buckle wrote that the idea of the Nation had deprived religion of its usefulness. It is surely not wrong to see religion, in its essentials, as a projection towards the future, ideologically veiled: an explicit scheme of social reproduction which must symbolically and ritually transmit a 'concrete transcendence'. Buckle probably did not believe that the memory, the traditions and the myths of the national pasts had in fact been substituted everywhere in Europe for such 'projection towards the future'. It is true, however, that in the science of this time the question of foreseeing and planning the future is almost absent, very markedly so in the new neoclassical or counter-classical economics.

The fundamental incompatibility that Buckle sensed between a nationalist ideology and religion did not really exist, not even in Germany, where in the upper spheres there was a prudish confessionalism, replicated in Victorian Britain and in Catholic France and Austria, according to which the supernatural element did not necessarily enter into conflict with the scientific outlook because there was a duality between reason and faith, between belief and knowledge. Those not pleased with such reconciliation with religion, could become idealist freethinkers, as 'Monists'. There was

---

[6] H. Haken has edited the proceedings of successive symposia held at Schloss Elmau in Bavaria on 'Synergetics: evolution of order and chaos in physics, chemistry and biology'.

almost always, also, a good pinch of chauvinism. Lack of a global and agreed-upon conception of social reproduction made it possible to use scientific debates ideologically by different groups. The 'principles of energy' were taken as proofs for 'idealism', 'spiritualism', even 'spiritism', and against 'materialism', evolution theory, social-Darwinism, economic liberalism, and social optimism. The second law of thermodynamics was used for theology, for pessimism. The subjective theory of value was taken to be psychophysically founded on Fechner's Law, and its ideological importance went well beyond economics. Somebody like Heinrich Treitschke could in the 1870s derive his anti-semitism from purported historical science. Anything and everything had ideological value, *n'importe quoi*. Meanwhile, the Marxists were developing a non-transcendental interpretation of the human historical process of social reproduction which implied at the same time a project for the future.

Clausius' friends and colleagues felt a strong call to take part in the production of such differing ideological groups, often in their inaugural speeches to scientific congresses or in academic ritual occasions. Clausius' friend Emil Du Bois-Reymond had given in 1872 his notorious speech, *Ignorabimus*, on the limits of scientific knowledge, a speech much recommended against unrepentant, fervent 'materialists' of 1848 vintage such as Büchner, Vogt, Moleschott, and also Strauss.

Hermann von Helmholtz, who had a difficult personal relationship with Clausius, became a sort of *Praeceptor Germaniae*, speaking on political and cultural questions, always as a pan-germanic, defending from a conservative political viewpoint, an ideal of academic freedom. Straying far beyond his own field of scientific competence, Adolf Fick also published his views on the problems of his time with a passion and intensity unparalleled among his circle. Rudolf Clausius did not do so. One factor might have been that Fick, Helmholtz, and Du Bois-Reymond were not only scientists, but medical doctors. So was also Clausius' faithful friend, the physiologist Jacob Moleschott, who had lived in Zurich in the same house, and who was known as a fervent Feuerbachian and materialist for his publications on 'the circuit of life' and who had been one case of *Berufsverbot* in Germany after 1848. He later taught in Rome. All of them, though they did not think alike politically, were involved in the institutionalization of scientific physiology and medicine. Does this explain their loquaciousness? Thus, Rudolf Virchow and Thomas Henry Huxley, in the same profession and of the same generation, were no less productive as ideologues. It was seen in chapter 2 how scientists of a previous generation, engaged in the institutionalization of the new chemistry, felt bound to speak on a variety of subjects and therefore became public figures.

The scientists educated as engineers, born around 1820 like the physiologists just mentioned, became similarly engaged in a process of institutionalization. Clausius' colleagues at Zurich, for instance Franz Reuleaux, or Gustave Adolphe Hirn in Mulhouse, or even more his best friend John Tyndall, wrote regularly for the general public and took part in the great debates on the time. Clausius did not lack opportunities, therefore, to engage in ideological polemics. He could have taken part in the discussions on Wilhelm Weber's 'relativist' law of energy, which Fick had greeted as the greatest innovation since Newton. He did not. In his time he could have become involved in two famous cases of academic exclusion in which science and ideology became inextricably mixed. One was that of the astronomer Friedrich Zöllner from Leipzig and his book on the comets. Zöllner found it expedient to draw some lessons against the decadent morality of some of his colleagues, and he also engaged in spiritist speculation based on the energy laws, working experimentally on such lines. Another case was that of Eugen Dühring, who lost his post at the University of Berlin. In his history of the principles of mechanics, he accused Helmholtz in 1873 of hiding, in his much admired work of 1847, Mayer's priority on the principle of conservation of energy. Dühring was a social democrat, but also a polemical anti-semite. His influence on the party and his work on the economics of the transition to communism provoked Engels' well known reaction in 1877. In 1880 Dühring published a verbose book on Julius Robert Mayer, against university science. Both Dühring and Zöllner had attacked Clausius, who merely troubled to publish concise amendments.

One man, one question; whether due to an inborn attitude or to an acquired political and philosophical conviction, Clausius was in any case that type of scientific worker. This may seem strange, given the habits among most of his colleagues, and the subject of his own work. Clausius' *grand bourgeois* teacher and friend, Gustav Magnus, an entrepreneurial figure of physics in Berlin, behaved in a similar manner at a time, not so distant from ours, when the transfer of ideology from science into the socio-political domain flourished. Science was a quarry for all kinds of social struggles and science claimed a cultural territory greater than ever before.

There were many reasons for a scientist to go beyond his subject: politics, professional strategy, religious beliefs. Clausius remained, however, a 'technical' writer.

The Kaiser's Birthday

The booklet 'On the stocks of energy in nature' (Clausius, 1885) merely explained the principle of conservation of energy and gave the physical reasons why energy stocks in nature were so important for the economy: energy did not exist in unlimited amounts. It did not even mention the second law, much less did it contain any theological speculation or any pronouncements on the destiny of humankind, neither in the pessimistic and entropic nor in the optimistic and ektropic vein. This parsimony had clearly been part of Clausius' personal code of behaviour. In a speech made somewhat earlier (and later published), 'On the relations between the great agents of nature', he described, with the same brevity, the relations between mechanical force, heat, electricity and magnetism as they were known at the time. Nothing else. There seem to be no other writings by Clausius for the general public.

The prologue remarks that the booklet 'On the energy stocks in nature' was the result of an academic celebration but its contents would be of interest to a wider public, because of the role of energy for the industrial development of today and the future. Some paragraphs had been omitted in publication (explained Clausius) because they were not related to the main theme. Those initial paragraphs which Clausius chose not to publish are included in the original manuscript.[7] They show that the booklet was first a speech made as Rector of the University of Bonn on 22 March 1885, on the Emperor's 88th birthday. The paragraphs not printed contain a eulogy to the Emperor. Certainly, then, an ideological document, though not published in its entirety by Clausius' own choice.

University professors, and above all, rectors, must make speeches. Clausius was able to choose a topic of general interest within his specialized field of knowledge. He discharged his due praise for the Emperor in two pages, delivered with conviction. He writes of him as a figure symbolic of peace and moderation, against all extremisms both in 1848 and in 1871, in revolution and in reaction. Clausius quoted the first Imperial Proclamation in 1871: 'to us and to our successors in the Crown, may God always grant to be promotors of the German Empire, *but not through war conquests. . .*'. The last words are underlined in Clausius' manuscript. He saw in them a promise which had been kept for the last fifteen years. Peace and security had promoted trade and industry, and therefore the standard of life had improved. In modern times this depended on the efforts made to put the forces of nature into use. *Ergo*, 'On the stocks of energy in nature and their use for productive work' (as written in manuscript), or 'On the stocks of energy in nature and their valorization for the benefit of humankind' (as amended in proof by Clausius and finally printed). A scientist for peace one hundred years ago.

The speech had been made in the Emperor's honour. But what had the Emperor to do with the 'coal question', with trade and industry? When

[7] In the Deutsche Museum, Munich, special collection.

Wilhelm, Louise and Friedrich Wilhelm's second son, got his 'baptism of fire' in 1815, Clausius had not even been born. When *raison d'état* forbade Wilhelm his great passion for Elisa Radziwill in 1824, Clausius, the son of a prolific pastor's family from Pomerania, was two years old. Wilhelm later married Augusta von Sachsen-Weimar. In the revolution of 1848, Wilhelm behaved as an absolutist prince, and in 1849 he entered Baden victoriously as commander-in-chief. Clausius had done his university studies in Berlin, at first finding it difficult to decide between history (taught by Ranke) and natural sciences. At the time of the revolution, he was teaching at the Friedrich Werder Gymnasium whose atmosphere Henry Adams was to catalogue shortly afterwards as miserable: 'the air was foul beyond all decency' – Adams wrote – and of the schoolboys 'none was noble or connected with good society'. Clausius would not have minded their social background. Clausius became later (1850–55) an instructor at the Artillery and Engineering School in Berlin. In 1857 there was the Neuchâtel crisis, when this city left Prussian domination, and in the same year Prince Wilhelm became regent because of his brother's mental illness. Clausius, teaching in Zurich (1855–67), wrote joyful and surprised observations on the democratic system in Switzerland and sent them to friends in Berlin. Wilhelm became King of Prussia in 1861 and German Kaiser in 1871. From early on, Wilhelm took an interest in industry, and someone like Werner Siemens (1816–92), the inventor of the dynamoelectric machine, found favour with him. Although at first he had been willing to emancipate himself from Prussian bureacracy, he in fact gave great impetus to Prussian hegemony; he became Bismarck's king and emperor. Between 1862 and 1866 he became involved in a constitutional conflict with the liberals over Army reform. Bismarck was successful in denying to Parliament functions of political control and legislation, thus setting a precedent which was to be invoked later in Germany in some politically exceptional situations. With the war against Austria, Bismarck drew even the liberals to a Prussian policy of military and economic power.

Clausius attained his chair at Würzburg in 1867, just after the Austrian war, and two years later he went to Bonn. He had been married since 1857 to Adelheid Rimpau, who was related to the Henneberg family, well known in the silk trade in Zurich. She died in 1879. Clausius married in 1886 Sofia Sack, his daughter's cousin-in-law. His daughter was married to a theologian at Marburg. Clausius died, like the Emperor, in 1888.

The Coal Question

After the triumph in the war against France in 1871, there followed a period known as the Great Deflation which began in 1873 and lasted nearly twenty years, during which the European economy suffered since the agricultural sector was depressed because of cheap agricultural imports from overseas. In Germany, a change in political, economic and social relations became imperative. This was to be expressed in the dilemma 'either civil war or forced industrialization', although the second part of the alternative appeared to go against the interests of an important section of the power élite, the landowners. The reorganization of the Prussian German State in the late 1870s was to be based on autocratic and corporative principles of pre-industrial origin, on loyalty to the King and to the State. In practice this meant that liberal ministers still in office were replaced by rigorous conservatives, that the bureaucratic organization was strengthened, and that public administration was cleared of free-traders. Bismarck also attempted to substitute a corporative Council of the State and the Economy for Parliament. Although not completely successful in his plans for political reorganization, Bismarck on the economic front was able to link the leaders of the new industrial economy to the Prussian State and to its traditional supporting forces, the landowners and the bureaucracy. Public order policy was based on repression: the laws against the socialists lasted for twelve years, from 1878 to 1890. Two attempts on the Emperor's life failed. The Rector of the University of Berlin, Hermann von Helmholtz, in his famous speech on 'The Facts of Perception' referred in passing to such odious crimes, 'which had naturally as their objective the chief of our Empire, only because in him is united all that deserves respect and gratitude'.

On the 'social question', neither internal repression, nor even joining the colonial powers' club in 1884, lessened the potential for conflict which industrialization had awakened and which the agricultural crisis made potentially more acute. Bismarck seemed to be walking towards a bloodbath, despite the introduction of illness and accident insurance in 1883 and 1884, and of disability insurance five years later, and despite the fact that in the mid-1880s the number of migrants to America was higher than ever before. In the 1890s, however, the traditional landed interests took a step backwards, there was a decision to force industrialization, and economic growth took off, though the German liberal bourgeoisie remained weak in comparison with France or Britain. In the period up to the First World War under Wilhelm II, who was to be the last Kaiser, Germany overtook her industrial competitors, despite having been a 'late starter', and the Socialist Party became domesticated to the extent of willingly entering the War; colonial exploitation of cheap labour, export of capitals and lack of markets, instead of lack of energy and material resources, characterized the capitalist economies.

In 1885, Germany's coal extraction was 73 million tons, while the United States' was 102 million tons and Great Britain's 162 million tons, a sign of Germany's delayed industrialization. Germany was mining as much coal as Great Britain in the 1850s. But with the industrialization fever of the 1890s, extraction of coal doubled between 1885 and 1900. The question of coal stocks had appeared repeatedly on the horizon much earlier. Depletion of guano and whale oil had given rise to concern during the mid-nineteenth century. Depletion of coal stocks would have unrivalled consequences. If this worried Clausius in 1885, it had already worried several British authors in the 1860s. Newspapers discussed it along with the many instances of miners' deaths and also of the great miners' strikes. In 1864, the periodical *Good Words* (Victorian, clerical and quite popular) pointed out that 'few questions can be more interesting than that of the duration of our coalfields, on which so much of the comfort and prosperity of the world depends'. William Armstrong had spoken to the British Association for the Advancement of Science, placing a limit of two hundred or three hundred years on coal extraction. E. Hull had considered as the annual limit of coal mining in Britain 100 million tons, thus securing eight centuries of supplies, provided that deeper fields could be exploited. In fact, discussion of coal by economists had begun in Britain in the 1830s. As Paul Christensen (1987) has indicated, J. R. McCulloch's review of Babbage (1832) in the *Edinburgh Review* (1833, pp. 328–9) admitted that, given the importance of steam 'as a moving power, an abundant supply of coal has become quite essential to distinction in manufacture', and his review two years later of Ure's *Philosophy of Manufactures* in the same journal (1835, pp. 455–60) drew attention to the physical 'causes' of

Table 9 *Coal extraction in major countries, 1865–1910 (million metric tons)*

	Germany[a]	Great Britain	United States
1865	28.3	99.7	24.7
1870	34.8	112.2	29.9
1875	48.5	135.4	48.2
1880	59.1	149.3	66.8
1885	73.6	161.9	102.1
1890	89.2	184.5	141.6
1895	103.8	194.3	171.7
1900	149.5	228.7	243.4
1905	173.6	239.8	351.1
1910	221.9	264.5	445.8

[a] Germany's figures include lignite.
Source: Bowden, Karpovich, Usher, 1937, p. 511.

industrial progress, including the possession of abundant supplies of the materials for iron, brass and steel, and of valuable and extensive coal mines. Lacking among the economists, perhaps, was the awareness of coal as one form of embodied sun energy, the production (as distinct from the extraction) of which involved a geological time scale, compared to the flow of solar energy incorporated regularly into agricultural produce or other rapidly renewable energy resources, such as waterfalls.

In 1865, William Stanley Jevons had published *The Coal Question*.[8] Jevons was immediately to become a tutor at Owen College in Manchester, and the book gave his career the initial push. Hans Peter Sieferle recently summarized Jevons' call to British entrepreneurial talent: that we must choose between greatness in the short run or continuous mediocrity. The book recommended a short increase of industrial use of coal in order to achieve a lasting base for Britain's industrial lead. It also recommended a protectionist policy against coal exports from Britain. Jevons' later book, the *Theory of Political Economy* (1871), which gave the foundations for the subjective theory of value (along the lines, it was later realized, of Hermann Heinrich Gossen's book *The Development of the Laws of Human Relations*), was concerned neither with any of Owen's hopes for the future of humankind (as was noticed), nor with the historical use of physical matter and energy in the human economy. It studied the formal rules of economic equilibrium. Its use of the mathematics of mechanics made of it, at the same time, paradoxically, one early example of the reductionist 'physicalization' of complex human relations which was then coming into vogue.

Clausius quoted William Siemens' figures for coal reserves in Britain but he did not quote other British antecedents of the 'coal question'. He would certainly have known some of them. He had friends in Britain, he had travelled to Britain many times, he had received the Copley Medal of the Royal Society in 1879. In contrast to Jevons, Clausius did not preach a short-term increase in coal extraction. He took, rather, a long-term view, and wrote that 'in economics, there is the general rule that consumption in one period of any good should not exceed its production in the same period'. He meant that production of coal was slower than its extraction. Perhaps he did not postulate increased coal output because he did not feel the urgency of the dilemma 'forced industrialization or civil war', which demanded more coal. Or perhaps he really believed, in 1885, lacking precise figures, that hydroelectricity could be an effective substitute for coal. Although hydraulic energy was more important in nineteenth-century industrialization that has been commonly assumed, the present supply of

---

[8] See also chapter 11.

energy from fossil fuels in the industrialized countries many times exceeds their hydroelectric potential. But the prospects for electrification were certainly exciting in 1885, when Berlin had seen the first electric works, of 540 kilowatts power, providing electricity to the Deutsche Theater and the Deutsche Bank. Emil Rathenau had founded the German Edison company in 1883, from which the AEG was born in 1887. However, electrification would make further demands on coal: Clausius merely drew attention to one alternative source, pointing out with enthusiasm the use of electricity from the Rhine in the town of Basle. In Britain, hopes for a municipal, decentralized socialism based on electrification were to be raised at the turn of the century, although perhaps the Clausius text should be seen rather an anticipation of the large-scale developments in the Dnieper basin or the Tennessee Valley.

If the 'enormous clouds from the chimney of the boiler house' where electricity was generated were but a symbol for *Die Neue Zeit*, the ecological and social meaning of electricity in modern times soon became clear: instead of economizing fossil fuel it opened unprecedented possibilities to spend it. The electrical revolution led to another qualitative step in consumption of unrenewable resources, conservationist hopes were radically disappointed and the hope for a decentralized socialism as well. A spiderweb of electrical lines was put on the landscape of many countries but a glance at these strategically designed networks not only teaches us where the spiders sit, it makes us also realize how the hopes for a decentralized socialism can be hampered by the actual mode of electrification. The power question remains unsolved, either technically or socially. In any case, the formula 'Soviets plus electrification' was not so new in 1917; it had an intellectual and a social history.

6

Patrick Geddes' Critique of Economics

Introduction

Are we really, to use Clausius' metaphor, behaving as rich heirs, who fritter away their fortunes? Is an adequate weight given to future demands in the present allocation of exhaustible resources and industrial waste? One early attempt at a critique of economics on such lines was made by Patrick Geddes, who was also one of the first authors to correlate periods of human history and expenditure of energy. Geddes' early economic writings will be considered in this chapter, though Geddes is mainly known by his later work on the ecological critique of urbanization. To study a process ecologically means to establish its energetic and material 'budget'.

Patrick Geddes, a Scot, born in 1854, died at Montpellier in 1932. He began his scientific career studying biology with T. H. Huxley (1825–95) in London. An eye disease contracted during an expedition to Mexico and his own interest in urban questions, which was first aroused in Edinburgh, led him to give up biology. In 1879 he had published an article entitled *Chlorophylle animale et la physiologie des planaires vertes* which indicates his familiarity from the beginning of his career with the principles of the utilization of energy by plants and animals.

In 1884 he published two articles on economic topics. Later he became an expert in town planning, working in Scotland, Cyprus, England, and India. His best-known book is *Cities in Evolution* (1915). In this chapter, Geddes as one of the first energy economists, is considered and the significance of his work for regional and town planning will not be discussed in detail. His articles of 1884 on the economy develop themes which may also be found, in abridged form, in his correspondence with Walras (1834–1910), the founder, with Jevons and Carl Menger, of neoclassical economics.

One of Walras' works had reached him through an economist (Foxwell, of Cambridge), whom Walras used in order to expand the circle of adepts of the new formalized marginalist economics. On 15 November 1883, Geddes wrote to Walras to thank him. (It was by reading this letter, nearly one hundred years later, that I learned of Geddes.) He explained his objections to Walrasian economics. The central paragraph of his letter, translated from the French, runs as follows. The mathematical economists thought that:

. . . they can do everything with no assistance from applied physics for studies of material production, no assistance from biology for the study of the organisms which make up society, with no assistance from modern psychology (a very different thing from the psychology of the old economists) or from the research done by the historical or anthropological school!

It is not necessary to agree with Geddes on the (dubious) benefit to be gained from biology in studying the evolution of 'social organisms', to accept the proposition that the study of material production requires the assistance of physics. Geddes suggested that Walras should make a distinction (discussing the application of mathematics to economics) between a) statistics, b) the theory of exchange (which might be called pure catallactics, said Geddes) and c) studies of the material resources of a country or the conditions of life of its inhabitants. The distinction between theory of exchange and studies of the utilization of resources is exactly the distinction between orthodox economics (or chrematistics) and ecological-institutionalist economics.

The idea that the value of things was determined by their 'marginal utility' led Walras and Jevons to believe that they had solved the 'paradox of water and diamonds' or why it is that although water is more necessary, a kilogram of water is cheaper than a kilogram of diamonds. Geddes thought that to talk about 'marginal utility' (the utility obtained from the last unit offered on the market and consumed) one first had to be able to talk about 'utility', a concept which seemed to him to be half metaphysical, half tautological, even when concealed behind a differential equation. And so he wrote:

Another objection, it has always seemed to me that Mr Jevons, by wanting to apply mathematics to the study of utility, is failing to recognize that this *Utility* is simply an abstraction which he has inherited from the metaphysical school and not a true scientific fact or generalization – that the *Utility* of a clock or of an opium pill is merely the 'clockness' of the one and the *virtus dormitiva* of the other. I do not deny that commodities are useful; they are, certainly, just as the animals and the plants which I deal with are alive, but I maintain that *Utility* is a rather unscientific abstraction, as pernicious to real progress in political economy as Vitality has been in biology and medicine.

Walras did not agree with these observations, which should perhaps be seen as objections to the commensurability of consumer goods in economics, but the discussion went no further. Walras hardly ever touched on physics except to point out frequently the formal analogy shown in his equations between static mechanical equilibrium and economic equilibrium. He had an interesting exchange of letters with Herman Laurent (a specialist in actuarial calculus), who wanted to know whether Walras would agree that an invariable standard of value would have to be based on physical realities. Walras did not want an invariable standard of value and repeated that value depended on supply and demand (and that behind the function of demand, there was a function of utility for each consumer, whose value these consumers would wish to maximize). Another of Walras' correspondents was Winiarski, an author – there were to be several around the turn of the century – who wrote about 'physic' or 'mental' energy, as if that had anything to do with the energy of the physicists and biologists or, on the other hand, with 'utility' or 'intensity of desire'. This was a confusion which even led him to say that Walras' equations expressed exchanges of that mysterious 'psychic' energy.

Walras was in close contact with Cournot, whom he considered his teacher in the development of mathematical economics. Cournot himself, however, drew a distinction between economics in the pecuniary sense (which he called, after Aristotle, *chrématologie*) and economics in the ecological sense of material and energy provisioning (cf. Naredo, 1987, on Cournot and the relationship between economics and the physical sciences). Walras, for his part, was a single-track economist, completely professionalized.

Ruskin and Geddes

Both Geddes and Soddy (see chapter 9) were admirers of *Unto This Last* by John Ruskin (1819–1900), a critique of conventional economics. The date of publication (1862) would have allowed an ecological critique of economic theory. Ruskin also published *Munera pulveris* in 1863, which is a critique of economics as the study of transactions in the market, pointing out that economics really should mean the study of material provisioning in human societies. It is not, however, an ecological critique with accounting of energy and materials.

Ruskin was a critic of the aesthetic disasters caused by industrial capitalism and rejected the idea that the market reflected the real needs of human beings to live surrounded by beauty. Therefore any accusation of physicalist or biological reductionism in the notions of need which are to be found in Geddes (and Soddy) is misplaced. To think that Ruskin's admirers had seriously proposed replacing economic – or rather chrematistic – calculus with energy accounting *and nothing else* would be absurd. Human energetics is in *no way* a theory of value, but a contribution to the critique of theories of value proposed by economists.

In his paper *John Ruskin, economist*, Geddes (1884) wrote that to say that a loaf of bread or a diamond have no value in themselves beyond their 'utility' is to say no more than that these specific phenomena share the idealistic aspect attributable to all phenomena. When economists maintained that objects possess solely 'utility' value, they were only expressing the indisputable fact that from that idealistic point of view they have no other aspect. The physical or physiological significance of the loaf or of the diamonds had never entered their heads. We should leave the academics in their cloisters and walk out into the world, look around us and try to see the loaf and the diamonds objectively, when it will be found that they have various properties: bread is a quantity of fuel and its heat-giving power can be measured in calories or units of work; the diamond is a sensory stimulus, which varies according to Fechner's Law.[1] Ruskin was trying to explain that intrinsic value is the absolute power of something to support life. An ear of corn has a certain value for sustaining the body; a cubic inch of air has a certain power to maintain the body's temperature[2] and a bunch of flowers has the power, through its beauty, to animate the senses and the heart.

Geddes went on to pay tribute to Stanley Jevons, because he had in fact argued, against his own 'marginal utility' theory, as it were, that coal was not merely an article with subjective value and consequent subjective exchange value; it represented a certain quantity of stored energy which imposed strict and calculable limits on modern industrial activity. The economics of coal, therefore, was not a question of increasing the wealth of the mine owners, as Ricardo would have explained with his theory of differential rent; nor was it a question of raising the miners' wages, as the trade union economists would say (not that there were many such economists); the question was the relation between reserves and present and future demand and a careful study of the nature and purposes of that demand; it was the taking of active steps to prevent wastage of energy

[1] Geddes' quotation of Fechner implies that one could measure in some way the 'sensory stimulus' given by diamonds; it is an unappropriate physicalism. Fechner (1801–87) was the founder of psychophysics, and proposed a law which relates stimulus and sensation (as in the logarithmic relation between noise, measured in decibels, and sensation). Max Weber, in 1908, in his campaign for separation between the sciences, was rightly to deny any possibility of basing marginal utility theory on this fundamental psychophysical law.
[2] Ruskin presumably was thinking of oxygen and the combustion of carbon in food.

(a wastage which might even amount to ninety-nine per cent), and to stop the spread of soot. Businessmen and their academic counterparts, the market economists, opposed such steps, with their advocacy of *laissez-faire*.

According to Geddes, Ruskin's clear vision of physical realities and his critique of the quality of production and of life, made him the legitimate heir of the physiocrats and the precursor of their rehabilitation with the aid of the physical and biological sciences. Moreover, by expressing the aims of practical economics as the improvement of the quality of life, and treating art criticism and other aspects of production from this point of view, and by stressing the essential unity of economics and morality and not their discrepancy, Ruskin had become entitled to be considered as an economist whose work would have permanent intellectual value.

This was an unrealistic appreciation. Ruskin is not read by economists. The paragraph points, however, to Geddes' critical programme of research on economics, ecological on the one hand and moral and aesthetic on the other. In the same year, 1884, he read *An Analysis of the Principles of Economics* to the Royal Society of Edinburgh (whose secretary was Peter Guthrie Tait) some forty pages in which he develops ideas presented three years before in *The Classification of Statistics*. In the chapter on 'physical principles' he wrote:

without ignoring the historic services of the physiocratic school, the application of the conceptions of modern physics to economics may be fairly said to date from Professor Tait's discussion of the sources of energy in nature, published about twenty years ago (. . .) The subject has been developed to some extent by other physicists, as Siemens, Thomson, etc., but seldom by economists, with the distinguished exceptions of Professor Stanley Jevons, whose investigations on the coal supply, and whose hypothesis of the correlation of sun spots and commercial crises, are both essentially from the present point of view. (p. 952)

The article by Tait which Geddes refers to, published in the *North British Review* (Tait, 1864), which was a review of literary criticism, is a thorough history of the discovery of the laws of energetics from Fourier (1768–1830), Rumford (1753–1814) and Sadi Carnot (1796–1832) to Clausius (1822–1888) and William Thomson (1824–1907), where Joule (1818–89) is given high praise and Mayer (1814–78) is ignored. It includes a classification of the sources of energy available for the production of mechanical labour (p. 364): fossil fuels, animal fodder, power from flowing water, tides, winds, ocean currents, volcanoes and geothermic water, and explains the physical origin of each one of these energy sources. The idea of the energetics of economic processes is implicit (for example, in comparing the efficiency of steam engines and the human body, p. 344). Geddes may have learned the history of the laws of energy by reading this article; however, Tait was not an ecological economist. Geddes proposed a comparison of historical periods, indicated in figure 1.

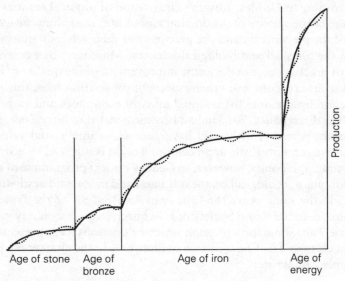

| Age of stone | Age of bronze | Age of iron | Age of energy |

Figure 1

There is here an implicit division of economic history into one period of utilization of renewable energy and another recent period of utilization of fossil energy. Notice, however, that Geddes did not draw exponential curves but logistic ones.

Geddes also proposed the construction of a type of input-output table in physical terms, inspired by the *Tableau Economique*. The first column would contain the sources of energy (according to Tait's classification, for example) as well as the sources of materials which are used, not for their potential energy, but for their other properties. Energy and materials are transformed into products in three stages: the extraction of fuels and raw materials; the manufacture; and the transport and exchange. The intermediary products used for the manufacture or transport of the final products must be subtracted from the final products. We need an estimate of the losses (dissipation and disintegration) at each stage.

It was legitimate to apply to the economy the quantitative concepts of physics which measure matter and energy. Production and consumption could be seen as mechanical processes (in fact, 'thermodynamic' or 'entropic' would have been more accurate words). The idea of society as a machine in which all phenomena are interpreted as the integration and disintegration of matter, accompanied by the transformation or dissipation of energy, opened up the possibility of complete quantitative systematization. A given quantity of matter is exploited, say, a units; so much is lost at each stage of production $(b + c + d)$ and the final product remaining is $(a - (b + c + d))$. Part of this will be available for recycling after consumption, in the form of scrap. Moreover, so many units of energy, a, are exploited; the processes of extraction, transport and so on cost so many units, b; the remainder $(a - b)$ is the available energy. The difference passes to the manufacturer, the materials and energy wasted by him are shown in the same way; the remainder, after a deduction for the losses incurred in the process of transport, represents the quantity of the final product, which could be separated into a permanent and into a transitory part (for immediate consumption).

The work done by human beings could also be expressed in physical units; from a physical point of view, they are heat engines (*automata*, said Geddes). The 'horse power' of a machine designated by pure convention, could equally well be called 'man power', and vice versa. Workers and machines were not only interchangeable but commensurable.

The quantity of energy and materials extracted during a given time and the part disintegrated or dissipated during the process were shown graphically in the diagrams by which Geddes explained his ideas. The quantity of the final product (or 'net' product, in physiocratic terms) might seem surprisingly small in proportion to the gross quantity of potential product. This disparity was intended to give an idea of the enormous losses of energy and materials, which often exceeded many times the final product, because of the inefficiency of these processes. Now, however, the losses at each stage were not accounted for, since what was being paid for at each stage was not the energy and matter lost, but only that available for that stage. For example, the energy from the coal which moves the machines is bought and accounted for in money, but not the other ninety per cent, which is dissipated. These losses of energy or matter were included in Geddes' accounting scheme, whereas they were excluded in conventional economics. The final product[3] was not 'added' value at all; it was the value remaining from the energy and materials available at the beginning once they had been through all the stages.

The part of the final product which took the form of capital (or productive apparatus, as Geddes called it) could be expressed in physical units. Certainly, if consumers were considered as automata, the needs essential to their maintenance could also be expressed in physical terms,

---

[3] What would be called 'added value' in modern national income accounting terms.

but human consumption could *not* be explained without introducing psychological and social considerations. Geddes observed great disparities in consumption between different peoples (pp. 959–60). For example, the Russians', Norwegians' and Scots' consumption measured in money were respectively 7, 14 and 30 pounds sterling per person per year. How could this huge difference be explained, given generally similar geographically conditions and similar needs for food and fuel? Consumption must be divided into 'necessary' and 'super-necessary': the variation in super-necessary consumption may be called the aesthetic element, and final products could be analysed in terms of their necessary and aesthetic elements. The paradoxical conclusion was thus reached that although production was fundamentally for maintenance, it was principally for art, a conclusion which obviously fits in with Geddes' praise of Ruskin, and makes it absurd to classify him among the partisans (assuming there are any) of a theory of calorie-value.

Other speculations in these articles written in the 1880s are rather unsatisfactory: economics considers egoism a fundamental psychological characteristic, whereas biology shows that altruism makes a contribution to the adaptation of species.[4] However, the *homo economicus* is nowadays a *déjà-vu* of little interest (which will be discussed in chapter 11).

Geddes found his epistemological inspiration explicitly in Comte (as shown, for example, by the classification of sciences which Geddes proposed in 1881); economics must be penetrated by the 'preliminary sciences', that is, by physics, chemistry and biology. Nevertheless, Geddes' critique of conventional economic accounting has value independently of the Comtean influence and independently also of his sometimes sloppy reasoning.

An Ecological Critique of Industrial Urbanization

Geddes' ideas on cities are fairly well known, especially through Mumford's work (Mumford, 1934; 1938; 1970) although they are less interesting as ecological critiques of economics than the articles of 1884. As far as we know, he never studied the urban energetics of a specific city; all the same, any urbanist who read his work could have begun the task many years ago. Cities have always lived from the energy (and materials) supplied by the countryside in the form of cereals and other types of food. The characteristic of the great modern cities is the size of this absorption, facilitated by modern transport (although the 'facility' of this transport is,

---

[4] Geddes was a friend of Kropotkin, although at the same time he was an admirer of the social organicism of Le Play.

to a great extent, no more than the result of the availability of chrematistically cheap energy).

Geddes' thoughts on urbanism, however, have a different starting point: the birth or growth of cities situated directly on top of coal fields. Durham, in the north of England, is an example, and there were others. The map of population in Great Britain had changed from the moment of inception of coal-based industrialization. But not only the cities near coal deposits had grown; others – especially London – had also grown enormously and become 'conurbations'; they were on the way to becoming 'megalopolises'. Coal had made this possible. This development had taken place against a background of belief in an unlimited industrial progress; in such a context, the objections of Carlyle, Ruskin and Morris could be dismissed as 'romantic' or 'aesthetic'. Their ideas were however more in accord with those of the physicists, although at odds with the conventional wisdom of the time.

Geddes was fond of bringing the assumed 'certainties' of the 'hard' sciences (including a most doubtful biology of human groups) to bear upon the unincisiveness of the economists, despite the fact that the natural scientists were, in general, enthusiastic partisans of industrialization and urbanization. This does not detract from the value of Geddes' conclusion, that there should be no confusion between the development of resources and the dissipation of energy. Such dissipation might produce extraordinary wealth in financial terms, but what did this really mean? An improvement in the quality of life? In the end, this wealth would turn out to have negative effects. The new type of economist on the other hand, would be concerned to preserve the real wealth of the nation by planting trees, for example, to replace those cut down; perhaps more so: the forest is a bank where real wealth grows.

Geddes was exercising here a leitmotif of ecological economics: the plants as the real capitalists, the economists' confusion between wealth and debt. He introduced also the distinction between 'palaeo-technical' or coal-based industrialization and urbanization, and 'neo-technical', but the neo-technologies were not specified (compared, for instance, to Popper-Lynkeus' detailed quantitative analysis) beyond eulogies of an integration of the cities with agriculture and optimistic visions concerning electricity (which may be considered a renewable source of energy only in the case of the use of water power). The neo-technical urbanism would create Eutopias; the old conurbations were really Kakotopias. Geddes gave no urbanistic prescription, just some concepts which were different from those advanced by the prevailing chrematistic economists and architects. His analysis of the evolution of cities is nearer a true human ecology based on the careful tracing out of the flows of energy and materials than the misnamed 'human ecology' of the school of urban sociology of Chicago of the 1920s, of Park,

Burgess and Hawley.[5] The new environmental sociology (Humphrey and Buttel, 1982) should adopt Geddes as a founding father. However, there was no systematic quantitative comparison in his work of the energy intensity of the two forms of urbanization, that is, of the calories or kilowatt-hours per inhabitant which would have to be brought from outside in order for the city to function. In later urban analysis and planning (see for instance, Lewis Mumford) such quantitative systematic comparisons are still missing. In Le Corbusier, the very idea of the relevance of ecological analysis disappeared; perhaps one of these days, coming full circle, we shall be able to read an apology for the great city (written perhaps by Jane Jacobs) seen as a true apotheosis of autopoiesis; organizing, cajoling, and increasing the flow of energy and materials from nearby or remote territories. There is nothing like a vision from the centre and from the top.

Towards the end of his life Geddes kept publishing copiously in the *Sociological Review*, often remarking that economics, and also geography, sociology and anthropology, should start from the study of the physical environment. He did not always express himself clearly, but he certainly had one distinctive point of view in economics. Over forty years after his most incisive work on economics was published, he wrote again: 'It is long since Stanley Jevons first called the attention of other political economists to the definite energy values of coal, for industrial prosperity and its continuance accordingly. Yet this physical view of economics, this doctrine of national economy, have not yet obtained their due and needful recognition from the conventional schools, with their persisting concentration on individual interests, and upon "the market", in which exchange-values are practically self-sufficient' (Geddes, 1926, p. 5).

Lewis Mumford claimed with reason that Geddes' many achievements included having anticipated Ostwald's and Soddy's social energetics (Mumford, in Defries, 1927, p. 2). Lewis Mumford himself could easily have written a history of human ecology, though he did not. His work on urban history and regional planning was to a great extent influenced by Geddes, and this qualified both master and disciple for membership in Hayek's list of 'social engineers' (Hayek, 1952, 1979 edn, pp. 171 and 226), potential Saint-Simonian dictators; a rather silly charge against authors who in fact belong to a tradition of lukewarm anarchism.

---

[5] The recent book by Amos Hawley (1986) is a further product of the Chicago tradition although with some modifications. For a pioneering study of ecological geography which links up a social analysis of class and political structure and a quantified description of energy flows, see Naredo, Gaviria et al., 1979. Students of Howard Odum have written theses and studies of regional human ecology; see for instance the detailed analysis of Gotland island by Jansson and Zuchetto (1986). See also chapter 15 below.

7

The Carrying Capacity of the Earth, according to Pfaundler

Introduction

Malthus' thesis was that the population would increase, if unchecked, up to the limit posed by the existence of 'decreasing returns' to the labour input. Although Malthus (1766–1834) and Ricardo (1772–1823) could not have made computations of the flow of energy, perhaps some readers will feel that the ecological critique of economics merely reiterates the traditional concept of 'decreasing returns' in a given production function. Malthus did not properly study human demography; neither did he contemplate the possibility that, as a consequence of increased demographic pressure, the agricultural production function would shift upwards, by the shortening of the rotation period (as in Boserup's thesis of 1965). His intention was not so much to do research on the carrying capacity of the earth, but rather to show that to improve the life chances of the poor was useless, because of their reproductive habits. The context was the aftermath of the French Revolution, and his *Essay on Population* (of 1798) is a contribution from the reactionary side (like Burke's), against authors such as Godwin and Tom Paine.

Marx, writing some sixty years later and from the opposite political point of view, would make clear – in the context of his praise for Liebig's 'agricultural chemistry' – how it made no sense to assume in Britain that the produce of the land would increase in a diminishing ratio to the increase of the labourers employed, because there was in fact a simultaneous increase in production and decrease in the number of labourers (1867, vol. I, chapter 13). What has happened since in the world, is made clear in Boserup's presentation (table 10). Production per hectare has increased while the number of workers in agriculture has decreased. At the same time, the input of fertilizers from outside the farms has increased enormously, and the amount of traction power per hectare has also increased greatly. Thus, from Boserup's rough figures, it is easy to see

Table 10 Agricultural productivity in selected countries, 1880–1970

	Hectares per male worker		Output per hectare		Output per male worker		Fertilizer (kgs/ha)	Workers per tractor
	1880	1970	1880	1970	1880	1970	1970	1970
United States	25	165	0.5	1	13	157	89	1
England	17	34	1	3	16	88	258	–
Denmark	9	18	1	5	11	94	223	2
France	7	16	1	4	7	60	241	3
Germany	6	12	1	5	8	65	400	–
Japan	1	2	3	10	2	16	386	45
India	–	2	–	1	–	2	13	2,600

Hectares refers to agricultural land, including pasture and fallow.
Agricultural output (which excludes fodder consumed by farm animals) is given in tons of wheat equivalent.
Chemical fertilizer is measured in kilograms of fertilizer content, per hectare of arable land only (excluding pastures and fallow).
Workers per tractor in India, 1961–65 average.
Source: Boserup, 1983

that in Denmark or France there would be some 2 horsepower/hectare (including tractors and other types of installed power, combine-harvesters, electrical equipment) while in traditional cereal agriculture in nineteenth century western Europe there would be at most a couple of horses (or perhaps oxen) for every 10 hectares.

Most economists, confronted with the facts set out in Boserup's table, would conclude that there has been a large increase in agricultural productivity per hectare and, especially, per worker; and they would point out that this was due to technical progress, that is, to upward shifts in the production functions.

To subsume the ecological critique of economic theory under the title of 'decreasing returns' or 'Malthusian problem' is misleading, since ecology consists of investigation of the flow of energy and the cycles of materials and Malthus, being an economist, was not an ecologist. Moreover, he could not have been an ecological economist because the concepts of natural sciences needed in order to analyse the flow of energy and the cycles of materials were not available until the 1840s and 1850s. Nevertheless, there is a line of filiation from Malthus to social-Darwinist ecologism. Darwin (1809–82) was grateful to Malthus as the inspiration for the idea of 'struggle for life'. The adaptation of a species to the environment is measured by its reproductive success, implying, its ability to make use of the available flow of energy and materials. One further and momentous step is needed: to consider not the human species, but human groups; 'races', nations, states, in order to extract a non-egalitarian outlook which links up evolutionary theory and ecology. There is certainly a continuity from the racism of Haeckel (1834–1919) to the idea of a *Lebensraum* introduced by the anthropo-geographer Ratzel in about 1900 (Capel, 1983, p. 290) and to the studies on world availability of raw materials in which the German economists established a tradition. When the limnologist August Thienemann (1941, p. 25–6) explained the origin and use of the word *Lebensraum* he appropriately included some praise for national-socialism.

If studies of population and resources show that there is not enough to go round, then it is convenient to believe that 'we' have some priority in use; because we are blonde, or because we are more intelligent and therefore more apt to develop new resource-saving or resource-augmenting technologies. In a more subtle manner, some ecological anthropologists who study in detail the 'adaptation' of some populations to very low levels of consumption of energy and materials, link up human ecology and social-Darwinism: unless such groups had 'adapted', natural selection would have reduced their numbers or would even have eliminated them. Because of their liking for isolated, small-scale human groups, anthropologists run the occupational hazard of forgetting that the poverty of some human groups is the reverse side of the prosperity of other human groups. It should not be forgotten, when commending the adaptive ability with which some groups use dung as a fuel that these same groups would very quickly learn to use kerosene or butane. Of course, one main point in human ecology and ecological anthropology is the emphasis on *cultural* mechanisms of adaptation to the environment (beyond purely biological adaptations, such as the ample thorax of the Quechua people to cope with the lack of oxygen at high altitudes). But, beyond this attempt to escape from biological reductionism, it should be realized that the study of human ecology and ecological anthropology is a study of social struggles over the distribution of energy and other resources among persons and human groups. An ecological history of humankind is not at all incompatible with the view of history as the history of class struggle, and as the history of conflicts between nations (or states), which should be explained socially (without ecological and ethological reductionisms).

As has been seen, the study of the flow of energy in human societies, an essential ingredient of human ecology, was born one hundred years ago. It was born as a critique of economics, emphasizing the issue of distribution. However, although the ecological point of view always leads to a discussion of human needs, it does not imply the adoption of either an egalitarian approach or a 'Malthusian' conclusion; that is, that some groups should barely cover their minimum biological needs and should disappear in the 'struggle for life', so that other groups might prosper and expand, as proposed by G. Hardin in his 'lifeboat ethics'. In fact, the ecological point of view – the careful study of the flow of energy and materials – shows that humanity is far from having reached the 'subsistence limit', even if no use were made of exhaustible resources. Rather, threats to human life arise from attempts to force upwards the exosomatic use of energy from nuclear sources.

One of the first realistic studies of the carrying capacity of the earth was published by Leopold Pfaundler (1839–1920) in 1902. Pfaundler was then a professor of physics in Graz (in Austria), and he had been the Rector of the University of Innsbruck. One of the best-known textbooks of physics of the time carries the names of Müller-Pouillet-Pfaundler, and Pfaundler was also to publish in 1904 *Die Physik des täglichen Lebens*. An instrument designed to measure electrically the specific heat of liquids is named after him. He was an expert in the game of Go, and he became interested in international languages (collaborating with Ostwald on this). He had studied in Paris with Regnault (1810–78). His father had been a well-known jurist in Innsbruck, and one of his sons became a professor of paediatrics in Munich, with the aristocratic surname Pfaundler von Hadermur granted in 1879.

The article of 1902 had the title, 'The World Economy in the light of Physics', and it was published in *Deutsche Revue*, a rather patriotic German publication for the general public, founded in 1877, which was issued in Stuttgart and Leipzig. The article's title was accurate enough – it could also have been called 'An Introduction to Biophysical Economics'.

Pfaundler began his article by remarking that the 'idyllic times' of the nomads, who only needed to look for new pastures, were over. There were signals that a time would come in which the surface of the earth would be full of humans who would obtain their food by struggling with each other. Some regions of the world were near saturation, and massive migrations to America were coming to a close. The time had come to study the carrying capacity of the earth, or of some regions, and to study to what extent such carrying capacity could grow through intensification of the economy. The first task, in such a study, was to determine the true objective of the 'struggle for life'. Specifically, what was the prize for the winner of this struggle? An answer to this question could be given by approaching it by a detour.

The Energy Cost of Horizontal Transport

Let us consider – wrote Pfaundler – how the maximum population which could live inside a given territory could be calculated. First, the average need of materials per person and the availablility of materials per square kilometre would be reckoned, and then the possible maximum population density calculated. Of course, the availability of materials would depend on the intensity of exploitation, and in any case, the general availability of such materials needed for human existence – carbon, hydrogen, oxygen, nitrogen, phosphorus, calcium, magnesium, potassium, etc., would not be of interest, but rather those which would become the limiting factor despite being exploited with the utmost intensity. Should, however, the hypothesis of this territory being closed be abandoned, then the calculus of carrying capacity would become more complicated, since materials lacking could be imported in exchange for those in excess of requirements. Such 'mutual aid' would increase the carrying capacity of all territories, but there were limits to the possibilities of such trade, since transport implied an expenditure of energy – this is where Pfaundler's article becomes interesting as an early statement of the 'energetic dogma'.

No work at all would be needed for horizontal transport (in the accepted sense of the word 'work'), were it not for friction. However, there is always a friction coefficient, as the Egyptians knew when they transported their enormous loads of stone on sleighs pushed on wood rails nearly frictionless by soapy water. The friction coefficient of a wheeled cart drawn with animals on a level road would be 1/20, that is, a force of one kilogrametre would have to be applied in order to transport 20 kilograms for one metre. In railways, the friction coefficient is much lower, perhaps 1/200. Let us imagine – wrote Pfaundler – that 1,000 kilograms of coal have to be transported on a level surface, by railway. Work equivalent to $1,000 \times 0.005 \times 1,000 = 5,000$ kilogrametres, for each kilometre of distance is required. How much coal would need to be burned in a steam engine in order to develop this force? One kilogram of coal would give about 6,000 kilocalories, but only about 4 per cent of this heat-energy would be transformed into work by the locomotive, that is, 240 kilocalories, which are equivalent to $240 \times 430 = 103,200$ kilogrametres.[1] Therefore, by using one kilogram of coal, one ton of coal could be sent: $103,200/5,000 = 20.6$ kilometres away. In other words, if it were required to send a given amount of coal 20,600 kilometres away (about half the circumference of earth), that same amount of coal would have to be burned. This example assumed transport by railway on a level surface, but apart from friction, mountains would have to be reckoned with, and the work required increased with the square of the slope over which the materials were transported. The coefficients of friction were lowest for water transport,

[1] 430 being the mechanical equivalent of heat, measured in kilogrametres and kilocalories, as it had been known since the 1840s.

and this was one factor in explaining, for instance, why stone from Bohemia was carried to Hamburg, downstream of the Elbe, while transport of stone over land was not attempted beyond the shortest distances.

Therefore, limits to the carrying capacity of the earth arose, not so much from the limited availability of some materials in some territories, but from the friction coefficients of transport (measured by the energy costs necessary to overcome them).[2] The increase of population in the world was due partly to new means of transport, mainly railways and steam boats. Pfaundler did not emphasize the difference between means of transport which used renewable energy (such as mules or sail boats), and means of transport whose competitive edge depended (for a given thermodynamic efficiency) on the price of coal, which in turn depended on the present evaluation of future demand. Be that as it may, Pfaundler reached here the conclusion that the carrying capacity of the earth would lie on a first approximation between two limits. The number of people who could live on each territory could be counted separately, by dividing the amount of materials available by the average need per person (considering perhaps only the materials in critical supply), and then reaching a total population for the earth as a whole by adding up the results of each territory. Alternatively, the earth could be considered as one single territory, which implied an assumption of costless mobility of materials. Using the first method, the estimated carrying capacity would be too low, since the possibility of overcoming local scarcities through trade would have been foregone. Using the second method, the result would be far too favourable, since the assumption of costless mobility of materials was unrealistic because of the energy costs of transport.

Pfaundler (writing in a relatively prosperous region of the world, and for a well-to-do pan-germanic readership) did not discuss what the carrying capacity would be if complete mobility of persons, not materials, were allowed for. The transport of persons implies an expenditure of energy (though, if they walked, the *extra* expenditure over that incurred to keep alive, would be small). It would be lower, in any case, than that required for the transport of food, year after year, to regions of the world lacking food. To see the plausibility of this point there is no need for a detailed calculation; it must only be considered that over twenty or thirty years,

---

[2] Apart from the coefficient of friction, that is, the energy needed to move the vehicle forward even on a flat surface, there is also a coefficient of air drag which arises from the fact that the vehicle must push its way through the surrounding air. Pfaundler did not mention it explicitly, though this does not change the general point he was making.

one person will consume food which weighs one hundred times more than the person himself.[3]

The Availability of Energy and the Energy Requirements of Humankind

Pfaundler, who began his article by trying to outline how a balance between material resources and human needs could be drawn up, shifted his line of argument by putting in the forefront the availability of energy, and no longer of materials. Boltzmann (1844–1906), to whose chair in Graz Pfaundler had acceded, had already stated on 29 May 1886 in a speech at the Imperial Academy of Sciences in Vienna that the struggle for life was primarily a struggle for available energy (cf. chapter 1, p. 10); therefore Pfaundler was not saying anything surprising when he reproduced Boltzmann's words. Perhaps Pfaundler was also influenced by Ostwald in his 'energetic' approach to the study of the economy, though according to Žmavc the influence ran the other way. Ostwald's main writings on energy and human history were to be published later, between 1908 and 1912. Pfaundler did not quote from any other author in the field of ecological economics, nor did he quote Clausius and William Thomson (nor Mayer and Joule). He was writing for the general public, and his article has the freshness of an original product, to which much thought had been given and which, therefore, could be expressed in simple terms.

Why give so much attention to the availability of energy and so little to the availability of materials? Pfaundler gave the following answer: When a piece of bread is being eaten, the carbon, hydrogen, oxygen, nitrogen, calcium, sodium, phosphorus, and chlorine, from which a piece of bread is basically formed, do not disappear; elements are indestructible, by the law of conservation of matter. When eating a piece of bread, the human body uses up energy, and throws away the materials, just as we throw away the skin of an orange we have eaten. The upper limit to human population does not depend, therefore, on the availability of materials, whose quantity does not diminish and which are, in fact, superabundant. For these materials again to become a piece of bread, a new quantity of energy is required: this happens, of course, with the action of solar rays which bring energy to the wheat field. The carbon dioxide in the atmosphere is broken up, the plants assimilate the carbon, and the oxygen becomes free and is able to be breathed in

[3] Twenty or thirty years seem a reasonable estimate for average prolongation of life span.

again by humans, in order to burn the carbon in the starch of the wheat grains.

Before being able to eat the wheat, we need of course – wrote Pfaundler – to convert the wheat grains into flour. This is done by the mill, or rather by the water which moves the mill-wheel. The human body also needs water. But does the mill really need water? If the miller complains that there is little water available, and he is taken to the seaside, he will say that this great expanse of water is of little use to him because it does not come down from a height. The only difference between water upstream and water downstream is the energy contained in it, which has been given up by milling. Water as matter is not of interest, but this energy is. If water comes from a height which is twice or three times as great, then correspondingly less water is needed. Water cannot be used again for milling unless it comes up again, and this happens through energy from the sun; the sun evaporates the water from the sea into the clouds.

Pfaundler's refusal to consider water as 'matter' made him forget the energy that could be obtained from water by separating the oxygen and hydrogen, and then burning the hydrogen. That a hydrogen economy, in this sense, had long been talked about, is shown in Marx's letter to Engels, of 2 April 1866, where he wrote that a certain M. Rebour had found the means of separating the oxygen from the hydrogen in water for very little expense; this idea had amused Clausius (1885) because of the energy requirements for electrolysis and is nowadays plausibly proposed as photolysis. In 1902 Pfaundler could not know about the prospects for using the hydrogen in water in another way, that is, through fusion energy. He could have mentioned, however, radioactive energy in radium and in other elements, and this silence shows that his exclusive preoccupation with the flow of energy was coupled with an 'anti-atomism' which he had shared with Mach and Ostwald.

His investigation placed exclusive weight on the conventional sources of energy. Thus, when wheat had become flour, there was still no bread; this further step was accomplished by means of energy from the baker's muscles, energy which came from the bread that the baker had eaten on the previous days. The dough would then go into the oven; the energy for the oven came from the combustion of wood collected in forests grown through solar radiation. Once the bread was ready, a knife would be needed to cut it. Pure iron was not found in nature (except in meteorites); blast furnaces would need energy from coal plus oxygen from the air. In the last resort, the energy in coal had also come from the sun. If our bread required to be buttered, energy would be needed to obtain butter from the milk by churning the milk; the milk itself had been produced by cows grazing in fields whose vegetation grew because of energy from the sun.

If salt were to be added to the buttered bread, exceptionally, in this case, the material required could be found in nature, although the evaporation of salt water and the transport of salt would also require energy.

If instead of food, clothes were considered, those of cotton or flax come from plants; those of wool, leather, and silk come from animals; and in all cases, ultimately, they come from solar energy. There is no scarcity of materials; on the contrary, there is generally a great excess; this proves that the struggle for existence is not directed towards the search for materials, but rather towards obtaining the energy needed in preparing the materials necessary for life.

From this monistically energetic point of view, the carrying capacity of the earth would basically depend on the conversion of solar energy by plants, as against the nutritional needs of humankind, and leaving aside such questions as the scarcity of water in vast regions of the earth (which scarcity could be made good if enough energy were available), and the availability of plant nutrients apart from those recycled from the produce of agriculture itself.

Pfaundler wrote that not only should the solar radiation used by agriculture be considered, but also the energy in coal, lignite, peat, and petroleum. The amount of coal mined per year was about 660 million tons at the turn of the century.[4] Taking a value of 6,000 kilocalories per kilogram, the heat produced by this coal being burned was $3,960 \times 10^{12}$ kilocalories, an amount of heat which – Pfaundler wrote – would allow nearly 40 cubic kilometres of iced water to be brought to boiling point. Shared equally by all the inhabitants of the earth (taken to be 1,611 million), that heat would be enough to bring 67 litres of iced water to boiling point every day for each of them.[5] Approximately one-third of all coal was mined in the United States, and another third in Britain, so that equal sharing was excluded, if only because of the energy cost of transport.

Coal fields were gradually becoming exhausted, and the development of peat and turf deposits was not able to keep pace with the use of coal by industry. Ill-informed people placed their hopes in electricity, whose transmission could make hydraulic power available over longer distances. But electricity is not an original source of energy; apart from the tides, all energy comes from the sun. Therefore it is important to consider the solar constant.

---

[4] Approximately one-fifth of the current rate of extraction in the 1980s.
[5] A more interesting comparison, some 0.4 TEC/person/year or (on Pfaundler's somewhat low estimate of calorific content) 2.4 million kilocalories/person/year.

Since the first researches by Pouillet in 1837, actinometry had become a discipline of its own.[6] The estimates made by Langley for the amount of energy from the sun measured in *gram*-calories per square centimetre and per minute, at the limit of the atmosphere, gave a value of around 3. Only a fraction of this reaches the soil, perhaps one-half in the equator on a clear day and much less in high latitudes in winter and on cloudy days. The energy reaching the soil throughout the year, as given by Crova and Saveliev (for Montpellier and Kiev, respectively) in kilocalories per square centimetre, would be 71.9 for Montpellier and 60.7 for Kiev. The average of these measurements, themselves belonging to moderate latitudes, would give 66.3 kilocalories/cm^2/year, that is, 6,630 million kilocalories/hectare/year; that is, more than the combustion heat of one million kilograms of coal.

Once the quantity of available solar energy had been established, the energy requirements of humankind could be considered. How much food energy was needed by the human body? The greater part of this energy was spent in maintaining the body's temperature, and in compensating for losses through radiation. Another part covered the expenditure of energy in work. According to Pfaundler, researches by Pettenkofer and Voit showed that a non-working human body would need 30 kilocalories per kilogram of weight per day, that is, a man weighing 70 kilograms would need, when not working, 2,100 kilocalories per day.[7]

So, in 1902, Pfaundler could assert without detailed explanation, that a worker working with average effort daily required, on average, 118 grams of protein (sic), 56 grams of fat, and 500 grams of carbohydrate (starch, sugar), which would combust to produce 3,055 kilocalories, and that this could be compared to the greater needs of a soldier at war, who would need about 3,500 kilocalories. On average, Pfaundler wrote, 3,000 kilocalories per day and per person, would be required as food energy,

[6] By 1840, the generally accepted rate of emission of solar energy was that determined by C. S. M. Pouillet (1790–1868). In 1912, Popper-Lynkeus gave as authorities on the solar constant and atmospheric absorption, Pouillet, John Herschel, Crova (in Montpellier), Violle (in Algiers), Langley, Abbot and Fowle (Popper-Lynkeus, 1912, pp. 720–1).

[7] By 1902, the notion that nutrition was a transformation of energy, and that the human body was a thermic machine, was over fifty years old. Karl Voit (1831–1908) had founded, with Pettenkofer (1818–1901), the *Zeitschrift für Biologie* in 1865, and he had written a section on the *Physiologie des allgemeines Stoffwechsels und der Ernährung* for Hermann's *Handbuch der Physiologie*. In the 1850s and 1860s, physiologists such as Adolf Fick (1829–1901), had done work on the thermodynamic efficiency of animal and human muscles, pursuing the idea of J. R. Mayer, Joule, Helmholtz, G. A. Hirn, first mooted in the 1840s, of the human body as a heat engine. At the time when Pfaundler was writing, the authority on nutrition was Max Rubner (1854–1932), Voit's student who had published a book in 1902 on *The laws of the use of energy in nutrition*.

although this would vary according to the race, intensity of work, sex and climate. It was much more difficult to calculate the energy needs for clothing. Rubner had established that by wearing clothes, man saves twenty per cent of the energy he would otherwise expend (in 'moderate' climates; perhaps such as Berlin, where Rubner taught). One other way of measuring the energy value of clothing was by calculating the energy used for the production of cotton, flax, or for the production of the animals which provide leather, silk, and wool. In order to estimate the energy spent on housing, the energy contained in wood and used in the extraction, manufacture and transport of stone, sand, cement, iron, etc., would have to be added up, and the energy used in fuels for heating and light included. To carry out such computations would be difficult. It could be assumed that the minimum daily energy need per person would be around 5,000 kilocalories, of which 3,000 kilocalories would be in the form of food. This would mean, per year, 1,825,000 kilocalories per person. At first sight, then, since it has been seen that the solar energy received per hectare/year was on average 6,630 million kilocalories and it has now seen that one person would need per year, as a minimum, about 1.8 million kilocalories, the mistaken conclusion could be reached that there could be a maximum population density of more than 3,500 human beings per hectare.

Limits to the Growth of Food Production

Pfaundler explained then how plants convert solar energy, introducing the reader to photosynthesis (a word which came into use in 1893, although the idea was much older). Pfaundler did not refer to the history of this idea. When Ingenhousz (1730–99) wrote that 'the plant by the help of sunlight betters foul air', the chemical world of those days became interested. Joseph Priestley (1733–1804), the well-known non-conformist, friendly with Thomas Paine, Mary Wollstonecraft and William Godwin, claimed that he had already observed that plants improve 'foul air', though he had missed the role played by light in the process of breaking up carbon dioxide and of returning the oxygen to the atmosphere. Ingenhousz already knew that the green portions of plants were responsible for capturing sunlight. The word 'chlorophyll' dates from 1818.

Ingenhousz did not realize at first the part played by carbon dioxide in photosynthesis, and he had a disagreement on this with Jean Senebier (1742–1809), from Geneva. A study of the role of water in photosynthesis and a first attempt to measure the yield of carbon fixation was made by Nicholas Theodore de Saussure (1767–1845), also from Geneva. But in the first half of the nineteenth-century the subject 'lapsed into almost complete quiescence' (Rabonovitch, 1945, chapters 1 and 2).

Chlorophyll acts as a 'photocatalyst'. By photosynthesis, which is the reversal of combustion, carbon dioxide and water are combined to produce carbohydrates; the energy in sunlight is converted into chemical energy, that is, the energy stored in the chemical bonds holding the atoms together in the molecules of carbohydrates. Plants provide energy for animals (unable to photosynthesize). This basic energetic relationship was formulated by J. R. Mayer (1814–78) in his booklet of 1845, published privately, *The organic motion in its relation to metabolism*, which is an essential work for quantitative ecology. Three years earlier, in 1842, J. R. Mayer had put forward (simultaneously with Joule and some other authors) the law of conservation of energy, publishing a paper on the mechanical equivalent of heat in Liebig's *Annalen*, but Liebig refused his long paper of 1845. In the second half of the nineteenth-century, some of the first studies of photosynthetic yield were to be carried out by Boussingault (1802–87) and by Engelmann, Reinke, Timiriazev, and Julius Sachs (cf. Lieth, 1975), some of which were quoted by Pfaundler. Pfaundler wrote that only a very small part of the energy reaching the earth could be converted by plants. Experiments made by Engelmann and by Julius Sachs showed that only 0.8 per cent of the radiation reaching the plants was incorporated as energy in the starch. Besides, plants did not cover the whole surface, since some space had to be left between the rows, and also much land was taken over by roads, buildings, etc. Morover, of all the energy in plants, perhaps only one-fifth could be used as food – the rest was inedible cellulose, mainly in forests. Thus, an approximate estimate would give an availability per hectare of 5.3 million kilocalories/year:

1   Energy radiated by the sun, reaching the soil (average for different latitudes): 66.3 $kcal/cm^2/year = 66.3 \times 10^8$ kcal/ha/year.
2   One-half of that energy which would fall on plants: 33.2×10^8 kcal/ha/year.
3   0.8 per cent assimilated by plants through the agency of chlorophyll: 26.5×10^6 kcal/ha/year.
4   One-fifth of this, as edible food: 5.3×10^6 kcal/ha/year.

This result could be checked by looking up statistics of cereal production, which (taking averages for different countries and different cereals) would give a figure of 1,220 kilograms of organic substance per hectare/year (excluding straw), which taking a value of 4,330 kilocalories/kilogram, would mean 5.3 million kilocalories/hectare/year. The implication was (in Pfaundler's discussion), that such agricultural yields were reached without any other energy input but solar energy and human and animal labour force.

Such yields would allow a maximum population density of some five persons per hectare, considering food needs only (at about 3,000 kilocalories per person and day, or about one million kilocalories per year). Assuming vegetarian diets, and assuming the working animals to feed on by-products this density could be compared to that actually observable in territories of intensive agriculture such as the Nile valley or some regions of China, with densitites of between two and three persons per hectare. This was a bit lower than the theoretical maximum, which was to be expected since the 'struggle for life' had not yet reached its extremes. On the other hand, a comparison with population densities of industrial regions were worthless, because such regions depended upon the import of food energy from neighbouring or distant territories. In industrial regions there was no equilibrium between population density and agricultural production.

How far was the distance from the limit of the carrying capacity of the earth? Statistics showed that there were 2,174 million hectares of arable and pasture land; 4,957 million hectares of steppes not yet cultivated, or unusable; 3,216 million hectares of forests; 3,305 million hectares of deserts and rocks; 450 million hectares in the polar regions and, finally, the lakes and seas which covered 73 per cent of the surface of the earth, which comprised, as a whole, 37,345 million hectares. Pfaundler's figures arc not far from those currently used. He also made the point that although pasture land would produce approximately the same amount of energy as agricultural land, this energy would arrive at humans in a roundabout way. On the other hand, it was doubtful whether agricultural yields could be sustained only with chemical fertilizers, without dung. The forests did not contribute to food energy, apart from mushrooms and some hunting, but they made an important contribution to the energy balance by providing wood for building, thus preventing losses of energy, and also wood for burning. Polar regions made no contribution, and the sea had already been characterized by Homer as sterile.[8] Pfaundler did remark, however, that the sun energy falling on the seas was useful in another way, by evaporating water which then came back in the form of rain. Water power moved many mills, and also produced electricity in the Niagara and in the Rhine, but this energy could not contribute directly to nutrition until mankind could learn to synthesize nutritive substances out of chemical elements.

The first and basic lessons of ecological economics is the study of the conversion of solar energy by plants, and the study of human nutrition.

---

[8] Pfaundler here repeated Liebig's mistake of not taking into account the plankton in the oceans.

Since Pfaundler wrote his article, the world population has increased three-fold, but Pfaundler's figures show that present population is well inside the carrying capacity of the earth, even assuming an agriculture which would make no use of non-renewable sources of energy. Pfaundler did not give unrealistic high values for carrying capacity, rather the contrary.

A Simple Account of the Second Law of Thermodynamics

By far the greatest proportion of energy from the sun falling upon the soil is not used by plants. Could this wasted energy not be concentrated and reused? This (somewhat rhetorical) question was Pfaundler's starting point in introducing his readers to the laws of energetics. Although by 1902 there was nothing new in his account, Pfaundler's explanation has a high didactic quality. He believed that an explanation of the 'law of entropy' was needed in order to be able to understand the economy.

The story was told that, when Liebig set up his laboratory in Munich after leaving Giessen, an observer wondered why it was that new supplies of sulphuric acid and of other materials were continuously brought in, and why they could not be used again, by separating them from the mixtures into which they were combined? The great chemists of the laboratory first took large portions and then smaller and smaller portions until the large bottles were nearly empty, when they sent for fresh supplies – of which all that did not escape up the chimney finally went down the drains. Could not a good chemist separate the acids again, by combining a stronger acid with the base? Of course he could do so; in general, chemical energy could be obtained again by expending a greater quantity of it. A chemical combination could be dissolved by increasing its temperature; however, in order to obtain this heat energy coal must be combined with oxygen, and more chemical energy is lost than is gained. The original materials are able to be recovered, but other materials will have escaped up the chimney or will have been lost down the drains.

Dissipated heat cannot do work again. This is what happened inside the steam engine, which produced mechanical energy from heat: the high-temperature heat, produced in the boiler through the combustion of coal, only partially transformed itself into work. One part of this heat was dissipated in the cold water of the condenser as heat of lower temperature. All attempts to concentrate this heat in order to make the boiler produce steam again, so that more work could be produced, were useless. An example – which Pfaundler took from Kelvin – would clarify this. A steam boat at sea allowed the steam, condensed into water, go into the sea. If the sea water had a temperature of 20 °C (for instance), the condensation water would be more or less the same temperature, and if its heat could be used again, so could the immense amount of heat contained in the sea water be used. All that would be required would be to use the heat of a very large amount of water so that its temperature would fall, for instance, from 20°C to 19°C, and to concentrate this heat for heating up the boiler in order to move the machinery. In principle, no coal at all would be needed on board, since sea water contains unlimited amounts of heat. However, this idea is impracticable because heat tends to dissipate when moving from bodies of high temperature to bodies of lower temperature; but heat never goes from a cold body to a warmer body by itself: it does not go 'without compensation', as the physicists said. An analogy would be to imagine that a miller would be able to pump up water leaving the mill, without an expenditure of energy. The water in the oceans is as useless to the engineer of the steam boat as it is to the miller.

The quantitative relations of this process were expressed by the second law of thermodynamics. Imagine – Pfaundler wrote – a Celsius thermometer whose scale has been changed, so that all its points would be 273 degrees higher: thus, 0°C would now be 273°, and the boiling point of water, 100°C, would now be 373°. These temperatures are called absolute temperatures by physicists, denoted by T. The second law of the mechanical theory of heat states that of a quantity Q of heat, at temperature T, only one fraction, q, can be transformed into work, and this fraction will be larger, the greater the difference between the initial temperature T and the final temperature T'. This relation can be formalized thus: $q/Q = (T - T')/T$. For instance, if half the heat Q is to be transformed into work, the final temperature T' should be half the initial temperature T. A steam engine whose boiler would be at a temperature T = 546° and whose condenser at T' = 273°, would achieve this. In the Celsius scale the boiler would be at 273°C and the condenser at 0°C, that is, the freezing point of water. For Q to be equal to q, T' would need to be equal to 0, that is, − 273°C. It is impossible to reach this temperature. In normal steam engines, the temperature of the boiler is about 169°C = 442°T, a temperature higher than the boiling point of water because the steam engines work under a pressure of about eight atmospheres. The cold water in the condenser would rarely be colder than about 12°C = 285°T, and therefore an impeccable steam engine would transform into work $q/Q = (442 - 285)/442$, that is, q = 35.5 per cent of Q. In practice, the best steam engines at most reach half this theoretical efficiency, because of various additional losses.

The same principle applies when an electric current passes through a conductor. According to Joule's law, the energy of the current will transform itself into heat, but this heat cannot be transformed again entirely into an electric current, without compensation. With this heat, the temperature of a junction of two wires of different metals, joined at the other end in another non-heated junction, could be raised, and the difference in temperature would make an electric current flow in the circuit. So, an electric current has produced heat, and a part of this heat was producing an electric current. However, much of the heat would be dissipated.[9]

A distinction must invariably be made – wrote Pfaundler – between the two directions in the transformation of energy. In one direction, the transformation could take place without compensation, by itself. In the opposite direction, the energy transformation required compensation; this did not contradict the law of compensation of energy because the total amount of energy always remained the same; its 'quality', however, varied. A system of bodies closed to the entry of energy from outside will always contain two types of energy: one which is still susceptible of transformation 'by itself', and one which can no longer be transformed without compensation. The first type was called 'free energy' by Helmholtz; the second type, of bound or dissipated energy, received the name of 'entropy'.[10] Solar radiation hitting the soil, or heat in sea water, can no longer descend to a lower temperature. If the heat which the earth radiates back found its way obstructed by a colder body, then the heat could still effect a transformation.

Thus, the most valuable type of energy is that coming from a very hot body, the sun, which emits an enormous amount of radiation energy, of which only a very small part reaches man, the rest being wasted in the heat-sink of space. This radiation energy drops from level to level, like water which falls from the top of a mountain and is able to move the wheels of the mills it encounters in its way down to sea level.[11] The struggle for life is, properly speaking, not a struggle for energy, but a struggle for *free* energy. One part of humanity, the agriculturalists, exploit the gradient of solar energy falling on earth, profiting from the process of carbon fixation by plants, a process still so full of secrets. Agriculturalists provide the raw materials for food and clothing. The food contains free energy which is transformed by human muscles. Another part of humanity, the industrial workers, exploit the free energy stocked in coal which has come also from the sun, working the raw materials into appropriate forms of food, clothing, and housing. A third group of people, those who engage in trade, exploit the free energy of coal, of animals, and of running water, in order to overcome

[9] This is known as the Seebeck effect, though Pfaundler merely described it as an instance of the operation of the Second Law, without mentioning names.
[10] Pfaundler did not quote Clausius, who had introduced this term.
[11] This metaphor had first been used by Sadi Carnot in 1824.

the 'friction' of transport itself and in order to distribute geographically those materials which contain free energy, and other materials.

In conclusion, all humanity needs energy from the sun. Even those who entertain the hope that nutritive substances could be made without the help of agriculture, have to admit that the energy needed for this process would come from coal, and therefore from the sun. The instinct of the peoples who identified the sun, which gives light and heat, with divinity, was thus totally confirmed by scientific enquiry. If coal ran out, humanity would be left, apart from hydraulic power, with a part of the surface of the earth which gives a right to a part of the energy radiated by the sun on it. Therefore, the future belongs mainly to the owners of the land, and the slogan in the struggle for life would be, 'Do not hide the sun from me!'[12]

Pfaundler's conclusion was certainly agreeable to landowners, or to those states bent on conquering or keeping other peoples' territories. An ecological analysis such as that carried out by Pfaundler is compatible with a variety of political and moral positions. One of its virtues, for energy economists, is that it did not consider only commercial, non-agricultural sources of energy. On the contrary, Pfaundler's analysis makes clear, that for the majority of humankind in history and at the time when he was writing (and still today), the main source of energy is direct solar radiation, and the most useful form it adopts is as agricultural produce (apart from background warmth).

It has been seen that Pfaundler was fond of the dreadful social-Darwinist expression 'the struggle for life'. Years later, Lotka's influential formulation (1925, p. 357) linked up the laws of thermodynamics and the evolution of species, as explained in the introduction. Some economy in the use of energy would be favourable to the reproductive success of a species; on the other hand, provided there was a surplus of available energy, any species which learns to use it would gain an advantage and would be able to increase its numbers. Therefore, the law of evolution takes the form of a law of maximum energy flow. However, it is unwarranted to apply this idea intraspecifically.

Students of the flow of energy in human societies have agreed in the view that humanity, as a species, is characterized by the possibility of enormous intraspecific differences in the exosomatic use of energy. Humanity is one single species, and socio-political struggles should not

---

[12] Pfaundler was probably in agreement with the sun-worshipping which the Monist League of Haeckel and Ostwald was to promote (cf. Gasman, 1971, p. 69). Sun-worshipping, if worship there must be, seems relatively harmless. More sun-worshippers have been killed by Christians than vice versa.

be reduced to a 'struggle for life', and to 'natural selection'. While I would dissociate myself from the link between ecological analysis and social-Darwinism (to which Pfaundler was prone), there is a more positive lesson to be drawn, in the field of economics, from Pfaundler's approach. Energy accounting was useful in order to understand the allocation of land and labour to different activities, it was also useful in order to discuss the prospects for economic growth. His article found no echo among the economists who did not consider the study of the carrying capacity of the earth as a part of their chrematistic, pecuniary business. Should Pfaundler not also appear in books on the history of human geography?

8

Henry Adams' 'Law of Acceleration' in the Use of Energy

Introduction

Henry Adams (1838–1918), a member of the Adams family which had produced presidents of the United States, was perhaps the first professional historian, though not the first author, to relate historical periods and the use of energy. He came upon this idea late in life. He knew and quoted the first psycho-socio-energetic speculations of Ostwald, but he never mentioned Geddes, Sacher, or Pfaundler. In spite of Lewis Mumford's eulogies (1970, chapter 9; 1979), Adams contributed more to the metaphysics created about the second law of thermodynamics than to an economic history firmly based on the analysis of the flow of energy.

In his correspondence, he attributed the first formulation of the 'law of acceleration' to his younger brother Brooks Adams, and the original inspiration to Marx (letter of 31 October 1899). Towards the end of 1902, Henry Adams wrote to Brooks Adams that his economic law of history was, or should be, an energy law of history (10 November 1902), and a few weeks later he wrote to Elizabeth Cameron:

My figures coincide in fixing 1950 as the year when the world must go to smash. This gives a comfortable margin for us to get out. As long as we can keep on, doubling up our horse-power every fifteen years, and our minerals do not give out, society will not collapse; but the longer it runs, the jollier the smash will be (. . .) We are the slaves of coal, and we must die with our master'. (25 January 1903)

In his own posthumous autobiography (written in the third person and edited by Henry Cabot Lodge) he explained that the Paris Exhibition of 1900 which he visited with Langley (the author of studies in the 'solar constant') made him see electric dynamos as symbols of a new era no longer characterized by the steam engine. He was also greatly impressed by the internal combustion engine. Modern men adored these symbols of energy, and Adams himself was no exception, though he still regretted the Mariolatry of the men who had built the cathedrals, the history of which (of Chartres, for instance) he had written.

In 1904, he wrote that some fifty years before, science had stated that the rate of increase in the use of energy could not be maintained. Although the world forgot about this, statistics were then still based on the belief that consumption would remain static: 'the coal-output of the world, speaking roughly, doubled every ten years between 1840 and 1900, in the form of utilized power, for the ton of coal yielded three or four times as much power in 1900 as in 1840', but nevertheless two generations had agreed with John Stuart Mill's views on the stationary state which was to follow the eruption of the new power embodied in coal and the steam engine at the end of the eighteenth-century. This belief in the stationary state had been encouraged by the mental inertia of science, which lasted until the discovery of radium had awoken people to the realization that power was inexhaustible. Also at the current rate of progress, bombs would double in number and power every ten years.[1]

His monographic writings on energy and history are entitled *The Rule of Phase applied to History* and *A Letter to American Teachers of History* (1909 and 1910), edited by his brother Brooks in 1919. They may be considered as the last thoughts of an old Bostonian aritstocrat who, impelled by his pessimism and comparative failure in life, discovered a passion for Lord Kelvin's thermodynamical theology which complemented that which he had long felt for St Thomas Aquinas' views on the social order of the world. If such order could not be maintained, the world could as well suffer a heat-death.[2] It is perhaps significant that Henry Adams did not give credit to Clausius for the second law of thermodynamics. He was searching for metaphysics and he would not have found them in Clausius.

The study of history from the point of view of energy flow should have taken into account the difference between thermodynamic systems which exchange matter and energy with the outside, those which exchange energy only (like the earth), and those which neither receive nor give energy or matter. Life on earth depends on solar energy, and at the time Adams was writing, the idea that the viability and prosperity of different forms of life depend on their capacity to use the flow of energy was nothing new. The extension of this idea to different groups of humans underlies the first endeavours to combine energy analysis and social-Darwinism. For instance, in the previous chapter some of Pfaundler's views in 1902 in this direction

[1] 'A Law of Acceleration', in *Education*, p. 490.
[2] See J. Needham (1941) for an account of similar views held in the 1930s by the Reverend W. J. Inge, Dean of St Paul's, London.

have been described, and nowadays some of the interpretations of *autopoiesis* seem to carry the practical implication that there is nothing to worry about in the waste of resources by the rich people of the North Atlantic countries. Each group of humans 'self-organizes' its flow of energy in the best interest of the survival of the fittest, if need be, by NATO military manoeuvres, or straight military intervention to secure the supply of energy from oil from the Gulf. But the societies (or social groups or persons) which dissipate most energy exosomatically are in no way inferior or superior on the 'evolutionary scale'. A good historian should not have forgotten that the majority of humankind lives almost exclusively from the annual revenue of solar energy.

It is blatantly ideological to threaten humankind with the Second Law, as Adams was fond of doing. So, he quoted the notes added by Eduard von Hartmann to the 1904 edition of his works:

> If the social consciousness of today rebels so strongly against the thought that vital processes will come to an end in the world, the chief reason is because society has indeed absorbed the first principle of thermodynamics – the conservation of energy – but not the second, the progressive degradation of energy by dissipation and levelling of intensities; and, in consequence, has erroneously interpreted the first law as though it contained an eternal guarantee of the endlessness of vital processes . . . In reality, the only question is whether, in the actual result, the world-process will work itself out slowly in [a] prodigious lapse of time, according to purely physical laws; or whether it will find its end by means of some metaphysical resource when it has reached its culminating point. Only in the last case would its end coincide with the fulfilment of a purpose or object; in the first case, a long period of purposeless existence would follow after the culmination of life. (Cited by Adams, 1919, pp. 151–2)

Such thoughts on 'some metaphysical resource' agreed with those proposed years earlier by some supremely qualified authors. For instance, Thomson and Tait had written biblically in 1860:

> . . . we have the sober scientific certainty that heavens and earth shall 'wax old as doth a garment' and that this slow progress must gradually by natural agencies which we see going on under fixed laws, bring about circumstances in which 'the elements shall melt with fervent heat'. With such views forced upon us by the contemplation of dynamical energy and its laws of transformation in dead matter, dark indeed would be the prospects of the human race if unilluminated by that light which reveals 'new heavens and new earth'. (Thomson and Tait, 1860, p. 7)

Taken in by some physicists' theological verbiage, Adams forgot to make what he could have, a careful presentation of the law of acceleration of the use of energy by different sections of humankind. In *The Rule of Phase* (a shorter piece than the *Letter to American Teachers of History*, whose

elaboration is well explained by Wasser, 1956), Adams made a metaphorical application of Gibbs' thermodynamics and insisted on the increase
in the use of energy, even drawing an unmistakable exponential curve
(1919, p. 292). A statistical exploration of such curves in different parts
of the world and at different times would have been a most interesting
contribution to the economic history of energy resources, including the
study of their utterly unequal use. As Adams presented it, his 'Law of
Acceleration' in the use of energy was more in the spirit of a *boutade* by
a rather hypochondriacal old man. It did not deserve, however, to be
dismissed by Karl Popper in a misleading footnote in *The Poverty of
Historicism* (Popper, 1962), which instead of complaining about the lack
of detailed empirical figures in Adams' work, silenced the substance of
Adams' argument by not mentioning the use of energy at all – a silence
perhaps explained by Karl Popper's revulsion in smelling the whiff of an
inductive historical law.

Henry Adams' character is reflected in his observation to his brother
Brooks that with an income of less than fifty thousand dollars a year, a
pessimistic pose was more appropriate; in order to be an optimist at least
a hundred thousand dollars a year were necessary (30 January 1910). It
is also in evidence in his observation that the suffragettes were a good
example of the principle of the degradation of energy. He was writing
all the time for his friends: although he took himself very seriously socially,
he does not appear to have taken himself seriously either intellectually or
politically. His presence in this book does not arise from his metaphysical
meditations on the second law of thermodynamics, nor from his tenuous
flirtation with energeticist social-Darwinism, but from his view that the
study of the use of energy would illuminate some aspects of human history.
On this count, he did better than his colleagues in the profession, including
the economic historians. He was, however, so self-congratulatory at the
discovery of his law of acceleration in the use of energy (which had already
been discovered at least two or three times) that he missed the opportunity
to engage a research assistant to compute some figures for him.

In Henry Adams' view, the Second Law said that the universe would
be turned into 'ashes'. Many people had chosen to disregard this, including
some physicists, who should have known better. Thus, John Tyndall (a
well known *ésprit fort*) had explained in *Heat as a Mode of Motion* (1862)
that the earth intercepted only $1/2,300,000,000$ of the total radiation of
the sun, and without worrying a jot about the degradation of the remaining
energy, had congratulated himself and humanity on the fact, that with
this tiny fraction, there would be enough, indefinitely, for the energy
requirements of humanity. On the other hand, Henry Adams wanted to
make a dramatic impact, by applying to human history the cosmological

speculations then in vogue. Thus, Adams insisted on the theory which purported to explain geological eras in terms of solar contractions, and made a great fuss about the more-or-less imminent cooling of the sun (Adams, H., 1919, p. 162ff). This was all rather silly, since existing explanations of the origins of solar energy were to superseded in the 1930s with the discovery of nuclear fusion, which is believed to be the source of the energy of the sun and of the other stars. The periodization of the sun's 'life span', which is certainly a subject which should interest historians, was not understood at the time Adams was writing.

This did not prevent him from going on to make his grandest announcement. If the Second Law announced the end of all life, even of all motion except that caused by gravitation, the theory of evolution explained, on the contrary, that there had been progress on earth in the adaptation of species to the environment. This supposed contradiction was the *leitmotif* of his 'Letter' of 1910. He wrote that William Thomson's famous paper, 'On a Universal Tendency in Nature to the Dissipation of Mechanical Energy' had been published in 1852. Seven years later, Charles Darwin announced his law of evolution. Darwinian evolution could be interpreted in the following terms: in each successive period of history, the inhabitants of the world had gained on their predecessors in the race of life, which meant that they were better adapted to environmental conditions. Their own vital forces had increased in the spontaneous struggle for life. Thus, the law of evolution contradicted the law of dissipation of energy, and even the law of conservation, since 'vital forces' increased without compensation (1919, p. 151). The physicists were either baffled by this increase in 'vital forces', or refused to acknowledge it as a fact. Adams wrote:

For human purposes, whatever does work is a form of energy, and since historians exist only to recount and sum up the work that society has done, either as a State, or as a Church, as civil or military, as intellectual or physical organisms, they will, if they obey the physical law, hold that society does work by degrading its energies. On the other hand, if the historian follows Haeckel and the evolutionists, he should hold that vital energy, by raising itself to higher potentials, without apparent compensation, has accomplished its work in defiance of both the laws of thermodynamics. (Adams, H., p. 156)

Life against Entropy

According to Adams, physicists would not agree with the proposition that humanity has the power to reverse the entropic process of nature. They would say that plants store energy, possibly too some animals, such as bees, but far more energy is 'stored' in the sun, and there is also energy stored in the radium atom, without any intervention from human beings or vital processes. What humans do – the physicist will claim – is to dissipate energy at an enormous rate.[3] It might even happen, as Kelvin claimed, that to burn coal, would mean the disappearance, in four or five centuries time, of all the oxygen from the air. But the evolutionist, who of course knew of the process of dissipation as well as the physicist, would nevertheless reply that the energy consumed by humans would not dissipate, but, on the contrary, would reappear in a more intense form of 'energy', which we may call 'Thought', 'Will', 'Vital Energy' (Adams, H., 1919, p. 219). Adams went astray here, perhaps carried away by the ideas of Ostwald and others who believed that there was a mental or psychic energy commensurable with physical energy; he was also possibly influenced by Bergson's metaphysics of the *élan vital*. Some of his examples make sense, however: 'The sun is an immense energy, but does its work on earth only by expending 2,300,000,000 more than equivalent energy in space, while Thought does more work without expending any equivalent energy at all. By placing a lens in the path of the sun's rays, it restores to any given intensity the radiation which had been indefinitely diffused' (Adams, H., 1919, p. 220). Also, he had wanted to ask Mme Curie to invent an engine attachable to her salt of radium, and pump its forces through it, as Faraday did with a magnet.

Adams, instead of doing accounts of the stocks and flows of available energy and their geographical and temporal distribution, preferred to produce a metaphysical scheme, in which the supposed contradiction between the Second Law and evolution (not only of species, but of humanity, and of different sections of humanity seen as 'social organisms') was solved by appealing to Thought:

> The physicist cannot more compromise with the evolutionist than Lord Bacon compromise with the Schools. Galileo could as well admit that Joshua had held up the sun, as Kelvin could admit the power of man to reverse the dissipation of solar energy, and thus to produce a new energy of higher potential, called Thought; yet even if, for the argument's sake, he had done so, the dispute would not have been settled. If Thought were actually a result of transforming other energies into one of higher potential, it must still be equally subject to the laws which governed those energies, and could not be an independent or supernatural force. (Adams, H., 1919, p. 220)

[3] Adams was thinking of North Atlantic humans.

Thus, even Thought was subject to a law of degeneration, and so he wrote:

. . . the American professor who should begin his annual course by announcing to his class that their year's work would be devoted to showing in American history 'a universal tendency to the dissipation of energy' and degradation of thought . . . might not fear the fate of Giordano Bruno, but would certainly expect that of Galileo, even though he knew that every member of the Cardinals' College of professors held the same opinion. The University would have to protect itself by dismissing him. (Adams, H., 1919, pp. 189–90)

The idea that there is a 'mental' or 'psychic' energy commensurable with heat-energy, or work-energy, is admittedly not useful at all (as Mach, Soddy, and other authors repeatedly asserted, disagreeing with Ostwald and others). However, in Henry Adams' words there could perhaps be found an intimation of ideas which are in vogue today. The notion of life, including human life, as a process contrary to the dissipation of energy was proposed, for instance, by Felix Auerbach (1856–1933), under the name of *Ektropismus*, a notion which applied the results of thermodynamics to biology.

There is, as yet, no history of biophysics or bioenergetics available (Wesley, 1974). Were there one, it would probably show that the idea of 'life against entropy' was in circulation in the 1890s. Vladimir Vernadsky (1924, p. 335) mentioned in this context the geologist John Joly (1857–1933).[4] Joly's brilliant essay dealt with the marked contrast between the living world and the inanimate world in their energy relations with the environment, making the point that the struggle for existence was a struggle for energy. This notion was applied intraspecifically to humans in a cautious passage:

Possibly in the present and ever-increasing consumption of inanimate power by civilized races, we see revealed the dynamic attitude of the organism working through the thought-processes. Whether this be so or not, we find generally in organized nature causes at work which in some way lead to a progressive transfer of energy into the organic system. And we notice, too, that all is not spent, but both immediately in the growth of the individual, and ultimately in the multiplication of species, there are actions associated with vitality which retard the dissipation of energy. (1915, p. 70–1)

This paragraph draws an analogy between 'civilized races', which at the time were multiplying faster than the less 'civilized', and species.

[4] His paper on 'The abundance of life' (1890), in vol. VII of the *Proceedings of the Royal Society of Dublin*, was published again as a chapter in a book: Joly, 1915, pp. 60–101. This book quoted Geddes and Soddy respectively on the evolution of sex and on isotopes, but not on ecological economics.

Bernard Brunhes

Auerbach's notion of *Ektropismus* has been taken to be an antecedent of systems theory (cf. Susiluoto, 1982, p. 24), anticipating Lotka and Bertalanffy, and contemporarily to Bogdanov, anticipating also Schrödinger's *What is Life?* (1944), in that it contains the idea of life overcoming disorder. Along a similar line of thought, Henry Adams (who was apparently unaware of Joly's paper of 1890) quoted with approval Bernard Brunhes' *La dégradation de l'énergie* (1908), a book which went through many editions, though its author died quite young. Brunhes (1867–1910) had also noticed the opposition between the doctrine of evolution and the principle of degradation of energy, but he had thought that the opposition could be reconciled while Henry Adams did not wish to take this way out. Brunhes, who was a physicist and a meteorologist, wrote altogether in a lower key than Adams. His work is a non-technical introduction to the study of the energy laws and their application in physics, chemistry and biology. In contrast to Henry Adams, he considered the hypothesis of a radioactive source for solar energy, but he still saw merit in Kelvin's views on the 'heat-death', and seems to have had religious beliefs. Brunhes wrote:

> Physical science presents to us a world which is unceasingly wearing itself out. A philosophy which claims to derive support from biology, paints complacently, on the contrary, a world steadily improving, in which physiological life goes on always growing perfect to the point of reaching full consciousness of itself in man, and where no limit seems imposed on eternal progress.

The constant loss of useful energy implied nothing contrary to the progressive transformation of species and the realization of more perfect organisms. Carnot's principle would not prevail against the fact of evolution. Raising the principle of Degradation of Energy to the status of a *unique* principle of development, was only a grandiose conception of some imaginative philosophers. In fact, though the world wears out, at the same time one could see 'the appearance on earth of living beings more and more elevated, and – in a slightly different order of ideas – the development of civilization in human society' (Brunhes, 1908, p. 193; cited by Adams, 1919, p. 225).

There would be little distance from the notion of *autopoiesis* and from the modern view of life as self-organization of the energy process, including the social-Darwinist touch ('in a slightly different order of ideas') which mistakes human groups for species. Henry Adams himself did not quite accept such views, he took rather a 'pessimistic' view, according to which there was no possibility of struggle against the Second Law (because even 'Thought', 'Will', and 'Vital Energy' were subject to a law of degradation). In his view, biologists stated quite clearly that:

The *Energetik* of the living organism consists, then, in the last analysis, in the fact that the organism, when left to itself, tends in the direction of a stable equilibrium under the surrender of energy to the outer world. The reaching of the stable equilibrium – even the mere approach to it – means death. In this respect the organism acts like a clock that has run down. (Reinke, cited by Adams, H., 1919, p. 152)

In Adams' view, the impossibility of restoration of energy applied to all organisms, including 'social organisms'. In this context, Joly, Auerbach or Brunhes are closer to Lotka and Prigogine in their effort to solve 'the paradox of Sadi Carnot versus Darwin' (Prigogine and Stengers, 1983, pp. iii, 133, 142, 263).

Although Brunhes was not a 'pessimist' of Adams' calibre, an interesting passage in his book complains about those who refuse to consider the practical implications of the entropy law on the grounds that Clausius' formulation, 'the entropy of the universe tends to reach a maximum', was faulty. It is certainly not known what happens to the energy of the universe. This was not a reason *pour quoi les critiques méritées par cette locution servent éternellement le fin de non-recevoir à ceux qui dénient toute portée au principe de la dégradation de l'énergie.* He came to realize that the entropy law (including also material 'entropy') would help to explain the *pentes raides du Puy de Dôme* – he was the directory of its Observatory – where sheep struggled to obtain a morsel of grass out of the eroded soil. This was not an example of 'the tragedy of the commons'; on the contrary, Brunhes quoted Proudhon's views on the Roman law of property which had caused deforestation and erosion in river basins. Not only private property was to blame, there was also *la complicité d'une opinion maintenue, à l'égard de l'avenir du monde matériel, dans un optimisme béat par l'ignorance systématique de l'idée de dégradation et par la répétition à contre-sens de la formule*: 'Rien ne se crée, rien ne se perd' (Brunhes, ed. 1912, pp. 357, 206).

Brunhes' book was reviewed with praise by Wilhelm Ostwald in *Annalen der Naturphilosophie* (vol. 10, 1911, p. 477), while Ostwald had been favourably mentioned by Brunhes in his book, but no school of human ecological energetics arose in France. Geography should have been the discipline where it took roots, since Bernard Brunhes' views on the flow of energy in human societies and on the notion of *Raubwirtschaft* were quoted in extenso by his brother, the geographer Jean Brunhes, professor at the Collège de France, in his widely known textbook *La Géographie Humaine* (1925, vol. I, p. 469).[5]

The view of 'life against entropy' has been taken up by some ecological economists (Norgaard, 1984; Swaney, 1985), who explicitly take issue with Georgescu-Roegen though not in defence of neoclassical economics. Norgaard is working on the idea of coevolutionary changes, with positive feedbacks between the social and the ecological systems:

> One way to look at the interaction of ecological and social systems is through energy flow . . . A surplus of energy would be defined as more than the ecological system needs to maintain its present mix of biomass and more than the social system needs to maintain the size and distribution of welfare of its population. The surplus energy may be either directed to, or fortuitously result in, a new interaction between the social and ecological systems. Coevolutionary development takes place when: 1) this new interaction is preferred by society by whatever combination of individual and collective means the society acts on preferences, 2) the interaction results in a continuing energy surplus, and 3) this surplus is directed toward further preferred changes. (Norgaard, unpubl., 1986)

Coevolutionary development (a notion proposed by Paul Ehrlich) is seen as the key concept for the integration between ecology and the social sciences, certainly beyond old-vintage social energetics. This theme would take us away from our modest endeavour, that is, the history of ecological economics, which will be continued in the next chapter by considering the views of Frederick Soddy.

[5] Few human geographers in France adopted an ecological perspective; see, for example, Claval, 1974, ch. IV. For an excellent account of the furtive relationship between geography and ecology, which discusses Bernard and Jean Brunhes and authors in Germany who developed the notion of *Raubwirtschaft*, see Raumolin, 1984.

9

Soddy's Critique of the
Theory of Economic Growth

Introduction

The ecological critique questions the definitions of the terms of economic discourse, such as 'production'.[1] To that extent, it has always been destructive of theories of economic growth, though this does not mean that the early ecologists were technological pessimists.

One persistent critic of economic theory who could not always be called a 'technological pessimist' was Frederick Soddy (1877–1956). From 1903 onwards, Soddy believed that radioactive energy from the disintegration of atoms could change the economic prospects of mankind, though he was doubtful about the possibilities of developing the technology for accelerating the rate of fission of the self-splitting atom. (More about his views on atomic energy will be learned towards the end of this chapter.) He had worked with Rutherford on the initial research into atomic disintegration in Montreal and later at Scottish universities. He discovered and named the isotopes, and obtained the Nobel Prize for Chemistry in 1921. In 1919 he had returned to Oxford as Professor of Chemistry; his second attempt to secure a chair at the university where he had been an undergraduate. Neither the scientists nor the economists paid any attention to his economic doctrines and to this day he remains an unknown name, even among the economists of his old university, despite recent articles by Trenn (1979) and Daly (1980).

He gave the significant title of *Cartesian Economics* to the lectures delivered to London School of Economics and Birkbeck College students in 1921, and which are quoted and paraphrased extensively in this chapter.

---

[1] For instance, it is geologically incorrect to say that production of oil in Mexico was about 2.7 million barrels per day in 1983 (135 million tons/year, one-third of which was exported to the United States) and that it should grow by 3.5 per cent a year during 1984–5 (*Financial Times*, 25 July 1984).

His critique of economics was not at all based on romantic gloom about technological prospects, but on a rationalist approach to economic categories and to economic science. The title he gave to his lectures should be emphasized, since it is now the fashion to set 'ecological thought' in opposition to scientific method and to analytical thought (for instance, in the work of the Californian mystic Fritjof Capra, who believes that 'the understanding of ecosystems is hindered by the very nature of the rational mind' (1982, p. 25), a fashion much favoured by the irrationalist philosophies of science prevalent in the 1960s and 1970s (cf. Newton-Smith, 1981).

Soddy took issue directly with Keynes' views on long-term growth, as set out in *The Economic Consequences of the Peace*. Soddy defined wealth as a flow, which could not be saved, but only spent. Real wealth came solely from the flow of energy from the sun, and was consumed as it arrived and could not be stocked. Part of this wealth took the form of so-called capital goods and was carefully measured as financial capital, that is, as credits against the community. Real wealth, in the form of a wheat crop, for instance, would rot if stored for any length of time, whereas the wealth which took the form of so-called capital goods, and was registered as financial capital, was supposed not to rot but, on the contrary, to grow independently at compound interest, *ad infinitum*. This was a convention of human society, subject to contingent ethical values; these were historically variable, but could not run permanently counter to the principles of thermodynamics. It could be agreed readily that a chauffeur had a spiritual life transcending the mechanism of his car, but if his spirit should move him to run the car on petrol already spent, he would be considered an ass.

The economists were victims of this delusion. Keynes seemed to believe that wealth – and not debt – increased according to the rules of compound interest, a 'fact' which he opposed to the Malthusian population'law'. He had written that one geometrical progression could overcome another, and that the nineteenth century had been able to forget the fertility of the human species because of the dizzy virtues of compound interest. Capital, according to Keynes, was something akin to a cake, which, one day, thanks to compound interest, would be large enough to satisfy everybody, unless it were prematurely consumed in a war. Once the stock of capital had increased sufficiently, excessive work, overcrowding and hunger would disappear, and mankind could devote itself to the exercise of its nobler faculties. Now we all know, remarked Soddy, that we cannot have our cake and eat it. Capital could not really be stored, as it was subject to a law of continuous decrement, because, in physical terms, it was energy embodied in certain objects, subject to the law of entropy.

What do 'Capital' and 'Investment' mean?

If part of an income is saved and invested, the stock of capital will be increased, that is, productive capacity will be increased. If demand is not lacking (and in the short run, demand will have been stimulated by investment itself), production will increase and in the long run it will be possible to remunerate that investment with a part of the increased production. Soddy was rather doubtful about this way of looking at the economy and implicitly asked whether we were not investing too much. Soddy's approach, in all his economic writings,[2] was different from that of the so-called 'technocrats', who emphasized that 'so far as production is concerned, our capacity is so great that practically any demand for goods can be met without delay. . . . Vast power, continuously expanding to vaster power, has been brought under control and is visibly up to its job if it gets its chance' (Henderson, F., 1931, pp. 10–11). Soddy was also worried about lack of effective demand caused by the ill-distribution of income, and his ecological critique of economics is directed against rentiers and capitalists. However, he emphasized supply problems, rather than lack of effective demand. His implicit question on excessive investment was not prompted by a worry that productive capacity would surpass effective demand. His thoughts ran in a different direction.

In a physical sense, investment means the expenditure of energetic and material resources on installations which are intended to increase productive capacity. In the financial sense, investment means the buying of a piece of paper which gives the right to an interest or dividend, and therefore to a part of production. Many investments said Soddy, do not increase productive capacity in the physical sense, rather they increase the destruction of non-renewable resources. Simultaneously, debts are increased. The economists believed that the issuing of shares and bonds, or of public debt, would increase productive capacity, provided that the money collected in this way were invested. Production would increase in the short run up to the limit fixed by productive capacity, due to the effect of the expenditure on investment, and it could increase in the long run *pari passu* with the increase in productive capacity.

Investment, that is, the expenditure of money on the buying of capital goods, ought to increase production in such a way that both interest (or dividends) and the principal of the debt itself could be paid over time. However, investment, with exceptions such as the construction of a water mill, did not increase productive capacity, rather it accelerated depletion of

---

[2] Including the second edition of *Wealth, Virtual Wealth and Debt*, published in 1933.

the stock of fossil fuels, both in the manufacture of the capital goods themselves and in their use once they had been installed and were fully functioning. The rule of a capitalist economy was that all credit advanced to firms or to the state in order for an investment to be made, had to be repaid and, in the interim, the credit was expected to earn at least the current rate of interest. Therefore if investment does not, in fact, increase production, but increases only debt, creditors, who are the owners of the scraps of paper called shares, bonds and public debt titles, will receive an increasing portion of a scarcely growing, stagnant or even falling production. To the extent that a large part of the investment was financed from the public debt, this leads to what would now be called a fiscal crisis for the state.

This was Soddy's analysis, and which naturally led him to deal with financial questions, since the value of such debts, in terms of production, depended on the stability of the value of money. Soddy's analysis was based on the impossibility of an accumulation of capital, not because of crises of effective demand and the consequent drastic oscillations in investment (and therefore in total demand) caused by excessive productive capacity due to such cumulative growth, but rather because of the physical absurdity of mistaking the expenditure of energy for the accumulation of productive capacity.

The 'social credit' proposals put forward by Major Douglas and A. R. Orage (the publisher of the review *New Age*) were interesting – wrote Soddy – but impractical, because they were based on the hypothetical virtues of compound interest which they wished to extend to everyone, and not just to a few owners of capital assets. Their idea of running the system not just for the benefit of its creditors but rather for the true creators of wealth was commendable, but misguided. Of course, all these writers lived in cities, far from any real contact with nature, and they thought that the peculiar customs and rules that were applied to urban businesses could be applied generally to the world economy. Any member of a rural community who knew how wealth was really produced – by the process of photosynthesis – would find it intellectually difficult to bow down in this naïve way before the institution of usury.

He wrote that economists who, as children, had been taught the myth of Genesis, were used to explain the origin of the first capitalist as a variety of Robinson Crusoe, a man of exceptional ingenuity and application. The advance of knowledge had shown, however, that if Adam were an animal, the first capitalist was a plant. Plants accumulated solar energy, whereas man expended it. Coal burned was burnt forever. It cannot be burned and kept in the cellar at the same time, and still less can interest continue to be accumulated on the value of burnt coal; this is precisely what happens with the economists' and entrepreneurs' so-called 'capital'. That wealth had not been saved, but spent, with a counterpart in the form of a receipt, and whose holder could go on earning interest every year on the amount of the debt: this was purely a social convention.

Not only entrepreneurs and shareholders were usurers, despite the genuine efforts made to increase wealth. All could be usurers; since during the war many people had learnt to buy war debt bonds, which paid interest. Such social conventions defied the laws of physics. Aristotle had despised usurers, but today even the rectors and wardens of the most ancient seats of learning, where Greek thought and culture were supposedly revered, were as enamoured of the virtues of compound interest as everyone else.

A favourite comparison of Soddy's was between the payment of interest and perpetual motion:

A man with, say, £20,000 invested at 5 per cent is in perpetual enjoyment without work of an income of £1,000 a year, and his heirs and successors after him. Consuming wealth every day of their lives, they always have the same amount as at first. This is not physics and it is not economics. Like all alleged examples of perpetual motion, it is a trick.

It was not, in any case, political economy applicable to the whole nation; it was perhaps individual economics, or 'the Art of acquiring a Livelihood as professed by Tutors and Mentors of Property Owners':

So used are they to living on the interest of the debt that they do not realize sufficiently the absurdity of everyone trying to do so. Whereas when we deal with the Wealth of Nations rather than Individuals – that is, with political economy in any real sense – . . . the views of the manual worker . . . are in strict accord with the facts of life and the physical laws which regulate the production of wealth. (Soddy, 1933, p. 86–7)

In other words, as implied by Soddy: a high rate of reward for savings could only be paid if the savings became financially high-yielding investments, that is, if there were a high rate of growth of the economy, that is, if there were a high rate of destruction of non-renewable resources, that is, if the present value of the future demand for exhaustible resources were drastically discounted. All this hung together; though rather precariously because it depended on continuing physical availability, technological change and ill-distribution of income (nationally and internationally).

Obviously, compound interest had never existed over long periods of time, as the story of the Emperor of China and the chessboard shows. The Emperor asked a man to teach him to play chess and then to name his reward. The man asked for one grain of wheat for the first square, two for the second, four for the third and so on. One pound sterling at 5.5 per cent rate of compound interest would double in 12.5 years, and in 250 years would pass the million pound mark. An economic system which allowed at least a part of the debt to grow at compound interest would have to be extremely prolific in scientific discoveries, as the nineteenth-century had been; even so, there was no way of escaping from the true economic principles of physics. Economics should not be mistaken for chrematistics, the art of making money, as Aristotle had explained. Perhaps Soddy had read Aristotle's *Politics*.[3] In any case, he believed in a science of economics which would not study the economy as regulated by the price system (this study could be called chrematistics), but as an analysis of the provision of the common wealth with the means of life which modern science made possible. A first step towards such a 'scientific utopia' would be to limit the rights of creditors.

Ruskin was Soddy's favourite economist, as he defiantly told his audience of economists in 1921. Ruskin had rightly said that in exchange there was no profit. A trader who sold hams with a mark up of ten per cent could buy eleven hams for the sum he would receive from selling ten, and could imagine that he had earned one ham. However, no ham has been produced in such a transaction. If there were ten hams at the beginning, there would be ten at the end, and these would be the profit on the entire lives of a certain number of pigs (two and a-half, to be precise), which would have been fed, according to nursery tradition, on potato skins; the potato skin's nutritive value is derived from radiation from the sun. The law of conservation of energy says that for each 'plus' there will be a 'minus'; in this case, however, the 'plus' was fortunately credited to the account of this planet, while the 'minus' was debited to the account of the sun. From the terrestrial point of view, this is equivalent to a creation of wealth. Wealth is always some form of useful energy embodied in an object. This is the only possible way of looking at things which the laws of energy and matter would allow.

Of course, the contrary proposition (for each 'minus' there is a 'plus') was not applicable to wealth: saving did not mean 'investment' in the sense of increase in productive capacity. It is known that there is a law which states that all useful energy – constituting wealth – is eventually dropped into the universal heat-sink at uniform temperature. Conventional economics could be criticized because the shadow was mistaken for the substance; in the same way that the old lady who, when her banker complained that her account was overdrawn, sent a cheque to him on the

[3] Or perhaps he had obtained Aristotle's distinction from Marx (*Das Kapital*, vol. I, ch. 4).

same account. This confusion has arisen from the very beginning of economic science, defined as the study of the 'Wealth of Nations'.

The most frequent form of debt, of course, is money, whose nature could be understood easily because of the war: an amount of money should maintain the same relation to the revenue of wealth as a ration coupon to the supply of food, or a theatre ticket to the capacity of the theatre. In fact, there is as little relation between money supply and revenue as between the barometer and the birth rate. For a chemist, it is difficult to believe in the almost mystical virtues of gold which accounted for the waves of economic expansion following each new discovery of a mine in California, South Africa or Australia. Of course, chemists are not versed in economic science, and hestitate to pronounce on such subjects, but it would seem that what really happened over the last century was that science increased the revenue of the world by leaps and bounds by the consumption of the store of energy preserved in coal

Now, if there were more food available while the number of ration coupons remained the same, coupon holders would receive more food, but if the supply of coupons were increased *pari passu* with the food supply, previous holders of coupons would receive the same as before, and new holders would receive the surplus of food. In that era of prosperity following the discovery of gold deposits, the money supply increased, not only because of the discovery of gold, but also because of the introduction of cheques and other forms of payment; thus the new prosperity was made available in part not only to old creditors but also to new ones.

Money is supposed to be a measure of value, a medium of exchange and a store of wealth. Wealth is, however, a flow, not a store. Humanity was crying for the moon when proposals were made to stabilize the value of currency without regarding the physical realities behind real wealth. Soddy explained inflation correctly as a means of making the payment of excessive debts bearable: an increase in the money supply, without an increase in real physical wealth, diminishes the creditors' share and therefore is blamed as inflation (he wrote), while a lower money supply increases their share and therefore receives the name of sound finance. We could identify a short-run and a long-run Soddy. What has been said applies in the short term: inflation favours debtors. In the long term, however, Soddy would have found the notion that increased nominal Gross National Product (GNP) has any relation to increased real GNP highly amusing. Financial expansion had no bearing upon the problems of the economy, linked to the availability of energy (and, perhaps, he could have said, to the increasing energy cost of the new sources of energy). He was a supply-sider in truly real terms. Thus, Soddy would have not agreed (possibly) with proposals (Meade et al., 1983) to set objectives for the growth of nominal GNP, preventing this growth from manifesting itself merely as an increase in prices by means of a social pact to keep wages down. Continuous growth might be achieved if the share of investment in production were adequate and if external payments were not to become unbalanced. The task of the government is to facilitate and control the money supply and to promote an incomes policy. This current mixture of monetarist and Keynesian-corporatist prescriptions would not have convinced Soddy, since it contains no consideration of the real flow of wealth.

'Cartesian economics' had to be scientific economics, far from the 'speculative philosophy taught in our schools'. In a more homely language than that of Descartes, the subject can be introduced by the following anecdote. An organist, enjoying rapturous applause from his audience, was very annoyed to see the blower appearing from behind the screen and saying, 'we have indeed played well'. The organist ordered him brusquely to disappear from public view. As the next piece was approaching its climax, the music suddenly petered out, and the blower appeared again to say, 'we both play, don't we?'. The point of the anecdote is that in modern times the human energy of the blower has been replaced by electrical energy; and energy, in any of its forms, should be the starting point of economics. In the eighteenth-century, the French school of philsophers known as the physiocrats did attempt to base economics in physical reality. They traced the origin of all wealth to the land, and calculated as exactly as the science of their time allowed. Karl Marx, contrary to common belief, did not attempt to show that the origin of wealth was human labour, but rather that the origin of exchange-value (or the money price of wealth) was human labour. Concerning wealth, Marx was perfectly correct – wrote Soddy – when he asserted 'that labour is not the only source of material wealth, of the use-values produced by labour. As William Petty said, labour is its father and the earth its mother' (*Das Kapital*, volume 1, chapter 1). Soddy thought in 1933 that 'it was rather the disciples of the prophet who forgot all about the mother, until their memories were jogged by the recalcitrance of the Russian peasant' (1933, pp. 73–4).

Soddy wavered in his appreciation of Marxist economics, which he sometimes considered as metaphysical as orthodox economics, although, now and then, his left-wing views on distribution led him to praise Marx, even to the point of writing that 'had Karl Marx lived after, instead of before, the establishment of the modern doctrine of energy, there can be little doubt that his acute and erudite mind would easily have grasped its significance in the social sciences' (1922, p. 13).[4]

Neither the physiocrats nor orthodox economics nor Marxist economics developed a relevant answer to the basic question: how does mankind live? The answer was, 'by sunshine'. Without the sun the world would be lifeless, not only because there would be no plants and animals, but also because even inanimate nature would stand still. The volcanoes would still erupt, the tides would ebb and flow in dead oceans, the newly discovered phenomena of radioactivity would persist, but there would be no rain and no wind. The starting point of economics should be the first and second laws of thermodynamics. Although Soddy did not pay attention to exhaustible resources other than fossil fuels and radioactive materials, he was not a partisan of an energy theory of value. He stated explicitly that he did not understand the proposals of those who wanted to substitute a system of 'energy certificates' for the prices system (1933, p. iv; cf. Chapman, 1980). In the unlikely event that he had been surrounded by economists converted to ecological reductionism, he would have quoted Ruskin at them with his eulogy of the aesthetic objectives of economic activity.

Although life followed the principles of the steam engine for its physical preservation, it was also 'the expression of the interaction of two totally distinct things represented by probability and free-will' (1922, p. 6). The natural sciences dealt with the phenomena of probability; there was room for sciences of intelligence and free will. Economists needed to understand the laws of physics, but they also needed to grasp the effect that the intelligent behaviour of humanity could have on the physical world. The biological and the human sciences had to study the equivalent of Maxwell's demon.

The Vital and the Laboral Uses of Energy

It was precisely the capacity of using energy externally, not only internally, like any other plant or animal, which made necessary a specific economic science, which could not be reduced to natural sciences. Soddy's distinction between the vital and the laboral uses of energy was introduced in his 1921

[4] However, Marx (1818–83) and Engels (1820–95) were contemporaries of J. R. Mayer (1814–78), Joule (1818–89), Clausius (1822–88), William Thomson (Kelvin) (1824–1907), and Helmholtz (1821–94). The establishment of the laws of energetics took place in the 1840s and 1850s, while the first volume of *Das Kapital* appeared in 1867. It is also known precisely, that Marx and Engels failed to grasp the significance of Podolinksy's work. For further discussion on Marxism and ecology, cf. ch. 14.

lectures, and it is similar to that of Lotka, so often quoted, between the endosomatic and the exosomatic uses of energy.

Vital use refers to photosynthesis in plants and to carbon oxidation in the nutrition of animals and human beings. Animals and humans cannot use solar energy directly (except to warm themselves), that is, they possess no chlorophyll. The laboral use of energy refers to the use of humankind of instruments which are moved by the wind, by waterfalls, by steam or internal combustion engines, etc. Such external uses of energy can also have recreative purposes, and this is why Lotka's distinction between 'endosomatic' and 'exosomatic' uses of energy is more comprehensive than Soddy's.

Soddy pointed out that, although the vital use of energy could not vary much from person to person, the laboral use varied enormously from one person, one country and one historical period, to another. This is something which had been noticed from the very beginning of ecological economics, by Podolinsky, Sacher and Geddes, and which is a specific characteristic of humankind. There was a discontinuity in the nineteenth-century, because before that period, the flow of solar energy had been exploited both for vital and laboral uses, whilst now, use was being made, for laboral purposes, of a stock. 'Wind power, water power and wood fuel are parts of the year-to-year revenue of sunshine no less than cereals and other animals foods. But when coal became king, the sunlight of a hundred million years added itself to that of today and by it was built a civilization such as the world had never seen' (Soddy, 1922, p. 20). The fundamental feature of this civilization was still that the 'internal combustion' of the human body could not directly be fed by fossil fuels, but only by vegetables, either directly or indirectly in the form of animal products. Water power or fossil fuels could certainly be used to make electricity and to manufacture nitrogenous fertilizer, which would increase crops, but the penultimate step must always be the storage of energy by plants. Photosynthesis marked the true limits of human welfare on earth.

Britain had been able to exchange commodities made with the energy stored in fossil fuels for food from other territories; by this process 'the whole world gradually drew more and more for its labour-use on the capital energy of fuel, and used it to widen the area under cultivation and to transport the harvests from the most distant regions of the world and so *indirectly* augmented the revenue of sunshine upon which it is still entirely dependent for its life-use' (Soddy, 1922, p. 11). This short-lived phase could be prolonged by imperialism, but nothing could change the fundamental fact: use of coal (or oil) meant using capital instead of revenue, and coal (or oil) could only be used indirectly for life. Thus there arose the paradox that capitalism was not 'capitalist' as regards the means of livelihood. It was, to coin a word, 'revenual' – this of course helped to explain the resilience of peasant farming, which was able to retreat successfully into subsistence by giving up the use of 'capital' (that is, non-solar forms of energy) which could be appropriated by the capitalists.

It was absurd, however, to talk of an 'accumulation of capital'. The capital stored in coal was spent, not accumulated. The flow of energy from the sun:

> may be embodied in some concrete commodity, in food which rots, in houses which fall into desuetude if not kept permanently under repair, and in all the tangible assets of our civilization, in railroads, roads and public works, factories, wharves, shipping and the like. All alike are subject to a process of compound decrement . . . The wealth is the revenue *and it cannot be saved.* (Soddy, 1922, p. 14)

The individual, however, although he will rarely have enough real wealth to keep alive for a single week, can store, not wealth, but currency, 'whether a cowrie stone or a metal counter, but now more and more, a simple paper note', and the community acknowledges the right that the holders of such tokens, who do not create real wealth, have to indent upon the revenue of wealth flowing through the markets at any given moment of time. The more wealth is spent, the greater the total amount of indebtedness, which becomes, as Ruskin said, 'power over the lives and labours of others' (1922, p. 15).

National Income Accounting

It could be argued, in answer to Soddy, that in economic accounting, that part of capital goods which is considered to depreciate yearly is subtracted from production. Thus, the GNP includes all investment; only a part of it will be counted as net investment, the rest being counted as amortization to be subtracted from GNP if it is required to calculate a measure of 'net production'. Therefore Soddy's strictures seem out of place, unless it is recalled that national accounts do not include any provision (or only a minimal one) for the depletion of natural resources, on the accounting convention that the discovery of new reserves compensates for the expenditure of that 'capital', which is therefore not amortized. The point is of such importance that it deserves a brief excursus; how a modern, influential, Keynesian macro-economist (Okun, 1981) deals with this question, which symptomatically receives cursory treatment, will be discussed.

Okun started from the premise that the economy, by itself, has an underlying 'prosperity trend line', and that crises can be costed by comparing actual production with the trend. This is the type of analysis which came into fashion in the first economic reports to President Kennedy. Okun would then wish to establish whether there is a discrepancy betwen the cost of a crisis, as measured by the actual loss in production compared to that of the trend line, and the 'social cost' of a crisis: perhaps there are some hidden benefits in a crisis, not captured by normal economic accounting. Okun would consider principally among such benefits, a lower degree of wear and tear of the capital goods (which, because of the crisis, work below full capacity utilization), and also the fact that the extraction of non-renewable resources will be lower than if the economy were to follow its prosperity trend line.

Imagine a farmer buying a tractor, which he thinks will last for five years. Part of his income will be set aside every year, in order for him to be able to buy a new tractor; otherwise, he will be losing capital. At the end of the period, models will possibly have changed, and perhaps he will be able not only to maintain his productive capacity (which is the objective of amortization), but even to expand it a little, making an involuntary net investment, if the new models are more effective. Assume now that there is a crisis, and that the farmer leaves some land idle because he anticipates difficulties in selling his produce. The tractor will work a smaller number of hours per year. It could seem that if the farmer carries on with his amortization plan (for instance, one-fifth of the cost of the tractor every year), then he would be amortizing too much, since the tractor is subject to less wear and tear. But although there will be less physical wear and tear, economic 'wear and tear' will continue just the same: the tractor will become obsolete, and the farmer will have higher production costs than farmers using newer tractor models. One part of amortization corresponds to physical wear and tear, and another part to technological obsolescence. In a period of economic crisis, physical wear and tear will be lower, a hidden benefit. Okun reached the following estimates: one-third of the total funds for amortization could be assigned to such 'user costs'; since the amortization of fixed capital (excluding housing) is approximately 7 per cent of Gross Domestic Product (GDP) in the United States, this implies that a fall of one per cent in GDP means a non-registered reduction in user costs of only 0.02 per cent of GDP (Okun, 1981, p. 274).

This is clear enough, and it serves as an introduction to the computation of the 'social benefit' which will accrue from the lower extraction of exhaustible resources, as a consequence of a crisis. It would seem that in principle the loss of capital by forgetting to amortize a tractor is quite similar to the loss of 'capital' by forgetting to amortize the oil taken from an oil well. However, Okun did not make any correction at all to the costs of the crisis on account of the lower extraction of exhaustible resources, on the grounds that the national accounts do not register any deduction for the depletion of exhaustible resources, since neither is the value of new discoveries of exhaustible resources included (before extraction) in the national accounts (1981, p. 275). This is an extraordinary convention.

The national accounts of a pastoral economy could be imagined. The cattle or sheep every year produce a certain number of youngsters, part of which we eat, and part of which remain in the herd to substitute for the old cattle and sheep which die a natural death. The accounting practice with exhaustible resources would be equivalent of considering as net production all the young sheep and cattle (eating them all up), without making any provision for 'amortization' (that is, for maintaining the productive capacity of the herd). In the case of oil or any other exhaustible resource, such accounting practices assume, in fact, that the resources are not exhaustible, that is, that new discoveries will keep up with current use. It might be argued, however, that a hidden 'social benefit' of a crisis in the developed countries would be that the destruction of oil and other resources would be slowed down somewhat.

(A symptom that new discoveries are not keeping up was the battle for the control of Gulf Oil in 1983 and early 1984. The Texan oil-financier T. Boone Pickens was offering to buy shares and, once in control, to change the company's policy, not expending so much money in new prospecting for oil which (in the United States territory) had not been successful, and instead investing the revenue from selling the considerable oil reserves of that company in more lucrative activities than that of looking for oil. Many shareholders were convinced. This policy, however, would not make sense for the economy as a whole, which still relies on oil as one of the cheapest sources of energy (in terms of energy costs, cf. Slesser, 1979) for laboral or exosomatic use. In any case, though, new discoveries do not seem to keep pace with current use, and in the five years between 1978 and 1983 the 'production' life of the United States oil reserve base had dropped from 11.1 to 9.4 years. Mr. Pickens' point was simple: since the big oil companies are 'producing' (in the United States) more oil than they are finding, the shareholders should be allowed to reap maximum benefit of this process of liquidation (*Financial Times*, 7 and 9 March 1984).)

The lower rate of depletion of exhaustible resources because of a crisis, should be given some credit in national income accounting, as a 'social benefit' not captured by market values. How it should be counted depends on how the present value of the demand of future generations is counted, a question which will be the subject of chapter 11, where both the micro-economic allocation of resources between generations and the construction of macro-economic National Income Accounts will be considered in more detail.

The First Illusions and Doubts about Nuclear Energy

This chapter on Soddy's economic thoughts would be incomplete unless his view were dealt with that the distinction between the vital and the laboral uses of energy would lose importance if enough energy were available to produce synthetic food. What are the prospects for a great increase in the availability of energy?

The extraordinary developments since the beginning of the century in the study of radioactivity and of the internal structure of the atom have proved that there is resident in ordinary materials amounts of energy of the order of one million times that which can be obtained from fuel during combustion, but to liberate this store the transmutation of the elements one into another must be first made possible. (1922, p.22)

The decisive factor was knowledge, since humanity had shivered with cold for thousands of years on top of coal mines, and nearly died of hunger next to the Niagara that now worked to produce more food through the manufacture of fertilizers. It was quite true that the future of civilization depended on the summer holidays of university teachers, who then had a few weeks for uninterrupted research. Soddy, it must be said, spent his time not in trying to split the atom, but in research on economics. His role in atomic physics, comparable in importance to that of Rutherford in the period up to the 1910s (Trenn, 1977), was negligible afterwards. It would be false, however, to say that this interest in the economy arose only in returning to the humanistic, philosophical, unscientific, political atmosphere of Oxford: in fact, he had from the very beginning of his career noticed the connection between the growth of the economy and the availability of energy.

He realized at the turn of the century that the newly discovered source of energy could change the history of humankind, but he thought all his life that warlike applications were more likely than peaceful ones. He asked himself what would be 'the effect of the discovery that, so far, we have been subsisting on the mere by-products of natural energy, and have remained ignorant even of the existence of the primary supplies in the atoms of matter' (1912, p. 240). The effect was likely to be destructive. H. G. Wells in *The World Set Free* (1914) used Soddy's warnings to anticipate not only the industrial employment of atomic energy, but also a universal atomic war. In 1917 Soddy wrote that if humanity succeeded in controlling this aspect of nature, war would probably cease to be the interminable agony it now was because a suitable section of the world, or the whole world if necessary, could swiftly and effectively be stripped of its population (Freedman, M., 1979, p. 259; Trenn, 1979, p. 267).His early alarm at the destructive possibilities of nuclear energy was not shared by many other scientists. Millikan, for example, himself a Nobel Prize winner and head of Caltech, openly ridiculed it (Sinsheimer, 1978).

Years later, in 1947, when Soddy was seventy years old, he gave a lecture in which he provided a detailed account of the discoveries of atomic theory, from Becquerel, Röntgen and J. J. Thomson between 1895 and 1897, to Otto Hahn in 1939 and the process of accelerated nuclear fission in the atomic bomb. There was a double achievement, 'both the sudden liberation of a sensible part of the atomic energy of uranium by the atomic bomb, and the controlled release by the uranium pile', that is, the graphite-moderated reactor. 'Of the effectiveness of the former for destruction the facts speak for themselves': more deaths from a single atomic bomb than from all the air-raids in Britain during the war. On the other hand, he was not hopeful 'so far as this one particular method of releasing atomic energy yet known is concerned, that it has any real technological application as a source of power for normal peacetime applications', and this for two reasons: the 'poisoning' of the reactor, which shortens its life, and 'the virtual impossibility of preventing the use of the non-fission products of the pile, such as plutonium, for war purposes' (1947, pp. 10–12).

Soddy believed in the progress of scientific knowledge, but he did not believe that it was synonymous with technical progress. He had long wished to discover why science had proved at least as much a curse as a blessing to mankind, in view of the contingency, which had seemed remote, but was now immediate, that the powers of destruction might suddenly be increased a million-fold. This line of enquiry had brought him to the idea that 'all history could be strung on the one thread, the growing power of men to control and use the energy of nature in supplement to their own relatively puny strength' (1947, p. 12). Soddy was not in the habit, in his economic writings, of observing scholarly conventions, and he did not quote either Podolinsky or Sacher (whom he did not know), or Patrick Geddes; or indeed Ostwald, whom he certainly knew. It is quite likely that Soddy independently made the connection between energy availability and the course of human history more or less at the same time as Ostwald, but stimulated by his own work on radioactivity (which was alien to Ostwald's outlook on chemistry and physics).

Be that as it may, by 1947 Soddy could complain of a double frustration in science: the technological benefits to be reaped from scientific work were not made available to humankind at large, because of the economic system which made for unequal distribution, and, moreover, some of the technological developments from scientific discoveries could not be more appalling. The destructive power of atomic energy was already here: 'we (should) wait for the natural orderly growth of technology to harness in due course the new source of power, rather than as now feverishly attempting to cook the hare before catching it', and 'rather than starting our engineers on a wild-goose chase elaborately cracking peanuts with steam-hammers, for purely political window-dressing as yet another carrot to keep the masses hopefully jogging along, it would be better to concentrate for a while on the purely research side' (1947, p.12).

In politics he apparently had no friends, and although (or because) he sometimes praised Marx, he was opposed to 'Soviet' 'communism'. In his lecture in 1947, he supported Bertrand Russell's conjectural proposal for the United States to prevent, by force if need be, the atomic armament of the Soviet Union. He died in 1956, just before the Campaign for Nuclear Disarmament was founded. Sometimes he had embellished his writings on the capitalist monetary and banking systems with unnecessary comments on Jewish bankers: he also occasionally alluded to the so-called 'white race' having to fight over sources of energy. I do not believe that these comments show other than run-of-the-mill Eurocentrism and anti-semitism, and Bernal and his friends thought well enough of him to ask for a preface to a collective work on the 'frustration of science' (Hall et al., 1935). He had at least one German 'disciple' (Brüggen, 1934) and he was mentioned by Žmavc (1926, p. 6), but his impact as a political economist and as an energy economist in Britain and outside was limited. He joined the Union of Scientific Workers, which was an unlikely step for an Oxford professor to take; he refused to pay the fee due to receive his MA, which meant that he was barred from attending the general meetings of the University; he was widely considered to be a strange character.

No doubt he was 'strange', as well as self-assured. He asked publicly how such people as economists who 'as regards real economics, as distinct from chrematistics . . . wittingly suppress rather than propagate the truth', could 'be tolerated in universities, the sole *raison d'être* of which is to seek out Truth and proclaim it though the heavens fall – for which service the students and teachers are relieved of the necessity of contributing a hand's turn of what they consume' (1947, p. 12). Despite such views, he did not pass totally unnoticed among economists (cf. Daly, 1980), and Hayek included him in his list of 'social energeticists' and 'neo-Saint-Simonians', together with Geddes, Hogben, Neurath and the so-called 'technocrats' of the 1930s.

Soddy, then did put forward the alternative (based on a rational critique of theories of economic growth) of either a radical questioning of distribution (to which he contributed a critique of the appropriation by capitalists and *rentiers* of part of production), or more economic growth (and therefore new sources of energy, a question on which he really was an expert and on which he held strong and varying opinions throughout his life). Wealth depended upon physical laws:

Because formerly ownership of the land – which, with the sunshine that falls on it, provides a revenue of wealth – secured, in the form of rent, a share in the annual harvest without labour or service, upon which a cultured and leisured class could permanently establish itself, the age seems to have conceived the preposterous notion that money, which can buy land, must therefore itself have the same revenue-producing power. (1933, p. 106)

The destiny of ideas often depends upon the social position of those who propose them, and seen from outside Soddy appeared to be in a favourable position: a Nobel Prize winner, a professor at Oxford, publishing in English. One reason for the lack of academic response, both from economists and fellow scientists, was perhaps that economics was already strongly professionalized. Professional biologists, and indeed plant and animal ecologists, were becoming interested in the study of energy efficiencies, but they would probably be alarmed by the call to invade the economists' and historians' terrain. Professionalization would not explain, however, the lack of political impact. The Marxists (in all relevant varieties) may have believed too strongly in economic growth (and in the Marxist theory of economic growth) to pay any attention. Soddy's ecologism in the modern sense was shown for instance in his remarks on agriculture, emphasising that it remained, as regards 'the internal energy of life', 'the key industry'; that all science could do was of indirect assistance; and that fundamentally it all remained unchanged, 'the collection of sunlight by the agency of chlorophyll and its transformation into the chemical energy of foodstuffs, either directly or through the intermediate transforming agency of animals' (1933, p. 38). This could have made him attractive to pro-peasant populists, who were, however, by the 1920s and certainly by the 1930s, a practically extinct species. The anarchists, in their few remaining strongholds, did not read books or at least did not read Soddy, and believed fervently in technical progress.

Digging up such precursors of contemporary ecologism as Soddy (much quoted by Foley, 1981, from whom I learned of him), has the virtue not so much of presenting arguments which by now might be familiar as of asking the question: why the silence, then and for so long after?[5] Why the

[5] In the history of social energetics, Alfred R. Ubbelohde's *Man and Energy* (1954), based on talks on the BBC Third Programme, has an honourable place, though it has less empirical material in the form of energy accounts than Cottrell's study (1955). The author, a physicist, an Oxford man, did not mention Soddy, who was still alive, and who must have felt disgusted if he had listened to the wireless or read the book. This is just one of many examples, in this case possibly deliberate.

lack of reception in academic circles and why the lack of ideological consumption of such ideas? Instead of an instance of social construction of a field of knowledge, it seems here to be an instance of persistent social resistance from many different quarters to the consolidation of this field of knowledge, that is, ecological economics. In the next two chapters will be considered some further examples of concern for the allocation of exhaustible resources, not only from outside the profession of economics, but from inside it, but first the American technocracy movement will be studied.

Technocracy, Inc.

As said before, Soddy did not emphasize, unlike the 'technocrats', lack of effective demand, but rather the long-run question of whether the increase in productive capacity which the economists attributed to investment was not a mirage:

Technocracy claims that by the use of the inanimate energy of Nature and by means of machines and mass production, man had become independent of his own physical exertions for his maintenance . . . that poverty *and* unemployment at one and the same time is now a horrible anachronism, that the average income and expenditure of the whole American nation could easily be multiplied many times with less hours of labour . . . In this it is similar to the thesis developed in the present book save, possibly, that I was and am more conservative, both with regard to the extent and rapidity with which the average scale of living can be augmented. (Soddy, 1933, preface)

Nevertheless, Soddy was considered one of their precursors by the technocracy movement which developed in the early 1930s in the United States, and which died away rather quickly in a welter of internal re-crimination and nonsense. Led by a man, Howard Scott, of no intellectual distinction but whose impressive physical size was complemented by a resonant voice (Benson, 1965, p. 135), the movement profited for some years from the collaboration of M. King Hubbert, then a young geophysicist at Columbia University, who over forty years later became widely known because of the prediction he had made in the 1950s that United States' domestic petroleum extraction would peak about 1970. In his work of the 1950s, he analysed the path of depletion of energy and material resources by means of bell-shaped curves, which show how much of total reserves are still available at any one time.[6]

[6] Many recent books on energy and environmental questions emphasize Hubbert's analysis (for instance, Foley, 1981, Ehrlich, Ehrlich and Holdren, 1977, Hall, Cleveland and Kaufman, 1986). Another well-known author who had some connection with the technocrats was Stuart Chase.

The disintegration of the technocracy movement after the Second World War was not a great loss, since there can be little doubt about its narrow nationalism, its anti-intellectualism, its cheap geopolitical approval for domination over Mexico and the Caribbean and further south (under the guise of 'continentalism'), its tendency to see a conspiracy of big business, Wall Street, the international bankers, and party politicians; all this embellished by Howard Scott's style ('technocracy smashes the price system'; 'the syphilis of business'; 'the dementia of democracy'). This curious, parochial group of people numbered a few thousands and was active in public life under the name of Technocracy, Inc. They organized cavalcades of grey cars, predicted the apocalyptic collapse of the system, and had an obsession with the Vatican. By the 1950s, what remained of the movement was so out of touch with reality that one of its periodicals claimed in 1959 that Fidel Castro was a Vaticanist fascist. The *Technocracy Study Course* (1940, p. 205) had described Ortega y Gasset as a Jesuit professor.

It is most painful to bring such uncultured people out of oblivion and into this book, but some of their themes in the early 1930s were certainly relevant. They emphasized the Veblenian theme of the role of technicians for the efficiency of production. They were on the whole optimistic about the possibilities for a great growth of production, which was frustrated by lack of effective demand; a strong theme at the time, which the policies of the New Deal took away from them. They strongly believed in the progress of automation, and they also put forward the 'viewpoint of social change as determined or limited by the amount of non-human energy available to society' (Elsner, 1967, p. 217). This was not at all a new viewpoint, but Elsner (himself an ex-technocrat) rightly points out that it had never before been used as an ideology by any political or semi-political group.

Technocracy's appearance was saluted by some 'energetic' jokes. In February 1933 *The Nation* published an article by Henry Hazlitt entitled 'Scrambled Ergs: An Examination of Technocracy', and in the same month and year 'a little book by John Lardner and Thomas Sugrue, *The Crowning of Technocracy*, had been published: in it the Technocrats were mocked from the Foreword by "Horace Power Ergenjoule, Soddy Professor of Implied Science", to the typesetters' note on the final page: This book . . . was made by one machine in five energy hours, using twenty-six British Thermal Units' (Elsner, 1967, p. 15).

M. King Hubbert's guiding theoretical light was mainly expressed in various editions (between 1934 and 1947) of the *Technocracy Study Course*.[7]

---

[7] The subtitle of this book is: 'An outline of those elements of science and technology essential to an understanding of our social synthesis, for members of Technocracy,

This is a summary of the section in that book which deals with social energetics.

Taking off from the physical science approach, the first few lessons in the book are concerned with the basic concepts and measurements of energy and its transformations and with the use of engines to convert energy into work. At this point the concept of efficiency is introduced (the ratio of work output to energy input). Man as an engine is discussed briefly and his approximately twenty-five per cent maximum efficiency is noted. Armed with these concepts, the student Technocrat approaches the network of life, energy, and resources. The flow of life-giving energy is traced from the sun through plant photosynthesis, herbivorous and carnivorous animal life. The 'dynamic equilibrium' or balance of nature established among the various life forms in a given area is examined. Man's place in this arrangement is described as uniquely disturbing in that he has increasingly learned how to divert a larger share of energy away from other animals to his own use. Domestication of plants and animals and the early utilization of metals and fuels is examined. Thus, the key to man's history is seen in his developing use of 'extraneous' energy – energy other than derived from the food he eats. Any people who have 'a superior energy-control technique' tend to dominate others with lesser abilities in this area. (Elsner, 1967, p. 117; see also Akin, 1977, chapter 4).

The jump from the study of the characteristics of the human use of energy compared to other animals, to the intraspecific analysis,[8] rings the familiar social-Darwinist bells of 'if there is not enough for everybody, there should be for us, because we are better at inventing new ways of using energy and other resources'.

In their economics, the limitation of resource availability for the growth of some industries was mentioned. The main emphasis – naturally enough in the early 1930s because of the Great Depression – was on the 'limitations of purchasing power imposed by price system distribution' (Elsner, 1967, p. 118). They realized that the ecological approach led to a discussion on

---

Inc.'. The 5th edition has 291 pages, with a bibliography on pp. 281–85. Lotka and Soddy were mentioned, Ostwald was not. Some titles of Technocracy's pamphlets include: *A thermodynamic interpretation of social phenomena* (New York, 1932), *The energy certificate* (1940), *Our country, right or wrong* (New York, 1946). There were apparently some German followers, as the following publications, which I have not seen, seem to indicate: *Technokratie*, Heft 1, Brünn: R. M. Rohrer, 1933 (which contains J. Werner: *Aufruf an die wissenschaftliche Weltintelligenz*), and *Technokratie, Zeitschrift der Deutschen technokratischen Gesellschaft*, bimonthly, from September 1933. They might contain some nasty stuff mixed with energy accounts, given the period and the country. For a German critique of Technocracy from a liberal point of view, see Kraemer (1933).

[8] Almost in terms of self-organization or autopoiesis of the energy process.

egalitarian principles of distribution. For instance, M. King Hubbert, who combined conservationist views with technological optimism, wrote in 1940:

> We can abandon the fiction that what one is to receive is in payment for what one has done, and recognize that what we are really doing is utilizing the bounty that nature has provided us. Under these circumstances we recognize that we are all getting something for nothing, and the simplest way of effecting distribution is on the basis of equality, especially so when it is considered that production can be set equal to the limit of our capacity to consume, commensurate with an adequate conservation of our physical resources.[9]

It is difficult to reconcile such egalitarianism with the belief expounded in the *Technocracy Study Course* of a natural 'pecking order' in the human species, also called a 'functional priority' in the chapter of that textbook devoted to such a cheap sociology. It was 'functionally' necessary to have a hierarchial ordering of society, but all levels would be open in principle to anybody: society would be in trouble – this was a truly techno-bureaucratic theme – if it mistook inherited social position for ability.

Here was a political group ready to use Soddy's reputation for their public relations; but although the technocrats recommended some of Soddy's books, Soddy did not collaborate with them, to judge from Elsner's, Benson's, Akin's and Berndt's research, and also from Soddy's own remarks in 1933 against 'energy certificates', one of the technocrats' pet ideas. Soddy did not share either the technocrats' unbounded technological optimism. One of the first official publications of technocracy[10] included Soddy's *Wealth, Virtual Wealth and Debt* in its reading list while refuting 'the hasty charge of plagiarism brought against technocracy in connection with this book' (first published in 1926; *Cartesian Economics* of 1922 is not mentioned), and emphasizing that Soddy did not adopt an energy theory of value, as if this were a mistake.

This last point is of such importance to the understanding of the present book that we must insist that an energy theory of value would not only mean to relapse into the 'energetic dogma', but would also precisely eliminate the difference in valuation of renewable and non-renewable (or slowly renewable) resources which is one starting point of ecological economics. Thus, it is easy to see that twelve months will produce the total world harvest and that the same amount of calories in the form of coal or oil is now taking many years to be produced (not meaning discovered and accounted for in proven reserves, but *geologically* produced). Why not

---

[9] Hubbert, M. King, *Man-Hours and Distribution*, Technocracy Inc., N. York, 1940, p. 28, quoted by Ernst R. Berndt, 1985.
[10] Scott Howard et al., 1933 (61 pp.).

a time-standard of value instead of a calorie standard, as suggested by Puntí (1982)? Ecological economics does not propose a *new* theory of value: it questions commensurability whether in terms of prices, calories or production time.

Another possible influence on the technocrats, apart from Soddy, might have been Ostwald's *energetische Imperativ* which neatly encapsulated what was to become one of the technocrats' main themes. As previously discussed, the connection between energy use and social development was not an original idea of Ostwald; it seems plausible that even the more learned of the group might not have known about some of his predecessors, but they must have heard about Ostwald, a truly 'technocratic' thinker in social matters.

Veblen's contribution to the technocrats' ideology was not related to the energy viewpoint, but was important (Scott had known Veblen in about 1920 in New York), so much so that disclaimers were issued: 'you cannot express Veblen's economic theory in terms of Scott's theory of energy determinants'. But Veblen's stand against the rationality of the price system and in favour of a technical rationality (particularly in *The Engineers and the Price System*), and his view that in the unlikely event of a revolutionary change, the technicians would have to play a decisive role, made him a clear source of inspiration, but only from the side of the social organization of production, so to speak, since the technocrats did not concern themselves with the analysis of 'conspicuous consumption'.

In conclusion, in this book, where shape is being given retrospectively to a school of human ecological energetics, it certainly is not pleasing to be obliged to include the technocrats, since they were a strident group of mentally uncouth people, but they cannot be left out. One note in their favour is that they – or perhaps simply M. King Hubbert – provided an American link between social energetics before the 1930s and the ecological study of population and resources of the 1960s and 1970s.[11]

Another American link of a much softer texture was provided simultaneously by Lewis Mumford in 1934 (when he published *Technics and Civilization*), which is not a monograph on social energetics but shows knowledge of the main contributions. The American conservationist line was prolonged in the 1940s, for instance by Fairfield Osborn (who published *Our plundered planet* in 1948) and by William Vogt (*Road to Survival*, 1948), names which do not strictly belong in the history of the relations between the study of energy flow in human societies and economic science. My self-imposed 'energetic' terms of reference cut out some interesting ecological authors.

---

[11] After the present book was finished, I saw an advertisement which *The Nation* runs in every issue (for instance, 22 November 1986): 'Technocracy – Technological Social Design available for $2 from Technocracy Inc., Continental Headquarters, Savannah, Oklahoma'.

10

Lancelot Hogben v. Hayek

In his articles in *Economica* (the review of the London School of Economics) of the early 1940s, Hayek wrote that the scientific advance of economics depended on the consistent application of subjectivism, and that neither commodities, nor money, *nor food* should be defined in physical terms, but rather in terms of the opinions held by people (1952, p. 31). Against whom was he specifically inveighing? One of Hayek's adversaries was Lancelot Hogben (1895–1975), who held a professorship of Biology and Society at the London School of Economics (LSE) in the 1930s. Biologists would doubtless find it perplexing that food should not be defined in physical and chemical terms.

Hogben did not believe that the depletion of natural resources posed any threat to economic development, and he cannot be classified as an 'ecologist' in the current sense, although he was a most coherent ecological critic of economics. In *Science for the Citizen* (1938, ed. 1946, p. 621) he had disparaging words for authors who wished to derive social consequences from the second law of thermodynamics, although he certainly realized that the introduction of coal had produced a profound change in what the biologist would call 'the ecological relations of mankind' (op. cit., p. 496). In common with most of the socialist scientists grouped in the *Visible College* (Werskey, 1978), that is, Bernal, Needham, Haldane, Hyman and Levy, he did not believe only in the progress of scientific knowledge, but also in the concomitant progress of technology. He did not doubt the possibility of an 'age of plenty', since modern science could find substitutes for all those resources which nature had located only in certain areas (1936, pp. 40, 66–7). His own definition of 'plenty' will be discussed later in this chapter, phrased in terms of energy costs and benefits, but his quarrel with the economists was not about the prospects for economic growth. Rather, it was based on the view that economists did not truly study the relationship between human needs and resources, since they lacked both a theory of needs and a scientific/technical knowledge.

He sometimes criticized his fellow scientists when they sang the praises of Soviet industrialization, which resurrected the discredited ideology of the first industrial capitalism (Werskey, 1978, p. 202). Hogben shared William Morris' opinion that not only did capitalism lead to injustice in the distribution of production and to periodic crises, but also that capitalism produced goods which it was undersirable for people to want. This is language which will make economists prick up their ears, since they believe that nobody but economic agents themselves should judge what is good and what is bad. This point will be discussed in the next chapter.

Hogben wrote that Morris had not been hypnotized by the liberal delusion that the things that people have been taught to desire by capitalist propaganda are the things that they need most. In the 1930s, there were few people ready to criticize capitalism, not for producing less than possible, but for producing the wrong things. Neo-classical economics refuses to consider this question. So does the Keynesian tradition, which argues in terms of aggregated effective demand, not considering therefore the origin of preferences revealed in the market.

Hogben's liking for William Morris matched his doubts about strict 'Bernalism', although he shared its technological optimism. Bernalism could be described as the belief that the economic and social structure of the capitalist world prevented technical progress being taken full advantage of, that the existing state of science had made possible. This could be expressed in Marxist terminology: science was a productive force whose application was slowed down by the existing relations of production. It was typical of Bernal to declare prematurely that the problem of energy production had been solved and to propose a pattern of urbanization wholly divorced from agriculture (Hall et al., 1935, pp. 57, 61). Hogben thought that the scale was a decisive consideration, over-riding the difference between socialism and capitalism (1949, pp. 14–15). Systems of transcontintental free enterprise and systems of socialism which planned for a whole continent (like the Soviet Union) should both be rejected. Even in the field of scientific 'production' Hogben reacted against the new centralism and the power of the great foundations, speaking openly against the transference of political authority to a scientific elite (1949, pp. 40–41).

Advanced technology did not imply an urbanized society, capitalist or socialist. There was the possibility of a decentralized, ruralized economy, the basis of which would be provided by hydroelectric energy, biochemistry and genetics. Liberals shared with socialists the Ricardian superstition that economists could pronounce on agricultural yields, with no help from the biochemists (1936, p. 43). Contemporary discussion on agriculture follows a different path; the so-called Green Revolution, as has been pointed out, was not politically green at all, either in the old populist sense or in the new ecologist sense. Nevertheless, despite Hogben's technological optimism (which biotechnology will perhaps justify in retrospect), there were clear differences between his views and 'Bernalism' which make him a more relevant author after the 'energy crisis' of 1973. The reader is referred to Werskey's excellent book (Werskey, 1978) for an account of the Bernalists' grandiose scale of thinking, which was very much the fashion by the Left in the 1930s. There are even better examples, and therefore Hogben's position is all the more remarkable. For example, the biologist H. J. Muller wrote (1936) that if food scarcity were not solved through synthetic chemistry, it would be solved by genetic engineering, with new types of plants. Some of his other prophecies (in electronic communications and automation, and in space travel) have already come true, but the increase in the productivity of agriculture is most doubtful; much depends on how it is measured, and this depends on how the future availability of energy and other scarce resources is seen and on how future demands are valued.

Muller (who won a Nobel Prize for discovering the effects of radiation on genetic mutations) joined the International Brigades in the Spanish Civil War as a doctor, and was certainly left-wing. He was also a eugenicist, believing in selection for intelligence, as well as for mutual help, a trait which he thought to be more widespread in the working class; while it was not possible to adequately measure intelligence by tests. Such a strange collection of beliefs, not atypical in 1930s, went with great hopes based on the piece of knowledge that Soddy and others had pointed out for the first time: the inconceivably great founts of energy which 'lie in the hidden recesses of the atom' (Muller, 1936, p. 76), and which would be available if the atom were 'unlocked'. The conquest of the forces in the atom nucleus was one of the most alluring fields of future endeavour; the preoccupation with fossil fuels was misplaced because of the 'practically inexhaustible physical sources of power (which) surround us', as yet undeveloped (Muller, 1936, p. 73).[1] Moreover, Muller resurrected old speculations about the recycling of energy that Rankine and Helmholtz had presented (and that Jevons also, as will be seen, had mentioned):

Astronomy also hints to us not only that the energy of the worlds may become scattered, as was formerly thought, but that there are places and occasions where it *may* gather together. If so, the second law of thermodynamics, with its pessimistic dictum that all energy must finally be dissipated until the universe attains a dead level of stillness, fails to have universal application. And so it may be that we shall yet find that fantasy of physics called 'Maxwell's demon' which can recollect for us in usable form the dissipated entropy of the cosmos. (Muller, 1936, p. 79)

[1] During the 1950s, H. J. Muller was to become very active in the attempts to ban atomic-bomb testing. Cf. Carlson, 1981.

In contrast, Hogben, even in the 1930s, was keener on 'soft' technologies than most other socialist scientists. He was not a eugenicist, either – almost the only socialist scientist not to be so. Moreover, he had an interest in the social sciences; he called Malthus 'the phlogistonist of demography' because his law of population was not based on empirical study, and he introduced demography into the LSE. His complaints against economists were twofold. Firstly, they proposed a theory of production without even a rudimentary knowledge of science and technology, which made them ridiculous; and secondly, they proposed a theory of consumption without a study of the origins of human needs; this made them noxious, because although they supposedly studied human needs, they did not do so, nor did anyone else. The fact that people have common needs was forgotten because there was a unilateral insistence on their having individual preferences (Hogben, 1936, pp. 18–19). This broke one of the points of contact between economics and the sciences, since biology could partially (but only partially) explain human needs. Why renounce this possibility of knowledge, hiding needs behind mysterious individual preferences which would be revealed only in the market?

Hogben tried to set up a Department of Population and Resources at the LSE, arguing that 'vital statistics' (a name taken from Petty, his favourite economist) and dietetics were not only medical disciplines but were also parts of the science of the wealth of nations. Economists left aside the reality of biological needs, which (reduced to absolute basics) could be measured by the calorific requirements of nutrition. Since a large part of the British population did not attain the minimum calorie intake established by the British Medical Council (Hogben, 1936, p. 71; cf. Webster, 1982), it was convenient to hide this reality under an avalanche of 'Austrian sophistication'.

Hogben would have agreed that in order to discuss the 'physiological needs of human nutrition', previous study of the history of physiology would be required. The allocation of resources to human nutrition could not then be explained in the way that it is (partly) explained now, before the study of cycles of materials and of applications of the laws of energetics to the human body. William Petty, the physiocrats, Adam Smith, Malthus and Ricardo were unable to discuss the energy needs of the human body. Marx, Jevons and Walras, with books published in the 1860s and 1870s, would have been able to include a discussion of calorie intake. Marx, for instance, could have expressed neatly in calories his distinction between the physiological minimum for survival and reproduction, and the cultural and social element historically variable in workers' remuneration. Interest in nutrition was widespread among left-wing 'materialists' – Moleshott had given the subtitle *Für das Volk* to a treatise on nutrition published shortly after 1848. Though the first investigations of nutrition placed more emphasis on *Stoffwechsel* (cycles of chemical elements), than onto energy conversion (*Kraftwechsel*), during the 1850s and 1860s quantitative work was carried out on the muscles, and the human organism as a whole, as heat engines. Thus, Edward Frankland (1825–99), a chemist with industrial connections in Manchester and London, was able to present, in 1866, a table establishing a hierarchy of about thirty different foodstuffs showing the monetary cost per unit of energy delivered, thus providing the basic data for an empirical economics of food consumption. As Coleman explains (1972, p. 136): 'While there is no discussion here of the needs of a balanced diet, there is a clear suggestion to the cost-conscious industrialist of how wages might be neatly weighed against the essential energy requirements of his labourers'.[2]

The science of nutrition as it is now, provides an explanation for the type and uniformity of the diet of the greater part of mankind. It is known why poor Mexicans eat maize and beans and why poor Brazilians eat rice and beans. Whatever their subjective preferences, a decision on their part to dedicate their income (or hours of work) to obtaining a diet of meat, fruit and vegetables instead of cereals, pulses and root crops can be excluded. However, orthodox economic theory would be reluctant, as Hogben complained, to distinguish between physiological needs (expressable in calories and grams of protein) and other types of needs. This distinction smacks of 'objectivism'.

The science of nutrition does not explain the alimentary prescriptions of Leviticus; reductionist explanations of the Hindu avoidance of beef or the Moslem taboo on pork, or indeed of Aztec cannibalism, are not necessary in order to establish the simple point that food consumption by human beings is partly explained by physiology. The history of the physiology of nutrition does not stand still. Twenty years ago the emphasis was on lack of protein; nowadays it is often said that undernourishment and malnutrition go together, in the sense that if calories are lacking, protein will be used for energy and not for building up tissue; and it was not until the end of the nineteenth century that vitamins were discovered and the study of deficiency diseases began. Few scientists have been as aware as Hogben himself of the history of science; he was one of the organizers of the congress in London in 1931, where the Soviet delegation, with Hessen and Bukharin, made such an impression.[3]

---

[2] Cf. elsewhere in this book, references to other important names in the history of the physiology of nutrition, such as Fick, Pettenkofer, Voit, Rubner. Cf. also McCollum, 1957.
[3] Bukharin (politically quite defeated by then) lived at Hogben's home during the conference.

Hogben did not think that human needs could be reduced to calories, or, generally, that biology sufficed to explain these needs. His emphasis on energy accounting was made as a polemical point against economists, who did not study the availability of resources and were not even aware of John Boyd Orr's research into calorie deficiencies in Britain. Thus, he wrote: 'The word "plenty" defined with reference to man's species has therefore a perfectly clear social meaning which remains in spite of the continued existence of Austrian economists. Plenty is the excess of free energy over the collective calorie debt of human effort applied to securing the needs which all human beings share' (Hogben, 1936, p. 71; 1939, p. 99). This definition was quoted by Hayek (omitting the reference to himself), in his articles against 'scientism' and 'neo-Saint-Simonism' in *Economica* in the early 1940s and in his book of 1952, allowing him to place Hogben in the list of 'social energeticists', and would-be dictators (1943, p. 40); a doubtful point to make against Hogben whom Werskey called an 'Orwell of the scientific left'.

Hogben's definition of plenty is identical to that proposed sixty years earlier by Podolinsky and Sacher. He must have been aware of Soddy's writings, and possibly of Patrick Geddes', but he did not quote them. He came to know Otto Neurath; and he clearly belongs to this group of writers. In common with them, he believed that a study of the energy flow in human society would cast doubts on conventional measures of value, but – also in common with them – he did not believe that economics should be reduced to the study of how the flow of energy and materials is used to satisfy biological needs. What was needed was knowledge of the biological base of human nature and *also* knowledge of the laws conditioning social habits and preferences. The study of human preferences could advance by its attention being turned to the materials offered not by biology so much as by social anthropology and history (1939, p. 101).

Economists claim to study the allocation of scarce resources to different human needs, but thermodynamics is not an educational requirement in the social sciences curriculum. How then could the economists identify 'scarcity' of resources? On the other hand, how could needs be analysed if attempts to educate the human race such that ostentation was no longer a distinctive trait of social behaviour, were condemned as an infraction of personal freedom?

Economists such as Hayek and Robbins made economics a deductive science, based on arbitrary hypotheses, rather like a game of chess (Hogben, 1936, pp. 6–7). They did not study the availability of resources. Robbins had declared, with the coy disdain of a débutante, that economics did not study the uses of dung (cf. Desai, 1978). Nor did such economists study human needs, refusing to classify them as physiological and ostentatious. Perhaps other economists, reluctant to descend into such obscurantist libertarian mysticism, would accept this classification of needs, but would point out that ostentation was characteristic of human nature. Here again, social history and anthropology could be of more help than biology. Nature did not condemn to failure the 'attempts to eradicate this unsconsionable nuisance and discord which arise from hypertrophied craving for personal distinction artificially fostered by advertizing propaganda and good breeding' (Hogben, 1936, p. 75; 1939, p. 101).

Hogben, therefore, was well aware of the fact that economics, based on methodological individualism, does not aim at explaining human preferences and valuations, but rather at accepting them as being revealed in market transactions. He was opposed to this methodology.

Now, if the definition of economics as the study of the human allocation of scarce resources to alternative ends is allowed, and if it is decided that this study cannot be separated from either the study of science and technology or the study of the establishment of socio-historical rules of consumption, nothing new is being proposed. Hogben is only one of a list of writers who have argued along these lines. What has been done in this book however, and which will be discussed in the next chapter is the extending of discussion on the methodology of economics to the question of inter-generational allocation of exhaustible resources.

11

Methodological Individualism and Inter-generational Allocation

Introduction

If part of this year's wheat crop is kept as seed, what happens to the rest (whether it is eaten, or squandered) has no influence on next year's crop, provided there is enough food for the agriculturalists. One barrel of oil used today is, however, one barrel fewer available for the future; it cannot be made good. One ton of bauxite taken from the soil and converted into aluminium does not seem to diminish future availability, since aluminium can be recycled. Let it be taken for granted that some resources are exhaustible (including material resources, since warning has already been given against the 'energetic dogma'); then see how economic theory is equipped to deal with their allocation across generations. A particular pattern of use of fossil fuels and other non-renewable resources implies a distributive choice between the present and future generations. The market gives a present value to future demands, and in that sense it is more generous with posterity than with impecunious contemporaries. But the present value of future demands is determined in a manner contrary to the rules of the methodological individualism characteristic of economic theory. It must be so determined, in the absence from the market of individuals who are not yet born.

In economic theory, prices play the role of signals for the allocation of scarce resources to alternative ends. For instance, should economic agents think that production techniques will not change, that population will be stable, and that preferences will not change, then it might be thought that the price pattern will make for an equal distribution of exhaustible resources among all generations. However, not only would some controversial assumptions have been introduced (including an estimate of how many generations there will be), but also a moral principle: an equal weight would have been given to the demands from all generations. Economic theory abhors moral principles. It studies the allocation of resources which results from transactions between individuals, whatever moral principles such individuals hold.

The first point to be considered in this chapter is whether the issue of the inter-generational allocation of exhaustible resources provides an argument against methodological individualism in economic theory. The market, it is assumed, does not impose types of conduct on individuals but grows rather out of such individuals' propensities to truck and barter. These individuals are either consumers who have the means to purchase goods, means which are distributed among various commodities according to the consumers' preferences; or they are producers who buy resources, combine them and sell the commodities thus produced. It may be considered, without loss of any important theoretical results, that individuals are both consumers and producers, provided they are not self-sufficient, since then no market would exist. Economic theory studies the pattern of quantities transacted and the accompanying prices. This has been the nucleus of economic theory from Adam Smith down to Arrow-Debreu by means of Jevons and Walras. This study has been carried out since the 1870s by differential calculus and, more recently, with games theory. Economic theory does not pay attention (in principle) to the physical characteristics of commodities. For instance, it should not be said that some commodities, because they are food commodities, are more needed than others, which are superfluous.

The demand for some goods perhaps will show the Giffen effect, that is, the demand will increase as prices go up. Giffen goods (or, less neutrally, 'inferior' goods) are defined as goods which generate a demand that shows negative income elasticity; that is to say, the higher the income of the consumer, the less is consumed. Textbooks quote bread and potatoes as examples, though margarine was also quoted (in pre-cholesterol days). Advanced texts in economics do not give examples. The genesis of the preferences of economic agents a, b, c for goods x, y and z is mysterious; and the physical characteristics of the goods do not enter into the explanation.

Food is eaten for physiological, social and symbolic reasons. Indeed, being fat has positive social value in some cultures, and, in general, in poor countries. In some North Atlantic countries, however, packets of food carry notices of their calorie content, the purpose being to spend a given amount of money in buying as little food energy as possible rather than to calculate a diet at minimum chrematistic cost. A biological-economic-cultural anthropology of human food habits is an interdisciplinary subject which is not taught: only historians and anthropologists are in a position to deal with it (Mintz, 1985).

The allocation of land and labour to basic agricultural products, which feed the poor, can only be understood by paying attention to their physical and chemical characteristics and to the physiology of nutrition. But economics does not wish to explain the origins of preferences; all it requires is that preferences are expressed according to rules which allow formal analysis. Economics becomes a science of choice between anything in general and nothing in particular.

This is the reason that other fields of study are becoming invaded by parodies of micro-economics, such as rational choice in political science (Barry, 1982); the application of games theory to nuclear strategy (Freedman, 1981, chapter 12); or to the study of amorous transactions in or outside the family (Becker, 1981). That economics makes the assumption of commensurability between things which are, perhaps, incommensurable from other points of view, comes out clearly in such studies, which push to the limit the principle of subjective valuation. We are asked to accept that, political leaders' assessment of the rationality of trade-offs between millions of deaths and territorial conquests (or political gains), has something in common with the trading-off, in elementary micro-economics, of apples and pears on an indifference curve. A second virtue of such studies is that they make clear that economics no longer needs to operate on the assumption of selfish economic agents. In the games of games theory (games such as 'chicken' or 'prisoners' dilemma'), selfishness can produce terrible results for everybody concerned, in a manner opposed to the operation of the 'invisible hand'. Thus, in what might be called the 'economics of war' – not in the substantive sense of a study of what happens or, rather, happened to economies in time of war (increase in non-productive investment, inflation, rationing), but in the formal sense associated with games theory and economists such as Morgenstern and Schelling – the agents might rationally choose a strategy of co-operation, instead of behaving as paradigmatic *homines economici*. The basic principle of economics is nevertheless still there; the economist will take as his only objective data the subjective inscrutable valuations of individuals.

When dealing with exhaustible resources, the principle that the allocation of resources should respond to the preferences of economic agents *encounters one ontological difficulty*: many of the relevant economic agents have not yet been born, therefore they cannot express their preferences and their 'willingness to pay'.

A given rate of discount of the future implies a given ethical attitude towards future generations. The question arises not only when considering the inter-temporal allocation of exhaustible resources, but also in growth economics. In the context of growth theory, the economist might be able to afford the moral luxury of not discounting the future, evading at the same time the egalitarian consequences that a zero rate of discount implies for the allocation of exhaustible resources. As Ramsey wrote: 'we do not discount later enjoyments in comparison with earlier ones, a practice which is ethically indefensible and arises merely from the weakness of the imagination' (Ramsey, 1928, p. 543). The point is that even without discounting the future (or overvaluing the present), the sacrifice that can be demanded from the present generation (in the form of reducing consumption in favour of investment) would be limited, provided *some* growth in consumption per caput is assumed, and this because of the principle of decreasing marginal utility. Economic growth, a consequence of today's savings, will make the future more prosperous and therefore the 'marginal later enjoyment' lower than today's.

In most models of economic growth, Ramsey's moral injunction is not followed. Both a more radiant future is assumed and its present value is discounted. However, when the closed discourse of the economics of growth is not being considered, but the economics of exhaustible resources, then it is not known whether the future will be more or less prosperous than the present. In fact, instead of being able to assume a more prosperous future, the reverse situation applies: a high rate of discount will mean quick depletion and therefore a less prosperous future.

In attempting to escape ethical presuppositions, it could be claimed that the rate of discount (whether high or low, zero, or even negative) reveals the economic agents' degree of preference for the present over the future. It would be as useless to argue with them as it would be to argue with anyone else about, for instance, the values given to different products in the diet. This is certainly not a matter of ethics, but of idiosyncrasies. In principle everybody is able to bid in the market. The economist will say that if the distribution of income is such that some people have so little market power that they starve, and if this is considered to be undesirable, this can be changed through the fiscal system (or, more radically, through changing the distribution of 'titles' to an income, such as property in land).

However, when the allocation of exhaustible resources is considered, it can be seen that the point is not only whether the pattern of prices and quantities which arises from the bidding of economic agents in the market will or will not deprive some of them of a minimum livelihood. It is also that those who have not yet been born, naturally cannot bid in today's market. Their future demands are given a certain (heavy? light?) weight today. Why that weight and not another? In the economics of exhaustible resources, the present value of the future demand of people who will *perhaps* be poorer than we, are being discounted (or not being discounted). Should future demand not be over- rather than undervalued? Today's economic agents cannot escape this moral dilemma.

Questions on the optimality of the inter-generational allocation of exhaustible resources cannot be separated from questions on moral values, against the basic rules of conventional economic theory. Let us imagine that we observe that one section of humanity does not care about the extreme poverty of another, large section of humanity (poverty expressed as a very low level of consumption not only of exosomatic but also of endosomatic energy). The rich are reluctant to admit that they are rich because the poor are poor. If they do not care about people who are alive, why should they care about people not yet born? 'What has posterity done for us'? There is one crucial analytical difference between the two situations; the poor of 'today' are able to come to the market had they money or something to sell; the poor (or the rich, *we do not know*) of 'tomorrow' cannot come to today's market. We *attribute* a value today to their future demand; they are not able to reveal their preferences. There is an allocation of resources to them without any transaction.

One possible line of work would have led to writing an essay in moral philosophy or in moral exhortation, or perhaps, more fruitfully, would have led to an investigation of the social distribution of different moral values on intra-generational and inter-generational economic equality (do they correlate with social class, income level, age, nationality, religion, gender?). In fact, the economist, in order to explain the historico-geographical allocation of exhaustible resources (and industrial waste), which is a major part of economic history over the past two hundred years, must become, certainly not a moralist, but a sociologist and a historian of the ethics of time-preference.

Economists should also become students of the history of science and technology, since economic agents will take their beliefs about technical change from this history (from where else?). If economic agents believe, for example, that 'soon there will be new sources of energy', a belief which will have an effect on the whole pattern of transactions and prices, the economists ought to be under the obligation of studying the social roots of this belief. For a long time there was no response to the warnings from outside the profession (and in some cases from inside it) that economic theory was forgetting that some resources are exhaustible.

Jevons

Let it be assumed that Jevons (1835–82) had developed, in *The Coal Question* (1865), an analysis in the form of equalizing the 'final degree of utility' (that is, marginal utility) from coal for all (or a certain number) future generations, so that the total utility obtained from the given stock of coal would be maximized. Apart from the necessary assumptions about future preferences, future techniques and future costs, it is likely that Jevons would have discounted the utilities that future generations would obtain from coal, at present value. Jevons already had a theory of interest based on individual time preference, that is, that economic agents are understood to hold the view that one unit of consumption in the future is less valuable than one unit of consumption today, this not because the future will be more prosperous, but because of subjective time preference.

Jevons believed that, should coal mining in Britain continue to increase at the same rate, and taking into account the greater thermodynamic efficiency of every new generation of steam engine, which would thus increase the competitiveness of coal against other fuels, British coalfields would not be able to sustain 'production' beyond the end of the century. Jevons, who, before going to live in Manchester, already had contacts with Owen College (where his cousin, the chemist Henry E. Roscoe, taught), must have known Joule and William Thomson by name from adolescence. He later had personal contact with Joule (1818–89). Jevons wrote that other countries lived on the annual regular income from the harvest, but Britain was living on capital; a capital which would not yield interest because once it was turned into heat, light and power, it disappeared forever into space (Jevons, 1865, p. 307). He did, however, entertain the thought that energy could somehow be 'recycled', despite the second law of thermodynamics. In *The Principles of Science* (Jevons, 1879, p. 751) he asked whether Rankine could have been right when he proposed that the universe could have a limit beyond which there would be only empty space. Heat waves would travel through the ether and, on reaching this limit, would be reflected back and concentrated in *foci*. This remarkable speculation (which had also been advanced by Helmholtz, cf. Harman, 1982, p. 68), was aimed rather at removing the pessimism about the 'heat-death' of the universe than of assuring mankind of a constant supply of energy on earth. It shows, however, that Jevons was perfectly aware of the second law, trying to combat, with Rankine's notion, W. Thomson's 'universal tendency in nature to the dissipation of mechanical energy'.

Jevons' book on coal contained forecasts of coal consumption in Britain which proved accurate for two decades (R. N. Adams, 1982, p. 36). He wrote the book in a single summer, clearly attempting to cause a sensation and intending to obtain a teaching job. Its immediate reception was remarkable. Gladstone wrote to say that he had found in it an excellent argument against the increase in the Public Debt. John Stuart Mill mentioned it in Parliament. John Herschel (1792–1871), who had long been helping Jevons with his career, wrote that 'we are using up our resources and expending our national life at an enormous and increasing rate and thus a very ugly day of reckoning is impending sooner or later', blaming the 'populations calling themselves civilized, but in reality luxurious and selfish' for the 'enormous and outrageously wasteful consumption of every other article that the earth produces' (8 January, 8 March 1866).

John Herschel, with Cambridge origins, a friend of Babbage, was a decisive organizing figure in the British scientific establishment. Leslie White (in Fried, 1959, p. 142) credits him with having noted, in 1833, in the first edition of his *Outlines of Astronomy*, that 'the sun's rays are the ultimate source of almost every motion which takes place on the surface of the earth'. He corresponded with Jevons on the possibilities of using the tides as a source of energy, taking a rather sceptical view. John Herschel's father was Sir William Herschel, the astronomer, who had made the original observation that there was a correlation between the appearance of sun spots and the movements in the price of corn (because, it was thought, sun spots meant increased heat, and increased vegetation on earth). This was a reasonable subject for Jevons to pursue as a statistical exercise to please one of his patrons (he had long been interested in price series, and had had correspondence with Laspeyres on index numbers). Unfortunately for the history of economics, Jevons' book on coal and his views on the trade cycle and sun spots tend to get confused as aspects of a single misguided attempt at physicalist economics.

Herschel chose to interpret Jevons' book as an attack upon the selfishness on the then current generation of (rich) Englishmen. Jevons himself was simultaneously engaged in developing economic theory as the 'mechanics of self-interest'. His first paper on marginal utility theory was written in 1862, before he wrote *The Coal Question*. An easy point could be scored by setting Herschel against Jevons; the 'mechanics of self-interest' did not produce an optimum allocation of resources over time. Nevertheless, Jevons did not treat the 'coal question' in a marginalist way, that is, he did not discuss which price-path of coal would lead to its allocation over time in such a way as to make its 'final degree of utility' (discounted or not) equal for all generations to come. Jevons did not ask which effects 'self-interest' would have on the pattern of depletion. In his marginalist economic theory, he considered demand synchronically, not over time. Though he did not foresee the use of oil in the internal combustion engine or the discovery of radioactivity at the end of the century, he had certain hopes concerning the 'recycling' of energy which perhaps help to explain why he did not develop the economic theory of exhaustible resources, which he was theoretically equipped to do in a non-egalitarian manner because of his time-preference theory of interest.

L. C. Gray, John Ise and American Conservationism

When discussing the inter-generational allocation of exhaustible resources, some economists have taken refuge neither behind the hypothesis of a radiant future nor behind subjective time-preference. Lewis C. Gray (1881–1952), an agricultural historian and a student of R. T. Ely, was the first economist to write (Gray, 1913; 1914) that in order to explain the pattern of use of exhaustible resources over time, one could assume that economic agents would compare price increases with the rate of interest (or of discount). His articles (as Smith, 1982, has made clear; also Crabbé, 1983) were contemporary with the conservationist movement in the United States during the presidencies of Theodore Roosevelt and Taft (Hays, 1959). Gray wrote that strict conservationism would imply giving equal importance to future and present needs. This was an absurdity according to him. Some positive rate of discount seemed necessary; otherwise, with a zero rate of discount, the period of utilization of exhaustible resources would grow to infinity and yearly use would be infinitesimal. The economist, however, could not adopt one particular rate of discount unless answers to the following questions were provided: what was the criterion of social value? how could the social value of present and future consumption of a commodity be compared? would society apply the same rate of discount as individuals? should social policy be determined by national or international welfare? It was difficult to say what the appropriate rate of discount should be without knowing the answers to such questions (Gray, 1913, pp. 515–19). Gray's contribution was praised by R. T. Ely (1918, p. 34) and by Stuart Chase (1936, p. 261), and it was analytically superior to Ely's chapters on conservation and economic theory (Ely, 1918, pp. 3–91) which were influential in the development of forest economics in the United States.

American conservationism was not in favour of diminishing the use of resources. Compared with today's 'green' movement, the emphasis then was not on distribution, but on growth. Thus, American conservationism furthered river-basin development, with the argument that hydroelectricity would replace coal. When somebody pointed out that the hydroelectric development of Niagara would spoil the river's beauty, a conservationist meeting expressed approval of Kelvin's view that it was practically an international crime to let so much energy run to waste. Gifford Pinchot wrote that forest science aimed at obtaining a sustained yield, and certainly not at preserving the climax vegetation (Hays, 1959, pp. 123–7).

The efficient use of a resource (in the sense of maximizing the resource's value over time) can clearly lead to some conservationist measures, for instance, against soil erosion and against total deforestation which denudes the soil and prevents forest growth. But the optimality of a path of use of the resource (and, in the case of exhaustible resources, of depletion) is always contingent on the rate of discount adopted and on hypotheses concerning technical change. This was clearly seen by another American economist, John Ise (born in 1885), who wrote books on forest economics, on oil policy and on national parks, and a textbook on general economics (1950). In an article published in 1925, he pointed out that future needs should be more-or-less discounted, due to uncertainties and contingencies; though it is doubtful, he wrote, whether we should value the needs of the next generation at half the value of our own; this is what a rate of discount of only two per cent per annum implies (assuming some thirty-five years between generations) (Ise, 1925, p. 285, cited by G. A. Smith, 1982, p. 491). His estimates of oil reserves in the United States were badly mistaken (Ise, 1925, p. 289): this does not mean that today's estimates are also mistaken.

Coming also from the field of forestry and soil conservation, for which the rate of discount is of paramount importance, there is other American material on the relations between economics and ecology before the 1940s. Aldo Leopold, who was analytically weak, wrote on conservation ethics in the *Journal of Forestry* (31, 1933, pp. 634–43) shortly after Franklin Roosevelt started a second conservationist movement with public subsidies and as part of the New Deal. Leopold realized that 'economic criteria . . . do not now suffice to adjust society to its environment', but he did not build upon Gray's and Ise's work.

Hotelling's Rule

Imagine a seller of oil who must decide whether to keep for 'tomorrow' a barrel of oil which he could extract and sell 'today'. The Saudi Arabian authority might be considered, who would decide whether to extract barrel number five million today, or to stop at one before that. If it is sold 'today', a revenue will be obtained which, invested at a rate of interest, will produce a certain extra revenue 'tomorrow'. The criterion for deciding whether or not to extract barrel number five million could be to compare the increase in price expected between 'today' and 'tomorrow' with the interest to be gained by selling 'today' and investing the proceeds. The application of this rule requires a knowledge of the rate of interest and a knowledge, or at least a reliable estimate, of future prices. If the markets establish a rate of interest, and if there is a futures market, the decision is easy. Even though existing futures markets do not provide prices for more than a few months ahead, nothing prevents sellers from having expectations of prices over long periods.

Introducing extraction costs does not change the rule. One would compare the revenue to be gained from the interest on the difference between the price and cost of the marginal barrel with the expected increase in net revenue if the sale of the barrel were postponed. This criterion bears the name of Gray-Hotelling, since it was explained by Gray (1913, 1914) and Hotelling (1931). Gray's position was, however, that one could not separate the economic efficiency in the inter-generational allocation of an exhaustible resource from the ethical problem, that is, from the study of the social distribution of ethical positions.

Perhaps a simple numerical example will clarify matters. Some of the assumptions needed in order to arrive at an inter-generational path of depletion of an exhaustible resource should be looked at.

Let us assume that at the present moment or generation, the buying intentions (or 'demand schedule') are as set out below:

p	q
15	0
14	1
13	2
12	3
11	4
10	5
9	6
8	7
7	8
6	9
5	10

That is to say, the demand function which expresses the quantities of that exhaustible resource which would be bought at different prices is $q = 15 - p$.

Let us assume that the total stock of q, which is a non-recyclable resource, is 10 units. Let us also assume that the seller is a monopolist, whether a private company or a planning agency is irrelevant here. Let us also assume that the average variable cost of extraction of this resource is constant, let us make it equal to one monetary unit. Being constant, it will be also equal to marginal cost. It would be more realistic to assume that marginal cost grows with extraction, but this would not change the essential points in the discussion.

The monopolistic seller will be then confronted with these data:

q	p	Total revenue	Marginal revenue	Total cost	Marginal cost
1	14	14	14	1	1
2	13	26	12	2	1
3	12	36	10	3	1
4	11	44	8	4	1
5	10	50	6	5	1
6	9	54	4	6	1
7	8	56	2	7	1
8	7	56	0	8	1
9	6	54	-2	9	1

Should the monopolist wish to maximize his profits, and should he only consider the present moment or generation, then he would extract and sell 7 units of this resource, at a price of 8 monetary units (should he sell 8 units, marginal revenue falls below marginal cost, and he makes less profit).

However, the shrewd business behaviour of this monopolist up to now leads us to think that he is not the sort of 'punk' who thinks that there is 'no future', but, on the contrary, that he is a responsible person who cares about his descendants, or about his nation, or about humanity. He knows that, after he dies, there will still be demand for this resource. How will he allocate the total amount $q = 10$, between the present and the future? It makes for nice simplification without loss of substance to assume that there are only two relevant moments or generations, t_0 and t_1. We shall also introduce a very unrealistic assumption, and this is that the conditions of demand, and the costs in time, t_1, as foreseen now in time t_0, are exactly the same as those obtaining now. We need to assume that the monopolist now makes some guess as to what demand and costs will be like in the future, and this assumption of identical conditions is as arbitrary as any other. Let us now see different allocative alternatives:

	q_0	q_1	Total revenue	Total costs	Profits
Initial allocation	7	3	92	10	82
	6	4	98	10	88
Chosen allocation	5	5	100	10	90
	4	6	98	10	88

We see that maximum profits are achieved by allocating 5 units to the present generation and 5 units to the future generation, that is, if the monopolist is a profit-maximizer, he will allocate the exhaustible resource with perfect equity between both generations, *provided* that he does not discount at all the present value of future revenue.

Should we observe that in the present generation 6 units are sold, leaving 4 units for the future generation, may we then say that the monopolist is not a profit maximizer? No, we may not (according to the rules of economic theory), since perhaps he is giving the same value (inscrutable subjective preferences) to 3 extra monetary units now as to 5 monetary units less in the future, that is, he is making $3(1+r)=5$, where r is the rate of discount (in this case, 66.66 . . . per cent, in the period between t_0 and t_1). The equal weight given to 3 monetary units now or to 5 monetary units in future might come from the fact that the extra revenue today, placed at interest, might compensate for the loss of revenue in future, and this is why we use 'rate of interest' and 'rate of discount' synonymously.

The conclusion is that for each r, there will be *ceteris paribus* a different allocation. Also, each allocation corresponds to a different r, and we could easily calculate which is the r which corresponds to more 'egotistical' allocations ($q_0 = 7$, $q_1 = 3$) or to more 'altruistic' allocations ($q_0 = 4$, $q_1 = 6$), a negative rate of discount in the second case. We could also assume that there are more generations: quite clearly, with the given demand and cost functions, and with $r = 0$, and assuming ten generations, one unit of resource would correspond to each generation. The important point is that an assumption is needed about the rate of discount.

This exercise could perhaps be considered an answer to a question set by Jevons in 1874 as external examiner for the Cambridge Moral Science Tripos (see *Papers and Correspondence*, 1972 vol. 7, pp. 132–3): 'The character of the demand being given, show upon what principles the price should be fixed, in order that the greatest gross profit may be made (by a monopolist) by the sale of the commodity. What modifications are required in the case . . . of a limitation in the commodity, e.g. coal?' Despite asking such a question, Jevons himself did not discover the Gray-Hotelling rule.

Should economic agents be Islamic fundamentalists who consider that the rate of interest should be zero, the application of Hotelling's rule will produce a slower time-path of depletion of exhaustible resources. Whether economic agents should behave as Christians or as Moslems is not for the economist to say, although he will be interested in analysing the different consequences of the economic agents' valuations.

Preferences are revealed in the market. Time preference will be revealed, for instance, in the market for savings, the amount of which will depend on the rate of interest being paid (although this does not mean that savings will be zero should the rate of interest be zero). Although some economists attempt to explain the ratio of savings to income using social class as a variable, orthodox economics, both macro- and micro-, is based on methodological individualism. Individual decisions on saving might depend on the family's development cycle, but these are still made individually.

In Karl Popper's words (1963, p. 341), the belief in the empirical existence of social collectives (such as the middle class, in the nice example he chose) is naïve collectivism which must be replaced by the principle that all social phenomena be analysed in terms of individuals, of their actions and reactions. This methodology is all too obvious in conventional economics, not only in the field of the allocation of exhaustible resources. This is why Hogben's discussion on the need to study the origins of economic agents' preferences was quite relevant to the main theme in this section, namely, the inter-generational allocation of exhaustible resources.

Since the so-called 'energy crisis' of 1973, the economic theory of exhaustible resources has flourished, and Gray's and Hotelling's rule may soon be introduced into textbooks. However, the question which Gray himself asked – what rate of discount of the future should be adopted – has no answer in economic theory, since it is equivalent to asking which weight should some economic agents (those already born) give to the demands of other economic agents, against the rule that all are entitled to come to market with their preferences and initial bundle of goods. This critique is (or should be) today mainly associated with Georgescu-Roegen's work, and in orthodox economic literature there is some reaction to his challenge after many years of near-silence. Thus, Dasgupta (1982, p. 104) writes that a zero rate of discount has been proposed by Georgescu-Roegen in order not to discriminate against the demand of future generations. He finds two reasons against this. The first reason in favour of a positive rate of discount is that consumption per caput will increase with time, and this provides a non-discriminatory rationale for discounting the present value of future consumption. However, a theory of growth would then be needed which would take into account the fact that some resources are exhaustible. Belief in the advance of scientific knowledge does not entail a belief in the discovery of substitutes for exhaustible resources at such a rate as to allow not only present patterns of consumption, but even their growth. Maintaining 'zero growth' in the over-developed countries already implies a remarkable speed of depletion of some exhaustible resources.

The second reason Dasgupta proposes for justifying a positive rate of discount is the second law of thermodynamics, attempting thus to turn the tables on Georgescu-Roegen. The day will arrive when there will be no more life on earth. There exists a possibility of the extinction of human life, which will grow as time passes. This is a reason for discounting the future. However, the second law will present no threat at all to human life for millions of generations, and over that period it cannot be invoked – except as a joke – to give a rationale for discounting the future. The paradox here is that if the future is now discounted and technical progress does not keep pace, the exosomatic use of energy and materials will possibly in future have to be curtailed below present levels, more than if the future were not discounted, or were discounted at a lower rate.

Clearly, it might be feared that a zero or a negative rate of discount would lead to some resources being left utilized. Then, as John Joly cheerfully put it, 'so long as there is free oxygen in the atmosphere, our coalfields might, at any time in the remote future, generate light and heat in the universal grave' (Joly, 1915). Uncertainty predominates in these matters over risks whose probabilities may be assessed. Georgescu-Roegen did not propose a zero rate of discount. His point was, rather, that the rate of discount is against appearances an extra-economic question or, to use his own categories, it is a subject fit for study by institutional rather than by analytical economics.

Some economic models assume that the agents do not know in which generation they will be born, and economists then discuss the consequences that the agents' preferences would have on the inter-generational pattern of allocation. Some authors have normatively proposed that, in order to correct for the selfishness or 'short-sightedness' of the present generation, a 'social' rate of discount should be adopted, lower than that determined in the market (for example, Fisher, 1981, p.68). Such proposals can be linked to an assumption that economic agents are located behind a Rawlsian veil of ignorance as to the generation into which they will be born, and therefore they would presumably be much less disposed to discount the future. Now, however, the historico-geographical decisions of actual economic agents cannot be explained by their ignorance as to whether they have or have not been born although to the extent that such moral exhortations are successful, the path of depletion of exhaustible resources will be slower. Rawlsian altruism towards the present generation could be interpreted in utilitarian terms: the rich of today will perhaps be driven by utilitarian calculus to insure against a revolution which would put them in the position of the poor, by allowing at least a fair livelihood to all their contemporaries, especially if they are citizens of the same state. But they will feel under no threat of revolution from those to be born in the distant future.

Other models feature economic agents who are hypothetically immortal, very much like amoebae reproduced by sporulation which are unable to 'say', 'when my poor mother died'. The economists' reluctance to separate commodities according to physical characteristics is overcome with a *fuite en avant*, since such an uncomfortable physical characteristic of economic agents as mortality is left aside. Then the intertemporal allocation could respond to the economic agents' individual preferences without leaving out of the game those who have not yet been born (Becker and Tomes, 1979; cf. Daly's critique, 1982). The trick is to show that the inter-generational allocation of exhaustible resources arises from the transactions between individual economic agents, all of them with their preferences. But it is nonsense to assume that unborn agents make transactions. Their demands, which lie in the future, are now *given* a certain weight by those agents who are alive at this time.

The economist should not become a preacher of the morality of *carpe diem*, or the morality consistent with a belief in immortality-on-earth, or a belief in reincarnation. The economist can agree that no 'science of ethics' exists which might teach the true ethical principle regarding future generations. Here, a primitive version of an 'emotivist' doctrine of ethics might prove an obstacle, if it is really believed that one can only persuade or fight, but cannot argue about the proper rate of discount of the future. Historical observation shows that ethical principles are argued about, and they change with time so that a sociological typology of their distribution among different groups of men and women can be attempted.

It is a sympton of methodological laziness to attribute preferences to the hypothetical individuals featured in the models of economic theory, never mind whether such preferences resemble those which would characterize an *homo economicus*, or whether they are altruistic. On the other hand, to set oneself the impossible task of researching the preferences and moral values of all real individuals, today and in the past, would be equivalent of committing methodological suicide, which is unnecessary because individuals belong to social collectives, and it is known that preferences and moral values are not randomly distributed.

A word is needed on models which purport to explain intertemporal allocation as arising from the transactions between 'overlapping generations'. Such models are not satisfactory, since they are forced to assume (in order to eschew the issue of attribution of preferences to distant generations) that the *whole* stock of exhaustible resources, owned by the older generation, is sold each time to the younger overlapping generation, in exchange for a part of the income the new generation is earning. This assumption implies an economy whose stock of exhaustible resources is small or dramatically undervalued.

The critique therefore, is *not* that economic theory operates with selfish economic agents, and future generations are sacrificed to present greed. Economic theory can operate assuming altruistic economic agents who apply a 'social' rate of discount lower than the market rate of interest, and who might even apply a zero or negative rate of discount. The critique is that economic theory is unable to deal with the inter-generational allocation of exhaustible resources relying only on the exchanges between agents whose behaviour accords with the postulate of rationality and utilitarian calculus, because non-born agents cannot bid in today's market. Since future demand today is given a certain value, the economist must necessarily become a sociologist of the ethics of valuing the future. Since the rate of discount will also be influenced by technical prospects, the economist must also understand where economic agents acquire their notions of technical change, that is, he must study the history of science and technology.

Neo-corporatist and Neo-liberal Macro-economics

Both orthodox micro-economics and macro-economics are based on methodological individualism, though it may seem that macro-economics is not, because it deals with the broad aggregates of the economy. For instance, neo-corporatist agreements on incomes policies, which attempt to determine the share of profits and the share of wages in national income, are signed by representatives of interest groups (workers' unions, employers' associations); it seems therefore that this excludes the individualistic approach. The main point of this section is however that macro-economic National Income Accounting needs prices, and prices (including the prices of exhaustible resources) come from micro-economics.

Consider first the notion of neo-corporatist economic policies. For the political scientist, corporatism means, mainly, an *extra-parliamentary* system of representation and intermediation of organized interests. In the 'old' corporatism, parliament itself would be substituted by a corporatist chamber, while political analyses of the 'new' corporatism have been focused on the relations between the system of political party representation and the system of organized interests. For an economist, corporatism is, to a large extent, synonymous with *extra-market* determination of prices and incomes. To the extent that economic theory (orthodox micro-economics, and Keynesian macro-economics, though not Marxian or Sraffian economics, nor the new ecological economics of Georgescu-Roegen) has been used to legitimize income distribution, the explicit notion that prices and incomes are a political matter is inconvenient. Perhaps this explains why corporatism, with its extra-parliamentary and extra-market connotations, has not been in recent times the explicit ideology of almost anyone.

In 1973, Aubrey Jones, a former conservative minister appointed by Harold Wilson to head the Prices and Incomes Board (a consultative body with the task of judging whether wage settlements were inflationary, and with the even more difficult task of determining criteria for wage differentials) published *The New Inflation*. Jones proposed a permanent corporative chamber where the representatives of capital and labour could meet and decide on an incomes policy. The assumption was that there would be a sufficient degree of social consensus. This proposal was interpreted as a change 'from Walras to Durkheim', that is, a change from the doctrine of general economic equilibrium to the functionalism of Durkheimian sociology, which in a capitalist society would demand extra-market (and extra-parliamentary) agreements between organized interests.[1]

Aubrey Jones' book carried the subtitle 'The Politics of Prices and Incomes'. Before jumping to the wrong conclusion in 1973 that, because of working class militancy in a period of full employment, corporatism was becoming *the* new capitalist ideology (including such amazing proposals as a corporatist chamber in Britain!) there should have been awareness of the imminent neo-liberal reaction. The extent to which Keynesianism was still alive as the ideology of informal neo-corporatist practices should also have been explored. The notion that growth depends on retained profits which are the source of investment and that, therefore, a given rate of desired growth determines a rate of profits (assuming some given incremental capital/output ratio) has been one of the main supports for neo-corporatist agreements. Its plausibility nowadays depends on how much credit the ecological critique of National Income Accounting and of economic growth will be able to muster.

In the second half of the 1970s, the neo-liberal reaction was growing, and in some countries the increase in unemployment made it attractive to attempt to do without social pacts. Neo-liberals were certainly entitled to the derogatory use of the 'corporatist' tag, because the first time that the word 'corporatism' was used as a term of abuse after 1945, in the Keynesian-social-democratic era in Europe, was probably by Hayek in 1960.[2] Hayek wrote that in countries where, because of the monopolistic behaviour of the unions, inflationary tendencies began to appear, there were increasing demands for an 'over-all wage policy'. Wages were to be determined by some conception of 'justice' rather than by the forces of the market. This would of course force unions to choose

between becoming the willing instrument of governmental policy, on the one hand, and being totally abolished, on the other. The former alternative is more likely

[1] Martinez-Alier (1973).
[2] Mendès-France had felt obliged to include some pages in *La république moderne* (1962) explaining why his proposals for concerted planning could *not* be described as corporatism, probably, in the French context, looking over his shoulder to the communists rather than to the Right.

to be chosen, since it would enable the existing union bureaucracy to retain their position and some of their personal power. But to the workers it would mean complete subjection to the control of a corporative state. (Hayek, 1960, pp. 282–3)

Free collective bargaining was contrasted by Hayek to an 'over-all wage policy' implemented by a corporatist state with the agreement of the union leadership (and not of the rank-and-file, since Hayek quite realistically thought that in a period of full employment they would not give permanent consent to a wage-norm). 'Corporatism' was used as an insult, and Hayek is certainly an exception to Shonfield's rule, that 'the corporatist form of organization seems to be almost second nature to the Austrians' (Shonfield, 1965, p. 193).

The word 'corporatism', whether analytically useful or not, has been embarrassing. In some cases, it is said to be 'unfortunate that both forms of interest organization and control (both forms being the "old" and the "new" corporatisms) go by the same name' (Giner and Sevilla, 1984). But whether or not its use is considered to be fortunate depends on the political position of author and reader, and on their judgements of historical trends. The distinction between descriptive and normative terms is difficult to make in political science; words are themselves part of the political contest. Thus, 'neo-corporatism' should be taken to be a contested concept, in Connolly's sense (1983).

The terms 'corporatist state', 'corporatist economy' and 'corporatism' have been used in the international debate since the mid-1970s more as terms of abuse than as terms of praise. Perhaps the word is losing this pejorative character. Thus, could be read in an unpleasant review of a book by Tony Benn: 'Of course post-war government depended on a corporatist consensus which has now broken down. That is a Thatcherite truism'.[3] And a favourable review of Shonfield's *In Defence of the Mixed Economy* (1984) states that he 'was a corporatist, and that is nowadays not a very fashionable thing to be'.[4] 'Corporatism', in the sense of liberal, social corporatism, therefore is not considered to be a bad thing *nor a bad word*, particularly in Ian Gilmour's book (1983) written as an explicit apology of corporatism from inside the Conservative Party against Thatcher's neo-liberalism while, in the United States, Felix Rohatyn is a tireless preacher of corporatism against the neo-liberal wave.[5] Compare, for instance, in the Spanish context, Julio Segura's angry reaction to a question from Julio Cotler

---

[3] *Times Literary Supplement* 11 September 1981.
[4] *Financial Times*, 25 February 1984.
[5] See, for instance, F. Rohatyn, 'Time for a Change', *New York Review of Books*, 18 August 1983.

on neo-corporatism in post-Franco Spain,[6] Segura being a well-known euro-communist (that is, euro-corporatist) economist.

Already in the 1970s, there were, however, cases in which the term was used with a positive connotation, at least for 'Iberian-Latin' countries (Pike, Wiarda, 1974). Also,[7] an editorial in the *International Herald Tribune* (21 June 1977) entitled 'Socialism – late style', praised West German social-democracy in these terms:

> The German socialists are not only economically moderate, they seem to be tending toward a new kind of corporative state – by no means fascist, but seemingly based on collaboration between unions and private corporations, under government control of sorts. It has worked quite well in terms of the West German economy, but the Socialists there are by no means in a very strong political position. The British Labour party – at least its governing right – seems to be adopting the same philosophy. Will the other Socialists do the same?

It would be foolish to say that German or British social-democracy were moving towards 'corporative states' without parliaments, after the pattern of Franco's Spain. The co-operation between unions, management, and government might rather be described as a 'corporatist structure' in the general politico-economic system (as Panitch and Kastendiek have written). The word 'corporatism' has been used in two different senses, which not only can be traced back (as Schmitter did in 1974) to Manoïlesco but also to Otto Bauer.

How are corporatist practices to be legitimized from a social-democratic point of view? Macro-economic theory has provided the main legitimizing platform for incomes policies. If National Income Accounting and economic growth theory fall in the next years into general disbelief, then the argument of wage-restraint in order to increase investment will cut little ice. Another possibility perhaps would be that of agreeing to permanent wage-moderation in exchange for a greater voice of workers' organizations in the running of the economy. This is where Otto Bauer's comments of 1933 come to mind. He wrote (certainly forced by circumstances) that the 'class struggle' in Austria at the time was a struggle on the interpretation of *Quadragessimo Anno*. Despite the Pope's praise for Italian fascism, a fundamental distinction should be made between the fascist corporative system (with appointed officials, without freedom of association and without the right to strike, without parties and parliament), and what would now be called liberal, or societal, or new corporatism, *berufständische*

---

[6] *Pensamiento iberoamericano*, 1983, 3, p. 130.
[7] Coincidentally, one week after the first parliamentary elections in Spain, on 15 June 1977, and at a time when the corporatist Moncloa Pact was already in the offing; the decisive moment in the recasting of bourgeois Spain after a period of military dictatorship and state-corporatism on behalf of the proprietary classes.

Selbsverwaltung (corporative auto-regulation, self-administration); a concept similar, as he explained, to 'organized capitalism' or to 'economic or industrial democracry'. Capitalists and workers would collaborate in a range of new institutions, with wide responsibilities which he discussed in detail. Such institutions would be similar to those which had grown out of collective bargaining (*Tarifgemeinschaften*), but would deal with many other questions apart from wages and work conditions; for instance, with the regulation of production and prices. *Berufständische Selbsverwaltung* was therefore not a 'road to socialism', which political conjuncture made impassable. It was a left-wing interpretation of *Quadragessimo Anno* rooted in social-democratic concepts and practices.

Bauer explicitly made the point that state-corporatism (he called it the 'Italian' *Korporationensystem*) would kill social corporatism. Since the Catholics held on to the anti-statist 'subsidiarity principle', he hoped that they would agree with him.

It would be calumnious to make Otto Bauer into a consistent partisan of corporatism as an ideology and practice of non-parliamentary political representation, and of permanent and structured socio-economic inequality. For instance, he wrote in 1923:

> Books like Othmar Spann's *Der Wahre Staat* and Ludwig von Mises' economic treatises represent the two types. The former wants to return to Adam Müller and romantic political thought, the latter to Bentham and the liberal Manchester school. Spann represents the flight into the romantic idea of a corporative state of a bourgeois intelligentsia ruined by currency devaluation. Mises, on the other hand, personifies the rediscovered self-consciousness of an entrepreneurial group carried upward by the boom resulting from the collapse of the currency and demanding the abolition of all restrictions imposed by the state and by the bargaining power of trade unions. (Cited by Diamant, 1960, p. 90)

Bauer should be considered to be a founding father of the ideology of social corporatism, because of his writings of 1933–4, although he distanced himself quite clearly from *state*-corporatism.

Gulick (1948, volume II, p. 1228) summarized Bauer's position as follows:

> Social Democracy was irreconcilable with a fascist corporative system but could readily come to an agreement with the idea of an occupational-estates self-management that does not destroy but presupposes the rights of free organization and of striking, and does not abolish but supplements political democracy. The foundation and starting point for such a system had to be freely elected works councils and employee representation. Appointment of workers' representatives by the government would contradict the whole self-administration idea . . . Bauer made the positive suggestion that public-law organizations of employers and employees be created to implement the occupational-estates self-management with which the Socialists were prepared to reach an agreement. As examples of the

functions of such bodies he offered the operation of labour exchanges, training of young workers, regulation of production and of the market, and representation of the trade or industry in matters of economic policy.

As can be seen, Gulick gave a cumbersome translation of *berufständische Selbsverwaltung*, as 'occupational-estates self-management'. The translation of *berufständische* in English is 'corporative' or 'corporatist'.

Bauer's pre-Keynesian, social-democratic proposals are relevant in that they made the distinction, even in 1933, between fascist, statist corporatism, and social 'new' corporatism, by bringing out explicitly the similarities between social-Christian and social-democratic corporatist proposals (the way Austrian and Spanish Catholics would behave in practice was not then known), by acknowledging the synonymity between 'organized capitalism', 'economic or industrial democracy', and corporative self-regulation' (that is, neo-corporatism) (this was a rare occasion of social-democratic linguistic honesty prompted by the political situation); and, finally, by emphasizing neo-corporatist arrangements beyond wage policies in a context of economic crisis, which makes them all the more contemporary. Bauer, however, did not go unchallenged; in the next issue of *Der Kampf*, Otto Leichter wrote against his attempt to compromise with Catholic corporatism, which in any case had become impossible after Dollfuss' takeover in February 1934 and the repression that followed. In normal political circumstances, for social-democracy to defend corporatism under this name represents a clear sign of intellectual bankruptcy.

However, there is nothing uniquely Christian or social-democratic in corporatist doctrine. The reaction against the liberal-individualist concept of society was many sided. Durkheim had predicted in 1902 that the conflicts created by the division of labour would affect the stability of capitalist society to such a degree that the society and the state would have to be organized along corporatist lines. This corporatism was compatible with parliamentary representation based on territorial universal suffrage, which would be complemented by the corporative representation of different professional interests, and which would make agreements to solve the conflicts arising from a market economy lacking the traditional norms of coexistence and morality. For Durkheim, there were social facts and institutions which could not be reduced to individual preferences and decisions.

The corporatist concept of society is different from the liberal-individualist concept. The former lays emphasis on social groups and on the harmonization of interests of the various collectives by means of negotiations outside the market. The latter expresses itself in an individualism which is not only methodological but ontological, and which often believes in the harmonization of individual interests by means of the operation of the 'invisible hand' in the market. The advocates of incomes policies fit much better into the corporatist concept, although many of them are economists who have used Keynesian macro-economics as the ideology of neo-corporatist agreements in the period after 1945.

The theory of economic growth used by economists is almost always Keynesian, developed after Harrod (1939), and it omits the question of availability of natural resources. If there is a lack of effective demand which does not allow full use of the installed productive capacity and of the available work force, the complementary outlay, from a short-term point of view, can come equally from extra consumption by wage earners, or from expenditure on investment or income from exports. The ideology which says that wage increases must be slowed down in order to increase investment is not short-term Keynesianism. Considering, however, the variations in installed productive capacity and in the active population, an outlay on investment, which animates demand in the short term, makes it possible, in the long term, to increase supply, if the investment is 'productive' (and is not digging holes and filling them in).

A growing economy allows a consensus, without inequality between classes disappearing. When an economic crisis comes truly from the supply side (for example, should market prices reflect the fact that available energy becomes increasingly expensive energetically, as seen in chapter 2), then illusions of continuous growth can lead to inflation. As Soddy wrote, we have confused the expansion of productive capacity with the expansion of debt (of financial capital). In the end, inflation does not act as a social lubricant, rather it introduces great uncertainty into plans for investment (since the monetary rates of interest that firms and governments have contracted may turn out to be extremely high if inflation subsequently falls).

So, neo-corporatist policies often have the halting of inflation as an overt aim. The theoretical basis is the 'Phillips' curve', interpreted as an inverse relation betwen inflation and unemployment. When, in the 1970s, inflation and unemployment started to increase simultaneously, this was interpreted as a displacement of Phillips' curve caused by the inclusion of expected rates of inflation in wage negotiations. It might seem that the phenomena described by Phillips' curve lend themselves more easily to a collectivist than to an individualist analysis. For example, the Phillips' curve can easily be translated into Marxian-Kaleckian terminology: the absence of an 'industrial reserve army' (in the 1960s) made it easy for the trade unions to bring pressure to bear on profits, pressure which, given oligopolistic market structures, can be transferred to prices. This analysis could easily adopt the language of Durkheim if the political conclusion drawn from it was the controlling of wages by means of corporative agreements between the social agents. From both politically opposed points of view, Marxian-Kaleckian and Durkheimian, the units of analysis are social collectives.

From the point of view of methodological individualism, on the other hand, it has been said that half-baked explanations of large-scale social phenomena (such as inflation) could be made in terms of other large-scale social phenomena (such as full employment), but a fundamental explanation requires resorting to propositions on the beliefs, dispositions, and relations of individuals (Watkins, 1959; Lukes, 1973).

For example, why do real wages not fall in spite of unemployment? There are possibly two different explanations. The first would be that the trade unions enforce the maintenance of wages which are not 'equilibrium' wages, or that the social norms of the working class puts 'undercutting' on a level with being a strike-breaking 'scab'. A second explanation would be found in looking for individualistic motives and analysing the behaviour of firms and workers; the literature on 'implicit contracts ' explains that companies often employ their workers and pay them higher wages than apparently needed because, if they hired others, the companies would incur search and training expenses. The micro-economic foundations of macro-economic phenomena have become fashionable. It is as if (Lukes' comparison), in order to explain the functioning of the army, methodological individualism were to study the soldiers' preferences – or that of the typical soldier with his curious predisposition to obey orders. Substituting 'industrial reserve army' for 'army', would help to make the obvious point that Marx was no methodological individualist (he believed in the explanatory power of class struggle). The 'methodological collectivist' would resort to the social norms and sanctions of the collective of workers or the collective of capitalists, to the monopolistic power in the products markets, and to concepts such as class consciousness and class struggle.[8]

It might be thought that no prior methodological discussion is needed if macro-economics is taken to be research on purely econometric laws. For example, whether the basic units of analysis are individuals or collectives seems a superfluous question if Kuznets' studies (1966) are considered, in which he correlated increases of GNP and the share of Net Investment for different countries and periods. Another example would be the extrapolation of the supposed Kondratiev cycles. The Phillips curve also started its career as pure econometrics. Nevertheless, in order to establish the magnitudes of National Income Accounting, it is necessary to add inputs and outputs; therefore they have to be given values. Thus, macro-economics can in no way dispense with micro-economics, not so much

---

[8] Cf. Sawyer, 1982, for a Kaleckian view of political economy.

in the sense of needing to explain the micro-economic foundations of the actions of economic agents – since such actions may be better explained if the agents are taken to be members of social collectives – but in the sense that macro-economics needs prices in order to aggregate macro-economic quantities, and prices appear to come from micro-economics.

There are simple economies, studied by anthropologists, whose national accounts can be expressed in physical units. For example, Salisbury (1962) calculated the total product and the respective parts of consumption and saving and investment in days of work in two different situations (with steel axes and without) in the New Guinea village which he studied. In the famous study by Rappaport (1967), total product was calculated in calories, inputs calculated in calories, and then the uses made of the total product (for subsistence, religious-ritual activities, etc.) studied. In this way the economy of the Tsembaga-Maring was explained. In a simple Ricardian economy, with a sole product, 'corn', which is also used as seed, the total product, the consumption, the investment (in the form of seed), the wages, the profits of the capitalist tenant farmers, and the rents of the landlords, could all be given in units of corn. It could be supposed that, from one year to another, consumption fell and investment rose (say, a larger part of the harvest was used as seed); the increase in the total product could be determined, and the rate of return on the investment (a sort of interest rate) calculated. The rate of return on the investment would presumably have compensated for the sacrifice of consumption in the present in exchange for increase in consumption at a later time, without use being made, in this case, of any exhaustible resource (assuming no loss of soil fertility).

However, there can be no macro-economics in monetary economies without chrematistic micro-economics, because the national accounts are calculated with prices. These prices are simply those of the market, or (in the case of exhaustible resources and industrial waste) may be prices which have been corrected to take into account the subjective ethical opportunity costs of present utilization which sacrifices future utilization.

Externalities

In this context, it is wrong to say that the ownership of a washing machine will not deprive anyone else of ownership of one; in contrast (to such alleged 'mass-consumer' goods), to the ownership of a cottage by the sea, which obstructs views of and access to the sea for other people.[9] The

[9] Barry and Hardin (eds), 1982, p. 157, commenting on Fred Hirsch's *Social Limits to Growth*.

external diseconomies created by cottages mean that their social value would be somewhat less than the sum of individual valuations expressed by their buyers' willingness to pay their prices in the market. It appears that washing machines produce no external diseconomies. But this is doubtful, if it is remembered that a washing machine uses some 300 kilowatt-hours per household/year (cf. Ramage, 1982, p. 52), which will have cost some 750,000 kilocalories at the power station. Washing machines are also 'positional goods'. To the unintended negative social consequences on the present generation of the use of some private goods, should also be added the ambiguity in the valuation (private or 'social') of the 'production' (or is it destruction?) of exhaustible resources.

The question of the valuation of synchronic externalities is methodologically different from the question of giving present values to future effects. In the first case, the market fails in valuing some costs and benefits; for instance, the present increase in traffic congestion and in atmospheric pollution attributable to the extra car, is a negative social effect which is not reflected in the price of the car. This is no reason for excessive alarm, since the art of cost-benefit analysis consists of inventing plausible extra-market valuations by using the criterion of 'willingness to pay'. The economist believes himself to be very much at home in such extra-market transactions, because his knowledge of the rules of rational choice is applied. He might point out that Arrow's general impossibility theorem states the conditions which will make impossible coherent choices through voting systems (against 'invisible hand' harmonies, but very much rooted in individualism).

If the diachronic dimension is considered, however, the present measurement of future effects, whether of the kind which nowadays usually go through a market (such as demand for barrels of oil) or of the type which the market does not capture, cannot be based on the interaction and aggregation of individual preferences, whether expressed in money, in extra-market willingness-to-pay or in some sort of voting or opinion poll system. Examples of external diseconomies (or economies) for future generations are the effects on the climate (whether good or bad) due to the increase in carbon dioxide, the effects of radioactive waste on human wealth, the impact on forests of the increase of sulphur dioxide. In all such cases, now *we* have to give values to the preferences of *other* unborn individuals.

At a time when the spread of nuclear energy sources continues, perhaps the emphasis on exhaustible energy resources in the present book is misplaced, because the main ecological problems might seem those of pollution rather than of depletion. However, it can be argued (as Soddy did) that nuclear energy is spreading before its technology has been made safe (a doubt remaining on whether it will ever be safe) precisely because of the desperate search for new energy sources, leaving aside for the sake of argument its military 'external economies'. Moreover, granting Singh's point (1976), that pollution does not spare the very generation which produces it, while resource depletion creates a problem largely for posterity, this does not mean that some forms of pollution have no future effects. One can assume the existence of Coasian markets (or some surrogate institution) which would value current external effects, but such markets would necessarily exclude the participation of non-born economic agents. In both cases (depletion and pollution), the higher the discount rate, the higher the rate of exaction of exhaustible resources will be, and the higher will be also the rate of insertion of pollutants into the environment. Therefore, there is a symmetry between the economic treatment of depletion and pollution.[10]

Conclusions

Let us summarize the conclusions reached in this long chapter. The orthodox economists' familiar initial gambit ('let us assume that two or more economic agents come into contact, each of them with an initial bundle of resources and a set of preferences') does not work, because unborn economic agents cannot come to today's market for exhaustible resources. Consideration of exhaustible resources is harmful to individualistic economic neo-liberalism because the question of economic efficiency in the allocation of resources cannot be separated analytically from the question of equity in the distribution of purchasing power.

Consideration of exhaustible resources also raises, therefore, basic doubts concerning the definitions of macro-economic quantities, and it damages the Keynesian ideology of macro-economic-oriented neo-corporatist consensus, in questioning something as fundamental as the definition of economic growth, and the way of constructing national accounts.

A discussion of neo-liberalism and Keynesian neo-corporatism inside capitalist countries, and of their possible undermining by the ecological critique, leaves aside, however, the most important question of international inequality (which will be discussed in chapter 15). Here, the ecological critique is able to create havoc, since the question of equal or

---

[10] Charles Perrings, *Economy and Environment*, Cambridge University Press, 1987.

unequal exchange is given a new twist, by asking the question of whether the market, by itself, is able to produce a path of depletion of exhaustible resources, and by asking the related question of the meaning of the disparity between productivity in energy terms and in chrematistic terms. In the next chapter, Max Weber's views precisely on this last question will be considered.

12

Max Weber's Chrematistic Critique of Wilhelm Ostwald

One of the few natural scientists who wrote on social energetics and had some impact on one of the social sciences (cultural anthropology), was Wilhelm Ostwald (1853–1932), a chemist and a great academic entrepreneur, famous for his editorship of a series of classic texts on physics and chemistry, and who was based in Leipzig for most of his active life. He was awarded a Nobel Prize for his studies on catalysis. He was active in the *Monistenbund* founded by Haeckel, over which he presided for a period. His anticlerical tendency even led him to participate in political meetings with Wilhelm Liebknecht, although he supported the war of 1914. An extreme 'monist' reductionist, he went so far as to believe that 'mental' or 'psychic' energy could be measured in physical units.

He developed the view that human history was linked to the growth in the availability of energy and the improvement in the efficiency with which it could be transformed. He wrote books along these lines, one of which was *Energetic Foundations of the Science of Culture* (1909) which foreshadowed modern evolutionist ecological anthropology, as Leslie White came to realize. Ostwald's views on economic history were not dissimilar to those propounded almost simultaneously by Soddy, who was twenty-five years younger, and which had also been propounded by Podolinsky, Sacher and Geddes in the 1880s, and by Pfaundler (with whom Ostwald was in contact) in 1902. Ostwald quoted none of them.

Ostwald's views on economic history, based on an energeticist critique of economic theory, were not strictly dependent on his 'energeticist' viewpoint in physics and chemistry, which denied the relevance of atomism before its experimental stage and for some years after the discovery of radioactivity by physical chemists. As mentioned earlier, Boltzmann's speech of 1886 linking up natural selection theory and availability of energy influenced not only Pfaundler but also Lotka, and therefore today's mainstream biophysics and ecological energetics. Nevertheless, despite such common ground, Ostwald and Boltzmann fought each other on the issue of atomism at Lübeck in 1895 as, respectively, a bull and a bullfighter, according to a contemporary. In any case, here Ostwald's energeticism in human history will be discussed, not his energeticism in the natural sciences, in the sense in which the word was used at the time, to deny any interest before the discovery of radioactivity to the study of the structure of matter. One thing has nothing to do with the other, as Soddy's work on human energetics patently demonstrates.

Ostwald had a talent for advertising his wares and coined a slogan which he described as an *energetische Imperativ* to be used not only as a moral guide but also as a principle of interpretation of the course of human history: *Vergeude keine Energie, verwerte Sie*! In it may be seen one step in the path from Boltzmann to Lotka and Prigogine linking up natural selection and use of energy. When applied not to different species but to humankind, it links energetics and social-Darwinism. Ostwald himself did not carry out any empirical analysis on how specific human groups and societies 'adapt' to the available flow of energy and how they modify it.

Max Weber (1864–1920), who wrote a review of Ostwald's *Energetic foundations of the science of culture* and published it in 1909 with the title *Energetische Kulturtheorien*, rightly criticized Ostwald for his failure to provide definite data, but he did not quote any of the writers (from Podolinsky to Pfaundler, apart from others who might have been missed in our research) who had worked empirically on the energetics of human societies. Max Weber explained Ostwald's main theses and defended the separation between the sciences, making fun of Ostwald's failed *salto mortale* from physics into economics. Weber reserved his fiercest irony for Solvay, the industrialist who had also written on energy and society, and he did not dwell excessively on Ostwald's nonsense about 'mental' energy, or on such 'monistic' flights of fancy as Ostwald's proposal for a universal language in order to save the energy spent on translations.[1] Ostwald dedicated his book to Solvay, to whom he had already given absurdly high praise in *Die Energie* (1908). Perhaps material incentives were involved. Between 1908 and 1913, Ostwald, who wanted to create a school of social energetics, devoted the last chapter of *Die Energie* and then three books (including the one reviewed by Max Weber), to the subject. I have not researched its reception in other countries, but *Die Energie* was already into its third edition in French (Alcan, Paris), in 1911, and it was also translated into Spanish. *Energetic Foundations of the Science of Culture*, which Ostwald had considered calling 'Energetic foundations of Sociology', was also translated into French.

---

[1] For a sycophantic account of Solvay's utterances, cf. Barnich (1919).

The development of culture, wrote Ostwald, depended on the availability of energy and upon the efficiency of its transformations. One of Max Weber's first points was that Ostwald forgot about the availability of materials; thus, Weber anticipated Georgescu-Roegen's strictures against the 'energetic dogma'. Ostwald began from the fact that almost everything that happened on earth took place because of energy radiated by the sun. Therefore, a permanent, viable economy ought to be based exclusively on solar radiation. Ostwald had written, however, that the rapid expenditure of solar energy, converted and stocked as chemical energy in coal, was of little importance. How could such squandering of an inheritance be of little importance? – asked Weber. The answer, according to Ostwald, was that the efficiency of the transformation of solar radiation was capable of enormous improvement, not so much because of an increase in the photosynthetic yield of plants, but because of the direct industrial application of solar energy through photovoltaic conversion. Perhaps Ostwald's view was correct, but why did he not analyse the reserves of iron, copper, and zinc which were so important for the transmission of electricity? Since Ostwald foresaw that future energy supplies would adopt the form of solar energy converted into chemical and electrical energy, it would have been useful to consider to what extent aluminium, the supply of which, Weber wrote, was practically inexhaustible, and the cost of which was falling rapidly and consistently, could replace copper and zinc. To summarize: although the flow of solar energy would not decrease in the relevant future, there was a need to consider the availability of materials, some of which were required for the transmission of energy itself. The law of entropy, wrote Weber, that is, of dissipation through use, applied to materials as much as to energy.

Moreover, if the prospects for the industrial use of solar energy, which up to then had only been used by live or fossil plants, were as good as Ostwald preached, why should there be any worry about the efficiency of the transformation of energy? Was thermodynamic efficiency not increasingly irrelevant, taking into account the fact that 'our' birth rates were falling? Weber's parochial slip may be interpreted as a complaint that Ostwald had not included a study of demography in his dynamics of human history.

Ostwald defined cultural progress as increase in the availability of energy and the substitution of human energy by alternative forms. He had also defined cultural progress in terms of increasing thermodynamic efficiency in energy use. About the first Ostwaldian criterion for cultural progress, that is, the increase in the availability of energy and the relative decrease in the use of human energy, Weber had little to say beyond a recommendation to bear in mind Sombart's arguments in his discussion of Reuleaux's concept of 'machine'.[2] Weber also remarked that a comparison between classical antiquity and the contemporary age would certainly show that there had been a great decrease in the relative importance of human energy and therefore that there had been 'cultural progress' if it were defined tautologically in this way. Paraphrasing Weber, it could be said that Ostwald could have saved himself some embarrassment by avoiding the use of the word 'culture', since his energetic definitions would make Austin, Texas in the second half of the twentieth century a more 'cultured' city that Florence in the Renaissance.

Weber's critique of the energetic definition of 'culture' can only be agreed with, but it is a pity that it distracted him from addressing himself to the useful question of whether any better understanding of human history, and particularly of economic history, is gained by the study of changes in the flow of energy in human societies.

The second Ostwaldian criterion of cultural progress, that is, the improvement in the thermodynamic efficiency of energy use, was, to Weber, more absurd than the first one. Although each generation of steam engines had certainly improved efficiency, many industrial processes which do not increase, but tend to decrease thermodynamic efficiency are, nevertheless, normally described as progressive. For instance – wrote Weber – if the energy radiated by the sun and contained in coal which had been transformed into kinetic, chemical and other forms of energy, including dissipated energy, were calculated for each unit of machine-woven textile and if a similar account for hand weaving were drawn up, it would be found that energetic efficiency in hand weaving was greater than in machine weaving, that is, that the energy unit cost was lower in pre-industrial processes. In an exchange economy, however, the relation between money unit costs, which are decisive for competitiveness, do not necessarily run in parallel to the relation between energy unit costs, though of course – wrote Weber with a smile – the energy spent would always have an 'energetic' influence on money costs. For instance, if Ostwald were right in saying that a device could be introduced to convert solar radiation into electrical energy, it was clearly possible that, even if its thermodynamic efficiency were much inferior to that of a steam engine, the economic competitive edge of this form of energy would be overwhelming. In fact, the most 'primitive' tool given by nature to humankind, the human muscle, was more efficient in the use of energy freed by the biochemistry of oxidation than the best electric dynamo, and yet it was unsuccessful by

[2] Franz Reuleaux (1829–1905) was director of the Technische Hochschule in Berlin, and author of *Theoretische Kinematik* (1875). Boris Hessen summed up Sombart's critique in 'the absurd idea that the essence of the machine consists of it being served by man' (Hessen, in Bukharin, 1931, p. 197).

economic comparison. According to Weber, study of prices and costs belonged to economics, and energetics was irrelevant. One obvious example could be added to Weber's list. Excluding solar energy, the input:output energy ratio of Mexican peasant maize is more favourable than the corresponding ratio in the United States. Nevertheless, the chrematistic or pecuniary cost relations might easily be the opposite, and in a free-trade market, American maize – perhaps grown with the help of cheap Mexican oil and natural gas – certainly undersells Mexican peasant maize.

Neither Max Weber nor Ostwald considered how the prices of exhaustible resources are determined. Weaving by hand was more expensive than weaving by machine because the steam engine had been invented and because coal was cheap. Why was coal cheap? If the answer was the abundance of supply, the allocation of coal over a period of time would have to be looked at. How was future demand valued at present? Weber did not go into this question.

With the benefits of hindsight, it can be seen that despite its low efficiency, the internal combustion engine gained a competitive edge in some parts of the world at a certain time, because oil was cheap owing to abundant supply and low extraction costs. But in order to understand why the supply of oil was considered to be abundant relative to demand, it has to be assumed that there was a belief in future discoveries of deposits at a rate equal to or higher than use at that time; or that there was a belief that, if oil ran out, it would be replaced by something else; or that the demand of future generations was discounted; or that the demand of the poor sections of humankind, not backed by money, could be ignored; or a combination of such beliefs and moral values. Only the most fanatic of methodological individualists, who really believed that subjective valuations were all that mattered and that the physical characteristics of commodities did not matter at all, could argue that, because a natural resource is cheap, it must be abundant. The economics of slavery (even at its most neo-classical) has to embrace the study of demography; the economics of natural resources has to embrace the study of the depletion of such resources.

Steam engines, at the time Weber was writing, had efficiencies as low as five per cent, whilst the human body can convert food energy into work with an efficiency of the order of twenty per cent, as has been known since the 1860s. Even today, if it is taken into account that a power station will have dissipated some two-thirds of the energy of coal or oil into space, as useless heat, and if the energy cost of extraction and transportation of coal or oil and losses in the transmission of electricity are also taken into account, it might transpire that work done with an electric engine is energetically less efficient than if done by human power.

However, it is obvious that the *amount* of work done in an industrial economy nowadays could not be done with human and animal power alone. This was in fact one of Ostwald's points: that greater availability of energy and a concomitant decrease in the share of human energy were signs of cultural progress. In societies with a generalized market system, the substitution of new forms of energy for human and animal energy has been brought about because the work done with machines powered by coal, oil, etc., is cheaper. But the market price of coal or oil and the resulting allocation of resources are firmly embedded both in the interpretation of the physical reality that economic agents take from the history of science and technology; and in the social distribution of moral values concerning the demands of future generations. A greater (or lesser) weight given to future needs or a less (or more) optimistic view of technical change could have pushed the price of coal or oil up (or down), thus changing the relations between costs which Max Weber thought decisive for an explanation of economic history. Max Weber's economics, in this particular piece of writing, should be called chrematistics or catallactics, the study of transactions by individuals, from which a pattern of prices and quantities transacted emerges without it being necessary to investigate the social causes of particular valuations.

It would be absurd, however, to blame Max Weber, of all people, for assuming that agents in history behaved as the ideal type of *homo economicus*. Besides, modern economic theory admits almost any kind of behaviour in its models, including altruistic behaviour (while excluding, to preserve at least a semblance of relevance, the participation of unborn persons in today's market). Max Weber, *qua* economic historian and sociologist, did research into actual types of behaviour which were not directed towards anything like the maximization of profit and utilities. Although it could be surmised that Max Weber would have had little sympathy for such parodies of micro-economics as 'rational choice' in political science, nevertheless he did not think that economic theorists were under an obligation to abstract the behaviour of economic agents in their models from the research of social and economic historians, or from the research of psychologists. Economic *theory* meant, for Weber, what it means in any Western university today – marginalist economics. At the beginning of his career, in his inaugural lecture in Freiburg (1895), he placed himself in the German historical school and not in the 'Austrian' school. However, his typology of social actions was much influenced by marginalist economics, and later on he adopted the view that economic *theory* was a set of deductive propositions derived from postulates about human conduct and hypotheses about the world which it was not fruitful to discuss, whatever psychologists, historians and anthropologists could say about real human behaviour and whatever the physicists said about the availability of resources. One can easily understand Hayek's eulogy (1952, new edn 1979, p. 171) of Max Weber's critique of 'social energetics', since Weber was ruling the accusation against economic theory of being disconnected from social, psychological, and physical realities out of order, and Weber was also to insist on the separation between the sciences of nature and the social, interpretive sciences, a constant position throughout his career.

This is the meaning of Weber's attack on Ostwald's 'Comtism'. Weber had first remonstrated with Ostwald because Ostwald had not carried out a detailed study of the use of energy by humankind throughout history, and particularly because he had forgotten to include exhaustible material resources in the analysis. Secondly, Max Weber had complained that Ostwald was unable to explain the introduction of new forms of energy, less efficient in energy terms, *not* more efficient, as Ostwald assumed in his definition of cultural progress; Ostwald's mistake came from not considering cost relations in money terms, that is, from not charting economic history with the help of economic theory rather than his preposterous energetics. In the third place, Max Weber took Ostwald to task because of Ostwald's belief in the Comtean hierarchy of sciences, a root cause of all his mistakes.

Launching into what was clearly a favourite topic, Max Weber wrote that although Ostwald had taken the precaution of saying that he would deal with only some aspects of cultural phenomena, a welcome self-restraint compared to the search for universal formulae of other naturalist thinkers, he still had the bad luck to believe in dated Comtism. The concepts of the 'general' sciences, which occupy the lower steps of the 'pyramid' of sciences, were supposed to be valid for the less 'general' sciences, which occupy the higher steps, and therefore become 'foundations' for the less general sciences; hence the title of Ostwald's book. Although Ostwald might be sceptical he should be informed that the 'basic' or 'fundamental' concepts of the 'general' sciences played no role whatever in economic theory, which was that part of the economic disciplines which set them apart from other sciences. For instance, it was irrelevant to economics whether astronomy adopted the Copernican or the Ptolemaic system. Nor did the validity of economic theory, a set of ideal-typical, hypothetical, theoretical propositions, depend at all on the findings of the physical theory of energy. The propositions of economic theory would remain valid whether or not the law of conservation of energy continued to hold for all physical, chemical and biological knowledge, or whether, at some highly unlikely future date, an 'anti-Rubner' reversed his experiments on the expenditure of energy in animals and humans. Weber was referring to Max Rubner (1854–1932), Koch's successor in Berlin, who had studied the use of energy in animal and human nutrition in detail, publishing *Die Gesetze der Energieverbrauchs bei der Ernährung* in 1902 (cf. chapter 7, p. 108). An 'anti-Rubner' would have discovered, for instance, that the energy in the food consumed by a horse would be less than the amount of work that that horse could do.

Weber went on to point out that the laws of energetics showed that there were scarcities; the implication being that economics, which studied the allocation of *scarce* resources through the price system, remained valid. Even under the absurd hypothesis of an 'anti-Rubner' showing, for example that the human body could use the energy from the same piece of bread time and time again, there would still be other scarce materials. Even given the existence of a *perpetuum mobile* – wrote Weber – that is, a source of energy from which free energy would flow at a given rate and at no energy cost – the validity of any single one of the hypothetical propositions of abstract economic theory would not be denied, and the practical value of these abstract, hypothetical propositions would only disappear, despite the colossal implications of such an energy source, if it were to provide: (a) any form of energy, (b) in any place, (c) at any time, (d) in unlimited quantity in any period, and (e) in the right direction for the desired effect. Any limitation of these conditions would give practical significance to the principle of marginal utility, that is, to a theory of value based on scarcity and subjective valuation.

Max Weber added that he had wasted some time in such nonsensical utopian constructions only because he wanted to make clear something often forgotten in discussions of method: that the Comtean hierarchy of sciences was the invention of an 'enormous pedant' who did not understand that each science dealt independently with an 'object of knowledge', using a set of hypothetical-theoretical propositions whose validity did not depend on the findings of any other science. Each science theorized knowledge obtained from experience of quite different and self-sufficient points of view. Of course, as soon as the territory of 'pure' theory was abandoned, the different disciplines overlapped as happened with the economic disciplines themselves.

By considering examples of unlimited supplies of energy, Weber had begged one question implicitly raised by Ostwald; what, if any, significance has the divergence in valuation in terms of energy costs and pecuniary costs? The Weberian examples of an 'anti-Rubner' and of the *perpetuum mobile* were meant to show that energetics would destroy economics only if the findings of physics denied the notion of scarcity. Even if energy were unlimited, what about materials? – had asked Weber, knowing full well that energy was limited. But the thrust of ecological economics from its very beginning, was *not* to deny scarcity – perhaps rather the contrary, despite Ostwald's optimism about the industrial use of solar energy. Therefore, Weber's examples do not address themselves to the ecological critique of economic theory, that the price system reflects scarcity of resources in a way in which a certain weight is given to the demands of future generations and in which particular expectations of technical change are relied on; the critique being, why that particular weight and not another? why those particular expectations?

If economics is to be of use in the study of economic history (in a way similar to the pure theory of biology being of use in study of the history of plants and animal species, and physics in the study of the history of the universe), then economics, defined as the study of the human allocation of scarce resources to present and future alternative ends, cannot be separated from either the study of the social distribution of moral values concerning the adequate path of depletion of exhaustible resources, or from the history of science and technology.

It must be admitted, however, that one of Weber's examples is puzzling. Would lack of knowledge of the motions of the planets and of the laws of gravitation influence economic theory, forcing a change in some of its propositions? In what way could a belief in a Ptolemaic cosmology alter opinions on available resources and, through this, change their allocation? On the other hand, it seems clear that a different physiology of nutrition would call for different explanations of some economic choices; for instance, it has been known for over one hundred years that at usual prices, root crops and cereals contain more energy (in kilocalories), and pulses and some cereals contain more protein per monetary unit than meat; this explains why root crops, cereals and pulses can be Giffen-goods and meat usually not; if the human body had a different physiology, such regularities would not be explained, as they are now, by physiology; perhaps an explanation in terms of the aggregate effects of mysterious subjective preferences should be made. Economists are taught to think that poor people's diets are a matter of subjective tastes, within a strict budgetary restriction. A moment of reflection would convince them (if they believe in the current findings of nutritional science) that poor people cannot choose a diet based on vegetables, fruits and meat, because they would not be able to buy amounts sufficient to supply minimum nutritional require-ments. They could choose such a diet only if nutritional requirements (or the calorific and protein values of different types of foods) were different. The study of agricultural economics, that is, study of the principles of human allocation of land, labour, etc., to different crops – cannot be separated from a study of current beliefs and findings on the physiology of nutrition, which also explains a good part of agricultural economic history.

In contrast to Max Weber's view on the separation of the sciences, and on the self-sufficiency of economics in order to explain the allocation of resources, Otto Neurath's views could be put forward; they are not Comtean and they are not reductionist. Neurath (1882–1945) is a familar name to philosophers, because of his role in the Vienna Circle. Of interest in connection with the present discussion, are his ideas on a 'cosmic history and unified science', of a 'history of the future' and a 'scientific utopianism', and his proposals, in economics, influenced by Popper-Lynkeus and Ballod-Atlanticus, of a *Naturalrechnung*. These three writers (Neurath, Popper-Lynkeus, Ballod-Atlanticus) are the main protagonists of the remaining chapters.

13

Ecological Utopianism: Popper-Lynkeus and Ballod-Atlanticus

Popper-Lynkeus

Josef Popper (1838–1921), a physicist and engineer, was born in Kolin, Bohemia; he lived in the Jewish ghetto until he was fifteen years old, and then became a student in Prague and Vienna. Since he was never appointed to a university post, he tried to make a living by selling his innovative improvements to the steam engine. As mentioned in chapter 5, he wrote a paper on the transmission of electricity in 1862, which he deposited with the Viennese Academy of Sciences, where it remained unpublished until 1884. He also wrote prolifically about the physical principles of aerial navigation. A friend of Ernst Mach, he had a considerable influence on the Vienna Circle. He was strongly humanistic and anti-religious, and often wrote on Voltaire. He adopted the pseudonym Lynkeus for his literary writings, some of which were considered pornographic, and which were appreciated by Freud, though Popper-Lynkeus showed no reciprocal appreciation of psychoanalysis.

Popper-Lynkeus, as a moral philosopher, developed an argument in favour of non-religious conscientious objection to military service. In a manner reminiscent of Hare's 'universalization principle', he gave maximum value in his moral theory to human life, and his characteristic *ad hominem* reproach against Herbert Spencer (1820–1903), was that it was unlikely that Spencer would propose the elimination of the weakest in the 'struggle for life' if Spencer himself belonged to the category of the weak and eliminable.

Popper-Lynkeus' ecologism, which proposed both the study of the economy in terms of the flow of energy and materials, and moderation in the use of exhaustible resources, was left-wing. He argued against the use of organic metaphors for the analysis of human society, and inveighed against Haeckel's social-Darwinism (Popper-Lynkeus, 1912, pp. 75–88) on the grounds that human social conflicts could not be analysed in terms of natural selection. When he advocated birth control, he took the trouble to point out that this had nothing to do with eugenesic proposals, and poured scorn on 'race improvement' (1912, p. 774). He wrote against anti-semitism. Popper-Lynkeus would have been opposed to the link between energetics and evolutionary theory as applied to different sections of the human species; he would have opposed the fundamental tenet of functionalist ecological anthropology, that one can understand human societies in isolation by studying how they 'adapt' themselves to, or modify, the natural environment in which they live, as if they were biological organisms.

In 1912, Popper-Lynkeus published a long book with the title *Die allgemeine Nährpflicht als Lösung der sozialen Frage*, developing ideas he had first presented in 1878 in one of the chapters of *Das Recht zu leben und die Pflicht zu sterben* (Popper-Lynkeus, 1878). A translation of the title and sub-title would be: 'On the general duty of nutrition as a solution to the social question, statistically researched, with a demonstration of the lack of theoretical and practical validity of economic theory'. *Die allgemeine Nährpflicht* gave a most detailed accounted of the resources available to the German economy just before the First World War with a double objective. The first was to calculate the human work requirement which would guarantee the whole population a subsistence minimum of food, clothing, housing and health services; this would be achieved by means of a *Nährpflicht* (instead of a *Wehrpflicht*), that is, by means of civil rather than military conscription. The second was to discover how the use of exhaustible resources could be gradually reduced, so that the economic system would be permanently viable, also taking into account that the population should not increase – clearly an anti-patriotic viewpoint in 1912.

The economy would thus be divided into two sectors. The basic-needs sector would provide the subsistence minimum, free of charge, to everybody, using the labour force of men and women. Popper-Lynkeus pointed out that such an extra-mercantile method of fulfilling basic needs would increase womens' freedom, provided that the distribution of basic goods was to adult individuals rather than to families. The necessary period of conscription was carefully calculated; here Popper-Lynkeus took issue with figures supplied by other writers who (in some cases) were both less utopian and less scientific: Hertzka, Bellamy, Anton Menger, and Bebel. There would be twelve years' service for men and seven for women, with a thirty-five hour week. This work would be organized by regional or state authorities. Therefore, Josef Popper-Lynkeus was not an anarchist, though some of his other views come near to anarchism. Thus, in *Das Recht zu leben*

(1878), he wrote that each soldier should decide by himself whether or not to take part in a war, not the government, nor parliament, nor a referendum, because only each individual should decide about his or her own health or life.

Since there would be resources and labour left over from those destined for the subsistence sector, the economy would have a second sector which would function according to market principles, though limits could be set to the amount of labour force that each single capitalist would be allowed to hire.

Karl Popper chose to classify Popper-Lynkeus' proposals as 'piecemeal social engineering', comparable to the introduction of a health service and subsidized housing, rather than 'utopian social engineering' (Popper, 1945, vol. I, p. 143), but it is doubtful whether the abolition of the vital need to sell labour and the proposal to diminish the use of exhaustible resources, to say nothing of the strongly egalitarian flavour of these proposals, can really be relegated to the category of 'piecemeal social engineering'. Neurath thought they were scientific utopianism, which is certainly what they would seem nowadays to the majority of mankind, who are far from attaining the subsistence minimum in terms of food, clothing, housing and health services which Popper-Lynkeus took as a perfectly achievable standard for Germany in 1912.

People who live in North Atlantic countries might remark that some of Popper-Lynkeus' more attractive proposals have already been put into practice in the shape of the 'Welfare State' without interfering with the freedom of the markets, including the market for the labour force. But Welfare States consist of a small proportion of humankind, and their prosperity in part has come from the use of exhaustible resources and possibly from the poverty of other peoples.

With the benefit of hindsight, the social acceptance – even by a majority of social democrats – of military conscription and the enormous, senseless slaughter of 1914–18 may seem far more strange and counter to human nature than the 'labour army' proposed by Popper-Lynkeus. In 1919, Neurath sent a telegram to him from Munich, with the joy and devotion of a disciple, announcing that the revolutionary council was going to implement his programme. If the will (and political strength) to do so had existed, one of the root causes of support for Nazism fifteen years later – the effect of unemployment on the standard of living – would have been removed.

Popper-Lynkeus himself (in his autobiography) explained the origins, intention and reception of his proposals. He had long been worried by the effects of so-called 'technical progress', and in 1888 he had published a long article on 'The aesthetic and cultural significance of technical progress', following a train of thought which had started at the world exhibition of 1883 in Vienna. Of course, judgements on artistic works were only expressions of subjective trends in taste; they did not contain any truth-value and could not be forced upon anyone. Perhaps the aesthetic thrill aroused nowadays by the laying down of the transatlantic cable, or by the solution to the flying problem, was quite analogous to that of the Athenians at the unveiling of a statue of Phidias or at the completion of a new public building. Nevertheless, his scepticism with respect to 'technical progress', which was very much in contrast to the mood of the times, had induced him to write some pages in *Das Recht zu leben und die Pflicht zu sterben* (1878) which dealt with the harmful effects of machinery and analysed the appetite for more and more technical progress. He had proposed that technical progress should be made harmless by appropriate socio-political institutions or, more correctly, by socialist institutions (1924, p. 62). This would be achieved by the separation of a so-called free private economy, that is, an economy with circulation of money and free competition, from an economy for existence, based on reciprocal obligations. This idea, which he later developed in *Die allgemeine Nährpflicht* and statistically had shown to be viable, depended on the introduction of 'conscription for food production' (*Nährpflicht*), by which all that was needed for a healthy and comfortable life would be produced and distributed to all citizens without exception, from birth to death, not in the form of money but *in natura*. All the rest, on top of such minimum needs, would belong to the private monetary economy, in which anyone could take part or not, as he or she wished, after having fulfilled service in the 'food production army' (*Nährarmee*).

Popper-Lynkeus complained that his proposals had been received by predictable reactions. The journal *Zukunft*, belonging to the German Marxists, had dismissed them as being only 'half-socialist', because they guaranteed only a minimum and not all necessities (1924, p. 81), while others (including the Austrian social democrats) had tried to annul and degrade the proposals by using the little words 'Utopia' or 'New Utopia', therefore avoiding the need for factual objections to their applicability (1924, p. 92). In the years after 1912, there was a small group of people in Austria and Germany who formed an *allgemeine Nährpflicht* society, dedicated to spread his scheme.

While some Austrian writers in the general field of economics, such as Otto Neurath (1882–1945), participated in the minor local cult of Popper-Lynkeus, others do not even mention him, in contexts where they might have done so. Thus Schumpeter, an almost exact contemporary of Neurath, did not include Popper-Lynkeus in his history of economic analysis (Schumpeter, 1954). Schumpeter's exclusion of Popper-Lynkeus, though it may have been provisional, since his history of economics was published posthumously, is perhaps indicative of the view that economics does not include the computation in physical terms of available resources and of their employment for the satisfaction of human needs over a period of time. Hayek, on the other hand, did not include him in his little list of 'neo-Saint-Simonian social engineers' (1952), although he included Neurath, who had arrived at his views through Popper-Lynkeus and Ballod-Atlanticus.

An examination of Popper-Lynkeus' proposals shows some similarities with economic planning in the Soviet Union from the late 1920s onwards; innumerable 'material balances' were in fact established by Popper-Lynkeus in his book (1912). But his emphasis on basic needs and especially his proposal not to increase so-called 'capital accumulation' and 'economic growth', but rather to diminish the use of exhaustible resources so that the economy would be permanently viable, are quite different from Soviet concepts of economic planning. Popper-Lynkeus' ecologism is most in evidence in the last one hundred pages of his book (in the 1912 edition) entitled 'The Future of the State of the Future'. The expression *Der Zukunftsstaat* was taken from Bebel and from Ballod-Atlanticus' book (first published in 1898), and Josef Popper-Lynkeus and Ballod-Atlanticus discussed each other's figures. In these hundred pages Josef Popper-Lynkeus explained the supply of solar energy to earth, with uncharitable comments towards those who wanted to turn the second law into metaphysics.[1] He put forward the hypothesis that solar energy had a radioactive source. He then calculated carefully the extent to which water power, wind power, etc. could replace coal. He carried out similar calculations for different metals and for fertilizers (calculating nitrogen in kilowatts). His conclusions tended to be on the 'pessimistic' side; he thought it would be very difficult to lessen coal consumption and maintain the standard of living; hence his emphasis on birth control.

When discussing the possibility of substituting renewable energy for coal energy, Popper-Lynkeus carried out a detailed analysis (1912, pp. 729–30) of the energy costs and value of *Kartoffel Spiritus*, alcohol from potatoes, giving estimates of the (very large) area which would be required to substitute *Kartoffel Spiritus* for coal for domestic heating. He criticized Kropotkin (whom otherwise he greatly admired) because he had claimed

[1]In 1876 Popper-Lynkeus had published a long review of the second edition of J. R. Mayer's *Mechanik der Wärme*. This review became famous as a text in the philosophy of science which anticipated the work of Mach and the Vienna Circle. Some paragraphs of this review had not been printed in 1876 (*Das Ausland*, 35) and Popper-Lynkeus restored them in his autobiography. One of these paragraphs very strongly attacked William Thomson's 'theological handling of Carnot's law'.

that enormous potato crops could be obtained by greenhouse farming. Josef Popper-Lynkeus pointed out that greenhouse farming in Northern Europe made use of such an amount of heat energy from coal, that its energy balance compared unfavourably with that of open-air agriculture. He made his own calculation in order to show where Kropotkin's mistake lay.

Writing on the 'Malthusian problem' (which he thought was misnamed, since Malthus had not made a proper study of the rules of human demography), Popper-Lynkeus (1912, pp. 754–5) entered the polemics on the carrying capacity of the earth. He quoted Franz Oppenheimer's studies published in 1901 where an estimate of 200,000 million persons was given as the upper limit, on the basis of the productivity achieved in greenhouse farming. Once again, Popper-Lynkeus emphasized (quoting Ballod-Atlanticus as support) that one could not extrapolate the results of greenhouse farming to the world at large, because of the required energy input from coal. This anticipates by some sixty years Gerald Foley's critique of Colin Clark's estimates on land use and population growth (Foley, 1981), based on the fact that Colin Clark had forgotten to consider the flow of energy into agriculture.

Popper-Lynkeus also suggested that the price system did not provide a good criterion for deciding whether alcohol from potatoes should be produced in large amounts. He pointed out that if alcohol from potatoes was used for heating, transport, etc., this would have the beneficial side-effect that no alcohol would remain for drink, but, on the other hand, it was possible that no potatoes would remain available as food. Controversies over the use of biomass for food energy or for fuel energy have a long history.

Nevertheless, even Popper-Lynkeus was capable, on occasion, of adopting a parochial outlook. He proposed (1912, p. 735–6) the eurocratic idea of importing peanut-oil from the German colonies in Africa and, somewhat surprisingly, from Spain, in order to burn it in diesel engines, since Rudolf Diesel had just announced (in 1912) that his engines could work on vegetable oils – an idea 'rediscovered' a few years ago, although sunflower oil seems to be preferred nowadays. Popper-Lynkeus, however, stated that this proposal was conditional on obtaining more information on yields and energy costs in peanut farming. Ecologists usually trace the first careful estimate of photosynthetic yield in agriculture, and not in laboratory conditions, that is, in maize growing in Illinois to Transeau (1926, in Kormondy, 1965). The following comment is of interest:

> The worry of Transeau's day was not only food but fuel also. Fossil fuels on which modern civilizations are based obviously would not last forever, and the exhaustion of the world then seemed more imminent than it does now because the total reserves were much underestimated. There was then no promise of atomic power to supply the needs of the future, and the only resource seemed to be to

grow fuel; to use the energy stored by contemporary plants rather than by those long dead. It became important to know how efficiently crops fixed solar energy in order to calculate the possibilities of producing fuel for power stations and motor cars by agriculture. (Colinvaux, 1973, p. 152–3)

One question is raised again, after reading Popper-Lynkeus' work: why did modern agricultural energetics not develop as a sub-discipline of agricultural science and of agricultural economics much earlier than it did?

Finally, although Popper-Lynkeus' proposals were directed to a German and Austrian readership, and his statistics did not refer to the world in general, and although, in fact, as has just been seen, he occasionally took an ethnocentric view, it must also be said that his proposals (in contrast to many other utopian writings of this period), were characterized not only by the thoroughness of the statistical work and by the ecological-conservationist aspect, but because they were addressed, if not to the whole world, at least to a considerable section of it. Popper-Lynkeus' utopia was not based on the migration of a small group of people from Europe to America or to Africa, as in the doctrines of the followers of Cabet's *Icaria* or in Hertzka's *Freiland* – where Kenya was the end of the journey for a small group of Europeans, without the residents having been consulted. Popper-Lynkeus' achievable utopia did not indulge in the literary fiction of abolishing scarcity and it was universal in intention, though not in calculation.[2]

Ballod-Atlanticus

Karl Ballod (1864–1933), who took the pseudonym Atlanticus from Francis Bacon's *Nova Atlantis* (1627), was an economist and demographer who lived in Berlin. Early in his professional life he made studies of colonization in Brazil and of the Russian economy. He published several editions of *Der Zukunftsstaat*, the first in 1898 with a different title and with a preface by Kautsky and the fourth in 1927. Possibly through his Russian connections, this book was also published in about 1905 in Russia.

Ballod-Atlanticus was an unusual utopianist in the sense that he chose to make a realistic description of the resources at the disposal of future society. His approach is 'scientific utopianism', as distinct from the approach of the writer of novels or science fiction. Equally clear is the

[2]There must be writings on Popper-Lynkeus' role in Jewish culture which would explain his reaction, if any, to Theodor Herzl's Zionism: 'although he never took an active part in the Zionist movement he bequeathed his substantial collection of books to the National Library in Jerusalem' (*Encyclopaedia Judaica*, Keter Publishing House, Jerusalem, vol. 13, 1972).

difference between Ballod-Atlanticus' approach, and planning as practised in so-called socialist countries, where it consists of adding a few percentage points to the levels achieved in the previous planning period, because radical changes are not expected in planning either in the institutions or in the composition of production.

Ballod-Atlanticus, in the 1920s at least, was simultaneously anti-Bolshevik and anti-social democrat, though he was neither a liberal nor an anarchist. His political position could be described as a somewhat technocratic ecologism. Popper-Lynkeus had written that Marx was an inspiration for him, more because of his egalitarianism than because of his capacity for historical prognosis; a socialist programme had to start from an ethical premise and ethical systems could not be derived from the march of history (Popper-Lynkeus, 1912, p. 322). Ballod-Atlanticus found the origin of his ideas in Marx, but Marx had not supplied a blueprint for the day after the revolution; he had thought out everything, but only until the critical day (Ballod-Atlanticus, 1927, p. 7). This was also a starting point for Otto Neurath's thoughts on the economy.

One difference between Popper-Lynkeus and Ballod-Atlanticus was that Ballod-Atlanticus only occasionally calculated costs in energy terms, supplementing his careful accounting in terms of materials. Another difference from Popper-Lynkeus, was that Ballod-Atlanticus was more 'technocratic', as his choice of pseudonym shows, since Francis Bacon had proposed a society ruled by the possessors of knowledge. Ballod-Atlanticus also gave Plato's *Republic* as an example. In this context 'technocrat' does not mean what it might mean in eastern Europe today, opposed to 'bureaucrat', where the 'technocrats' are the economists and engineers who favour a greater role for the price system than for planning in physical terms.

Ballod-Atlanticus disliked economists. In some ways he anticipated the American 'technocrats' of the 1930s. He admired Henry Ford, a capitalist who really profited from the possibilities opened up by increased productivity and market growth, and who was therefore totally opposed to cartelization and restriction of output. Ballod-Atlanticus, writing in Germany in the 1920s, was full of enthusiasm for synthetic textiles and synthetic protein, and for mechanized agriculture, combined, nevertheless, with a pattern of dispersed urbanization and a multitude of domestic gardens. He was also – and this is crucial – opposed to the private car, despite his admiration for the type of capitalist that Ford represented.

The nucleus of Ballod-Atlanticus' book is a calculation of the number of people who could be nourished with the production from a standardized farm of 500 hectares; a *Normalgut*. Such a farm was assumed to have rather unfertile soil (a realistic assumption for northern Germany), and to use mechanical traction, the reason for this being that a great deal of land would be required to feed the animals. If rotation were intensive enough, this land could be used instead for human nutrition. If tractors were used, oil from outside the farm would of course be necessary – Ballod-Atlanticus reckoned the value of this oil in energy units, but did not quite establish the global energy balance of this model farm. Assuming the use of tractors, two thousand people could be nourished from 500 hectares, though the number would naturally depend on the importance of meat in the diet.

How would this pattern of mechanized model farms fit in with the rest of the economy? Ballod-Atlanticus was opposed to industrial and urban concentration, on the grounds that it led simultaneously to the construction of large numbers of new apartment buildings in the great cities and to the deterioration of abandoned rural housing. Such workers' quarters were built so close together that it became impossible for their inhabitants to contribute to their own food supply. As a rule, cities should not have more than one hundred thousand inhabitants, thus saving most of the materials used for the high-rise buildings and for the urban infra-structure of the growing large cities. This type of consideration had arrived a little late for Berlin in the 1920s, but Ballod-Atlanticus' book would still repay close study by urban planners in Mexico, Brazil and other countries. There is nothing 'romantic' in it, only a collection of rather arid calculations, showing, for instance, the amounts of materials of different sorts which would be needed to house all Germans in towns and cities of moderate dimensions, within a framework of mechanized model farms and domestic gardens. Ballod-Atlanticus criticized Ebenezer Howard because the gardens in his 'garden cities' were too small to allow any significant contribution to food intake. He did not quote Patrick Geddes, and neither Geddes nor Lewis Mumford – whose erudition casts a wide net – quoted him, perhaps as a result of the triple censorial alliance of liberal economists, social democrats and Stalinists (and Leninists in this particular context) who relegated such writers as Ballod-Atlanticus and Josef Popper-Lynkeus, to the attic of our intellectual past even in Germany itself and among the generation of 1968.

Another drawback of industrial and urban concentration, was that the waste from the big cities was not used for fertilization of agricultural land. In the pattern of settlement which Ballod-Atlanticus proposed, each *Normalgut* would support a community nearby. In contrast, he calculated the units of nitrogen, phosphorus and potassium produced annually by *Gross Berlin* in the form of human excrement and other waste, which would have been enough to fertilize 200,000 hectares (1927, p. 170), but which in fact became a huge and costly urban disposal problem. This is a calculation which would have pleased both Liebig and Marx. Ballod-Atlanticus also calculated the needs of nitrogen, phosphorus and potassium for the whole German economy.

Ballod-Atlanticus' attack on the forms adopted by industrial urbanization had little in common, in my view, with the anti-rational, anti-technology and anti-democratic tendencies in Germany and elsewhere at the time. Ballod-Atlanticus' dung accounts may scarcely be called 'romantic nature-loving' after the fashion of the Wandervögel and the Artamanen, allegedly a German disease to which even Social-democracy was prone.

In the German-Austrian context it is important to separate Ballod-Atlanticus and Popper-Lynkeus from such romantic, conservative, religious nature-loving. It was a characteristic of the struggle for free thought in Europe in the nineteenth century (although perhaps difficult to understand in Anglo-Saxon countries) that agnosticism was not simply substituted for religion. Attempts to substitute science or pseudo-science for religion were made by Comte in France and, later, by the Monist movement (or parts of it) in Germany. Since Haeckel was prominent in this attempt, and since it was also he who introduced the word 'ecology' into scientific discourse, it is worthwhile again to emphasize his distance from writers such as Ballod-Atlanticus and Popper-Lynkeus.

Haeckel and Popper-Lynkeus were almost exact contemporaries, but this was the only trait they had in common. Haeckel was a conservative social-Darwinist, and in 1918, when he was about to die, he had time for this outburst:

> The prettiest role in the whole tragi-comedy (of the revolution in Munich) is now being played by the new founder of the 'Bavarian Republic', Herr Salomon Kuchewski, a Galician Jew, who under the pseudonym Kurt Eisner has named himself president . . . How is it possible for such a degenerate swindler to be able to tyrannize the whole Kingdom of Bavaria for four weeks? (Gasman, 1971, p. 25)

Popper-Lynkeus probably did not in the least mind Haeckel's *kulturkämpferisch* views (for instance, in his famous *The Riddles of the Universe*, 1899), such as that Christ had an Aryan father. But Popper-Lynkeus strongly opposed anti-semitism and social-Darwinism, and he was also opposed to attempts to substitute science for religion – he felt that there was a basic difference between scientific and metaphysical propositions.

Both Ballod-Atlanticus and Popper-Lynkeus clearly remained aloof from the reaction against rational scientific analysis and specialized learning, and in this they were closer to Marxism and to anarchism in the Kropotkinian tradition than to conservative, mystic 'back to nature' movements. The wish to develop 'a comprehensive new outlook which stressed the larger coherence of things and which would grasp the essential inter-related unity of all existence' (a phrase of uncertain meaning which is borrowed from Stark, 1981, p. 175, so similar to characteristic utterances of today's believers in holy and holistic 'ecologism') was a conservative view; thus, Bölsche, occupying the most mystic wing of Haeckel's Monism, was published by the right-wing publisher Diederich (while Ballod-Atlanticus was published by Dietz Verlag, in 1898), and it was Diederich who commissioned Bölsche's extremely successful *Das Liebesleben der Natur* (1898–1902). From here there was little distance to the Theosophy and Anthroposophy of Rudolf Steiner, which joined with the irrational, apocalyptic 'ecologism' in which 'back to nature' is taken to mean 'back to God and religion'.[3]

In his well-judged effort to exonerate Haeckel and other monists from any direct responsibility for Nazism despite their social-Darwinism, Kelly (1981, p. 134) pointed out that German socialists gave paradoxical support not only to Haeckel, but even to writers as reactionary as Bölsche, and therefore that these writers' views had a much wider and diffuse influence than that assumed by the partisans of an exclusive and direct Monist-Nazi intellectual connection (such as Gasman, 1971). As Kelly puts it, social-democratic support for Haeckel and Bölsche meant at least tacit party sanction for locating the origins of workers' problems in urbanization rather than in class exploitation. Several points arise here.

Overcrowding, struggling for green space, for better urban transport, and for rent rebates, are all aspects of the class struggle in an urban context as Manuel Castells and David Harvey have shown. The critique of urbanization and the critique of capitalist exploitation could be brought together in this sense, traditional in Marxism since Engels wrote on the appalling living conditions of workers in Manchester and on the housing question in general. The analysis of industrial urbanization can also be accommodated into the Marxist framework as part of a critique of the concept of 'productive forces', which in the present book has been developed from the point of view of energy flow. Social-democratic 'nature-loving' – such as it was – did not carry religious overtones with it, but it did *not* produce either such ecological critique, perfectly compatible with an appeal to reason, totally alien to the mystical brand of 'ecologism'.

When Ballod-Atlanticus considered the costs in materials and energy of alternative transport systems, he left his technocratism and his Fordism to one side. He made a case against the expansion of the motor car industry and implicitly against the motorways which were subsequently built in accordance with an economic and social ideal which, in spite of the

[3] I am grateful to Anna Bramwell (Trinity College, Oxford) for discussions on this point. She is currently writing a *Political Theory of Ecology*.

repeated use in its rhetoric of the words 'blood' and 'soil', proposed concentrated industrial urbanization and intensive use of exhaustible resources from German or foreign territories, which would, presumably, last out the thousand years of the Reich. It is a fact that the memory left by Hitler among the older German generation is much more that of *Blut und Autobahnen* than of *Blut und Boden*.

Ballod-Atlanticus explained (1927, p. 262) that there were 20 million cars, or one for every six persons, in the United States, 778,000 in Great Britain, 574,000 in France and 308,000 in Germany. Germany then imported 1.2 million tons of oil per year (which might be compared with the 100 million tons of oil and oil products imported per year in 1985 by West Germany alone), and Ballod-Atlanticus thought that the figure could possibly be doubled. Since one car consumed about 1,200 kilograms of petrol per year, plus lubricant oil, the number of cars would be able to increase very slightly, supposing a continued dependence on imported oil. Oil from coal, however, could in principle allow a considerable increase in the number of cars, perhaps up to ten million. But Ballod-Atlanticus thought that relative lack of water power in Germany made it advisable to keep coal for the production of electricity. Besides, the air pollution caused by cars, which could already be smelled, was worse than the plague, and this was a further argument in favour of public transport (Ballod-Atlanticus, 1927, p. 266).

Ballod-Atlanticus' prediction with regard to cars was spectacularly mistaken. There are now about 20 million cars in West Germany alone and, not less remarkably, there are also a few million in East Germany. However, from a world perspective, the present ratio of cars to population (1 car per 17 persons, about 300 million cars to 5,000 million inhabitants) will be difficult to increase and it has possibly decreased since 1973. Economics and geology (which describes the history of oil) might lead to contradictory conclusions about the future of the motor car. Of course, the ratio varies considerably both from one country to another and from one social class to another within some countries, not excluding the so-called socialist countries. It is doubtful whether cars will become generally available, and it might be argued that a car is a 'positional' article in Fred Hirsch's sense and not because of the diseconomies of traffic congestion but because of oil consumption; if you have one, you are *eo ipso* depriving somebody else from having one, either now or in the future. Ballod-Atlanticus would have agreed, and therefore he can hardly be classified as an all-out technocratic Fordist thinker.

He certainly did not envisage a future of poverty. His calculations include, for example, the number of workers (one hundred thousand) who would be needed for the construction of pianos for Germany's musical needs.

He had bitter words (in the 1927 edition of his book) for the socialists who had failed to take advantage of the revolutionary moment in 1918. He had sat on the Commission for Socialization and had seen at close quarters that the socialists had not even nationalized coal. They had switched to free market principles and, what was worse, they favoured cartelization in practice. This they tried to hide under the name of 'economic democracy'. Some of Marx's epigones, Berstein for instance, had taken the view that the lack of development of productive forces made the socialization of the economy impossible, and thus saved themselves the trouble of thinking how it should be organized.

Ballod-Atlanticus proposed a mixture of state, provincial and communal public enterprises (including the model farms), reserving an important position for the technicians. No egalitarian, he suggested that technicians should be paid more as an incentive to education. He was aware that his attitude of favouring technicians would be criticised. During the war, he had suffered criticism because of his recommendation that the number of pigs should be cut down so that more calories and protein would be directly available for human consumption; a recommendation which had earned him, with others, the name of *Schweineprofessoren*.[4] His discussions with Moltke on protein requirements (in which he included accurate calculations) had led to nothing because Prussian officialdom lacked understanding in such matters (1927, pp. 27–9). It was preferable to trust technicians rather than bureaucrats; or economists for that matter; the Austrian school, which had finally triumphed among the German university professors of economics, was *neo-Manchestertum* and *Scholastik*.

Ballod-Atlanticus' utopia did *not* presuppose the elimination of the premise of economics, scarcity – at the same time, he violently opposed the economist's way of dealing with scarcity, through the functions of the market or market surrogates. However, Hayek failed to include him in his list of 'neo-Saint-Simonians'. I learned of him through the writings of Neurath and Popper-Lynkeus.[5]

Among the writers studied, one difference between the German, the Austrian and the British (Geddes, Soddy) stands out. The Germans and the Austrians, because of the relevance of social revolution, in some cases (such as those of Ballod-Atlanticus and Popper-Lynkeus) drew up detailed, *global* economic plans which went beyond their ecological critique of conventional economics. 'Plans' is not quite the appropriate word, however, since there was an element of 'scientific utopianism' (which Otto Neurath found appealing)

---

[4] A play on words: the Darwinist professors had been known as *Affenprofessoren*.
[5] Cf. also the summary of the 1919 edition of Ballod-Atlanticus' book in Rolf Schwendter (1982, vol. 1, p. 228 f).

14

The History of the Future

Unified Science and Universal History

The tradition of the writers considered in this book is carried on by Georgescu-Roegen, who often remarks that the aim of economic activity is the enjoyment of life (which he translates into French as *la joie de vivre*). The formulation is deliberately vague. We can talk about the need for nitrogen, phosphorus and potassium, for water and solar energy, for carbon and oxygen, all of which are required for a plant to develop; we use the same language about people's physiological needs; but we cannot physiologically account for people's desires, which vary historically and culturally. Economics should not be reduced to human ecology. Economics, as the study of the human allocation of scarce resources to alternative ends, should be human ecology, and should *also* be the study of the cultural, social and ethical influences on production and consumption. Such ecological political economy bridges some of the gaps between the natural and the human sciences, and tends to integrate them.

At times, the question of the unification of science has been discussed as though it were a question of unification of language; for example, if explanations based on the 'vital principle', were used in biology, its language would be very different from the languages of physics and chemistry. Modern biology uses the language of physics and chemistry. This language, moreover, makes use of the languages of mathematics and logic. When Jevons and Walras established the equations that relate 'marginal utilities' and prices, they were proud of the formal analogy with the equations of mechanics. Economists make use of Lagrange's multipliers in their models, although they also make use of mathematics which are not those of mechanics. (Faber and Proops, 1985). Certain physicists and biologists discovered formal mathematical analogies between pure economic theory and mechanics (Helm, 1887, p. 72; Lotka, 1921; Winiarski, 1900), and were led to query whether economic theory dealt with the equilibrium conditions of real 'forces'.

Despite the similarity in mathematical form between parts of economics and parts of physics, the language of economics has been at most 'pseudo-physicalist' because economics has not used concepts of physics. For example, while biologists seek to study the flow of energy, economists have not been interested in doing so.

Neurath's proposals, explained in 1944, near the end of his life, tended neither towards 'physicalism' (in the sense of a 'unified language') nor reductionism, as his many disclaimers of Comtean 'pyramidism' make clear. Although each science has specific objectives and, when necessary, a different language and research techniques, his proposal was to integrate them into a 'unified science' which would include, as in an encyclopaedia, all the propositions of 'cosmic history'. 'Universal history', meaning the global history of humanity, and including the natural history of the universe and of the earth, is perhaps preferable to Neurath's dramatic turn of phrase.

Another question is that of the unification of method, that is, whether the facts considered by the social sciences can be studied scientifically in the same way as those considered by the natural sciences. Though many of the research techniques are the same (for instance, the statistical corroboration of hypotheses), the social sciences – this is my own view – use an additional research technique: that of listening, translating and understanding, which there is no need to glorify into an exclusive methodology called hermeneutics. Neurath believed in a strict unity of method, but this question can be left aside.

What did 'encyclopaedic' integration of the various sciences within one unified science mean? Neurath explained that all scientific propositions could be seen as connected (or co-ordinated, though without 'pyramidism') with one another in such a way that they appeared to be parts of a single science which dealt with the stars, the Milky Way, the earth, plants, animals, human beings, woods, natural regions, tribes, and nations; in short, the result of such an agglomeration of scientific propositions would be a very general universal history. This would not be just a collection of separate and different groups of propositions, since it could never be known beforehand when it might be useful to take propositions from other sciences into consideration when analysing certain experiences (Neurath, 1944, p. 9). Neurath gives an example: in order to study human migrations, propositions from different sciences would be used. The journeys of Genghis Khan cannot be explained in isolation by his psychological make-up, or by the social structure of his people, or by the exhaustion of pastures in Central Asia, or by meteorology, but by a mixture of propositions from psychology, sociology, and ecology which is free from contradictions. Another example of predictions being unable to be made based on knowledge of only one branch of science, is the case of the manufacture of cars (Carnap, 1938, in 1969, p. 61). A good history (of the past and the future) of the motor car would have to include the history of the internal combustion engine, with an analysis of its efficiency, compared for instance with the steam engine. It would also be necessary to include an analysis of the development of urbanization. The geological and human history of petroleum could not be omitted, neither could the proposals for replacing fossil fuels. Therefore, the social triumph of a morality which allows a choice between the production of food for people and of fuel for cars would have to be explained. An analysis of the ostentatious or symbolic value of the car would need to be added and clarification of what lies behind the phrase, so common among some social groups in certain parts of the world, that 'the car is a necessity'.

The demographic implications of the history of the motor car should also be considered. The assistance of a sociologist or historian of ethics might be needed to explain the introduction of moral values which, in spite of initial protests, brought about an eventual acceptance by society of the increase in mortality caused by the motor car among some age groups which would otherwise have a longer expectation of life. Chrematistic reductionism might lead economists to think that accident insurance premiums, or the compensation paid to victims of accidents or their heirs, may be an accurate measure of the effects of the car on 'vital statistics'; or they might wish to gauge such social costs of the motor car not incorporated into prices paid by motorists, by valuing the accident victims in terms of the 'human capital' that they represent. Some exceptionally enthusiastic economists might attempt to fit all the effects of the motor car – not only the deaths caused by accidents, but also carbon dioxide emission, etc. – into financial calculations, even though there is no market for these 'products'.

There are others who think that cost-benefit analysis is unable to value so many deaths, so much petroleum destroyed, so much agricultural land misused, so much extra carbon dioxide, in the same units. Some economists would agree that not only the evaluations, but also the selection of negative and positive externalities and even their classification as negative or positive, need the help of other sciences. Synchronic externalities are difficult enough for the chrematistic outlook. When events which affect our descendants are being dealt with, valuations cannot be made by taking even notionally, our descendants' preferences into account, because they are not yet alive and so cannot be economic agents now.

Therefore, although the simple application of economic theory does not allow the past and future of the motor car to be explained, a general history could be made of it from which would emerge, perhaps not predictions, but at least ideas which could be used to separate possible from clearly impossible futures. The findings of different sciences would have to be combined.

In unified science there would be *no* propositions other than those coming from the different sciences. It is not a question of creating a super science. Neurath's proposal, as he himself said (1944, p. 20), has no relation with the metaphysical speculation (strong words) of a *Ganzheitslehre*, or holism. The aim was to produce an encyclopaedia. Within his encyclopaedia might be found propositions from one science establishing laws and predicting events contrary to the laws and predictions of another science, and the aim would be to clarify these situations instead of simply putting up with such reputedly incompatible approaches. One homely example which comes to mind is the article on 'women, subordination of'.

If written by a socio-biologist, it might state that the root of the double standard of sexual morality was that 'human females, as good mammals who produce few, costly, and therefore, precious offspring, *are* choosy about picking mates who will contribute maximally to their offspring's fitness, whereas males, whose production of offspring is virtually unlimited, are much less picky' (Barash and van den Berghe, 1977). Another interpretation could be that women's subordination is due to the inferiority of domestic labour, hence, the advocacy of women's incorporation into so-called productive labour and the elimination of the gender division of labour as the path to women's emancipation. A third interpretation would argue that 'by attributing women's subordination to the inferiority apparently inherent in domestic labour . . . one ends up taking one of the effects of women's subordination in class society as its cause'. The true cause would be the 'naturalization' of social inequality. Liberals tend to attribute structured social inequality to physical degeneration (a belief manifest in the eugenicist movement at the beginning of the twentieth century) and hence the contradictory attitude of liberals towards the family. On the one hand, the liberal, individualist ethos preaches freedom, which should include free love and indeed free reproduction (with no attention being paid to marriage, family names, etc.). On the other hand, control of female sexuality is still needed in order to preserve, if not 'purity of blood', at least an appropriate genetic endowment for one's children and grandchildren, so that the privileges given by socio-economic inheritance be explained (away) by biological heredity, maintaining the liberal myth of 'equality of opportunity' in a context of social and economic inequality.

The socio-biologist would presumably argue that nothing short of new reproductive technologies (which would for instance reduce gestation periods to a few days, so that maternal energy and material 'investment' per son or daughter would fall drastically) will overcome the inequality in sexual moral standards which natural selection has imposed. The social anthropologist or the social historian would point out that the obstacle to be removed in order to achieve women's liberation is inherited social inequality, and that increased freedom is a sign of greater social mobility. The duty of the editors of an Encyclopaedia of Unified Science would be to edit out such inconsistencies in the interpretation of the past and in the predictions (or guides to action) for the future. The successful *practice* of women's liberation might help the editors of the Encyclopaedia. (Quotations and ideas have been taken from Stolcke, 1981.)

Another example, central to this book, and which bears repetition in this context, is that arising from agricultural energetics. Economic science has explained agrarian history and made predictions about the agrarian economy which run along these lines: when 'productivity' in agriculture increases, the low income elasticity of demand for food means that agriculture is able to transfer workers and other resources to other sectors of the economy, and this is part of the process of economic growth. But it is doubtful whether this economic law helps in understanding the past, or in predicting a feasible and desirable future, because (excluding the direct input of solar energy) the energetic efficiency of modern agriculture is inferior to that of traditional agriculture. The productivity of modern agriculture (using the word 'productivity' in the usual economic sense) must be calculated with the price of the inputs (including fossil energy) and the price of the outputs established by the markets (leaving aside government interventions which bring the prices down or up a little). The economist may say that the economic and ecological conclusions would come fairly close to one another if the energy and materials used in modern agriculture were valued not at the market price, but at an opportunity cost which 'adequately' took into account future supply and the need which future generations will have for them. This brings us back once again to a discussion of the sociology of the distribution of moral values. There are economists who will say (as Max Weber said) that energetic efficiency is of no interest when it comes to explaining economic phenomena, to which they might add that no-one can have better (and cheaper) information than that provided by the markets; they are supporters of the separation of the sciences, fundamentalist chrematistic economists.

A global programme of agrarian history which could be used to make the 'history' of possible futures would first have to explain the physical history of solar radiation and photosynthesis; it would have to incorporate the cultural and biological history of food; it would have to explain the history of 'agrarian chemistry' and the ideology of chemical fertilizers. It would be history (into which the social history of the sciences relating to agriculture and nutrition would also enter) which would co-ordinate the propositions of the different sciences, while trying to eliminate their contradictions, preventing that something which is described as an increase in 'productivity' with one set of analytical instruments, being described as an increase in 'destructivity' with another set of analytical instruments.

Which propositions of economic science are contradictory or appear doubtful from an ecological standpoint? This task is carried on today by Georgescu-Roegen, among others. Which modifications should be made to economic theory, and particularly to input-output analysis, taking into account the laws of physics, including the 'impossibility of total recycling of materials'? This does not mean the reduction of economics to physics. For example, the theory of consumption of products by human beings would need to be connected with studies not only of physiology, but also of cultural anthropology. There is no need for holistic metaphors such as 'the whole is greater than the sum of the parts', but there must be elimination and overcoming of contradictions between the propositions of different sciences in the perspective of understanding the past and the present, and of influencing the 'history of the future'. Neurath's idea was that 'the propositions which do not connect, without contradictions, with the general structure of laws, have to disappear' (1973, p. 326). It is not a question, therefore, of simply compiling an encyclopaedia of all the propositions and laws from the different sciences; there is a further step, which arises when it is required to explain history, or to predict a specific spatio-temporal process, or when it is wished to give the future a 'push' in a specific direction. The Marxist methodology for the study of human history, that is, the study of the dialectic between the changes in productive forces, the relations of production and social- and class-consciousness, in the perspective of a not very long march towards equality and freedom, inspired Neurath's idea of a 'unified science', that is to say a 'universal history'. There is therefore a strong connection between logical empiricism and Marxist historicism, which Karl Popper has done his best to sweep under the table (with great success, helped by uncomprehending 'anti-Machian' Marxists). Both Hayek and Karl Popper would condemn the attempts at an Encyclopaedia of Unified Science. Karl Popper (1963, p. 269) had some unpleasant words to offer, while Hayek let his hair down with:

The enthusiasm for physicism (it is now called physicalism) and the use of 'physical language', the attempt to 'unify science' and to make it the basis of morals, the contempts for all 'theological', that is anthropomorphic, reasoning, the desire to organize the work of others, particularly by editing a great encyclopaedia, and the wish to plan life in general on scientific lines are all present [in Saint-Simon]. One can sometimes believe that one is reading a contemporary work of an H. G. Wells, a Lewis Mumford, or an Otto Neurath. (Hayek, 1952, new edn 1979, pp. 225–6)

Neurath's *Naturalrechnung*

The Vienna Circle's original name was the Ernst Mach circle. Lenin's attack on 'Machism' in 1909 repeated by cohorts of opportunistic scribblers in the Soviet Union and elsewhere, certainly helped later to isolate left-wing logical empiricists like Otto Neurath from much of the Left. The glories of Vienna, with some suitable modifications and omissions, have been inherited in part by such anti-Marxist, anti-'historicist' philosophers as Karl Popper. A logical empiricist defence of Marxism as a theory of history (Cohen, 1978) was not written until much later. It is a poignant fact that Neurath, born in Vienna in 1882, died in Oxford in 1945, on the verge of the rise of the school of philosophy in which Ayer (not at all a conservative, and philosophically educated in Vienna) played an important role. In Oxford there was, perhaps incongruously, apart from Cole, at least one of the father-figures of the British school of Marxist historiography, Christoper Hill (who even wrote a book on Lenin). Nevertheless, it would be unfitting to think of Oxford or indeed of Britain as a place where the Vienna Circle–Marxist dialogue on 'unified science', 'universal history', 'ecological utopianism', or the 'history of the future' has been pursued. In France and in Germany the situation was even less conducive to this dialogue. (This was not so with Sacristán in Barcelona.)

Lenin's diatribe of 1909, which emitted more smoke than light, against the 'idealism' of Bogdanov (and the empirio-criticism of Mach), contains an interesting footnote, which says:

Mach speaks in favour of the bureaucratic socialism of Popper (Josef) and Menger (Anton) which guarantees the 'freedom of the individual', whilst he thinks that the doctrine of the social-democrats [in the sense accepted before 1914, the Bolsheviks were still social-democrats] can be 'unfavourably compared' with that socialism, and is a threat of a 'slavery even more universal and more oppressive than that of a monarchic or oligarchic State'.[1]

Ernst Mach deserved neither Lenin's sustained and misjudged philosophical attack nor Lenin's incidental political assault. Mach rarely wrote on social matters, but the commentary quoted by Lenin was preceded by a paragraph which has relevance to our main theme. Noticing the growth of installed

[1] Lenin (1909), n. 2, chapter 6. The reference is to Mach's *Erkenntnis und Irrtum* (1906), p. 80–1. Anton Menger (brother of the 'marginalist' economist Carl Menger), rector of the University of Vienna, was a moderate social reformer. Mach quoted his *Neue Staatslehre* (G. Fisher, Jena, 1902). He was also the author of *Das Recht auf den vollen Arbeitsertrag in geschichtlicher Darstellung*.

horsepower in industry,[2] Mach pointed out that this growth had not achieved Aristotle's dream of a society without slaves. The reasons had been explained by Josef Popper-Lynkeus:[3] the colossal performance of the machines was not directed towards the sustenance of humanity, but on the contrary was employed for the satisfaction of the needs for luxury of the domineering part of humanity. The speed of the trains, the facilities of the post, the telegraph and the telephone, were most convenient, but only for the minority who enjoyed them. There was another consideration. The whizzing wheels of the factories, the tramways and the electric lights could not be viewed with pure pleasure when the vast amount of coal which went into the air every hour was recalled. The 'savings from the youth of the earth' were fast being spent. Would we go back to barbarity? Or would humanity become wise and learn to 'keep house', to budget properly? Material and cultural progress was generally introduced by persons who had a certain independence, who were not overburdened by the search for subsistence. New ideas had one delightful property which material improvements did not: they could easily reach that part of humanity burdened with work, and it was quite likely that with fresh knowledge of existing conditions, that part of humanity would unite against the domineering part, in order to demand equal and suitable shares of the common patrimony. Josef Popper-Lynkeus had proposed a programme to this end; his objectives were the same as those of the original social-democracy, but he placed more emphasis on the freedom of the individual. Here Mach added the commentary denounced by Lenin.

It was Lenin and not Mach who used the expression 'bureaucratic socialism' for Popper-Lynkeus' scheme. The context of Lenin's passionate attack on such a sensible and left-wing person as Mach, a retired professor who was nearly seventy years old, and not at all a political competitor, was Lenin's opinionated defence of a materialist ontology against Bogdanov's 'idealism'. Lenin's outbursts of 1909 against Mach and Bogdanov would not have mattered very much (Mach was certainly unperturbed) had they not been published again in the Soviet Union after the Revolution of 1917, now in the context of the political debate against Lunacharsky's and Bogdanov's *Proletkult*.

Apparently Lenin made no other reference to Josef Popper-Lynkeus and this one (whose context has been explained), was made before Popper-Lynkeus published the detailed version of his scheme in 1912, which he had first announced in 1878 and which Mach must have followed closely.

[2] Quoting the statistics in Bourdeau, *Les forces de l'industrie*, Paris, 1884.
[3] In: *Die technischen Fortschritte nach ihrer ästhetischen und kulturellen Bedeutung*, 1888, p. 59 f, 'a beautiful and illuminating piece of writing'.

It is not known what influence Josef Popper-Lynkeus had on Bogdanov (1873–1928), when Bogdanov, who was living with Lenin at the time and who was an important person in the party, was preparing his utopian novels, *The Red Star* and *Engineer Menni*, in the years following 1905. However Bogdanov was certainly influenced by Ballod-Atlanticus, and he used the expression *Zukunftsstaat* (which Bebel had also used) (Grille, 1966, p. 158, n. 2). Bogdanov chose to express his vision of the future not on the basis of a detailed statistical investigation of available resources and of necessities (in the manner of Josef Popper-Lynkeus and Karl Ballod-Atlanticus), but in the form of novels, arguing that technical progress was bound to make concrete plans for the organization of the 'state of the future' rapidly obsolete. This is certainly a good argument against 'scientific utopias' as mandatory blueprints for evermore, but not against the view (which was also Neurath's) that there is room for *diverse* 'scientific utopias' to allow choice between them, and that there should be continuous production of new ones. Some tendencies in Marxism have always insisted on the strict separation of 'utopian socialism' from 'scientific socialism'. However, it is quite possible that 'scientific utopias' make a more accurate guess at the future. (Neurath, 1944, pp. 31, 32, 44).

Utopian novels can be marvellously educative (for instance the anarchist utopia of *The Dispossessed* by Ursula Le Guin), but novels are not 'scientific utopias', neither when they assume the abolition of all scarcities nor when (as in Le Guin's case) they assume poverty. They do not include empirical calculations of resources and human needs, essential ingredients for the realistic 'education of desire'. Why should they, being novels, works of fiction, even works of science fiction? Therefore, H. G. Wells (1866–1945) has not been given a chapter in this book although he was sometimes on the point of embarking on a critique of economics from a physical point of view. He came close to it in the section on 'Utopian economics' in *A Modern Utopia*, where he proposed a society ruled by a non-hereditary techno-bureaucracy, and where he wrote:

It has been suggested by an ingenious thinker (did he mean Soddy?) that it is possible to use as a standard of monetary value no substance whatever, but instead, force, and that value might be measured in units of energy . . . Now the problems of economic theory will have undergone an enormous clarification if, instead of measuring in fluctuating money values, the same scale of energy units can be extended to their discussion, if, in fact, the idea of trading could be entirely eliminated. In my Utopia, at any rate, this has been done, the production and distribution of common commodities have been expressed as a problem in the conversion of energy, and the scheme that Utopia was now discussing was the application of this idea of energy as the standard of value to the entire Utopian coinage.[4]

These were really crackpot schemes unaccompanied by any empirical research into the availability and distribution of energy and material resources. Here again, the solidity of British capitalism probably made concrete proposals for an achievable utopia irrelevant.

In other instructive utopian writings, such as Morris' *News from Nowhere*, despite the gentle vision of a green England in summer which Morris conveys, the ecological perspective (that is, the analysis of the flow of energy and materials) was also lacking. This is also unfortunately the case in Chayanov's *Journey of my brother Alexei Kremnev to the land of peasant utopia*, written in 1921, which is assumed to take place in 1984, after a 'counter-revolution' in the Soviet Union against the party bureaucrats has created a universal peasant society of small-holders, the population of Moscow being reduced to a few hundred thousand inhabitants with dwellings set in the midst of domestic gardens. This is not an ecological utopia, because some crucial technological details are not properly explained; for instance, how very high agricultural yields are achieved. Similar comments are applicable to Havemann's delightful *Morgen* (1980), a touching book in itself, and because it was written in the tense unstable reality of Berlin, where perhaps one day Rudi Dutschke's dream of a free (and red-green) commune, empty of foreign or native troops, will come true. Havemann assumed a multitude of small nuclear-fusion power stations scattered over the countryside, but he provided no technical explanation. The function of 'scientific utopian' writing should be not only to suggest new and desirable social relations based on the old moral values of equality and freedom, but also to specify feasible and viable productive bases for such societies, and for the whole world. Some energy and material accounting *in natura* is an essential ingredient of 'ecological utopianism'.[5]

[4] No date is given (Odhams Press, London, p. 349–50) in this edition, but works on Wells give 1905 as year of publication.

[5] Orwell's well-known utopia, entitled *Homage to Catalonia*, describes the revolutionary social values compatible with the birth of an egalitarian society, with a relatively low level of consumption of exosomatic energy and materials, organized on anarcho-syndicalist lines, but there is not (nor could there be, because of the civil war) a statistical description of the normal provisioning of this society, nor a discussion of how the collectivized economy would function. Some writings on rural Spain after the revolution of 1936 come much closer to the concept of empirical ecological utopias, writ small, because they do not only explain the change in property relations and systems of work, and the change in social values, they also explain the techniques of production, the yields achieved in the collectives, etc. (cf. for instance, Gaston Leval, 1977; Bernecker, 1982).

But if one criterion of ecological or scientific utopianism is accountancy, then the question arises: what is the difference with an exercise in economic planning? One of Max Weber's arguments against socialism (apart from that of the extension of the power of the bureaucracy) was that a socialist economy would lack the means of rational calculation insofar as it involved physical allocation of resources rather than the use of money or a price mechanism (T. Bottomore, 1984, p. 133), an argument which was developed by L. von Mises and Hayek, and which Oskar Lange attempted to answer in a famous debate. The allocation of exhaustible resources was not considered by either side in that debate.

Neurath wrote that Popper-Lynkeus' and Ballod-Atlanticus' computations showed how an economic plan based on statistics could be established. Because there was much room for realistic choice, there should be many different 'scientific utopias'. Consider for instance, housing plans to accommodate a given population. Those plans which, with the same human effort, would require more materials and energy would be discarded. When a greater expenditure of resources goes with a smaller quantity of human work there is a difficult decision: should the coal mines be protected or should human labour be spared? The answer will depend on whether it is decided that water power, or perhaps solar radiation, would be utilized more efficiently in the future. If this is so, then coal can be used more freely now and human work will not be squandered where it can be replaced by coal. However, if it is feared that thousands upon thousands will freeze to death in the future, should the present generation use too much coal, then more human energy and less coal can be used now. Considerations of this type, together with many other non-technical considerations, will determine the selection of one of the technically feasible plans. A capitalist factory would decide which of two production plans to adopt by comparing the net amount of money it would make from each. Production plans for the economy, however, could not be based on a common unit of measurement. How could we compare, unless in different units, the protection of human labour with the protection of coal deposits? (1928, edn 1973, p. 263).

Such *Naturalrechnung* denies the commensurability (synchronic and diachronic) of elements in the economy. For example, Neurath adds that books and pears cannot be compared in the same units. Since Neurath lived in the midst of a generalized market system and not on a Trobriand island with discrete spheres of exchange, he knew quite well that pears and books could be compared in money terms, since they had prices. At first sight the market would also determine the depletion path of coal. Economists will discuss whether a monopolistic market will make for a slower rate of depletion, but they will never deny commensurability. Neurath's purpose was nothing less than to put the economists out of business.

Suitable cheating of the classification and the valuation of externalities (such as the effects of the large-scale build-up of carbon dioxide) and discount rates can produce an appearance of commensurability in money of different forms of energy. For instance, when costing kilowatts from nuclear energy compared to other sources, by-products such as plutonium should be included, though it is unclear whether this is a negative or a positive externality. It is certainly effective against one's enemies. It has also a long radioactive life, so that the question of the present value of its future effects also arises. But it will be said that in a generalized market economy, commensurability is not a fiction, it is an observable fact; there *are* prices of pears and books, there are also prices for human labour, for coal and for other forms of energy. It is the market which (at least at first sight) provides the criterion for the temporal use of coal deposits.

Suppose that the economy were socialized. In principle (though not in practice) there would be no market for coal and no market for wage labour. The economist would not be alarmed. He would point out that Neurath could not have known, at the time when he wrote that text, that an input-output analysis, assuming certain objectives of production and given certain inputs and the functions that indicate the possibilities of substitution among them, will attribute implicit prices to all inputs. However, it is obvious that the genesis of objectives of production has not been explained. The usual practice is to plan 'from the achieved level' (Birman, 1978) adding a few *ad hoc* percentage points to the levels of the preceding period. It is also obvious that the decision as to which inputs of exhaustible resources are available 'today' implies the adoption of a particular temporal horizon and a discount (or no discount) of the present value of future demand. How many generations are included in the objectives of production? Moreover, how should the present and future effects of some of the outputs (the *garbojunk* and *waste* of Georgescu-Roegen's input-output tables) be valued? The prices of natural resources in socialist economies have often been criticized (by Dobb and Nove) because they were fixed according to the average cost (and not the marginal cost) of extraction. This leaves aside the question of optimization of their inter-generational allocation which, both in the East and the West, is not separable from the social distribution of moral principles and from the interpretations of the history of science and technology.

For instance, if the 'Soviet' leadership were to become 'green', then they would follow a different policy of depletion of exhaustible resources and they would give a different value to the present and future diseconomies of nuclear power stations. Such change would add much social force to the arguments of the present book. But, where do their moral views come from? And their beliefs in technical progress? Not from random individual idiosyncrasies, which would give a wider spread of attitudes instead of such a uniform pattern.

Marxism and Ecology

Marxists certainly should have no commitment to methodological individualism. Therefore, it would be strange to hear a Marxist defence of a particular rate of interest or discount of the future in terms of the preferences revealed in the savings market. The distribution of production, the consumption and the investment and even the prices are explained by Marx in an institutional way. In the Marxist view, capitalism is a passing historic system and the capitalist economy cannot be understood in isolation from social organization in conflicting classes, one of which is forced to sell its labour power since it lacks its own means of subsistence; the market value of production is appropriated by the capitalists, who have to pay the inputs used and the labour power; this last is paid according to the cost of its reproduction including a historically variable surplus above physical subsistence, though not including the cost of 'free' domestic work usually supplied by women. The capitalists' profits go partly on luxury consumption and partly on investment or accumulation of capital which allows them to become even more wealthy. It may easily happen that the capitalists' activities have contradictory results, because accumulation of capital may be high and yet consumption by the exploited wage workers relatively low, which provokes crises and possibly wars for the domination of external markets. The workers may change from being a class in themselves to being a class for themselves, organized and aware of their historic goals; therefore capitalism, subject to periodic crises, may give way to socialism after a revolution. Then, eventually, the state, which is always an instrument of class domination, will fade away. Within this Marxist scheme, actions are explained by the class position of the participants.

Marx wrote sometimes that capitalism misused natural resources, but this did not seem to him to be a relevant fact in explaining capitalist dynamics. The concepts required were those of exploitation (based on the theory of labour value), class struggle, crises of over-investment or under-consumption (words are tricky – in any case, *not* pre-capitalist crises of subsistences). Crises were a sign that the relations of production were blocking the development of productive forces. Marxists tend to believe that the protests of the ecologists against capitalism are of the same order as the moral and aesthetic protests of Ruskin, Morris and the 'utopian' socialists. They may agree with them, but they find that they are of no use in *analysing* the dynamics of the capitalist system. The social actors of that system are really motivated by the desire to accumulate capital and to increase production, so as to sell more and make more profits. They are also motivated by the desire to increase workers' exploitation (or to resist it).

Marx's starting proposition was that total production exceeded what was required to replace used means of production (such as seed, in an agricultural economy), and to sustain the producers (and their dependants) not only in the capitalist system, but also in feudalism, in slavery, and in fact whenever social differentiation exists. In capitalism, the surplus of work was not as obvious as in other types of relations of production, it adopted the form of surplus value, disguised by the sale of labour power in the market as a commodity.

Marx analysed the capitalist system with theoretical instruments which were outside capitalist accounting, and outside the frame of mind of at least some of the social participants: labour value, exploitation, commodity fetishism, alienation. The very concept of 'capital' did not refer to 'produced means of production' (even less to financial capital), but to a social relation specific to the capitalist stage in human history. In contrast, Marx's discourse on 'production' and on 'productive forces' is historically unspecific.

Production and surplus production were concepts which did not belong specifically to the analysis of capitalism. One interesting line of discussion – which will not be pursued here, as it is irrelevant to the theme – is that suggested by Sahlins, that surplus production arises historically not so much because of the 'development of productive forces' as because incipient political structures force an intensification of work. One line of discussion has been opened up by pointing out that Marx 'imported' the concept of production and of surplus production into industrial capitalism without giving a place in analysis to the question of replacement of used-up means of production. The meaning of workers' maintenance was clear enough: physical subsistence, plus a cultural, historically variable element, not excluding gains obtained by class struggle. But there is nowhere in Marx, nor in later Marxists, an analysis of the replacement of used-up means of production in an economy based on exhaustible resources, that is, resources which cannot be replaced, at least in the sense that corn seed or a mule can be replaced.

To the extent that Marxist economics has preoccupied itself with natural resources, the treatment has not been an ecological one (that is, consideration of availability of resources, of waste disposal and of inter-generational allocations), but a Ricardian one, that is, how rent paid to the owners of natural resources would alter the pattern of distribution of income, and of savings and investment (Massarrat, 1980).

The Marxist schemes of 'simple' and 'expanded' reproduction do not take into account whether the availability of exhaustible resources would put a limit even to 'simple' reproduction. This merely reflects the metaphysical status that the concept of 'production' has in Marxist economics, no different from that of mainstream economics. This is also applicable to Sraffa's schemes of 'production of commodities by means of commodities' whose intention was to show that the distribution of income cannot be explained as a by-product of price formation in the market because prices will be different if distribution is different. The question of exhaustible resources and inter-generational allocation could probably be fitted into Sraffa's schemes, but it was not.

In conclusion, Marx believed that it was possible to talk about investment and about increased production not only in the language specific to capitalists, or in a language appropriate only for the analysis of capitalism, but in a language applicable to all economic systems, even to socialist economies (in his not-abundant writings on socialism and communism). The first models of economic growth which were used for planning in the Soviet Union, based on the division of the economy in sectors (for example, consumption, 'light' industry, 'heavy' industry, as in Feldman's model which preceded Keynesian theories of growth) are truly of Marxist origin: a preoccupation with the intertemporal allocation of exhaustible resources is generally absent from Marxist economics, and this is not because the 'problem' did not 'exist' before 1973.

Although Marxists would be in principle in a good position to mistrust the market's perceptions, this does not mean that a 'technologically determined' Marxism, or an even more restricted 'energy-flow determined' Marxism, could exist, because judgements on technology and on the availability of energy cannot depend only on the 'facts', they also depend on social structure and social interests. One relevant question is, whose perceptions are substituted for the market's myopic and class-biased perceptions? How is scientific and technological knowledge socially constructed and socially used?

It is recognized that it is easy to document Marx's and Engels' interest for ecological questions. Marx knew the work of the so-called 'vulgar materialists', Moleschott (1822–93), Büchner (1824–1901), Vogt (1817–95). Although Marx did not quote him, Moleschott influenced Marx's use of the expression 'metabolism (*Stoffwechsel*) between man and earth'. Marx was opposed to the notion of decreasing returns, on the grounds that modern British agriculture showed an increase in production and simultaneously a decrease in the number of workers employed: Malthusian conclusions were, thus, most inappropriate (*Das Kapital*, vol. 1, p. 457). However, Marx mentioned that the concentration of population in the great cities damaged the natural conditions for the fertility of agriculture, and he quoted Liebig's notion of an agriculture of spoliation in contrast to an agriculture of restitution. In volume 3 (chapter 47), Marx showed himself in favour of Liebig's argument for small-scale agriculture in terms of its greater capacity to return fertilizing elements to the ground, as compared with large-scale agriculture producing for large and distant cities. Alfred Schmidt (1978, p. 86–9) was therefore right in pointing out that Marx's use of the expression 'metabolism between man and earth' was not metaphorical: it referred specifically to the cycles of plant nutrients. However, this approach, which in any case did *not* also comprise the flow of energy, was not integrated into Marx's view of history, and this is why there has been no school of Marxist ecological historians or economists.

In Engels, some early references to the flow of energy can be found, perhaps the first one in a letter to Marx of 14 July 1858, from Manchester, where Engels mentioned Joule and the law of conservation of energy. Joule of course also lived in Manchester. Writing thirty years later to Nicolai Danielson (15 October 1888), Engels said that the nineteenth century would be remembered as the century of Darwin, Mayer, Joule and Clausius; it had been not only the century of the theory of evolution but also of the theory of the transformation of energy.

The second law was mentioned by Engels in some notes written in 1875 which became, posthumously, famous passages of the *Dialectics of Nature*. Engels referred to Clausius' entropy law, found it contradictory to the law of conservation of energy, and expressed the hope that a way would be found to re-use the heat irradicated into space. Engels was understandably worried by the religious interpretations of the second law. In a letter to Marx of 21 March 1869, when he became aware of the second law, he complained about William Thomson's attempts to mix God and physics.

It is risky to judge anybody's views from private notes, and the significance of such passages by Engels on the second law together with his comments on Podolinsky, have to be viewed rather in their reception. Thus, in a book published in 1925 on Engels as a 'natural scientist', on the occasion of the publication of *Dialectics of Nature* and on thirtieth anniversary of Engels' death, the Austrian Marxist Otto Jenssen printed Engels' letters to Marx on Podolinsky, and explained that in these letters Engels had anticipated a critique of Ostwald's social energetics before Ostwald himself appeared on the scene (Jenssen, 1925, p. 13).[6]

---

[6]The Russian I. K. Luppol (a 'Deborinist', as opposed to a 'mechanist' in the polemics of the 1920s, cf. Joravsky, 1961) also mentioned Engels' letters in 'Zur Frage des Verhältniss des Marxismus zur Naturwissenschaft', *Unter dem Banner des Marxismus*, 1928, p. 197, but he did not discuss Podolinksy's article.

Engels' reaction to Podolinsky's article (which was considered briefly in chapter 3), was certainly a crucial missed chance in the dialogue between Marxism and ecology. Engels' position was that the energy productivity of human labour (which Podolinsky had calculated for an agriculture which did not make use of a large input of energy from fossil fuels) would depend 'only on the degree of development of the means of production' (as he wrote on his letter to Marx of 19 December 1882). It could amount to 5,000 kilocalories, to 10,000 kilocalories, to 20,000 kilocalories, or to one million kilocalories per day. Of course such figures were not given by Engels as reasoned estimates. But it is fair to infer that (given the adequate relations of production) he saw no limits to the amount of energy which could be harnessed by the work of a man. Oil workers, or workers at nuclear power stations or hydroelectric works, would show extremely high ratios of energy output to direct human energy input. Such types of work did not exist in 1882, but coal mining certainly did, and Engels referred to it: he wrote to Marx that: 'Podolinsky has completely forgotten that a man who works does not only incorporate *present* solar heat, he is rather a great squanderer of *past* solar heat. How we squander energy reserves, coal, minerals, forests and so on, you know better than I do'. It is certainly not true that Podolinsky had forgotten this, though he did not extend his energy accounts to industrial activities. Although Engels understood perfectly how a calculus of energy inputs and outputs could be established in hunting and in agricultural activities, even to the extent of remarking that the calculus would be difficult in agriculture because one should include the energetic value of fertilizers and other auxiliary means, he thought on the other hand that 'the energetic value, according to their cost of production, of a hammer, a screw, a needle, is a quantity which cannot be calculated'. Whatever the practical difficulties of such calculus, this is what is done in energy accounting.[7] Not only the energy analysis of industrial processes, but that of agriculture also would be impossible if the energetic worth of machines, pesticides, fertilizers, etc., could not be calculated. But Engels was prejudiced against this: 'In my view' he wrote 'the wish to express economic relations in physical terms is quite impossible'. Podolinsky had only managed to show one fact already well known, that the industrial producers had to live from the products of agriculture: this 'could be translated, if one so liked, into the language of physics, but little would be gained by it'. This is how Engels ended his second letter to Marx on Podolinsky, and many economic historians

---

[7] Max Weber understood how it should be done, when he compared the energy cost of a piece of cloth woven by hand and by machine (Weber, 1909), although Weber also denied the relevance of energy accounting for economics.

would have agreed with him until recently. Agriculture feeds the towns, and greater agricultural productivity (because of 'technical progress', 'growth of productive capacity', 'development of the means of production') will allow industrial expansion and greater incomes for those peasants and land workers still left behind. Each agricultural worker would be able to feed ten, twenty, fifty or one hundred town dwellers. This was taught by economics (with the sociological corollary that small-scale or, rather labour-intensive agriculture, was a leftover from the past). But when the facts are translated into the language of physics (*ins Physikalische übersetzen*, as Engels wrote), what in economic language is called 'greater productivity' should be called 'smaller productivity'.

Although Marxism is clearly inter-disciplinary history, it has not encompassed 'natural history' or the history of the natural sciences. The Marxist concept of *Produktivkräfte* may be translated as productive forces or productive powers (Wittfogel, 1985), and it is not related to the meaning of *Kraft* as force or power or energy. G. A. Cohen has written (1978, p. 104–5) that Marx complained that Ricardo's views on diminishing returns and differential rent reckoned without the further development of fertilizers. This complaint shows that the Marxist explanation of economic processes must not abstract *on principle* from the physical processes underlying them. Cohen quotes Marx's letter to Engels of 13 February 1866, where he stated that Liebig's agricultural chemistry was more important for the discussion of diminishing returns than all that the economists had said. Even if it is agreed that the separation of economics from physics was not a matter of principle for Marx (nor for Engels, despite his polemical asides against Podolinsky), the question is whether the physical processes used to overcome diminishing returns in agriculture should qualify as productive forces. This point is symptomatically not discussed at all by Elster (1985). This writer, who deals with a peculiarly ahistorical, or perhaps posthistorical Marxism, feels no need to define 'production', 'productivity' or 'productive forces'.

Perhaps it could be said optimistically that Engels understood the principles of agricultural energetics though not of industrial energetics, also that he clearly understood the difference between spending the energy stock in coal and using the flow of solar energy, and that he was far in advance of many later economists, sociologists and historians in his knowledge and interest in science. But it must be said that Marx and Engels had the opportunity of reading one of the first attempts at ecological Marxism, and that they did not use it profitably. Of course, it was very late in their lives. Marx, in 1880–2, was still quite active intellectually – his letter to Vera Zasulich on the role of the peasant commune in socialism was drafted in March 1881. A proper definition of increases in agricultural productivity would have been of the essence in order to analyse social differentiation in the countryside (as it nowadays appears so clearly in India and in China). Marx was to die in 1883. Engels died in 1895. It should have been left to later Marxists to modify Marxism in the light of the ecological critique of economics, but there have been epistemological obstacles (the use of categories of political economy) and ideological obstacles (the vision of a two-stage transition to communist equality) to such an undertaking.

The ideological obstacles can be sensed in the *Critique of the Gotha Programme*, of 1875. The Marxist idea is that 'production' would increase according to the 'development of productive forces', which capitalism would in due course be unable to increase further, but which socialism would increase in such a way, that at the end, distribution according to need would be possible after a period of distribution according to the quantity and quality of work. Both Kropotkin (in *The Wage System*) and William Morris (in *The Policy of Abstention*) argued explicitly against distribution 'according to work', on the grounds that while inequality in capitalism lacked legitimacy from the workers' point of view, the Marxists seemed bent upon giving a positive sanction to inequality after the revolution, for the sake of 'revolutionary' principles. Though Kropotkin shared in the vision of future abundance he was simultaneously in favour of immediate equality. A Marxist discussion of *Kommunismus ohne Wachstum* ('communism without growth', Harich's expression introduced in 1975) is still pending. While Marx, writing in 1875, would adjourn communist distribution until the development of productive forces would have proceeded further, some of his followers, writing later, would even adjourn the first stage, socialism (in the sense of expropriation of the means of production), waiting for further growth in the productive forces.[8]

Also, Plekhanov lacked awareness of the flow of energy and materials in his writings of the 1880s and 1890s. His 'monism' had nothing to do with Ostwald's and it was a 'purposively clumsy' word used instead of 'materialism' in order to deceive the censor. 'Materialism' was not used by Plekhanov in an ecological sense, that is, it did not imply the study of the cycles of materials. Lenin's critique of Ostwald and of energy analysis in general in the context of his attack on Bogdanov and

---

[8] This debate became familiar in a different context to the generation of 1968, because of the Cuban polemics on the management of the economy (between Guevara and Mandel on one side, and Bettelheim and the 'old communists', on the neo-'Bernsteinian' side) and also because of the Maoist emphasis on moral incentives and communal agriculture and the subsequent reaction against it on the part of 'intellectual workers' and party bureaucrats. Such debates on whether the relations of production could go beyond the limits set by the development of productive forces, did *not* include a discussion of exhaustible resources.

Mach in 1909, was a further step in the unauspicious start to the dialogue between Marxism and ecological economics.

Bogdanov and Bukharin

Bogdanov's utopian novels have been mentioned earlier. His theoretical writings are one of the origins of 'general systems theory'. This grew out of the links between thermodynamics and biology, cornerstone of Bertalanffy's position, anticipated by Felix Auerbach's concept of *Ektropismus*.[9] Bogdanov (1873–1928) suggested the link between the study of energy flow and natural selection, and he was not averse to applying this notion to changes in human societies. This was influenced by Ostwald, and this is why Lenin's attack on Bogdanov (in *Materialism and Empiriocriticism*, 1909), reached Ostwald too. In fact, there were good reasons for an attack on Ostwald's notion that there was one 'universal substance', energy, rather than matter, and on his reductionist, 'monist' approach to human history. Ostwald's views on 'mental' energy as a form of physical energy – which Bogdanov did not repudiate, rather the contrary – were rightly criticized by Lenin. The link between energy analysis and social-Darwinism must also be pushed aside strongly, it is – as Lenin put it (1909, 1927 edn, p. 339) – 'an indescribable mess'.

Lenin also pushed aside *another* question, which Bogdanov and some of his colleagues had, somewhat confusedly, introduced, that is, whether there could be a definition of 'productive forces' in terms of energy availability. Lenin dismissed this idea and came close to dismissing the very concept of energy (1909, 1927 edn, pp. 339, 346), because Lenin's attack on Bogdanov also became an attack on Mach's 'empirio-criticism', taken to be philosophical idealism in contraposition to good materialist ontology. In Mach's theory of knowledge, the energy laws were not presented as realities of nature but as mental constructions – as all other physical, chemical and biological laws – meant to explain, with as much 'economy of thought' as possible, the data of our senses. Lenin's refusal of Mach's so-called idealism was a pity, not only because the Leninist cloud of suspicion towards 'Machism' thickened around the concept of energy, and even more around social energetics, but also because Mach's theory of knowledge allows the history of science to

---

[9] Cf. *General Systems. Yearbook of the Society for Advancement of General Systems Theory*, vol. I, 1956 to vol. XXIX, 1985, published under Bertalanffy's editorship, and including several articles by Kenneth Boulding.

be fitted into a Marxist view of history much better than an immovable materialist ontology such as that proposed by Lenin.[10]

Bukharin (1888–1938) – as prominent in the Bolshevik party in the post-revolutionary period as Bogdanov had been before the Revolution – became aware of the possibility of translating some aspects of 'historical materialism' into the vocabulary of social energetics. In 1921, in his widely known book *Theory of Historical Materialism*, in the chapter which deals with the relation between nature and society, he wrote that human society must, wherever it exists, extract material energy from its environment. The more energy society extracted from nature, the better society adapted to nature. Society spent the energy of human work in this process and gained a certain quantity of appropriated natural energy. It was evident that this balance was of decisive importance to the development of the whole of society. Did the income exceed the expenses? If so, by how much? This exchange of energy was the proper way to interpret the idea of metabolism between nature and society, which allowed the process of social reproduction. (Bukharin, 1921, chapter 5, paragraphs 31 and 32). Clearly, Bukharin was on the point of asking: is this energy 'income' really an income or is it part of 'capital'? And, whether flow or stock, how is this surplus of energy 'produced' and shared by humans?

Bukharin also presented a typology of stable and moving social equilibria phrased in terms of social energetics. The growth of society required that more energy be extracted from nature than it put back in, while a society might also stabilize its functioning at a low level of consumption of energy. Neither Bogdanov nor Bukharin carried out quantitative work on energy flows, but both of them realized that the Marxist concept of 'productive forces' could be partly re-tooled in terms of the availability of energy, which they both thought would grow enormously.[11] A comparison between Bogdanov's and Bukharin's ideas on social organization would show that both regarded technology as the most important driving force in society (Susiluoto, 1982, p. 85). Bogdanov thought that in order to cope with the enormous 'machinery for the transformation of energy' which humankind was creating, there would be a need for establishing a rational social system: his utopia was born of fear and we might speculate on how Bogdanov (who was strongly anti-statist) would have seen the creeping advance of the 'nuclear state' (in Jungk's sense). Bukharin's utopia

---

[10] For a defence of 'materialism' against 'idealism' (i.e. logical empiricism) at a much later date and in 'cold war' style, see for instance Cornforth, 1955; also, Chattopadhyaya, 1979.

[11] Bogdanov (in his *Short Course of Economic Science*, 1919, translated 1923, pp. 378–80) was enthusiastic about atomic energy, as Vernadsky (who popularized the concept of 'biosphere') had already been in 1910 (cited by Vucinich, 1970, p. 392).

was born of hope: it was desirable and inevitable that the availability of energy be increased, but this would create no unsurmountable social problems, rather the contrary. Reviewing Roberto Michels' book (on the 'iron law of oligarchy'), Bukharin wrote that there was no reason to worry unduly about the growth of a germ of class division in the post-revolutionary society, since social differentiation would melt away, not only because of the end to the monopoly of education but also because of superabundance.

The basic theoretical elements for an ecological Marxism were present in such formulations, because they made it possible to understand the relations between society and nature in terms of human ecology (while, of course, the relations of production, and social consciousness, *cannot* be studied as human ecology). But even such prominent authors failed to start a debate. There were other attempts. So, Sergei Perov, a biochemist and a 'mechanist' in the debate on philosophy of science of the 1920s, 'searched in the empirical sciences for the universal principle that would furnish an ontological and methodological basis for the unity of all science, and he claimed to find it, somewhat as Bogdanov did, in the work of the American chemist Willard Gibbs', that is, in thermodynamics (Joravsky, 1961, p. 155). A. K. Timiriazev (the son of the biologist K. A Timiriazev), another 'mechanist', wrote in 1928 that one of Deborin's 'dialectical' formulations, 'there is no dispersion of energy without its concentration' – clearly connected to the reception of Engels' views on the energy laws in *Dialectics of Nature* – was a vague and diffuse expression, on a level with 'there is no action without a reaction' (Joravsky, 1961, p. 159).

It would be strange if Marxist theory eternally stood still, and Neurath wrote that Marxist propositions about 'productive forces' should be converted into propositions about the flow of energy in agrarian and industrial production: 'it is possible that a later elaboration of materialist sociology (his name for Marxism) in the spirit of unified science would bring about a transformation of the propositions referring to 'infra-structure' into propositions referring to the energy cycle of nutrition, of domestic heating, etc.' (1931, edn 1973, p. 353). Neurath had Popper-Lynkeus' calculations in mind, and for that reason mentioned domestic heating, which is perhaps not the most interesting example.

Proof of the absence of an ecological Marxism could be found in the practice of economic planning in the Soviet Union, where discussion on the inter-generational allocation of exhaustible resources does not exist.[12] One more telling proof is the absence of an ecological approach in the great Marxist historians, whose successes since the 1940s (for instance, Dobb's contribution to the understanding of the transformation of feudal

[12] For an East German contribution, see Graf, 1980.

relations of production, or E. P. Thompson's contribution to the study of the birth of working class consciousness), were based of course upon concrete empirical historical studies. There is no comparable empirical and analytical work in Marxist historiography addressed to a clarification of the notion of 'productive forces' or 'productive powers'. It cannot come only from 'bibliocentric exegesis' (Lukes' phrase) but from concrete historical ecological anthropology and human ecology. A debate on ecology and Marxism is anticipated in the USSR and other eastern European countries, in China, also in Cuba where Engels' remarks on soil erosion in the coffee plantations of Oriente province, perhaps inspired by Lafargue, are well remembered. Cuba has been a net exporter of energy for much of the nineteenth and twentieth centuries. Podolinsky's article, Engels' perceptive though sceptical response to it, the debates of the 1920s and other materials introduced in this book, will all play roles in this discussion.[13]

Ecological Anthropology

While the best known ecological anthropologists (Vayda, Rappaport) have been functionalist, researching the biological and cultural 'adaptations' to the flow of energy and materials available for human groups studied in isolation, there is also a historical ecological anthropology (Orlove, 1980). The functionalist tag is certainly not an original critique, and such a splendid study in ecological economics as Rappaport's *Pigs for the Ancestors*, where many students have learned the concept 'caloric return to caloric input', should not be belittled.

An example of Marxist and therefore historical ecological anthropology is Richard Lee's research on the Kung San (1979). Lee computed the energy accounts for the Kung San, unaware that this methodology had not been invented by the academic ecologists between the 1920s and the 1940s but by Podolinsky and Sacher about 1880. No doubt Lee would have quoted Engels' sensible comments on the energetics of hunting and gathering societies, had he been aware of them.

Leslie White, who with Julian Steward was the father of modern ecological anthropology, analysed human history in terms of the interplay between technological development (defined by the availability and the efficiency in the transformation of energy), the social system, and the cultural-symbolic level. The social system was defined as relations of

[13] Engels' letters to Marx on Podolinsky were quoted by Ilya Novik, 1981, p. 113, but Podolinsky's work itself was not mentioned.

production, though Leslie White did not use this terminology because of the danger of being a Marxist dissident in the American academic world. In fact, he was openly denounced as a Marxist by a colleague, Morris Opler.

Leslie White was inspired not by a knowledge of physics or biology but by Morgan and Tylor as evolutionary anthropologists, and he collected all the references to the use of energy he could find in both authors: the harvest was meagre. He became aware, after his 1943 article was published, that his views coincided with those of previous authors, mainly with Willhelm Ostwald's. He also realized that Soddy was a precursor, but he did not mention the *Technocracy Study Course* authored by M. King Hubbert. Leslie White accurately characterized Winiarski as somebody who 'seems merely to present social systems as analogous to physical systems, to describe them in the language of physics, rather than to apply physical concepts to gain new insights and understandings of socio-cultural systems' (White, in Fried, 1959): that is, Winiarski did not study biophysical or ecological economics but rather the formal analogies between physics and economics.

Leslie White attributed to an American physicist, Joseph Henry (1797–1878), first secretary of the Smithsonian Institution, whose main work was on electricity, an energy theory of cultural development introduced in 1873 in which he was supposed to have outlined 'stages of evolution in terms of harnessing energy in increasing magnitudes and in various forms'. Joseph Henry's collected papers are being published at present by the Smithsonian Institution and perhaps one will be able to find in them a quantified analysis of human ecological energetics. His writings of 1844, 'On the origins and classification of the natural motors' (referring to Babbage, Liebig, Dumas and Boussingault for a description of forms of power, making the point that animal power comes from combustion of vegetables which have grown by the 'decomposing energy of the sun's rays'), and also his writings of the 1850s with the general title of 'Metereology in its connection with Agriculture', make Leslie White's claim quite plausible. Nevertheless, his 1873 piece is merely a one-page statement in the context of a speech for a farewell banquet for Professor John Tyndall:

It is a fundamental principle of political economy that the physical state of man can only be ameliorated by means of labor or, in other words, by the transformation of matter from a crude to an artificial condition. But this cannot be effected, except by expending what is called *power* or energy. In ancient times, almost the exclusive source of this energy was muscular force, derived from compulsory human labor; and all the monuments and objects that have been left to us, as marks of ancient civilization, are the results of organized systems of slavery . . . Now, we owe the abolition of this condition of humanity, in the higher civilized nations of the world at the present day, to the study of the laws of the operations of Nature. By a knowledge of these laws the energies of the elements of Nature are substituted for human labor, and by this substitution man is not only relieved from brute force, but also given control of energies which enable him to produce effects which could only result from the muscular power of beings of a superior order. It may be shown by a simple calculation that about fifteen tons of anthracite coal burned in the furnace of one of our best steam engines exerts an energy equal to that of an able-bodied slave working ten hours a day for thirty years of his active life. It is this substitution of the energies of Nature for the power of the human muscle that, as we have said, has abolished slavery and elevated humanity to a higher plane than was ever dreamed by the wisest sages of ancient times.[14]

Readers of the present book will easily agree that Leslie White's search for the roots of his own views, and his praise for what amounted to an inspiring thought but not to an elaborated theory of social energetics, was a typical endeavour for anybody trying to found a new school of thought. Unfortunately, Leslie White was prevented by Cold War restrictions to intellectual freedom from creating a research school on the relations between Marxism and ecology, and this is why American ecological anthropologists and human ecologists have been unaware of Podolinsky's and Engels' ecological energetics (cf. Vayda, 1969; Hardesty, 1977; Orlove, 1980; Ellen, 1982; Young, 1983), which did not lie hidden in obscure archives but had been, on the contrary, well publicized in the 1920s. Engels' letters to Marx on Podolinsky were published in English in the 1930s and again in 1942.[15] Possibly, anthropologists of the Soviet Union aware of Marvin Harris' 'cultural materialism' have connected it to Podolinsky–Engels and also, perhaps, to Lenin–Bogdanov–Ostwald, but research on this point has been insufficient.[16]

While Marxist anthropologists and historians could have become aware of Podolinsky's ecological economics through Engels' corres-pondence with Marx (published in German in 1919), or by his article in *Die Neue Zeit*, ecologists had another route of access: Vernadsky (1863–1945), a major figure in Russian science before and after 1917, mentioned Podolinsky with praise in his book *La Géochimie* (1924, pp. 334–5) and no doubt in other untranslated texts, as somebody who had studied the energetics of life (in the footsteps, he wrote, of J. R. Mayer, W. Thomson and Helmholtz) and attempted to apply such ideas to the

[14] *A scientist in American life: Essays and lectures of Joseph Henry*, ed. by Arthur P. Molella, Nathan Reingold et al., Smithsonian Inst., Washington DC, 1980, p. 103.
[15] In vol. XXIX of the Marxist Library, International Publishers, New York.
[16] The writings of Iu. Bromley have been consulted, hampered however by lack of competence in Russian.

study of economic phenomena. Vernadsky gave the references to the French and German versions of Podolinsky's article and he accurately described him as a *savant et politicien ukrainien mort jeune* placing him politically in Drahomanov's circle.[17]

The present book partly grew out of a desire to provide a scientific and social context for Podolinsky's work. It could have been written some sixty years earlier by older authors of Marxian or ecological backgrounds, with some training in economics: leaving aside the discussion on National Income Accounting, other economic concepts considered in this book such as the discount rate (Gray, Ramsey) and externalities (Pigou) were already part of the economists' stock-in-trade by the 1920s.

[17] Jacques Grinevald, who kindly provided this reference, has suggested that there might be a link from Podolinsky to mainstream ecological energetics through Vernadsky's son (who taught Russian history at Yale) and Alexander Petrunkevitch, to G. E. Hutchinson and to R. Lindeman, and then to E. and H. Odum, Ramon Margalef, etc. The main influence, however, was clearly A. Lotka, himself influenced by Ostwald's social energetics and by the group of authors around Ostwald who published between 1905 and 1910 in the *Annalen der Naturphilosophie* (J. Žmavc, S. Heryng, Oskar Nagel), and probably by Pfaundler and Boltzmann. There is a discussion of the genesis of Lindeman's paper of 1942 (reprinted in Kormondy, 1965) by R. E. Cook, 1977, p. 22–6.

15

Political Epilogue

Introduction

An ecological approach questions the definition of 'productive forces', but it does not give a new theory of value; it destroys theories of value by asking the question of how the exhaustible resources which are susceptible of inter-generational allocation should be valued. There is nothing (in the East or the West) which forces scientifically to 'commodity fetishism', and thus to establish equivalences between, for example, two days' less work 'today' against an extra kilogram of coal used 'today' and therefore a kilogram of coal less available for 'tomorrow'. The rates of exchange can be imposed only by the historic existence of the generalized market and the ethics of that market.

The 'history of the future' of humanity cannot be reduced to blind confidence in the rationality of the market or to an economic planning exercise which imposes a false commensurability. The question of incommensurability posed by Neurath cannot be solved with an energetic theory of value either. An economic planner would be mistaken if his objective were to minimize the dissipation of energy or to maximize the flow of energy utilized; indeed, any objective expressed only in units of energy, would be mistaken.

Planning 'according to needs' is not immediately helpful either, even leaving aside the question of future demands. Apart from minimum biological needs, all other needs are cultural creations whose genesis requires explanation before they are taken as a point of reference for a plan. Studies by anthropologists of closed spheres of exchange (Barth, 1970; Douglas, 1970) show that the possibility of trade offs (three kilograms less of beans in exchange for five more litres of ethanol) is also a cultural creation. Veblen produced the theory of ostentatious consumption, which may operate in reverse: when poor people know that they cannot consume certain products, they may decide that they do not need them. Elster (in

Sen and Williams, 1982, p. 219) called this *sour grapes*. Felt needs, cannot be a starting point, because they depend on other people's levels of consumption.

A discussion of what alternative ends, present and future, should be served with the scarce resources available cannot, therefore, take as given the needs expressed in the market or the needs shown in opinion polls, influenced by the desire for imitation, by the hopelessness of the poor, by the economists' propaganda on consumer sovereignty and on the allocative virtues of the market.

What Hayek called 'social engineering' and Karl Popper 'utopian social engineering' is what Neurath called 'construction of (many) scientific utopias'; which preferably would be called 'ecological utopias'. The discussion of achievable utopias and the study of ecological economics have been suppressed in secondary and university education. The construction of 'ecological utopias' requires accounting *in natura*, an explicit discussion of moral principles and an education in the history of science and technology, accepting, however, in the face of the irrationalist philosophies of science which have been in fashion, that there is progress in scientific knowledge (Newton-Smith, 1982).

This position is compatible with technological 'optimism', or with technological 'pessimism' in a double sense; some technologies may be dangerous and other technologies may never reach viable development. For example, the progress of scientific knowledge established the impossibility of a *perpetuum mobile*. There were, for instance, successive approximations to the truth in the theories on the source of solar energy which have made an incidental appearance in this book. On the one hand, there were J. R. Mayer's and William Thomson's meteoric hypothesis, and Helmholtz's idea that the sun's energy originated in its gravitational contraction, which Henry Adams still entertained about 1900. On the other hand, there were the notions of 'chemical dissociation' (which Podolinsky took from Secchi), of a radioactive source, that is, nuclear fission (mentioned by Popper-Lynkeus), and the explanation accepted since the 1930s, of nuclear fusion. Technological replication has been successful so far only in the hydrogen bomb, but not in controlled industrial use. Knowledge of the chemistry of gunpowder explosions did not entail a gunpowder engine. The hopes expressed by many of 'our' writers for the chemical synthesis of foods have not been yet fulfilled.

Scientific or ecological utopias have no need to rely on 'miraculous' technologies, because they incorporate empirical research into scarcities, and therefore, they must ask specifically about the aims of humankind. Women and men are genetically able to consume exosomatically, enormously diverse quantities of resources; there could be discussion how to share these resources among those who are alive now, and between us and those who have not yet been born; we are bound to take sides in the struggles on distribution by default, if nothing else.

Utopias can pursue different goals, they can serve extra-human ideals, the greatness of God, the greatness of the Nation and its dominance over other nations, but they can also take as their starting point a description of a world where human beings, with all their defects and weaknesses, can live with all possible happiness allowed by natural circumstances, the land and the sea, raw materials and the climate, the size of the population and the spirit of new discoveries, education and the will to work. One can praise this attempt to achieve happiness and joy, or one can find it a vulgar, inferior goal; in either case, it is possible to study scientifically the effects of social institutions on human happiness. The construction of utopias on realities which are possible in the coming years could well make a great contribution to the development of a general theory of happiness. (Neurath, 1919, edn 1979, p. 239).

Ecological Neo-Narodism and Sustainable Development

Inspired by such lofty visions, the contemporary relevance of the history of ecological economics may have been overstated, and the fact forgotten that it exhibits a somewhat alarming trait compared with historical studies of established disciplines, in that it is the history of a non-established subject. There have never been university chairs in ecological economics. Our writers lacked an academic forum (because of the separation and professionalization of the sciences) where their arguments could be presented. There was also a crucial absence of plausible political groups, outside academia, which could adopt them as ideologues. There is no school without disciples. A new field of knowledge must be constructed not only intellectually but socially. At least, in the short-term, it is of little use publishing if you do not fit into an academic or political group; 'parish or perish'.

The writings of a remarkable collection of critics of economics who shared an interest in the study of the flow of energy in human societies have been paraphrased, commented on, and explained. In this epilogue, social-Darwinist ecologism is left aside, and the existence of a strong current of egalitarian ecologism emphasized. Therefore the explanation for the lack of political acceptance of this view in Third World countries has been sought, hence the question on the plausibility of international ecological neo-narodism as an ideology for the dispossessed of the earth. It is doubtful, however, whether ideas originating in the First World are fit for consumption in the Third World. Who will be the intermediaries, what distortions will take place in transit?

The main political ideologies (apart from nationalism) of Third World leaders, have been the ideologies of economic development and Marxism, often with an emphasis on economic growth rather than on international and internal redistribution. A new ideology, which still has shaky empirical ecological foundations, appeared in the 1960s. It was the ideology of 'appropriate technologies' (cooking with solar collectors, producing biogas from dung) in order to fulfil 'basic needs'.[1] The question is asked whether 'appropriate technology' is a more appropriate ideology than the old peasant redistributive dreams against landlords and urban dwellers; a world 'black repartition' of resources such as land and oil.

If modern agriculture means 'farming with petroleum' (and natural gas), then it could be argued that it cannot be extended to the world at large, at least as a permanent solution. Hence, the argument that labour-intensive agriculture has an important role to play in feeding the world population. This requires, of course, detailed empirical work on the changing energy and material requirements for agriculture; but in principle the case has been made by Pimentel and others (Vermeer, 1976), that the old economists' vision of a world fed by an active agricultural population which would comprise only five or ten per cent of total active population was unrealistic.

United States' or European agriculture might seem to be a model for disaster, if generally adopted. It combines a very high use of non-renewable energy with the actual or potential production of surpluses which are difficult to dispose of, in a market economy based on the principle that demands only count if backed by money. It could seem that neo-narodism makes a virtue out of the necessary resilience, indeed of the functional role of labour-intensive farming for the world economy. This argument on the functionality of traditional agriculture for permanently solving the world food problem is not satisfactory. Given the carrying capacity of the earth, hunger anyway is a social, not an ecological problem, motivated by restrictions of geographical mobility, high meat consumption and consequent wastage of cereals, and the unequal distribution of purchasing power and titles to income.

Neo-narodism is interpreted not only in the pro-peasant sense, but also in the redistributive sense; many of the most painful labour-intensive tasks of traditional agriculture would disappear, if even a small part of annual petroleum extraction were channelled to this end, rather than to ostentatious

---

[1] One influential spokesman for 'intermediate technologies' was E. F. Schumacher (1911–77) who had been at Oxford in the early 1930s and again in the 1940s, but who apparently was not influenced by Soddy; one more clear case of discontinuity in the building of ecological economics. (Cf. Kirk, 1982 and Schumacher, 1973).

consumption. Even though modern agriculture means 'farming with petroleum', there is enough petroleum to modernize all of the world's agriculture to some extent, without future energy availability being jeopardized. It is a question of priorities, given present techniques and present population and needs. Distributive compulsions can be swept under the carpet by either of two opposing methods: by assuming miraculous technical change and economic growth in the future, or by singing the praises of energy-efficient traditional methods of production.

In fact, for a world population of five thousand million or even ten thousand million, an energy subsidy from fossil fuels of 0.2 or 0.3 TEP per head/year for the agricultural and food system does not seem to be impracticable, when compared to present fossil fuel consumption in the over-developed countries.[2] All that would be required would be a re-distribution of resources towards agriculture (for fertilizers and for some mechanization) in order to increase yields and to eliminate the hardest types of human work. Instead of preaching the impossibility of modern agriculture everywhere, I would take the view that what appears to be impossible, is its permanent universal extension while preserving the very high levels of non-renewable energy consumption in some regions of the world. For instance, in the United States, the food system (agriculture and animal production, plus distribution) takes up only about 15 per cent of all primary energy, despite being very energy-intensive. More precisely:

To feed each American, about 1500 litres of oil equivalents are expended per year. Furthermore, a total of 17 per cent of United States energy is expended to supply the population with food. Of this, agricultural production uses about 6 per cent, food processing and packing use another 6 per cent, while distribution and home preparation account for the remaining 5 per cent. (D. and S. Pimentel, in Dahlberg, 1986, p. 278)

Perhaps a term like 'ecological Maoism' would have been better understood a few years ago, rather than neo-narodism; as it is interpreted in a similar sense, as an egalitarian ideology against the belief in economic growth which helps to preserve inequality. However, there is no neo-Maoist dress to put on. My point is, simply, that the social conditions of existence of the inhabitants of the world who have failed to profit from the exosomatic bonanza of fossil fuels, and who have difficulties even in reaching the minimum endosomatic energy intake, could cause them to interpret the human history of the last two hundred years in terms of growth of destructive forces to the benefit of a minority; thus, they would lose faith in economic growth or in the development of productive forces, and this would activate their redistributive urgencies.

[2] Cf. the accounts explained in chapter 2.

I am puzzled by the fact that left-wing ecologism has grown in the 1970s, and it is still growing, not so much in the Third World as among part of the youth of some of the most over-developed countries. This book, though born and grown to such lengths out of scholarly curiosity, is probably also a by-product of 'German' political ecologism. The questions of why the 'green' movement has had such an extremely long gestation period, and why it has ignored some quite impressive ancestors could be asked. But why was it born at all in the early 1970s? Why was a history of ecological economics not written long ago? Why is it possible that several similar books are now being written, more or less at the same time?

It is a fact that the ecological critique only started to bite politically shortly after the student rebellion of 1968 which spread from Berkeley to Berlin. It is also unfortunate that it coincided with an anti-empiricist, anti-rational passing fashion in which, so to speak, astrophysics was less valued than astrology, and the study of the physiology of nutrition was less appreciated than the latest food fad.

Nowadays, a kind of ecological Marxism such as that proposed in the present book is rapidly gaining ground in Berlin, though certainly not at all in Berkeley. There is some inconsistency about caring for conservation of world resources while enjoying the average standard of living of prosperous Frankfurt, Amsterdam or Berlin. Perhaps consciousness is not strictly determined in all cases by social circumstances. 'Green' politics is now stronger in some European countries than in the United States, but most of the ecological literature, scientific and political, of the late 1960s and early 1970s came to Europe from America. Barry Commoner deserves a special mention. The wilderness mystique of the 1960s was part of the hippies' pacifist communalism, particularly in California: the growth of the so-called 'counterculture' was described as 'the greening of America' by Charles Reich's book of 1971, but North American environmentalism wilted in the 1980s. This is not surprising in a country whose citizens recovered their usual self-congratulatory mood blissfully unaware (in the best of cases) that their average standard of living is not replicable in the rest of the world because it implies such a disproportionate use of the earth's resources. Back in the 1960s, however, the old Sierra Club, Friends of the Earth (founded in 1969), and countless other groups, cared for environmental protection with a fervour unknown in Europe, where the activists of 1968, students like Cohn-Bendit in Paris or Rudi Deutschke in Berlin or the editors of the *New Left Review* in London, were still unaware of the basic principles of human ecology.

However, some of the themes and writers of 1968 prepared the terrain for the ecological critique. Not only Maoism and Guevarism, but also, for instance, Bloch's Marxian utopianism, which dates back to 1918; the revival of anarchist communalism, though in some versions (Murray Bookchin's) it was initially based on an ethno-centric North American assumption of abundance; the 'dependency' school of international relations (or the 'development of under-development' in A. G. Frank's words), though it paid no attention to ecological economics; and, perhaps mainly, Marcuse's critique of the 'uni-dimensionality' of man under modern capitalism, which was certainly a critique of commodity fetishism (the fiction of commensurability) even though it did not emphasize the depletion and unequal distribution of resources.

An alternative explanation of the success of left-wing ecologism is not so much the preparatory work of 1968, but the reality of 1973: the 'energy crisis'. But this term could as well mean the lack of endosomatic consumption of satisfactory amounts of food energy; in this sense, the year 1973 is irrelevant. Even if only fossil fuels for industrial use were considered, the amounts available were not significantly lower or higher in 1973 than in 1963 or in 1983, and OPEC had been founded some years earlier. If the price of oil increased in 1973, it was because the perception of reality changed in some quarters. It could have changed earlier, should ecological economics have become an accepted academic subject and/or a basis for a political ideology.

As this book has emphasized time and again, the ecological critique of economics was already experiencing a minor boom a few years before 1973. Boulding's, Daly's and Georgescu-Roegen's contributions are well known to economists, but the writings of Barry Commoner, Paul Ehrlich, Amory Lovins, Howard Odum, Earl Cook, Ignacy Sachs, Ivan Illich, Malcolm Caldwell, Barbara Ward, became better known among a wider public.[3] If one reads the thorough survey of environmentalism by O'Riordan (2nd edn, 1981) with its impressive bibliography, one is struck by its relatively narrow geographical focus on Britain and the United States. Why are there not strong ecological movements in India, in Africa? Why has the question of unequal exchange not been posed in ecological terms until quite recently (Bunker, 1985), and still without political consequences? Despite the changes in post-Maoist China, the idea of a Third World 'ecopopulism' has grown over the last few years, for instance in the work of Narindar Singh (1977), who wrote on the 'malignancy of overdevelopment', Riddell (1981), Redclift (1984), but so far there are almost no ecological social movements with roots in the Third World.

---

[3] For a list of works on energy, the economy and society in the 1950s and 1960s, especially from the United States, cf. Cutler J. Cleveland, 'Biophysical economics: historical perspective and current recent trends', in Costanza and Daly, eds, 1987.

Coming back to Europe, while a current of competent and persistent ecological politics keeps growing in Germany and other countries, there is the puzzle of the failure in France of a link between the traditions of the Marxist left and the new ecologism, in contrast to Germany. This is important for Latin America and parts of Africa, and also for southern Europe where the Left has traditionally relied so much on Parisian intellectual fashions. John Rodman's persuasive review of André Gorz's *Ecology as Politics*, a book first published in French in the mid-1970s, explains that it contains 'readable popularizations of the ideas of more original thinkers (most importantly, Ivan Illich). In their day, they may have puffed fresh air into the musty Marxian closet of the Parisian intelligentsia, but breathless, uncritical enthusiasm for new revelations dates quickly' (Rodman, 1984, p. 318–25).

In the next upsurge of the political cycle (perhaps in the 1990s after the present trough), left-wing ecologism possibly will go on growing, and will put down roots also in environments more natural to it than Berlin or Amsterdam. Should this happen, it will not be because we know now about resource exhaustion and we did not know before. 'We' have known, or could have known, all the time; what matters is how facts of the history of nature are ascertained and interpreted in human history, and not their disembodied reality. The new ecological economists (such as Georgescu-Roegen and a few others) anticipated 1973 by a few years, though they had initially (and have even now) little impact. They themselves were largely unaware of the old ecological economics which have been studied in this book. Depletion of resources, the flow of energy and materials, are historical phenomena; their perception is also historical.

Signs that perceptions are changing and that a kind of ecological neo-narodism is beginning to grow (intellectually, rather than politically) can be seen in Mexico, where dependence on imports of cereals (not mainly as animal feedstuffs, as in the Soviet Union, but for direct human consumption) has grown to about twenty per cent of total consumption. At the same time, Mexico is exporting and is planning to export large quantities of oil and natural gas to the United States, where their cereals come from. Another spectacular case is Morocco, where, at the beginning of 1984, there were food riots and several hundred deaths, because of price increases in the context of stabilization policies inspired by the IMF and the World Bank as conditions for the renegotiation of the external debt. In this particular country, large imports of wheat go together with exports of phosphates. The calculus of comparative advantage would give different results if the Mexican peasant's work were counted at an opportunity cost in which the scarcity of jobs in the cities and the negative externalities of extreme urban congestion were taken into account, and if exhaustible resources were valued within a longer time horizon and with lower rates of discount of the present value of future demand.

Schejtman has argued that in countries where the rural population is still over 30 per cent, and where malnutrition is widespread in urban as well as in rural areas, the food supply should not depend on the capitalist sector and imports; the peasantry should become the main pillar of a strategy of national and individual food security.[4] There is the fact (which Schejtman himself analysed and which other writers, for instance in the context of the discussion on sharecropping, have also pointed out) that peasants use their own labour power and that of their families with greater intensity than under conditions of wage-labour. There is the further fact that the external non-renewable energy subsidy for traditional agriculture is much less than for 'modern' agriculture.[5] Not only have the imports of cereals increased, there is also an increasing payments deficit on account of imports of fertilizers, pesticides and agricultural machinery in Latin America.[6] Schejtman points out (1983, pp. 178–80) that to imitate the United States' food systems models in Latin America, both with regard to methods of production and patterns of consumption, would imply (on the basis of the Steinharts' calculation, Steinhart, 1974) that feeding the Latin American population would require the equivalent of seven million barrels per day of oil (that is, about seven times Brazil's imports, and four times Mexico's exports in the mid-1980s). Such quantities are large, but not implausibly large. Even the most intensive agriculture finds limits to growth in the capacity of the human body for consumption of food, though such limits can be pushed far through meat consumption, and even further if the fact that the conversion of fossil fuels into slightly larger quantities of ethanol makes chrematistic sense is taken into account.

The energy subsidy required to put the Latin American food system on a United States standard is about 20 per cent of the United States' consumption of fossil fuels for all purposes. Therefore it is not wildly unrealistic to believe in the full modernization of Latin American agriculture, already a relatively industrialized urbanized and peasantless continent.

[4] Cf. Schejtman , 1983. Alex Schejtman, an Oxford graduate, is a leading author in the economics of peasant farming; he was a member of the Allende administration in Chile between 1970 and 1973, and currently works for FAO and CEPAL.
[5] Initial accounts of Mexican agrarian neo-populism under the SAM programme did not yet mention the energy-intensity argument. Cf. Redclift, 1980; Durnston, 1983.
[6] It has been asserted that in the so-called developing countries, 'for every one per cent growth in the food production system there is an approximately two per cent growth in commercial energy use'. United Nations Research Institute for Social Development, 1983, p. 25. This looks too low, on the basis of Campos' and Naredo's work in Spain (Naredo and Campos, 1980, cf. ch. 2 above).

However, since it seems unlikely, for socio-political and chrematistic reasons, that such resources will be made available by the Good Neighbour or anybody else, energy accounting is now beginning to provide a tenable argument in favour of the persistency of the peasantry, in terms of its role in feeding the population with minimum use of non-renewable forms of energy. The ancient vision of the best-known agricultural economists,[7] that a decrease in the share of population in the 'primary sector' is in principle to be welcomed as a sign of viable and permanent economic development, will now be strongly questioned. This vision was based on non-ecological definitions of agricultural 'production' and 'productivity'.

The term 'ecological neo-narodism' will be embarrassing to Marxists, because one characteristic of agrarian populism has been to underplay cumulative social differentiation and class struggle in the countryside. Research on Podolinsky's life done for this book shows the *narodniki* to have been close to egalitarian ecologism. Marx himself, at the end of his life, thought they were genuine friends of the people (Shanin, 1983).

It could be argued, however, that 'ecological' is an unsuitable word to apply to peasants, especially to poor peasants. Forced by the land tenure system and by the restrictions on emigration to richer countries (so obvious in the Mexican or Moroccan cases), peasants are driven onto the mountain slopes or, as in Brazil, towards fragile tropical soils which they rapidly spoil. Where the practices associated with shifting cultivation are coupled with heavy pressure on the land, final deforestation follows. However, in the restricted sense in which the material has led me to use it in this book (as it mainly concerns the study of the flow of energy), 'ecological' is a suitable word because of the indisputable superiority of traditional peasant agriculture for the conservation of fossil fuels. Nevertheless, the peasants' virtues, which are once more appreciated (their capacity to be exploited, their use of renewable energies), are virtues only in the social context of an extremely unequal national and international distribution of resources. The survival of hard-working peasant agriculture is possibly becoming an adaptive ecological imperative for the nutrition of the world's population *only* because of the very high consumption of exhaustible resources by *some* people, in *some* areas, mainly for non-agricultural purposes. After all, the use of non-renewable forms of energy in the food systems of the over-developed countries is enormous, compared with its use for *all* purposes in poor countries, but it is a *small* proportion of total non-renewable energy use in the rich countries and in the world.

---

[7] Johnston and Mellor, 1984. Hard to believe, but there is no reference in this article to (for instance) David Pimentel's work.

Redistribution of the world's resources would be most swiftly achieved by allowing free movement of populations, although mainstream political philosophy does not consider free migration to be a right. With this question taken off the agenda, the case against conservation of resources becomes easier to make. The argument runs as follows: 'There is no real hope of bringing about a just distribution of resources in the world in the immediately foreseeable future. To ensure that the unjustly treated majority of persons in the world today will enjoy their rights, we must greatly increase resource use in the Third World. If that occurs, conservation could then be achieved only by massive cutbacks in resource use in the affluent countries of kinds which are socially, economically, and politically such as to be practically impossible to achieve. Given these facts, the demand for conservation will in effect become what is already is in the writings of its exponents, a demand that resource use be pegged as near present levels as possible, with roughly the present distribution' (McCloskey, 1983, p. 86). However, such a collection of unexplained 'facts' cannot satisfy a social scientist, and moreover a Third World perspective would certainly include among the facts to be explained not so much the existing migratory currents as the *lack* of mass migration from states where most people are poor to states where many people are rich. Being a student of ecological ethics and politics, McCloskey is aware that the distribution of population is an important issue, but he considers free migration to be not a right but rather a benevolent political action on the part of the recipient countries on a level with removal of tariffs or technological aid (ibid., p. 87).

The Social Base of Ecologism: Examples from the Andes

There are two sets of questions which should be discussed before bringing this chapter to a close. First, will the new biotechnologies increase yields without increasing energy intensity? Will they be neutral concerning scale or will they favour large farms, as with the misnamed Green Revolution of the 1960s and 1970s? What effects will the release of new genetic materials have on the environment? Such questions go beyond the scope of this book, but their answers *might* deprive agricultural energetics of its social relevance.[8] Thus, in Brazil, although the debate on the energy intensity of 'modern' agriculture has been more intense than elsewhere because of the ethanol programme, the main topic of debate among agricultural experts is not, as in Mexico and Peru, the virtues of 'traditional'

---

[8] Cf., for example, Buttel, Kenney and Kloppenburg, 1985, Doyle, 1985, Kenney, 1985, Wolf, 1986.

agriculture for sustainable development, but on the contrary, the promises offered by the new biotechnologies. With exceptions such as the group around Fernando Homem de Melo, and also José Lutzenberger, the debate centres on whether national capitalism will be able to control and develop biotechnologies or whether foreign domination will increase (Sorj and Wilkinson, 1984; Sorj, Wilkinson and Coradini, 1984; Ozorio de Almeida, 1984).

From the point of view of maintaining and increasing genetic variability, traditional agriculture has been manifestly superior. Norgaard has remarked:

> In the context of our coevolutionary agricultural past, the conflicts between economic and ecological thinking suggest radical changes. Rather than simply modifying existing economic systems to reduce the rate of extinction, the co-evolutionary perspective indicates how people could return to their role as active participants in the creation of diversity . . . A shift to an evolutionary world view will encourage an emphasis on particulars, regional differentiation, and the reestablishment of locally unique ecosystems which foster biological diversity. (Norgaard, 1986, unpubl.)

In the second place, are there any signs anywhere of the growth of ecological neo-narodism as an effective movement with social roots and not merely as the speculation of North Atlantic Marxists reconverted to ecologism?[9] Because of my familiarity with the Andean region, I have attempted to find such signs in that area, rather than in Asia or Africa, or in other areas of Latin America (cf. Bunker, 1985, on the Amazonia). However, the following pages should be seen merely as an introduction to a new research project, and not as a finished essay on Andean ecological neo-narodism.

Bolivia and Peru are suitable countries for the study of quite diverse ecosystems, since they contain highlands, Andean valleys, and tropical lowlands. Already a substantial amount of work has been done on Andean human ecology, because of the research on the biological adaptations and cultural practices associated with living at high altitude, and also because of the interest in the exchanges between different ecological levels, in pre-hispanic and post-conquest days: John Murra's 'vertical economy' (Brush, 1974, 1982; Brooke Thomas, 1976; Millones and Tomoeda, 1982; Masuda, Shimada and Morris, 1985). In Bolivia, research on human ecology has been promoted by the Instituto de Ecologia, in La Paz, which is a joint undertaking of the University of San Andrés and the University of Göttingen. The Institute publishes a review, *Ecologia en Bolivia*, and

---

[9] See for example Helmut Thielen, 1985, on Nicaragua.

it has also published the proceedings of a symposium held in 1982,[10] including one article by Franz Augstburger on 'Agrobiology as a new perspective', which compared the 'Green Revolution' to agrobiology. The 'Green Revolution' increased energy inputs, decreased the fertility of the land and increased erosion, and contaminated food and environment with pesticides and waste from fertilizers. Augstburger shows the feasibility of 'agrobiology' in Bolivia by drawing up detailed balances of the availability and use of organic fertilizers and he praises pre-hispanic agriculture, by which 'fewer than thirty per cent of the population produced food for the whole empire'. This is a generalized view today in the Andes (Antunez de Mayolo, 1981) which might be described as a retrospective utopianism (Flores Galindo and Burga, 1982; Flores Galindo, 1987).[11]

Even the common traveller becomes aware of the erosion and salinization in the Bolivian highlands, and the long history of spoliation by foreigners or to the benefit of foreigners (from Potosi to the tin mining of today), is well known. Colonial and contemporary mining in Bolivia is a good instance of the principle that 'the power to exploit the natural environment and the power to exploit other humans are closely related' (Bunker, 1985, p. 14). Bolivian society, like Peruvian society in the age of guano, has not been able to produce a successful social power structure which would struggle effectively in order to conserve resources and in order to increase their pecuniary export value. The miners of Catavi and Siglo XX will go down fighting but nevertheless their numbers and political clout are about to be drastically reduced as the mines become exhausted. June Nash (1979, p. 17) pointed out that Bolivian miners see the history of their country as the exploitation of national riches and of their own physical forces for the enrichment of others. An interesting survey by Mansilla (1984) on the perception of ecological issues by entrepreneurs, unionists, students and journalists in Bolivia shows, however, that there is little environmental awareness. The survey did not include peasants, and this leads to be asked the crucial question for the success of ecological neo-narodism; will it find a social base among the peasanty?

An answer to this question may be seen, rather hazily, in the following account by John Earls, an anthropologist working in the Andes:

In the first months of 1977 I was in the Comunidad de Sarhua (Victor Fajardo, Ayacucho). One of the inhabitants told me why the 'ancients' had built so many terraces on the hills and mountains overlooking the Qaracha river. Such walls, built I believe in the Wari period, are nowadays almost completely destroyed though

---

[10] Geyger and Arce (eds), 1982.
[11] Augstburger spoils his praise of ecological agriculture with an unnecessary reference to Steiner (1924). He also quotes Howard (1948).

their outline can still be traced. My sarhuino friend took a handful of soil, so sandy that it was of no use for agriculture, and he told me that the Sarhua soils are becoming more and more like this, because the governments of today do not care for the walls, and every year the rains wash out the soil and carry it down to the Pampas and Apurimac rivers, towards the Amazon . . . Besides, in Sarhua and in the whole Sierra the people need food but they eat more in Lima where they produce scarcely any food at all: one day of hunger will arrive, when the people from Lima will come back to the Sierra to work on useful things, such as walls and water ditches, as in ancient times.

John Earls continues:

At that time of the year, the rains had not yet come and it seemed as if there would be a drought. The government had sent an agricultural officer to the communities in the region, to report on the food situation. When I asked him why the terraces were not rebuilt – having in mind the conversation with the peasant – he replied that this work would not pay. There is no doubt whatever [concludes John Earls] on whose theory, regarding the relations between the speeds of change of factors which are basic for sustainable agricultural production, is really acceptable: the peasant's theory and its catastrophic prediction would accord with the ecologist's view. (Earls, 1977, in Lajo, 1982, pp. 26–7; see also Burga and De la Torre, 1986)

A different assessment of the present value of future benefits is seen here. In terms of economic theory, the peasant was making use of a lower rate of discount than the government's agricultural officer. At least some peasants, when asked the right questions, give ecological answers.[12]

It is not known whether this is or will become the general peasant outlook.[13] In any case, some local agronomists, influenced perhaps more by anthropologists than directly by peasants, share wholeheartedly in such Andean agronomic pride. Thus, it has been written that the domestication of maize, potatoes, *olluco*, *mashua*, *quinua*, *ají*, *camote*, *oca*, cassava, tomatoes, cotton, beans such as *frejol* and *pallares*, and of animals such as the llama, the alpaca and the guinea pig, were first made in the Andes. Set against such initial achievements, contemporary genetic improvements of the same species are of little consequence. Agriculture is believed to have begun in the Andes 8,000 years ago, earlier than anywhere else (Grillo, in Lajo, 1982, p. 229–30; also Grillo, 1985, p. 7–56). The 'Western' attitude towards technology, as an instrument of domination of nature, would be alien to the Andean concept of reciprocity between

---

[12] For an empirical appraisal of erosion in the Andes, with particular reference to a region in Bolivia, see R. Godoy, 1984. p. 359–83.
[13] Cf. Richards, 1985 (on Africa).

humankind and nature. The 'non-Western' attitude is based upon the self-regulation of needs and the education of desires, so that resources may be maintained and improved, creating conditions for a better valorization of solar energy in biological cycles (Grillo, in Lajo, 1982, p. 227–8).

Now, however, there is no doubt, against such 'non-Western' views, that human ecology as a science, that is, the study of the 'metabolism' between humankind and nature, started, as we have seen, in Europe. But the question is not so much the historical geography of scientific knowledge as the current politics of egalitarian ecologism. Will Podolinsky, Popper-Lynkeus, or even Georgescu-Roegen, be more useful politically in the North Atlantic or in the Third World, in Berlin or in Cusco, in Nicaragua or in Amsterdam? Should the FAO and CEPAL officials succeed in selling to governments the concept of 'food security', partly defined by 'sustainability' (cf. also Douglass, 1984, and particularly Senayake on Sri Lanka, 1984; also Bayliss-Smith on Karnataka, India, 1984), then a political pro-peasant ecologism would be closer. One may doubt, however, whether international bureaucrats will really become the organic collective intellectuals of a new revolutionary subject, the world's rural poor. The social traits of the peasantry and agricultural proletariat, and the political repression which hinder their organization should also be kept in mind.

In Bolivia, the Túpac Katari movement, favourably inclined towards the Indian peasantry, is receptive to political ecologism (Rivera Cusicanqui, 1984), while in Peru, in my view there is not much distance between political pro-peasant ecologism, and the extremely radical Maoism, which takes as its main point the critique of 'bureaucratic capitalism' and which is the ideological nourishment of the Sendero Luminoso movement. Thus, the agronomist Antonio Díaz described in 1969 the hacienda Allpachaka in the department of Ayacucho in the following terms:

The owner sold the hacienda to the University . . . In this way, the culture of the city, of the *mestizos* and *criollos*, 'white' culture, reached the hacienda where sixteen peasant families with their own indigenous, rural, autochthonous culture had been living. The cultural values of both groups are very different. Their behaviour also. Agronomists and students of agronomy will take barely notice of the peasants, they see them as working tools. They measure development by the number of tractors, by yields, in terms of capitalist rationality. They could not care less for the culture of such 'inferior indians'. (Díaz Martinez, 2nd edn, 1985, p. 39)

The author was reaching for a concept of 'cultural erosion' due to Westernization, modernization of techniques (and, in this case, Castilianization), that is, the loss of knowledge of traditional agronomic practices which often goes with the loss of varieties of plants – 'genetic erosion'.[14]

Without connection to Sendero Luminoso, but rather to the more moderate United Left, there grew among agrarian experts in Peru in the early 1980s the view that the central role in a policy of 'food security' should be played by the peasantry, and that this should go together with a change in food habits away from imported foodstuffs (such as wheat and powdered milk). The motivation is mainly anti-imperialist; the arguments fit well with ecological economics. Thus, Manuel Lajo stressed that

if the question were how to apply the principle of comparative advantage to the allocation of the resources of Peruvian agriculture, then we would probably choose sugar, coffee, cotton, wool. Production of . . . basic products for the nutrition of the population would be irrational, according to the theory of comparative advantage, since it is cheaper to import them from the overdeveloped and subsidized agriculture of the United States, Europe or New Zealand. (Lajo, 1982, p. 15)

There is an implicit question here, which goes far beyond the debate on export-led growth (or non-growth) versus substitution of imports: what is the *measure* to be used in order to calculate costs? While European exports are certainly subsidized, this is not the case for New Zealand's exports and it is not always the case for the United States' exports, unless we would reasonably consider the 'low' price of non-renewable inputs as a hidden subsidy.

In energy terms, production from the over-developed countries is not cheaper, but more expensive, though a chrematistic standard of measurement might give different results. This could have been common knowledge for a long time. How should we explain, therefore, the poor academic and extra-academic reception of human ecological energetics and of ecological economics for about one hundred years? How should we explain that no political use has been made of their findings, in contrast, for instance, to Marxism, neo-classical economics, and Keynesianism, in contrast also to social-Darwinism? Why may one legitimately put the question today as to whether such political use is about to be made, in a new ecological narodism, which can be combined without excessive difficulty with some varieties of anarchism and of Marxism? The original contribution made in this book, if any, does not lie in the answers which may be given to such questions but, rather, in the questions themselves.

---

[14] This paragraph was written a few months before Antonio Díaz Martinez's assassination in prison in Lima, in June 1986, with three hundred other political prisoners, apparently on government orders. He was also the author of a book on Chinese agriculture, an extended report of a long field trip, published in 1977. I had known him since 1970; we were friends.

Bibliography

Adams, Henry, 1918: *The Education of Henry Adams: an Autobiography*, ed. Henry Cabot Lodge, Houghton Mifflin Co. (The Riverside Press, Cambridge), Boston and New York (Sentry edn 1961, introd. D. W. Brogan).

Adams, Henry, 1919: *The Degradation of the Democratic Dogma*, with introduction by Brooks Adams, Macmillan, New York.

Adams, Henry, 1938: *Letters*, vol. II, ed. Worthington Chauncey Ford, Houghton Mifflin Co., repr. Kraus, New York, 1969.

Adams, Richard N., 1975: *Energy and Structure: a Theory of Social Power*, University of Texas Press, Austin and London.

Adams, Richard N., 1982: *Paradoxical Harvest. Energy and Explanation in British History*, Cambridge University Press.

Adams, Richard N., 1984: *The Eighth Day: Human Society and the Self-Organization of the Energy Process*, unpublished MS.

Adler, F. W., 1905: 'Bemerkungen über die Metaphysik in der Ostwald'schen Energetik', *Vierteljahrschrift für wissenschaftliche Philosophie und Soziologie*, Reisland, Leipzig, 29, III, 287–333.

Akin, William E., 1977: *Technocracy and the American Dream: the Technocrat Movement*, University of California Press, Berkeley.

Altieri, Miguel, 1985: *Agroecología: Bases científicas de la agricultura alternativa*, CETAL, Valparaíso, (English edn, Berkeley, Ca, 1983).

Anais do IV Simposio Internacional sobre Tecnologia dos Alcoois como Combustivel, 1980: Guarujà, São Paulo, Oct.

Anthony, Peter, 1983: *John Ruskin's Labour: a Study of Ruskin's Social Theory*, Cambridge University Press.

Antúnez de Mayolo, Santiago Erik, 1981: *La nutrición en el antiguo Perú*, Banco Central de Reserva del Perú, Oficina Numismática, Lima.

Arkright, Frank, 1933: *The ABC of Technocracy*, Hamish Hamilton, London.

Armytage, W. H. G., 1968: *Yesterday's Tomorrows: a Historical Survey of Future Societies*, Routledge and Kegan Paul, London.

Babbage, Charles, 1971: *On the Economy of Machinery and Manufactures* (1832), Augustus Kelley, New York.

Baker, Paul T. and Little, Michael A., 1976: *Man in the Andes: a Multidisciplinary Study of High-altitude Quechua*, Dowden, Hutchinson & Ross, Stroudsburg, Penn.

Ballestrem, Karl G., 1969: 'Lenin and Bogdanov', *Studies in Soviet Thought*, 9, Dec.

Ballod, Carl, 1898: *Produktion und Konsum in Sozialstaat*, with preface by Karl Kautsky, Dietz, Stuttgart.

Ballod (Atlanticus), Karl, 1927: *Der Zukunftsstaat: Wirtschaftstechnisches Ideal und Volkswirtschaftliche Wirklichkeit*, 4th edn, Laub, Berlin.

Baracca, A. and Rossi, A, 1978: *Materia ed energia*, Feltrinelli, Milan.

Baracca, A., Ruffo, S. and Russo, A., 1979: *Scienza e industria 1848-1915*, Laterza, Bari.

Barnich, G., 1919: *Essai de politique positive basée sur l'energétique sociale de Solvay*, Lebègue, Brussels.

Barry, Brian and Hardin, Russell, eds, 1982: *Rational Man and Irrational Society? An Introduction and a Sourcebook*, Sage, London.

Barth, Frederick, 'Economic spheres in Darfur', in Firth, 1970.

Bauer, Otto, 1933, 1934: *Werkausgabe*, vol. 7, pp. 496–517, vol. 9, p. 341f, Vienna.

Bayliss-Smith, Tim, 'Energy Flows and Agrarian Change in Karnataka: the Green Revolution and Micro Scale', in T. Bayliss-Smith & Sudhir Wanmali, eds, *Understanding Green Revolutions: Essays in Honour of B. H. Farmer*, Cambridge University Press, 153–72.

Bazukis, Egolfs, 1969: 'Forestry viewed in an ecosystem perspective', in Van Dyne, 1969, 189–258.

Bebel, August, *Die Frau und der Sozialismus* (1883), English edn, Schocken, New York (Appendix on Population and Resources).

Bebel, A. and Bernstein, E., 1919: *Der Briefwechsel zwischen Friedrich Engels und Karl Marx*, Dietz, Stuttgart.

Becker, Gary S., 1981: *A Treatise on the Family*, Harvard University Press.

Becker, Gary S. and Tomes, N., 1979: 'An Equilibrium Theory of the Distribution of Income and Inter-generational Mobility', *Journal of Political Economy*, 87.

Benson, Norman F., 1965: *The Origins and Impact of an American Radicalism: a History of Technocracy Inc.*, doctoral thesis, Ball State University, Muncie, Indiana.

Bernal, J. D., 1939: *The Social Function of Science*, Routledge and Kegan Paul, London.

Bernal, J. D., 1954: *Science in History*, Watts, London.

Berndt, Ernst R., 1985: *From Technocracy to Net Analysis: Engineers, Economists, and Recurring Energy Theories of Value*, MIT Center for Energy Research Policy, Cambridge, Mass., Reprint Series no. 54.

Bernecker, Walther, 1982: *Colectividades y revolución social*, Crítica, Barcelona.

Berneri, Mari Louise, 1951: *Journey through Utopia*, Beacon Press, Boston.

Bertalanffy, L. von, 1950: 'The Theory of Open Systems in Physics and Biology', in F. E. Emery, ed., *Systems Thinking*, Penguin, 1969.

Birman, Igo, 1978: 'From the Achieved Level', *Soviet Studies*, XXX, April.

Blaug, M., 1982: *The Methodology of Economics*, Cambridge University Press.

Boardman, P., 1978: *The Worlds of Patrick Geddes*, Routledge & Kegan Paul, London.

Bogdanov, A., *A short course of economic science*, Labour Publishing Co., London, 1923; *Allgemeine Organizationslehre*, S. Hirzel, Berlin, 1926; *Essays in Tektology* (English trans. by G. Gorelike), Intersystems Publishing Seaside, Ca. 1984; *Der rote Stern, ein utopischer Roman*, Verlag der Jugend-internationale, Berlin, 1923; *La science, l'art et la classe ouvrière* (présentations par Dominique Lecourt et Henry Deluy), Maspéro, Paris, 1977. (Bogdanov's writings on Marxist philosophy before 1909 have apparently not been translated from Russian into West European languages).

Bohm, R. A., Clinard, L. A. and English, M. R., 1982: *World Energy Production and Productivity: Proceedings of an international Symposium*, Ballinger, Cambridge, Mass.

Boland, Lawrence, 1982: *The Foundations of Economic Method*, Allen & Unwin, London.

Bölsche, W., 1898–1902: *Das Liebesleben in der Natur*, Diederich, Leipzig.

Boltzmann, Ludwig, 1905: *Populäre Schriften*, Barth, Leipzig.

Bonilla, Heraclio, 1974: *Guano y burguesia en el Perú*, IEP, Lima.

Boserup, Ester, 1965: *The Conditions of Agricultural Growth*, Chicago University Press.

Boserup, Ester, 1981: *Population and Technological Change: a Study of Long-term Trends*, Chicago University Press.

Boserup, Ester, 1983: 'The Impact of Scarcity and Plenty on Development', *Journal of Interdisciplinary History*, XIV, 2.

Bottomore, Tom, 1984: *Sociology and Socialism*, Wheatsheaf, Brighton.

Boulding, Kenneth, 1966: 'The Economics of the Coming Spaceship Earth', in H. Jarret, ed., *Environmental Quality in a Growing Economy*, Johns Hopkins Press, Baltimore.

Boulding, Kenneth, 1972: 'Toward the Development of a Cultural Economics', *Social Science Quarterly*, 53 (2), 267–84, reprinted in *Collected Papers*, vol. VI.

Boussingault, J. R., 1845: *Rural Economy in its Relations with Chemistry, Physics and Meteorology; or An Application of the Principles of Chemistry and Physiology to the Details of Practical Farming*, Baillière, London.

Bowden, Witt, Karpovich, Michael and Usher, Abbot Payson, 1937: *An Economic History of Europe since 1750*, American Book Co., New York.

Brown, L. R., 1980: *Food or Fuel: New Competition for the World's Cropland*, Worldwatch Paper 35, Washington DC.

Brüggen, Nikolaus Freiherr von der, 1934: *Wohlstand für Alle: Grundsätzliche Orienterung über eine neue Nationalökonomie nach Professor F. Soddy*, Riga.

Brunhes, Bernard, 1908: *La dégradation de l'énergie*; 2nd edn Flammarion, Paris, 1912.

Brunhes, Jean, 1925, *La Géographie Humaine*, 3rd edn, Alcan, Paris.

Brush, Stephen, 1974: 'El lugar del hombre en el ecosistema andino', *Revista del Museo Nacional*, XL, 279–301, Lima.

Brush, Stephen, 1982: 'The Natural and Human Environment of the Central Andes', *Mountain Research and Development*, II (1).

Brush, Stephen, 1986: 'Genetic Diversity and Conservation in Traditional Farming Systems', *Journal of Ethnobiology*, 6 (1), 151–67.

Budyko, M. I., 1980: *Global Ecology*, Progress Publishers, Moscow.

Bueno de Mesquita, Bruce, 1983: 'The Cost of War: a Rational Expectations Approach', *American Political Science Review*, 77 (2).

Bukharin, N. I., 1922: *Theorie des Historischen Materialismus*, Verlag der Kommunistischen Internationale, Hamburg.

Bukharin, N. I., 1927: *La théorie du matérialisme historique*, Editions Sociales Internationales, Paris.

Bukharin, N. I., Hessen, Boris et al., 1931: *Science at the Crossroads: Papers presented to the International Congress of the History of Science*, Kniga, London (new edn, Frank Cass, London, 1971).

Bunge, Mario, 1980: 'Tres concepciones de la sociedad', *Epistemologia*, Ariel, Barcelona.

Bunge, Mario, 1982: *Economía y filosofia*, Tecnos, Madrid.

Bunker, Stephen, 1985: *Underdeveloping the Amazon: Extraction, Unequal Exchange and the Failure of the Modern State*, University of Illinois Press, Urbana and Chicago.

Burga, M. and De la Torre, C., 1986: *Andenes y camellones en el Perú andino*, CONCYTEC, Lima.

Buttel, Fred, 1980: 'Agriculture, Environment and Social Change: some Emergent Issues', in F. Buttel and H. Newby, *The Rural Sociology of Advanced Societies*, Croom Helm, London.

Buttel, Fred, Kenney, Martin and Kloppenburg, Jack, 1985: 'From Green Revolution to Biorevolution: Some Observations on the Changing Technological Bases of Economic Transformation in the Third World', *Economic Development and Cultural Change*, 34 (1).

Bynum, W. F., Brown, E. J. and Porter, R., 1983: *Dictionary of the History of Science*, Macmillan, London.

Caldwell, Malcolm, 1977: *The Wealth of Some Nations*, Zed, London.

Cannon, S. F., 1978: *Science in Culture: the Early Victorian Period*, Dawson, Kent.

Capel, Horacio, 1983: *Filosofia y Ciencia en la Geografia contemporánea*, Barcanova, Barcelona.

Capra, Fritjof, 1983: *The Turning Point: Science, Society and the Rising Culture*, Fontana, London.

Cardwell, D. S. L., 1971: *From Watt to Clausius: the Rise of Thermodynamics in the Early Industrial Age*, Cornell University Press, Ithaca, New York.

Carlson, E. A., 1981: *Genes, Radiation and Society: the Life and Work of H. J. Muller*, Cornell University Press, Ithaca, New York.

Carnap, Rudolf, 1969: *Foundations of the Unity of Science*, vol. I, University of Chicago Press, orig. *International Encyclopaedia of Unified Science*, ed. Otto Neurath, Rudolf Carnap and Charles Morris, 1938.

Carnot, Sadi, 1978: *Réflexions sur la puissance motrice du feu et sur les machines propres à développer cette puissance* (1824), ed. Robert Fox, Vrin, Paris.

Carreras, A., Maluquer de Motes, J., Nadal, J. and Sudrià, C., 1987: *El dilema energètic en la industrialització catalana*, L'Avenç, Barcelona.

Carson, Rachel, 1963: *Silent Spring*, Hamish Hamilton, London.

Cawson, Alan, 1983: *A Preliminary Bibliography on Modern Corporatism*, Sussex Working Papers on Corporatism 1, University of Sussex, April.

CEPAL/FAO, 1985: División Agricola Conjunta, *Análisis y diseño de la política alimentaria: lineamientos de un enfoque sistémico*, Taller sobre Análisis y Diseño de la Política Económica en el Sector Agroalimentario, Lima, 6–9 August.

Chapman, Peter, 1975: *Fuel's Paradise: Energy Options for Britain*, Penguin, London.

Chase, Stuart, 1936: *Rich Land, Poor Land: a Study of Waste in the Natural Resources of America*, McGraw Hill, New York.

Chattopadhyaya, Debiprasad, 1979: *Lenin the Philosopher*, Sterling, Calcutta.

Childe, V. Gordon, 1941: *Man Makes Himself*, Watts, London.

Christensen, Paul, 1987: 'The Materials-energy Foundations of Classical Theory', in R. Costanza and H. Daly, eds, 1987.

Cipolla, Carlo, 1974: *The Economic History of World Population* (1962), 6th edn, Penguin, London.

Clark, Colin, 1969: *Population Growth and Land Use*, Macmillan, London.

Clausius, Rudolf, 1885: *Über die Energievorräthe der Natur und ihre Verwerthung zum Nutzen der Menschheit*, Verlag von Max Cohen & Sohn, Bonn.

Claval, Paul, 1974: *Eléments de Géographie Humaine*, Génin, Paris.

Cleveland, C., Costanza, R. and Kaufman, R., 1984: 'Energy and the US Economy', *Science*, 225.

Coates, Ken, ed., 1972: *Socialism and the Environment* (incl. article by M. Caldwell), Spokesman, Nottingham.

Coddington, A., 1970: 'The Economics of Ecology', *New Society*, April.

Cohen, G. A., 1978: *Karl Marx's Theory of History: a Defence*, Oxford University Press.

Cohen, Robert S., 1963: 'Dialectical Materialism and Carnap's Logical Empiricism', in Paul A. Schlipp, ed., *The Philosophy of Rudolf Carnap*, Open Court, La Salle, Illinois.

Coleman, W., 1986: *Biology in the 19th century* (1971), Cambridge University Press.

Colinvaux, Paul, 1973: *Introduction to Ecology*, Wiley, New York.

Colinvaux, Paul, 1976: book review in *Human Ecology*, 4 (3).

Colinvaux, Paul, 1983: *The Fates of Nations: a Biological Theory of History*, Penguin, London.

Connolly, W., 1983: *The Terms of Political Discourse*, 2nd edn, Martin Robertson, Oxford.

Conselho Nacional de Desenvolvimento Cientifico e Tecnologico, 1980: *Avaliacão tecnológica do álcool etílico*, Brasilia, 2nd edn.

Cook, R. E., 1977: 'Raymond Lindeman and the Trophic-Dynamic Concept in Ecology', *Science*, 198, pp. 22–6.

Cornforth, Maurice, 1955: *Science versus Idealism*, Lawrence & Wishart, London.

Costanza, R., 1980: 'Embodied Energy and Economic Valuation', *Science*, 210, 12 Dec.

Costanza, R. and Daly, Herman, eds, 1987: 'Ecological economics', special issue of the review *Ecological Modelling*.

Cottrell, Fred, 1955: *Energy and Society: the Relations between Energy, Social Change and Economic Development*, McGraw Hill, New York.

Cournot, A. A., 1861: *Traité de l'enchaînement des idées fondamentals dans les sciences and dans l'histoire*, Hachette, Paris.

Crabbé, Philippe J., 1983: 'The Contribution of L. C. Gray to the Economic Theory of Exhaustible Resources and its Roots in the History of Economic Thought', *Journal of Environmental Economics and Management*, 10, 195–220.

Crosby, Alfred, 1986: *Ecological Imperialism: the Biological Expansion of Europe, 900–1900*, Cambridge University Press.

Crouch, Colin, 1982: *Trade Unions: the Logic of Collective Action*, Fontana, London.

Dahlberg, Kenneth, ed., 1986: *New Directions for Agriculture and Agricultural Research: Neglected Dimensions and Emerging Alternatives*, Rowman & Allanheld, Totowa, NJ.

Daly, Herman, 1968: 'On Economics as a Life Science', *Journal of Political Economy*, May.

Daly, Herman, 1972: *Toward a Steady State Economy*, Freeman, San Francisco.

Daly, Herman, 1977: *Steady-state Economics: the Economics of Biophysical Equilibrium and Moral Growth*, Freeman, San Francisco.

Daly, Herman, 1980: 'The Economic Thought of Frederick Soddy', *History of Political Economy*, 12 (4), 1980.

Daly, Herman, 1982: 'Chicago School Individualism versus Sexual Reproduction: a Critique of Becker and Tomes', *Journal of Economic Issues*, XVI (1).

Daly, Herman, 1985: 'The Circular Flow of Exchange Value and the Linear Throughput of Matter-Energy: a Case of Misplaced Concreteness', *Review of Social Economy*, Dec. 279–97.

Daly, Herman and Umaña, Alvaro, eds, 1981: *Energy, Economics, and the Environment*, AAAS Selected Symposium, Westview Press, Boulder, Colo.

Darmstadter, J. et al., 1977: *How Industrial Societies Use Energy – a Comparative Analysis*, Johns Hopkins University Press, Baltimore and London.

Dasgupta, P. S., 1982: *The Control of Resources*, Basil Blackwell, Oxford.

Dasgupta, P. S. and Heal, G. M., 1979: *Economic Theory and Exhaustible Resources*, Cambridge University Press.

Daub, Edward E., 1971: 'Rudolf Clausius', in C. Gillispie, *Dictionary of Scientific Biography*, III, 303–11, Scribners, New York.

Davis, J. C., 1981: *Utopia and the Ideal Society*, Cambridge University Press.

Debeir, J. C., Deléage, J. P., Hémery, D., 1986: *Les servitudes de la puissance. Une histoire de l'energie*, Flammarion, Paris.

Defries, Amelia, 1927: *The Interpreter Geddes: the Man and his Gospel*, Routledge, London.

De Gleria, Silvana, 1985: 'Prodotto netto ed energia netta (ovvero: dogma fisiocratico e dogma energetico), *Economia Politica*, II (2).

Desai, Ashok, 1978: 'Development and Energy Consumption', *Oxford Bulletin of Economics and Statistics*, 40.

Deutsch, Karl, ed., 1977: *Ecosocial Systems and Ecopolitics*, UNESCO, Paris.

Diamant, Alfred, 1960: *Austrian Catholics and the First Republic*, Princeton University Press.

Díaz Martínez, Antonio, 1985: *Ayacucho, hambre y esperanza*, 2nd edn, Mosca Azul, Lima.

Dobb, Maurice, 1973: *Theories of Value and Distribution since Adam Smith*, Cambridge University Press.

Douglas, Mary, 1970: 'Primitive rationing', in Firth, 1970.

Douglass, Gordon K., ed., 1984: *Agricultural Sustainability in a Changing World Order*, Westview Press, Boulder, Colo.

Durnston, John, 1983: 'Il Sistema Alimentare Messicano: un nuovo modello di sviluppo sociale o rurale?', *La Questione Agraria*, 9.

Earl, D. E., 1975: *Forest Energy and Economic Development*, Clarendon Press, Oxford.

Earls, John, 1982: 'La coordinación de la producción agrícola en el Tawantisuyu', in Lajo, Ames and Samaniego, 1982.

Easlea, Brian, 1983: *Fathering the Unthinkable*: *Masculinity, Scientists and the Nuclear Arms Race*, Pluto Press, London (ch. 2 on Soddy and Rutherford).

Eden, R. et al., 1981: *Energy Economics*, Cambridge University Press.

Edwards, Paul, 1972: 'Josef Popper-Lynkeus', *Encyclopaedia of Philosophy*, Macmillan, London.

Ehrlich, Paul, Ehrlich, Anne H. and Holdren, John P., 1977: *Ecoscience*: *Population, Resources, Environment*, Freeman, San Francisco, 2nd edn.

Ellen, Roy, 1982: *Environment, Subsistence and System*: *the Ecology of Small-Scale Social Formations*, Cambridge University Press.

Elsner, Henry, 1967: *The Technocrats*: *Prophets of Automation*, Syracuse University Press, Syracuse, New York.

Elster, Jon, 1983: *Explaining Technical Change*: *a Case Study in the Philosophy of Science*, Cambridge University Press.

Elster, Jon, 1985: *Making Sense of Marx*, Cambridge University Press.

Ely, R. T., Hess, R. H., Leith, C. K. and Carver, T. N., 1918: *The Foundations of National Prosperity*: *Studies in the Conservation of Permanent National Resources*, Macmillan, New York. (Carver's article in this volume is not concerned with energy, despite its title).

Engel, Barbara A. and Rosenthal, Clifford N., 1975: *Five Sisters*: *Women against the Tsar*, Knopf, New York.

Engels, F., 1925: *Dialektik der Natur*, MEW edn., vol. 20, Dietz Verlag, Berlin, 1972.

Engels, F., 1882: Letters to Marx, 19 and 22 December 1882, MEW edn, vol 35, Dietz Verlag, Berlin.

Entropie, 1982: Numero Hors Série, Actes du Colloque Thermodynamique et Sciences de l'Homme, Paris.

Esteva, Gustavo, Barkin, David et al., 1980: *La batalla del México rural*, Siglo XXI, Mexico.

Esteva, Gustavo, Barkin, David and Prieto, Ayari, 1984: *Por una nueva política alimentaria*, Sociedad Mexicana de Planificación, Comité promotor de investigaciones para el desarrollo, Mexico.

Faber, M. and Proops, L. R., 1985: 'Interdisciplinary Research between Economists and Physical Scientists: Retrospect and Prospect', *Kyklos*, 38, 599–616.

Falk, Jim, 1982: *Global Fission*: *the Battle over Nuclear Power*, Oxford University Press.

FAO, 1980: 'Energy Cropping versus Agricultural Production', *16th Regional Conference for Latin America*, Havana, Aug.–Sept.

Fedorov, E. K., 1980: *Man and Nature: the Ecological Crisis and Social Progress*, International Publishers, New York.

Fick, Adolf, 1906: *Gesammelte Schriften*, Stahelsche Verlag, Würzburg.

Figner, Vera, 1928: *Nacht über Russland*, Malik Verlag, Berlin.

Firth, Raymond, ed., 1970: *Themes in Economic Anthropology*, Tavistock, London.

Fisher, Anthony, 1981: *Resource and Environmental Economics*, Cambridge University Press.

Flores Galindo, Alberto, 1987: *Buscando un Inca: Utopía e identidad en los Andes*, Casa de las Américas, Havana.

Flores, Galindo, Alberto and Burga, Manuel, 1982: 'La utopía andina', *Allpanchis Phuturinca*, Cusco, XVII (20).

Fluck, R. C. and Baird, D. C., 1980: *Agricultural Energetics*, Avi Publishing Co., Westport.

Foley, Gerald and Nassim, Charlotte, 1981: *The Energy Question*, 2nd edn, Penguin, London.

Footman, David, 1954: *Red Prelude: a Life of A. I. Zhelyabov*, Cresset Press, London.

Frank, André G., 1959: 'Industrial Capital Stocks and Energy Consumption', *Economic Journal*, LXIX, 170–4.

Freedman, Lawrence, 1981: *The Evolution of Nuclear Strategy*, Macmillan, London.

Freedman, Michael I., 1979: 'Frederick Soddy and the Practical Significance of Radioactive Matter', *British Journal for the History of Science* XII (42).

Freitag, Heiko and Martinez-Alier, J., 1982: 'Proálcool – ein Energieprogramm für Brasilien?', *Peripherie*, 9.

Friedman, Milton, 1953: 'The Methodology of Positive Economics', in Hahn and Hollis, 1979.

Frolov, I. T. et al., 1983: *Society and the Environment*, Progress Publishers, Moscow.

Fuchs, Albert, 1949: *Geistige Strömungen in Österreich*, Globus, Vienna.

Fulton, John F. and Wilson, L. G., 1966: *Selected Readings in the History of Physiology*, 2nd edn, Ch. Thomas, Springfield, Ill.

Ganapathy, R. S., ed., 1981: *Agriculture, Rural Energy and Development*, Symposium of the International Association for the Advancement of Appropriate Technology, University of Michigan.

Gardiner, P., 1959: *Theories of History*, Free Press, New York.

Gasman, Daniel, 1971: *The Scientific Origins of National Socialism: Social Darwinism in Ernst Haeckel and the German Monist League*, Elsevier, New York.

Geddes, Patrick, 1881: *The Classification of Statistics and its Results*, A. & C. Black, Edinburgh.

Geddes, Patrick, 1884: *John Ruskin, Economist*, W. Brown, Edinburgh.

Geddes, Patrick, 1885: *An Analysis of the Principles of Economics*, Proceedings of the Royal Society of Edinburgh, read 17 March, 7 April, 16 June, 7 July 1884, reprinted by Williams and Norgate, London.

Geddes, Patrick, 1915: *Cities in Evolution: an Introduction to the Town Planning Movement and to the Study of Civics*, Williams & Norgate, London (new edn, Benn, London, 1968).

Geddes, Patrick, 1926: 'A National Transition', *Sociological Review*, XVIII (Symposium on Coal).

Georgescu-Roegen, Nicholas, 1971: *The Entropy Law and the Economic Process*, Harvard University Press.

Georgescu-Roegen, Nicholas, 1976: *Energy and Economic Myths: Institutional and Analytical Economic Essays*, Pergamon, Oxford.

Georgescu-Rogegen, Nicholas, 1979a: 'Energy Analysis and Economic Valuation', *Southern Economic Journal*, 45.

Georgescu-Roegen, Nicholas, 1979b: 'Comments', in V. Kerry Smith, ed., 95–105.

Georgescu-Roegen, Nicholas, 1979c: *Demain la décroissance: entropie, écologie, économie* (trans. & intr. J. Grinevald & Ivo Rens), Favre, Lausanne.

Georgescu-Roegen, Nicholas, 1982: 'Energetic Dogma, Energetic Economics and Viable Technologies', in J. R. Moroney, ed., *Advances in the Economics of Energy and Resources*, vol. 4, JAI Press, Greenwood, Conn.

Georgescu-Roegen, Nicholas, 1983: 'La teoria energética del valor económico: un sofisma económico particular', *El Trimestre Económico*, L (2), 1983.

Gerasimov, I. P., 1975: *Man, Society and Environment*, Progress Publishers, Moscow.

Geyger, Erika and Arce, Carlos, eds, 1982: *Ecologia y recursos naturales en Bolivia*, Centro Portales, Cochabamba.

Gillispie, C. ed., 1970–1980: *Dictionary of Scientific Biography*, Scribner, New York, 15 vols.

Gilmour, Ian, 1983: *Britain Can Work*, Martin Robertson, Oxford.

Giner, S. and Sevilla, E., 1984: 'Spain: from Corporatism to Corporatism', in A. Williams, ed., *Southern Europe Transformed*, Harper & Row, New York.

Ginger, Theodor, 1905: 'Beitrag zur Theorie des wirtschaftlichen Wertes: Versuch einer energetischen Formulierung desselben', *Jahrbücher für Nationalökonomie und Statistik*, III (29), G. Fischer, Jena, 740–56.

Godoy, R., 1984: 'Ecological Degradation and Agricultural Intensification in the Andean Highlands', *Human Ecology*, 12 (3), 359–83.

Goldemberg, J., 1978: 'Brazil: Energy Options and Current Outlook', *Science*, 200, April.

Goldemberg, J., Johansson, T. B., Reddy, Amul K. N., and Williams, R. H., 1986: 'Toward an Energy Strategy for a Sustainable World', *Journal 86: the Annual Report of the World Resources Institute*, Washington, DC.

Gomes da Silva, J., Serra, G. E., Moreira, J. R., Gonçalves, J. C. and Goldemberg, J., 1978: 'Energy Balance for Ethyl Alcohol Production from Crops', *Science*, 201, Sept.

Göricke, Fred and Reimann, Monika, 1982: *Treibstoff statt Nahrungsmittel: wie eine falsche energiepolitische Alternative den Hunger vermehrt*, Rowohlt, Hamburg.

Gossen, H. H., 1854: *Laws of Human Relations and the Rules of Human Action Derived Therefrom*, MIT Press, Cambridge, Mass., 1983 edn.

Graf, Dieter, 1980: *Ökonomische Bewertungen der Naturressourcen im entwickelten Sozialismus – ein Beitrag zu methodologischen Grundlagen*, Akademie Verlag, Berlin.

Graham, Loren, Lepenies, Wolf and Weingart, Peter, eds, 1983: *Functions and Uses of Disciplinary Histories*, Sociology of the Sciences Yearbook, Reidel, Dordrecht and Boston.

Gray, L. C., 1913: 'The Economic Possibilities of Conservation', *Quarterly Journal of Economics*, 27.

Gray, L. C., 1914: 'Rent under the Assumption of Exhaustibility', *Quarterly Journal Economics*, 28.

Green, Maurice, 1978: *Eating Oil: Energy Use in Food Production*, Westview, Boulder, Colo.

Gregory, Frederick, 1977: *Scientific Materialism in 19th Century Germany*, Reidel, Dordrecht and Boston.

Grigg, David, 1982: *The Dynamics of Agricultural Change: the Historical Experience*, Hutchinson, London.

Grille, D., 1966: *Lenins Rivale: Bogdanov und seine Philosophie*, Verlag Wissenschaft und Politik, Cologne.

Grillo, Eduardo, 1982: 'La producción agropecuaria de alimentos', in Lajo, Ames and Samaniego, 1982.

Grillo, Eduardo, 1985: 'Perú: agricultura, utopía popular y proyecto nacional', *Revista Andina*, 3 (1).

Grinevald, Jacques, 1976: 'La révolution carnotienne: thermodynamique, économie et idéologie', *Revue européene des sciences sociales et Cahiers Vilfredo Pareto*, 36.

Grinevald, Jacques, 1979: *Note historique sur le concept de travail mécanique (avec un supplément bibliographique sur la problématique énergétique)*, Institut Universitaire d'Etudes du Développement, Geneva.

Grinevald, Jacques, 1984: *Dimensions historiques et culturelles de la problématique énergétique en Europe*, unpublished MS with 123 long footnotes on the socio-cultural history of thermodynamics.

Gringmuth, Werner, et al., 1974: *Reproduktion der natürlichen Umweltbedingungen*, Akademie Verlag, Berlin.

Grout, Paul, 1981: 'Social Welfare and Exhaustible Resources', in J. A. Butlin, ed., *The Economics of Environmental and Natural Resources Policy*, Westview, Boulder, Colo.

Gulick, Charles, 1948: *Austria: From Habsburg to Hitler*, University of California Press, Berkeley, Ca.

Hahn, Frank and Hollis, Martin, eds, 1979: *Philosophy and Economic Theory*, Oxford University Press.

Hall, Charles, Cleveland, Cutler J. and Kaufman, Robert, 1986: *Energy and Resources Quality: the Ecology of the Economic Process*, Wiley, New York.

Hall, Daniel, Crowther, J. G., Bernal, J. D., Motram, V. H. Charles, Enid, Gorer P. A. and Blackett, P. M. S., 1935: *The Frustration of Science*, Allen & Unwin, London.

Hardesty, Donald, 1977: *Ecological Anthropology*, Wiley, New York.

Harich, Wolfgang, 1975: *Kommunismus ohne Wachstum*, Rowohlt, Reinbek bei Hamburg.

Harman, P. M., 1982: *Energy, Force and Matter: the Conceptual Development of Nineteenth-Century Physics*, Cambridge University Press.

Harrod, Roy, 1939: 'An Essay in Dynamic Theory', *Economic Journal*, 49.

Haswell, Margaret, 1981: *Energy for subsistence*, Macmillan, London.

Havemann, R., 1964: *Dialektik ohne Dogma*, Rowohlt, Reinbek bei Hamburg.

Havemann, R., 1980: *Morgen: die Industriegesellschaft am Scheideweg: Kritik und reale Utopia*, Piper Verlag, Munich.

Hawley, Amos, 1986: *Human Ecology: a theoretical Essay*, University of Chicago Press.

Hayami, Yujiro and Ruttan, Vernon, 1985: *Agricultural Development: an international perspective*, Johns Hopkins University Press, Baltimore, 2nd edn.

Hayek, F. A. von, 1941: 'The Counter-Revolution of Science', *Economica*, VIII (29), (30), (31).

Hayek, F. A. von, 1942–4: 'Scientism and the Study of Society', *Economica*, IX, 267; X, 34; XI, 27.

Hayek, F. A. von, 1949: *Individualism and Economic Order*, Routledge & Kegan Paul, London.

Hayek, F. A. von, 1952: *The Counter-Revolution of Science: Studies on the Abuse of Reason*, Free Press, Glencoe, Ill. new edn Liberty Press, Indianapolis, 1979.

Hayek, F. A. von, 1960: *The Constitution of Liberty*, Routledge & Kegan Paul, London.

Hays, Samuel P., *Conservation and the Gospel of Efficiency: the Progressive Conservation Movement 1890–1920*, Harvard University Press.

Helm, G., 1887: *Die Lehre von der Energie, historisch-kritisch entwickelt*, Veit, Leipzig.

Helm, G., 1898: *Die Energetik nach ihrer geschichtlichen Entwickelung*, Veit, Leipzig.

Henderson, Fred, 1931: *The Economic Consequences of Power Production*, Allen & Unwin, London.

Henderson, Hazel, 1978: *Creating Alternative Futures*, Putnam, New York.

Henry, Joseph, 1886: *Scientific Papers*, Smithsonian Institute, Washington DC (2 vols).

Henry, Joseph, 1980: *A Scientist in American Life: Essays and Lectures of Joseph Henry*, ed. Arthur P. Molella, Nathan Reingold, et al., Smithsonian Institute, Washington DC.

Hermann, Ludimar, 1879–83: *Handbuch der Physiologie*, 6 vols, Vogel, Leipzig.

Heryng, S., 1911: 'Die Logik der sozialen Ökonomie (Zusammenfassende Ergebnisse): Analyse der ökonomischen Grundbegriffe vom energetische Standpunkte', *Annalen der Naturphilosophie*, 10, 20–58 (summary of book published in Polish – does not contain empirical work, more concerned with exchange than with production).

Hicks, J. R., 1976: 'Revolution in Economics', in Spiro J. Latsis, *Method and Appraisal in Economics*, Cambridge University Press.

Hicks, J. R., 1969: *A Theory of Economic History*, Oxford University Press.

Himka, John Paul, 1983: *Socialism in Galicia: the Emergence of Polish Social Democracy and Ukrainian Radicalism (1860–1890)*, Harvard University Press.

Hirn, Gustave Adolphe, 1962: *Exposition analytique et experimentale de la théorie mécanique de la chaleur*, Mallet-Bachelier, Paris.

Hirsch, Fred, 1976: *Social Limits to Growth*, Routledge & Kegan Paul, London.

Hofstadter, Richard 1944: *Social-Darwinism in American Thought*, rev. edn Beacon Press, Boston, 1955.

Hogben, Lancelot, 1936: *The Retreat from Reason* (Conway Memorial Lecture), Watts, London.

Hogben, Lancelot, 1938: *Science for the Citizen: A Self-Educator based on the Social Background of Scientific Discovery*, Allen & Unwin, London (new edn 1946).

Hogben, Lancelot, ed., 1938: *Political Arithmetic: A Symposium of Population Studies*, Allen & Unwin, London.

Hogben, Lancelot, 1939: *Dangerous Thoughts*, Allen & Unwin, London.

Hogben, Lancelot, 1949: *The New Authoritarianism* (Conway Memorial Lecture), Watts, London.

Hollis, M. and Nell, E. J., 1975: *Rational Economic Man: a Philosophical Critique of Neo-classical Economics*, Cambridge University Press.

Hopkinson, C. S. and Day, J. W., 1980: 'Net Energy Analysis of Alcohol Production from Sugar Cane', *Science*, 207, Jan.

Hotelling, H., 1931: 'The Economics of Exhaustible Resources', *Journal of Political Economy*, 39.

Howard, Albert, 1948: *An Agricultural Testament*, Oxford University Press.

Howorth, Muriel, 1958: *Pioneer Research of the Atom: Rutherford and Soddy in a Glorious Chapter of Science. The Life Story of Frederick Soddy*, London.

Hudson, J. C., 1975: Barbados Sugar Producers' Association, 'Sugar cane: its energy relationships with fossil fuels', *Span*, 18 (1).

Hudson, Michael, 1975: *Economics and Technology in Nineteenth-Century American Thought: the Neglected American Economists*, Garland, New York.

Humphrey, C. R. and Buttel, F., 1982: *Environment, Energy and Society*, Wadsworth, Belmont.

Hunt, Shane, 1984: 'Guano y crecimiento en el Perú del siglo XIX', *HISLA: Revista Latinoamericana de Historia Económica*, 4.

Hunter, Louis C., 1979: *Waterpower in the Century of the Steam Engine*, vol. I of *A History of Industrial Power in the United States, 1780–1930*, Virginia University Press, Charlottesville.

Hutchinson, Keith, 1981: 'W. J. M. Rankine and the Rise of Thermodynamics', *British Journal for the History of Science*, 14 (1).

Immler, Hans, 1984: *Natur in der ökonomischen Theorie*, Westdeutscher Verlag, Opladen/Wiesbaden.

Immler, Hans and Wolfdietrich, Schmied-Kowarzik, 1983: *Marx und die Naturfrage*, Kasseler Philosophische Schriften, 10, Kassel.

Instituto Nicaragüense de Recursos Naturales y del Ambiente, 1984: *Forjando una política ambiental: pensamiento de Sandino y Carlos Fonseca*, Managua.

Ise, John, 1925: 'The Theory of Value as Applied to Natural Resources', *The American Economic Review*, XV, 284–91.

Ise, John, 1950: *Economics*, Harper, New York.

James, Preston, E. and Martin, Geoffrey J., 1981: *All Possible Worlds: a History of Geographical Ideas*, 2nd edn, New York.

Jansson, Ann-Mari, ed., 1984: *Integration of Economy and Ecology: an Outlook for the Eighties*, Proceedings from the Wallenberg Symposia, Askö Laboratory, University of Stockholm.

Jansson, A. M. and Zuccheto, J., 1985: *Resources and Society: a Systems Ecology Study of the Island of Gotland, Sweden*, Springer Verlag, New York.

Jantsch, Erich, 1980: *The Self-organising Universe*, Pergamon, Oxford.

Jayawardena, S. A., 1982: *Reference Books for the History of Science: a Handlist*, Occasional Publications, Science Museum Library, London.

Jensen, Kenneth, 1978: *Beyond Marx and Mach: Aleksandre Bogdanov's Philosophy of Living Experience*, Reidel, Dordrecht & Boston.

Jenssen, Otto, ed., 1925: *Marxismus und Naturwissenschaft: Gedenkschrifts zum 30. Todestage des Naturwissenschaftlers Friedrich Engels, mit Beiträgen von F. Engels, Gustav Eckstein und Friedrich Adler*, Verlagess. des Allegemeinen Deutschen Gewerschaftsbundes, Berlin.

Jevons, W. Stanley, 1865: *The Coal Question*, Macmillan, London & Cambridge.

Jevons, W. S., 1871: *The Theory of Political Economy*, ed. R. D. Collison Black, Penguin, Harmondsworth, 1970 edn.

Jevons, W. Stanley, 1879: *The Principles of Science: a Treatise on Logic and Scientific Method*, 3rd edn, Macmillan, London.

Jevons, W. Stanley, 1965: *The Coal Question: an Inquiry Concerning the Progress of the Nation, and the Probable Exhaustion of our Coal Mines*, reprint of the 3rd edn, Augustus Kelly, New York.

Jevons, W. Stanley, 1972: *Papers and Correspondence*, ed., R. D. Collison Black, Macmillan, London, 7 vols.

Johnston, Bruce and Mellor, John, 1984: 'The World Food Equation: Interrelations among Development, Employment and Food Consumption', *Journal of Economic Literature*, XXII, June.

Johnston, William M., 1972: *The Austrian Mind: an Intellectual and Social History*, University of California Press, Berkeley.

Joly, John, 1915: *The Birth-time of the World and other Essays*, Dutton, New York.

Jones, Aubrey, 1973: *The New Inflation the Politics of Prices and Incomes*, Penguin, London.

Jones, Greta, 1980: *Social-Darwinism and English Thought: the Interaction between Biological and Social Theory*, Harvester, Brighton.

Joravsky, David, 1961: *Soviet Marxism and Natural Science 1917–1932*, Routledge & Kegan Paul, London.

Jurisch, Konrad W., 1908: *Salpeter und sein Ersatz*, S. Hirzel, Leipzig.

Kapp, K. William, 1963: *Social Costs of Business Enterprise*, 2nd edn, Asia Publishing House, London.

Kastendiek, H., 1980: 'Neokorporatismus?' *Prokla* (Berlin), 38.

Kauffman, George B., ed., 1986: *Frederick Soddy, 1877–1956*, Reidel, Dordrecht & Boston.

Kautsky, Karl, 1899: *Die Agrarfrage: eine Übersicht über die Tendenzen der modernen Landwirtschaft und die Agrarpolitik der Sozialdemokratie*, Dietz, Stuttgart.

Kelly, Alfred, 1981: *The Descent of Darwin: the Popularization of Darwinism in Germany 1860–1914*, University of North Carolina Press, Chapel Hill, NC.

Kenney, Martin, 1986: *Biotechnology: the University–Industrial Complex*, Yale University Press, New Haven.

Khozin, G. S., 1979: *The Biosphere and Politics*, Progress Publishers, Moscow.

Kirk, Geoffrey, ed., 1982: *Schumacher on Energy*, Jonathan Cape, London.

Kitchen, P., 1975: *A Most Unsettling Person: An Introduction to the Ideas and Life of Patrick Geddes*, Gollancz, London.

Kneese, A. V. and Sweeney, J. L., eds, 1985: *Handbook of Natural Resources and Energy Economics*, vols I, II, North Holland, Amsterdam.

Kopp, Anatole, 1979: *Architecture et mode de vie: textes des années vingt en URSS*, Presse Universitaires, Grenoble.

Kormondy, Edward J., 1965: *Readings in Ecology*, Prentice-Hall, Englewood Cliffs, NJ.

Kraemer, Erich, 1933: *Was ist Technokratie*, Kurt Wolff Verlag, Berlin.

Kraft, Max, 1902: *Das System der technischen Arbeit*, Arthur Felix, Leipzig (encyclopedic study with full author and subject index).

Krass, A., Boskma, P., Elzen, B. and Smit, W., 1983: *Uranium Enrichment and Nuclear Weapon Proliferation*, SIPRI/Taylor & Francis, London.

Krohn, W. and Schaefer, W. 1978: 'Ursprung und Struktur der Agrikulturchemie', *Starnberger Studien* Band 1, Suhrkamp, Frankfurt.

Krohn, W., Taylor, Edwin T. and Weingart, Peter, eds, 1978: *The Dynamics of Science and Technology: Social Values, Technical Change and Scientific Criteria in the Development of Science*, Reidel, Dordrecht & Boston.

Kropotkin, P. A., 1889: 'The Wage System', in *The Conquest of Bread*, introd. Paul Avrich, Allen Lane, London, 1972 edn.

Kropotkin, P., 1903: *Modern Science and Anarchism*, Social Sciences Club, Philadelphia.

Kropotkin, P. A., 1974: *Fields, Factories and Workshops of Tomorrow*, introd. Colin Ward, Allen & Unwin, London.

Kuznets, Simon, 1966: *Modern Economic Growth: Rate, Structure and Spread*, Yale University Press, New Haven.

Lajo, Manuel, Ames, Rolando and Samaniego, Carlos, eds, 1982: *Agricultura y alimentación: bases de un nuevo enfoque*, Pontificia Universidad Católica, Lima.

Landes, David, 1969: *The Unbound Prometheus: Technological Change and Industrial Development in Western Europe from 1750 to the Present*, Cambridge University Press.

Lang, W., 1981: 'Spanien nach Franco: vom autoritären zum liberalen Korporatismus?', in Ulrich v. Alemann, ed., *Neokorporatismus*, Campus, Frankfurt.

Leach, Gerald, 1975: *Energy and Food Production*, IPC Science & Technology Press, Guildford.

Lee, Richard, 1979: *The !Kung San: Men, Women and Work in a Foraging Society*, Cambridge University Press.

Léger, Danièle, 1982: 'Apocalyptique écologique et "retour" de la religion', *Archives des Sciences Sociales des Religions*, 53 (1).

Lehning, Arthur, ed., 1974: *Archives Bakounine*, III, IV, V, E. J. Brill, Leiden.

Lemkow, L., 1981: *Environmental and ecological concepts in social theory: a sociological and historical analysis*, doctoral thesis, Universidad Autónoma de Barcelona, Bellaterra, Barcelona.

Lenin, V. I., 1909: *Materialism and Empiriocriticism*, Interscience Publishers, New York, 1927.

Leval, Gaston, 1977: *Colectividades libertarias en España*, Aguilera, Madrid.

Lewis, C., 1977: 'Fuels from Biomass: Energy Outlay versus Energy Return: a Critical Appraisal', *Energy*, 2, 1977.

Liebig, Justus von, 1859: *Letters on Modern Agriculture*, ed. John Blyth, Walton & Maberly, London.

Liebig, Justus von, 1863: *The Natural Laws of Husbandry*, ed. John Blyth, Walton & Maberly, London.

Lieth, H. and Whittaker, R., 1975: *Primary Productivity of the Biosphere*, Springer Verlag, Berlin–Heidelberg–New York.

Lind, Robert C., ed., 1982: *Discounting for Time and Risk in Energy Policy*, *Resources for the Future*, Johns Hopkins University Press, Baltimore.

Lindsay, Robert, ed., 1975: *Energy: Historical Development of the Concept*, Dowden, Hutchinson & Ross, Stroudsburg, Penn. (a collection of the basic early papers).

Lockeretz, William, ed., 1982: *Agriculture as a Producer and Consumer of Energy*, Westview, Boulder, Colo.

Loomis, R. S., 1984: 'Traditional Agriculture in America', *Annual Review of Ecology and Systematics,* 15, 499–78.

Lotka, A. J., 1911: 'Die Evolution vom Standpunkte der Physik', *Annalen der Naturphilosophie*, 10, 59–74.

Lotka, A. J., 1921: 'Note on the Economic Conversion Factors of Energy', *Proceedings National Academy of Sciences*, 7, 192–7.

Lotka, A. J., 1925: *Elements of Physical Biology*, Williams & Wilkins, Baltimore.

Lotka, A. J., 1934: *Théorie analytique des associations biologiques*, Hermann, Paris.

Lukes, Steven, 1973: 'Methodological Individualism Reconsidered', in Alan Ryan, ed., *The Philosophy of Social Explanation*, Oxford University Press.

Lukes, S., 1984: 'Marxism and Utopianism', in P. Alexander and R. Gill, eds, *Utopias*, Duckworth, London.

McCloskey, H. J., 1983: *Ecological Ethics and Politics*, Rowman & Littlefield, Totowa, NJ.

McCollum, Elmer V., 1957: *A History of Nutrition: the Sequence of Ideas in Nutrition Investigations*, Houghton Mifflin, Boston.

Mach, Ernst, 1891: *Die Prinzipien der Wärmelehre historisch-kritisch entwickelt*; 3rd edn, Barth, Leipzig, 1919.

Mach, Ernst, 1905: *Erkenntnis und Irrtum: Skizzen zur Psychologie der Forschung*, Barth, Leipzig.

Mach, Ernst, 1978: *Wissenschaftliche Kommunikation, Die Korrespondenz Ernst Machs*, ed. Joachim Thiele, A. Henn, Kastellaun.

Machlup, F., 1951: 'Schumpeter's Economic Methodology', in S. E. Harris, ed., *Schumpeter, Social Scientist*, Harvard University Press.

Madden, Patrick, 1986: 'Beyond Conventional Economics: an Examination of the Values Implicit in the Neo-classical Economic Paradigm as Applied to the Evaluation of Agricultural Research', in Dahlberg, ed., 1986.

Maier, C., 1975: *Recasting Bourgeois Europe: Stabilization in France, Germany and Italy in the Decade after World War I*, Princeton University Press.

Maier, C., 1978: 'The Politics of Inflation in the Twentieth Century', in F. Hirsch and J. Goldthorpe, *The Political Economy of Inflation*, Martin Robertson, Oxford.

Maiguashca, Juan, 1967: *A reinterpretation of the guano age, 1840–1880*, D. Phil. thesis, Oxford.

Mairet, Ph., 1957: *Pioneer of Sociology: the Life and Letters of Patrick Geddes*, Hyperion Press, Westport, Conn., 1979.

Major, Jack, 1969: 'Historical Development of the Ecosystem Concept', in Van Dyne, 1969, 9–22.

Makhijani, Arjun and Poole, Alan, 1975: *Energy and Agriculture in the Third World*, Ballinger, Cambridge, Mass.

Mansilla, H. C. F., 1984: *Nationale Identität, gesellschaftliche Wahrnehmung natürlichen Ressourcen und ökologische Probleme in Bolivien*, Wilhelm Fink Verlag, Munich.

Manuel, F. E. and Manuel, F. P., 1979: *Utopian Thought in the Western World*, Blackwell, Oxford.

Margalef, R., 1963: 'On Certain Unifying Principles in Ecology', in Kormondy, 1965.

Margalef, R., 1977: *Ecologia*, Omega, Barcelona.

Marglin, Stephen, 1963: 'The Social Rate of Discount and the Optimal Rate of Investment', *Quarterly Journal of Economics*, 77.

Marsh, George Perkins, 1965: *Man and Nature*, ed. D. Lowenthal, Harvard University Press.

Martinez-Alier, J., 1973: 'El fin de la ortodoxia en teoria económica y sus implicaciones políticas', *Cuadernos de Ruedo ibérico*, 41–2.

Martinez-Alier, J., 1977: 'El Pacto de la Moncloa: la lucha sindical y el nuevo corporativismo', *Cuadernos de Ruedo ibérico*, 58–60.

Martinez-Alier, J., 1983: 'La ciencia económica y el análisis energético: discusiones antiguas y recientes', *Papers: Revista de Sociologia*, 19.

Martinez-Alier, J., 1984: *L'ecologisme i l'economia: Història d'unes relacions amagades*, Edicions 62, Barcelona.

Martinez-Alier, J and Naredo, J. M., 1982: 'A Marxist Precursor of Energy Economics: Podolinsky', *Journal of Peasant Studies*, 9, Jan.

Marx, Karl, 1867/1894: *Das Kapital*, vol. I (1867), vol. III (1894), Ullstein Verlag, Frankfurt-Vienna-Berlin, 1969.

Marx, K. and Engels, F., 1975: *Cartas sobre las ciencias de la naturaleza y las matemáticas*, Anagrama, Barcelona.

Mason, S. F., 1953: *A History of the Sciences: Main Currents of Scientific Thought*, Routledge & Kegan Paul, London.

Massarrat, Mohssen, 1980a: 'The Energy Crisis: the Struggle for the Redistribution of Surplus Profit from Oil', in P. Nore and T. Turner, eds, *Oil and Class Struggle*, Zed, London.

Massarrat, Mohssen, 1980b: *Weltenergieproduktion und die Neueordnung der kapitalistischen Weltwirtschaft*, Campus, Frankfurt.

Masuda, Shozo, Shimada, Izumi and Morris, Craig, eds, 1985: *Andean Ecology and Civilization: an Interdisciplinary Perspective on Andean Ecological Complementarity*, University of Tokyo Press.

264 *Bibliography*

Mathew, W. M., 1968: 'The Imperialism of Free Trade: Peru, 1820–1870', *Economic History Review*, XXI (3), 562–79.

Mathew, W. M., 1970: 'Peru and the British Guano Market, 1840–1870', *Economic History Review*, XXIII (1), 112–28.

Mayer, J. R., 1845: *Die organische Bewegung in ihrem Zusammenhang mit dem Stoffwechsel*, Heilbronn, published also in *Die Mechanik der Wärme*: *gesammelte Schriften*, Stuttgart, 1893, and in Ostwald, *Klassiker der exacten Naturwissenschaften*, Akademische Verlag, Leipzig, 1911.

Meade, J. E., 1983: *Demand Management*, Allen & Unwin, London.

Meijer, J. M., 1955: *Knowledge and Revolution: the Russian Colony in Zürich, 1870–1873*, Van Gorcum, Assen.

Melo, Fernando Homen de and da Fonseca, Eduardo Gianetti, 1981: *Proálcool, energia e transportes*, Livraria Pioneira, São Paulo.

Melo, Fernando Homen de and Pelin, Eli Roberto, 1984: *As solucões energéticas e a economia brasileira*, Hucitec, São Paulo.

Millones, Luis and Tomoeda, Hiroyasu, eds, 1982: *El hombre y su ambiente en los Andes centrales*, National Museum of Ethnology, Suita, Osaka.

Mintz, Sidney, 1985: *Sweetness and Power: The Place of Sugar in Modern History*, Penguin, Harmondsworth.

Mises, Richard von, 1931: 'Josef Popper-Lynkeus', *Neue Oesterreichische Biographie 1815–1918*, Almathea Verlag, Vienna (Band 31).

Mishan, E. J., 1981: *Introduction to Normative Economics*, Oxford University Press.

Moleshott, Jacob, 1850: *Lehre der Nahrungsmittel. Für das Volk*, Enke, Erlangen.

Moleshott, Jacob, 1852: *Der Kreislauf des Lebens*, Von Zabern, Mainz.

Morris, W., 1910–15: 'The Policy of Abstention', 1887, in *The Collected Works*, introd. May Morris, Longman, London.

Moscovici, S., 1968: *Essai sur l'histoire humaine de la nature*, Flammarion, Paris.

Mouchot, A., 1869: *La chaleur solaire et ses applications industriels*, Gauthier-Villars, Paris, 2nd edn 1879.

Muller, H. J., 1936: *Out of the Night: a Biologist's View of the Future*, Gollancz, London.

Mumford, Lewis, 1934: *Technics and Civilization*, Harcourt & Brace, New York.

Mumford, Lewis, 1938: *The Culture of Cities*, Harcourt & Brace, New York.

Mumford, Lewis, 1948: 'Patrick Geddes, Victor Branford and Applied Sociology in England: the Social Survey, Regionalism and Urban Planning', in H. E. Barnes, *An Introduction to the History of Sociology*, Chicago University Press, 1948.

Mumford, Lewis, 1962: 'Apology to Henry Adams', ch. 32 of *Interpretations and Forecasts 1922–1972*, Harcourt, Brace & Jovanovich, New York, 1979.

Mumford, Lewis, 1970: *The Myth of the Machine: the Pentagon of Power*, Harcourt, Brace, New York.

Musson, A. E., 1976: 'Industrial Motive Power in the United Kingdom, 1800–1870', *Economic History Review*, 29.

Nagel, Paul, 1983: *Descent from Glory: Four Generations of the John Adams Family*, Oxford University Press.

Naredo, J. M., 1987: *La economía en evolución: Historia y perspectivas de las categorías fundamentales de la ciencia económica*, Siglo XXI, Madrid.

Naredo, J. M., Gaviria, Mario, et al., 1979: *Extremadura saqueada: recursos naturales y autonomia regional*, Ruedo ibérico, Barcelona.

Naredo, J. M. and Campos, Pablo, 1980: 'I ⅃ energia en los sistemas agrarios', *Agricultura y Sociedad*, 15.

Naredo, J. M. and Campos, Pablo, 1980: 'Los balances energéticos de la agricultura española', *Agricultura y Sociedad*, 15.

Nash, June, 1979: *We Eat the Mines and the Mines Eat Us*, Columbia University Press, New York.

Nash, Roderick, 1967: *Wilderness and the American Mind*, Yale University Press, new edn 1973.

Needham, Joseph, 1941: 'Evolution and Thermodynamics', in *Moulds of Understanding: a Pattern of Natural Philosophy*, ed. Gary Werskey, St Martin's Press, New York, 1976.

Neurath, Otto, 1925: *Wirtschaftsplan und Naturalrechnung: von der sozialistischen Lebensordnung und vom kommenden Menschen*, Laub, Berlin.

Neurath, Otto, 1944: *Foundations of the Social Sciences*, University of Chicago Press, 1970.

Neurath, Otto, 1973: *Empiricism and Sociology*, ed. Marie Neurath and R. Cohen, Reidel, Dordrecht & Boston.

Neurath, Otto, 1979: *Wissenschaftliche Weltauffassung, Sozialismus und Logischer Empirismus*, ed. Rainer Hegselman, Suhrkamp, Frankfurt.

Newcombe, Ken, 1977: 'Nutrient Flow in a Major Urban Settlement: Hong Kong', *Human Ecology*, 5 (3).

Newton-Smith, W. H., 1981: *The Rationality of Science*, Routledge & Kegan Paul, London.

Norgaard, R. N., 1984: 'Coevolutionary Development Potential', *Land Economics*, 60 (2), May.

Norgaard, R. N., 1985: 'Environmental Economics: an Evolutionary Critique and a Plea for Pluralism', *Journal of Environmental Economics and Management*, 12.

Nove, Alec, 1977: *The Soviet Economic System*, Allen & Unwin, London.

Novik, Ilya, 1981: *Society and Nature: Socio-ecological problems*, Progress Publishers, Moscow.

Novikov, G. A. et al., 1970: *Ocherki po istorii ekologii* (Essays on the History of Ecology), Institute for the History of Science and Technology, Academy of Sciences, Moscow.

Nowell-Smith, P. H., 1959: *Ethics*, Pelican, London.

Odum, Eugene P., 1968: 'Energy Flow in Ecosystems: A Historical Review', *American Zoologist*, 8, Feb.

Odum, Eugene P., 1971: *Fundamentals of Ecology*, 3rd edn, Saunders, London.

Odum, Eugene P., 1975: *Ecology: the Link between the Natural and the Social Sciences*, 2nd edn, Holt, Rinehart & Winston, New York.

Odum, Eugene P., 1977: 'The Emergence of Ecology as a New Integrative Discipline', *Science*, 195, 1289–93.

Odum, Howard T., 1971: *Environment, Power and Society*, Wiley, New York.

Odum, Howard T., 1983: *Systems Ecology: an Introduction*, Wiley, New York.

Offord, Derek, 1986: *The Russian Revolutionary Movement in the 1880s*, Cambridge University Press.

Okun, Arthur, 1981: *Prices and Quantities*: *A Macroeconomic Analysis*, Blackwell, Oxford.

Olson, Mancur, 1971: *The Logic of Collective Action*, Harvard University Press.

O'Riordan, T., 1981: *Environmentalism*, 2nd edn, Pion, London.

Orlove, Benjamin, 1980: 'Ecological Anthropology', *Annual Reviews in Anthropology*, 9, 235–73.

Ostwald, Wilhelm, 1909: *Energetische Grundlagen der Kulturwissenschaft*, Alfred Kröner, Leipzig, (French trans., Giard & Brière, Paris, 1910).

Ostwald, Wilhelm, 1912: *Der energetische Imperativ*, Akademische Verlagess. Leipzig.

Ostwald, Wilhelm, 1913: *Die Philosophie der Werte*, Alfred Kröner, Leipzig.

Ozorio de Almeida, Anne Luise, ed., 1984: *Biotecnologia e Agricultura*, Vozes-Biomatrix, Petropolis.

Page, Talbot, 1977: *Conservation and Economic Efficiency*: *an Approach to Materials Policy*, Johns Hopkins University Press, Baltimore.

Palerm, Angel, 1980: *Antropologia y marxismo*, Casa Chata, INAH, Mexico.

Panitch, L., 1981: 'Trade Unions and the Capitalist State', *New Left Review*, 125.

Parfit, Derek, 1985: 'The Social Discount Rate', in *Reasons and Persons*, Oxford University Press, Oxford, pp. 480ff.

Parsons, H. L., 1977: *Marx and Engels on Ecology*, Greenwood Press, Westport, Conn.

Passet, René, 1979: *L'économique et le vivant*, Payot, Paris.

Passmore, J. A., 1974: *Man's Responsibility for Nature*: *Ecological Problems and Western Traditions*, Scribners, New York.

Pearce, D. W., 1976: *Environmental Economics*, Longman, London.

Pearce, David, 1987: 'Foundations of ecological economics', in Costanza and Daly, eds, 1987.

Perelman, Michael, 1977: *Farming for Profit in a Hungry World*, Allanheld, Montclair, NJ.

Pfaundler, L., 1902: 'Die Weltwirtschaft im Lichte der Physik', *Deutsche Revue* (ed. Richard Fleischer), 22 (2), April–June, 29–38, 171–82.

Phillipson, John, 1966: *Ecological Energetics*, Arnold, London.

Pike, F. and Stritch, T., eds, 1974: *The New Corporatism*: *Social and Political Structures in the Iberian World*, Notre Dame.

Pimentel, D. and Pimentel, M., 1979: *Food, Energy and Society*, Arnold, London.

Pimentel, D. and Hall, C. W., eds, 1984: *Food and Energy Resources*, Academic Press, London.

Pimentel, D. and Pimentel, S., 1986: 'Energy and other Natural Resources Used by Agriculture and Society', in Dahlberg, ed., 1986.

Pimentel, D. et al., 1973: 'Food Production and the Energy Crisis', *Science*, 182, pp. 443–9.

Pires, Carlos Borges, 1984: 'Energia e agricultura: a cultura do trigo no Alentejo nos ultimos sessenta anos', *Revista Crítica de Ciências Sociais*, 14, Nov.

Plekhanov, G., 1895: 'The Development of the Monist View of History', in *Selected Philosophical Works*, vol. I, Lawrence & Wishart, London, 1961.

Podolinsky, Serhii, 1880a: 'Le socialisme et la théorie de Darwin', *Revue Socialiste*, March.

Podolinsky, Serhii, 1880-3: 'Le socialisme et l'unité des forces fisiques', *Revue Socialiste*, June 1880; 'Il socialismo e l'unità delle forze fisiche', *La Plebe*, 1881; 'Menschliche Arbeit und Einheit der Kraft', *Die Neue Zeit*, March–April 1883.

Poggendorf, J. C., 1863-1904: *Biographisch-Literarisches Handwörterbuch zur Geschichte der exacten Wissenschaften*, Barth, Leipzig, many vols.

Polanyi, Karl, 1944: *The Great Transformation: the Political and Social Origins of our Time*, Beacon Press, Boston, 1957.

Popper, Karl, 1944-5: *The Poverty of Historicism*, orig. articles in *Economica*, XI and XII; Routledge & Kegan Paul, London, 1962.

Popper, Karl, 1945: *The Open Society and its Enemies*, Routledge & Kegan Paul, London, (2 vols).

Popper, Karl, 1963: *Conjectures and Refutations*, Routledge & Kegan Paul, London.

Popper-Lynkeus, Josef, 1878: *Das Recht zu leben und die Pflicht zu sterben*. 3rd edn Reissner, Dresden, 1903.

Popper-Lynkeus, Josef, 1884: *Physikalische Grundsätze der elektrischen Kraftübertragung*, Hartleben, Vienna.

Popper-Lynkeus, Josef, 1888: *Die technische Fortschritte nach ihrer ästhetischen und kulturellen Bedeutung*, Reissner, Leipzig.

Popper-Lynkeus, Josef, 1912: *Die allgemeine Nährpflicht als Lösung der sozialen Frage: eingehend bearbeitet und statistisch durchgerechnet*, Reissner, Dresden (one later edn is not complete).

Popper-Lynkeus, Josef, 1924: *Mein Leben und Wirken: eine Selbsdarstellung*, Reissner, Dresden.

Pouillet, C. S. M., 1838: 'Mémoire sur le chaleur solaire, sur les pouvoirs rayonnants et absorbants de l'air atmosphérique et sur la temperature de l'espace', *Comptes Rendus*, 7, pp. 26–65, cited by Frank A. J. L. James, 'Thermodynamics and Sources of Solar Heat 1846–1862', *British Journal for the History of Science*, 15, July 1982.

Prigogine, Ilya and Stengers, Isabelle, 1979: *La nouvelle alliance*, Gallimard, Paris (references are to Spanish edn, Alianza, Madrid, 1983).

Puntí, Albert, 1982: 'Balance energético y coste ecológico de la agricultura española', *Agricultura y Sociedad*, 23.

Puntí, Albert, 1983: 'Energia y fuerza de trabajo', *Mientras Tanto*, 15.

Rabinovitch, Eugene I., 1945: *Photosynthesis and Related Processes*, Interscience Publishers, New York.

Ramage, Janet, 1983: *Energy: a Guidebook*, Oxford University Press.

Ramsey, F. P., 1928: 'A Mathematical Theory of Saving', *Economic Journal*, XXXVIII.

Randall, G. W., 1984: 'Role of Crop Nutrition Technology in Meeting Future Needs', in B. C. English, J. A. Maetzold, B. R. Holding and E. O. Heady, eds, *Future Agricultural Technology and Resource Conservation*, Iowa State University Press, Ames, Iowa, 354–67.

Rappaport, Roy, 1967: *Pigs for the Ancestors: Ritual in the Ecology of a New Guinea People*, Yale University Press (new edn 1985).

Raumolin, J., 1984: 'L'homme et la destruction des ressources naturelles: la Raubwirtschaft au tournant du siècle', *Annales E. S. C.*, 39 (4) (essential bibliography).

Redclift, Michael, 1980: 'Agrarian Populism in Mexico: the Via Campesina', *Journal of Peasant Studies*, 7 (4).

Redclift, Michael, 1984: *Development and the Environmental Crisis*, Methuen, London.

Reipricht, Kurt, 1969: *Die philosophisch-naturwissenschaftlichen Arbeiten von Karl Marx und Friedrich Engels*, Dietz, Berlin.

Richards, Paul, 1985: *Indigenous Agricultural Revolution*, Hutchinson, London.

Riddell, Robert, 1981: *Ecodevelopment: Economics, Ecology and Development, an Alternative to Growth Imperative Models*, Gower, Farnborough, Hants.

Rivera Cusicanqui, S., 1984: *Oprimidos pero no vencidos*, HISBOL, La Paz.

Robbins, Lionel, 1932: *An Essay on the Nature and Significance of Economic Science*, Macmillan, London, 1952.

Roca, Jordi, 1984: *Els pactes socials: cap a un nou corporativisme? El cas de l'Estat espanyol 1977–83*, master's thesis, Universidad Autónoma de Barcelona, Bellaterra, Barcelona, 1984.

Rodman, John, book review, *Human Ecology*, 12 (3), 1984.

Rodnyj, N. I. and Solowjew, I. L., 1977: *Wilhelm Ostwald*, Teubner, Leipzig.

Ronge, Grete, 1955: 'Die Züricher Jahre des Physikers Rudolf Clausius', *Gesnerus*, 12, 83–108.

Rosa, Luiz Pinguelli, ed., 1984: *Energia e crise*, Vozes, Petropolis R. J.

Rose, Hilary and Rose, Steven, 1969: *Science and Society*, Allen Lane, London.

Rose, Hilary, 1983: 'Hand, Brain and Heart: a Feminist Epistemology for the Natural Sciences', *Signs* 9 (1).

Rossiter, M. W., 1975: *The Emergence of Agricultural Science: Justus Liebig and the Americans, 1840–1880*, Yale University Press.

Rothman, Harry, Greenschields, Rod and Rosillo, Francisco, 1983: *The Alcohol Economy: Fuel Ethanol and the Brazilian Experience*, Pinter, London.

Rubner, Max, 1902: *Die Gesetze des Energieverbrauchs bei der Ernährung*, F. Deuticke, Leipzig.

Ruskin, John, 1872: *Munera Pulveris: Six Essays on the Elements of Political Economy*, Smith, Elder & Co., London (first published in *Fraser's Magazine*, 1862–3).

Ruskin, John, 1861: *Unto this Last: Four Essays on the First Principles of Political Economy*, Smith, Elder & Co., London.

Ryan, Alan, ed., 1973: *The Philosophy of Social Explanation*, Oxford University Press.

Sacher, Eduard, 1881: *Grundzüge einer Mechanik der Gesellschaft*, Gustav Fischer, Jena.

Sacher, Eduard, 1899: *Die Gesellschaftskunde als Naturwissenschaft*, Pierson's Verlag, Dresden & Leipzig.

Sachs, Ignacy, ed., 1972: *Political Economy of Environment: Problems of Method*, Mouton, Paris – The Hague.

Salisbury, R. F., 1962: *From Stone to Steel: Economic Consequences of a Technological Change in New Guinea*, Melbourne University Press.

Sapir, Boris, ed., 1974: *Lavrov: Years of Emigration, Letters and Documents* Institute of Social History of Amsterdam, Reidel, Dordrecht.

Sapir, Marc, Steenhout, Anne and Vanderborght, Jean-Pierre, 1983: *L'ecosystème Belgique: Essai d'écologie industrielle*, CRISP, Brussels.

Sawyer, M., 1982: *Macroeconomics in Question*, Wheatsheaf, Brighton.

Scalon, Tony, 1982: 'Outlook for Soviet Oil', *Science*, 217, 23 July.

Schejtman, A., 1983: 'Análisis integral del problema alimentario y nutricional en América latina', *Estudios rurales latinoamericanos*, 6 (2–3).

Schieck, Hans, 1972: 'Die Behandlung der Sozialisierung Frage in den Monaten nach dem Staatsumsturz', in E. Kolb, ed., *Von Kaiserreich zur Weimarer Republik*, Kiepenheuer & Witsch, Cologne.

Schmidt, Alfred, 1978: *Der Begriff der Natur in der Lehre von Marx*, 3rd edn, EVA, Frankfurt – Cologne.

Schmitter, P. and Lehmbruch, G., eds, 1979: *Trends toward Corporatist Intermediation*, Sage, Beverly Hills.

Schumacher, E., 1973: *Small is Beautiful*, Blond and Briggs, London.

Schumpeter, J. A., 1912: *The Theory of Economic Development*, Oxford University Press, 1961.

Schumpeter, J. A., 1954: *History of Economic Analysis*, Oxford University Press.

Schwarz, Richard, 1919: *Rathenau, Goldscheid, Popper-Lynkeus und ihre Systeme zusammengefasst zu einem Wirtschaftsprogramm*, Anzengruber, Vienna.

Schwendter, Rolf, 1982: *Zur Geschichte der Zukunft. Zukunftsforschung und Sozialismus*, Syndikat, Frankfurt (2 vols).

Scott, Howard et al., 1933: *Introduction to Technocracy*, John Lane, The Bodley Press, London.

Sen, A. K., 1961: 'On Optimising the Rate of Saving', *Economic Journal*, LXXI, Sept.

Sen, A. K., 1980: *Collective Choice and Social Welfare*, Oliver & Boyd, London.

Sen, A. K., 1981: *Poverty and Famines: an Essay on Entitlement and Deprivation*, Clarendon Press, Oxford.

Sen, A. K. and Williams, B., eds, 1982: *Utilitarianism and Beyond*, Cambridge University Press.

Senayake, Ranil, 1984: 'The Ecological, Energetic, and Agronomic Systems of Ancient and Modern Sri Lanka', in Douglass, ed., 1984.

Serbyn, Roman, 1982: 'In Defence of an Independent Ukrainian Socialist Movement: Three Letters from Serhii Podolinsky to Valerian Smirnov', *Journal of Ukrainian Studies*, 7 (2).

Shanin, Teodor, ed., 1983: *Late Marx and the Russian Road*, History Workshop Series, Routledge & Kegan Paul, London.

Shonfield, A., 1965: *Modern Capitalism*, Oxford University Press.

Shonfield, A., 1984: *In Defence of the Mixed Economy*, Oxford University Press.

Sieferle, Rolf, 1984: *Fortschrittsfeinde? : Opposition gegen Technik und Industrie von der Romantik bis zur Gegenwart*, Beck, Munich.

Siemens, Werner von, 1892–95: *Scientific and Technical Papers*, J. Murray, London.

Singer, C., Holmyard, E. J., Hall, A. R. and Williams, Trevor, 1954–78: *A History of Technology*, Clarendon Press, Oxford (7 vols).

Singh, Narindar, 1976: *Economics and the Crisis of Ecology*, Oxford University Press, Delhi.

Sinsheimer, R., 1978: 'The Presumptions of Science', *Daedalus*, Spring.

Slesser, Malcolm, 1979: *Energy in the Economy*, Macmillan, London.

Slicher van Bath, B. H., 1966: *The Agrarian History of Western Europe, 1500–1850*, Arnold, London.

Smil, Vaclav, 1979: 'Energy Flows in Rural China', *Human Ecology*, 7 (2).

Smil, V., 1983: *Biomass Energies: Resources, Links, Constraints*, Plenum Press, New York.

Smil, V., 1984: *The Bad Earth: Environmental Degradation in China*, Zed, London.

Smil, V., 1985: *Carbon, Nitrogen, Sulphur: Human Interference in Grand Biospheric Cycles*, Plenum Press, New York.

Smil, V. and Knowland, W. E., eds, 1980: *Energy in the Developing World: The Real Energy Crisis*, Oxford University Press.

Smith, Erasmus Peshine, 1853: *Manual of Political Economy*, G. P. Putnam, New York, reprinted Garland, New York, 1974.

Smith, E. A., 1979: 'Human Adaptation and Energetic Efficiency', *Human Ecology*, 7 (1).

Smith, Gerald Alonzo, 1982: 'Natural Resource Economic Theory of the First Conservationist Movement (1895–1927)', *History of Political Economy*, 14 (4).

Smith, V. Kerry, ed., 1979: *Scarcity and Growth Reconsidered*, Johns Hopkins University Press, Baltimore.

Soddy, Frederick, 1912: *Matter and Energy*, Williams and Norgate, London.

Soddy, Frederick, 1922: *Cartesian Economics: the Bearing of Physical Science upon State Stewardship*, Hendersons, London.

Soddy, Frederick, 1926: *Wealth, Virtual Wealth and Debt*, Allen & Unwin, London, 2nd edn 1933.

Soddy, Frederick, 1947: *Atomic Energy for the Future*, Constitutional Research Association, London (15 pages, Bodleian Library 22283 e 438 (7).

Solvay, Ernest, 1906: *Note sur des formulles d'introduction à l'Energétique physio et physio-sociologique*, Travaux de l'Institut Solvay, Misch et Thron, éditeurs, Brussels.

Sorj, Bernardo and Wilkinson, John, 1984: 'Agrobusiness, Biotechnologies, and Rural Structures', MS.

Sorj, Bernardo, Wilkinson, John and Conradini, Odacir, 1984: 'Biotechnologies in Brazil', report submitted to the National Research Council (CNPQ), Institute of International Relations, Rio de Janeiro.

Stalley, Marshall, 1972: *Patrick Geddes: Spokesman for Man and the Environment: a Selection*, Rutgers University Press, New Brunswick, NJ.

Stark, Gary D., 1981: *Entrepreneurs of Ideology: Neoconservative Publishers in Germany 1890–1933*, University of North Carolina Press, Chapel Hill, NC.

Steiner, Rudolf, 1924: *Geisteswissenschlaftliche Grundlagen zum Gedeihen der Landwirtschaft*, Rudolf Steiner Verlag, Dornach, 1975.

Steinhart, J. S. and Steinhart, C. E., 1974: 'Energy Use in the US Food System', *Science*, 184, 307–16.

Stepan, Nancy, 1982: *The Idea of Race in Science: Great Britain 1800–1960*, Macmillan, London.

Stern, Alfred, 1944: *La filosofía de los valores*, Minerva, Mexico, (chapter on W. Ostwald).

Stickers, J., 1913: *Was ist Energie? Eine erkenntniskritische Untersuchung der Ostwald'schen Energetik*, Hans Schnippel, Berlin.

Stoddart, D. R., ed., 1981: *Geography, Ideology and Social Concern*, Blackwell, Oxford.

Stolcke, V., 1981: 'Women's Labours: the Naturalization of Social Inequality and Women's Subordination', in K. Young, C. Wolkowitz and R. McCullagh, *Of Marriage and the Market*, Routledge & Kegan Paul, London.

Sudrià, C., 1987: 'Un factor determinante: la energia', in J. Nadal, A. Carreras and C. Sudrià, *La economía española en el siglo XX*, Ariel, Barcelona.

Sunkel, Osvaldo and Leal, José, 1986: 'Economics and Environment in a Developmental Perspective', *International Social Science Journal* (issue on Environmental Awareness), 109.

Susiluoto, Ilmari, 1982: *The Origins and Development of Systems Thinking in the Soviet Union: Political and Philosophical Controversies from Bogdanov and Bukharin to Present-day Reevaluations*, Suomalainen Tiedeakatemia, Helsinki.

Swaney, J. A., 1985: 'Economics, Ecology and Entropy', *Journal of Economic Issues*, XIX (4), Dec.

Tait, Peter Guthrie, 1864: 'The Dynamical Theory of Heat', 'Energy', *North British Review*, XL, 40f. and 337f.

Tamanoi, Yoshiro, Tsuchida, Atsuchi and Murota, Takeshi, 1984: 'Towards an Entropic Theory of Economy and Ecology: Beyond the Mechanistic Equilibrium approach', *Economie appliquée*, XXXVII, 2, 279–94.

Taylor, Keith, ed., 1975: *Henri Saint-Simon 1760–1825: Selected Writings on Science, Industry and Social Organization*, Croom Helm, London.

Thielen, Helmut, 1985: *Agrarreformen in Lateinamerika zwischen Oekonomie und Oekologie: Modelfall Nicaragua*, Hagg & Herchen, Frankfurt.

Thienemann, August, 1941: *Leben und Unwelt*, Band 12, Bios, ed. A. Meyer-Abich, Barth, Leipzig.

Thomas, R. Brooke, 1976: 'Energy Flow at High Altitude', in Baker and Little, 1976.

Thompson, E. P. 1977: *William Morris*, Merlin Press, London.

Thomson, W and Tait, P. G., 1860: *Energy* (7 pages), Bodleian Library d.86 (14).

Tiezzi, Enzo, 1984: *Tempo storico e tempo biologico*, Garzanti, Milan.

Trenn, T. J., 1977: *The Self-Splitting Atom: a History of the Rutherford–Soddy Collaboration*, Taylor & Francis, London.

Trenn, T. J., 1979: 'The Central Role of Energy in Soddy's Holistic and Critical Approach to Nuclear Science, Economics, and Social Responsibility', *British Journal for the History of Science*, XII, 42.

Truesdell, C., 1980: *The tragicomical History of Thermodynamics*, Springer, Berlin.

Tsuru, Shigeto, 1972: 'In Place of GNP', in Sachs, ed., 1972.

Tvardovskaia, V. A., 1978: *El populismo ruso*, Siglo XXI, Madrid.

Tyndall, John, 1863: *Heat Considered as a Mode of Motion*, Longmans, Green & Co., London.

Ubbelohde, Alfred R., 1954: *Man and Energy*, Hutchinson, London.

'Ueber die Anwendung des Gesetzes des mechanischen Aequivalents der Wärme auf die Nationalökonomie', 1877: *Das Ausland*, Augsburg, 50, 298, without author's name.

Ullrich, Otto, 1980: *Weltniveau: in der Sackgasse des Industriesystems*, Rotbuch Verlag, Berlin.

United Nations Research Institute for Social Development, 1983: *Research Notes*, no. 6, Geneva.

Van Dyne, George, 1969: *The Ecosystem Concept in Natural Resource Management*, Academic Press, New York.

Vayda, Andrew P., ed., 1969: *Environment and Cultural Behaviour: Ecological Studies in Cultural Anthropology*, Natural History Press, Garden City, New York.

Veblen, Thorstein, 1921: *The Engineers and the Price System*, Huebsch, New York.

Veermer, Donald E., 1976: 'Food, Farming and the Future: the Role of Traditional Agriculture in Developing Areas of the World', *Social Science Quarterly*, 57, 383–96.

Venturi, Franco, 1952: *Roots of Revolution: a History of Populist and Socialist Movements in Nineteenth Century Russia*, University of Chicago Press, 1983.

Verdet, M., 1863: *Exposé de la théorie mécanique de la chaleur*, Hachette, Paris.

Vernadsky, Vladimir, 1924: *La Géochimie*, trans. from Russian, Alcan, Paris.

Vernadsky, Vladimir, 1926: *La Biosphère*, trans. from Russian, Alcan, Paris.

Vogt, William, 1948: *Road to Survival*, William Sloane, New York.

Vucinich, A., 1970: *Science in Russian Culture 1861–1917*, Stanford University Press.

Vucinich, A., 1976: *Social Thought in Tsarist Russia: the Quest for a General Science of Society 1861–1917*, University of Chicago Press.

Wachtel, Henry I., 1955: *Security for All and Free Enterprise: a Summary of the Social Philosophy of Josef Popper-Lynkeus* (with introduction by Albert Einstein), Philosophical Library, New York.

Wagensberg, Jorge, 1980: *Nosotros y la ciencia*, Bosch, Barcelona.

Wald, F., 1899: *Die Energie und ihre Entwertung: Studien über den Zweiten Hauptsatz der mechanischen Wärmetheorie*, W. Engelmann, Leipzig.

Walicki, A., 1969: *The Controversy over Capitalism: Studies in the Social Philosophy of the Russian Populists*, Clarendon Press, Oxford.

Walras, L., 1965: *Correspondence of Léon Walras and Related Papers*, ed. W. Jaffé, Amsterdam.

Wasser, Henry, 1956: *The Scientific Thought of Henry Adams*, Thessaloniki.

Watkins, J. W. N., 1959: 'Historical Explanation in the Social Sciences', in Gardiner, ed., *Theories of History*.

Watt, Kenneth, Molloy, L. F., Varshney, C. K., Weeks, D. and Wirosardjono, S., 1977: *The Unsteady State: Environmental Problems, Growth, and Culture*, East-West Center, University of Hawaii Press, Honolulu.

Weber, Max, 1909: 'Energetische Kulturtheorien', *Archiv für Sozialwissenschaft und Sozialpolitik*, 29, in Weber, *Gessammelte Aufsätze zur Wissenschaftslehre*, J. C. B. Mohr (Paul Siebeck), Tübingen, 3rd edn 1968.

Webster, C., 1982: 'Healthy or Hungry Thirties?', *History Workshop Journal*, 13, Spring.

Weinstein, D. A., Shugart, H. H. and Brandt, C. C., 1983: 'Energy Flow and the Persistence of a Human Population: a Simulation Analysis', *Human Ecology*, 11 (2).

Werskey, Gary, 1978: *The Visible College: the Collective Biography of British Scientific Socialists of the 1930s*, Holt, Rinehart & Winston, New York.

Wesley, J. P., 1974: *Ecophysics: the application of Physics to Ecology*, Charles Thomas, Springfield, Ill.

White, Leslie, 1943: 'Energy and the Evolution of Culture', *American Anthropologist*, 45 (3).

White, Leslie, 1948: 'Lewis Henry Morgan: Pioneer in the Theory of Social Evolution', in H. E. Barnes, *An Introduction to the History of Sociology*, Chicago University Press.

White, Leslie, 1959: 'The Energy Theory of Cultural Development', in Morton H. Fried, ed., *Readings in Anthropology*, Thomas Y. Cromwell, New York, vol. II, 139–46.

Wiarda, H. J., 1974: 'Corporatism and Development in the Iberic-Latin World', in Pike and Stritch, eds, 1974.

Williams, Trevor, 1982: *A Short History of Twentieth Century Technology*, Clarendon, Oxford.

Winiarski, L., 1900: 'Essai sur la mécanique sociale: l'énergie sociales et ses mensurations', *Revue philosophique*.

Winiarski, L., 1967: *Essais sur la mécanique sociale*, textes réunis et présentés par Giovanni Busino, Droz, Geneva.

Wittfogel, Karl, 1985: 'Geopolitics, geographical materialism and Marxism', trans. G. L. Ulmen, *Antipode: a Radical Journal of Geography*, 17 (1).

Woeikof, A., 1901: 'De l'influence de l'homme sur la terre', *Annales de Géographie* 50 and 51.

Wolf, Edward C., 1986: *Beyond the Green Revolution: New Approaches for Third World Agriculture*, Worldwatch Institute, Washington, DC.

Worster, Donald, 1977: *Nature's Economy: the Roots of Ecology*, Sierra Club Books, San Francisco, new edn Cambridge University Press, 1986.

Wortman, Richard, 1967: *The Crisis of Populism*, Cambridge University Press.

Yergin, Daniel and Hillenbrand, Martin, 1983: *Global Insecurity; a Strategy for Energy and Economic Renewal*, Penguin, London.

Young, Gerald L., 1983: *Origins of Human Ecology*, Hutchinson & Ross, Stroudsburg, Penn.

Young, Robert M., 1969: 'Malthus and the Evolutionists: the Common Context of Biological and Social Theory', *Past and Present*, 43.

Žmavc, Johann, 1905: 'Vorbemerkungen zu einer Neugrundlegung der Wirtschaftswissenschaft', *Annalen der Naturphilosophie*, IV, 386–402.

Žmavc, Johann, 1906: 'Die zwei Hauptprobleme der Wirtschaftswissenschaft', *Annalen der Naturphilosophie*, V, 111–18.

Žmavc, Ivan, 1926: *Die energetischen Grundlagen der Soziotechnik: die allgemeine Lehre von der menschlichen Arbeit als dem Element der wissenschaftlich begründeten Gesellschaft*, Sudetendeutscher Verlag Karl Kraus, Reichenberg i.B.

Index

Index by Jacqueline McDermott